The Authors

Bill Bateman

Virgil and Dolores Albertini

TOWERS IN THE NORTHWEST

The Administration Building

Orval Heywood

TOWERS IN THE NORTHWEST

A History of Northwest Missouri State University
1956-1980

By
VIRGIL ALBERTINI
and
DOLORES ALBERTINI

NORTHWEST MISSOURI STATE UNIVERSITY
Maryville, Missouri

Printed by
RUSH PRINTING COMPANY
MARYVILLE, MISSOURI

CONTENTS

ILLUSTRATIONS

FOREWORD

Dr. J. W. Jones expressed his "earnest hope" in the foreword to Miss Mattie Dykes' *Behind the Birches* "that the inspiration of the first 50 years will be an inspiration to us all to work steadfastly for the welfare of the College so that the future of Northwest Missouri State College will be even more illustrious than the past." As one studies Virgil and Dolores Albertini's history of Northwest Missouri State University during the immediate past 25 years, it certainly would appear that Dr. Jones' "earnest hope" has been and is being fulfilled.

An understanding of history is so essential to any enlightenment of the future. *Towers in the Northwest* greatly enhances one's understanding of the great institutional strengths and traditions of excellence which have become the standard of acceptance at Northwest.

In its brief, but significant, 75 years Northwest has made a substantial mark on history. The formation of that history, the eyes of this documentation and the collective strengths of Northwest's many publics including students, faculty, staff, alumni, parents, donors and friends provide an impressive foundation as the University's attention begins to focus on the 21st Century.

Thomas Jefferson wrote: "I like the dreams of the future better than the history of the past." Part of Northwest's history is the way in which it leans into the winds of the future at times. As one finishes reading this very well-written historical account, it seems to leave a feeling of confident anticipation of Northwest's next chapter of history.

B. D. Owens
President

Preface

Histories can be organized in several ways. The numerous histories of other colleges and universities have shown a great variety of emphases. *Towers in the Northwest* is an interpretive, chronological history written for Northwest Missouri State University alumni, students, faculty, staff, and friends. We have not attempted to provide an in-depth institutional history, and we feel that no one can really claim a great degree of objectivity in writing a history on something as complex as a university; we can only try to weigh the evidence as honestly as possible. The writers recognize, to be sure, that histories by their very nature have to be selective, and that there is considerable subjectivity involved merely in deciding what to discuss and what not to include.

Detail and supporting facts have sometimes been sacrificed in favor of our attempt to capture the spirit and the flavor of Northwest's development and maturation. Our concern has been to show the tone and character of the University's last twenty-five years. This work does not trace the twisting path of curriculum building at Northwest. The inclusion of curricular specifics would, it was feared, be tedious for the readers. The appendix does offer a guide for those who wish to identify particular administrators, regents, and faculty.

This history is based largely on primary source material. Particularly valuable have been the catalogs, alumni bulletins, the *Northwest Missourian,* the *Tower* yearbook, the *Daily Forum,* the Board of Regents minutes, the Faculty Senate minutes, diaries, letters, files, scrapbooks, funeral home and nursing home records, and the collected clipbooks in the News and Information Office. One of our best primary sources has been the personal interview. Helping us capture certain time periods in American history was Eric Goldman's *The Crucial Decade—and After,* D. Duane Cummins' *Consensus and Turmoil: The 1950's and 1960's,* and William L. O'Neill's *Coming Apart.* We have also been able to draw on our own experience at Northwest, covering a little more than sixty percent of the twenty-five year history. We have found, too, that abundant historical records exist on campus. Since some of these records are casually stored here and there, a University Archives needs to be established in order that materials are systematically organized and made more accessible to researchers.

Apologies are extended to the many administrators, faculty, staff, students, alumni, regents, and friends who merit mention but do not receive it. Our debts are many. We owe much to President B. D. Owens who conceived the idea of a twenty-five-year history and urged its writing. Mr. Bob Sunkel, chairman of the Seventy-Fifth Anniversary Committee, recommended us to the President to write this history. Dr. George English, vice president for academic affairs, arranged for a semester of release time from classes so that the male counterpart of this project could concentrate on the writing. Professor Emeritus Mattie Dykes was the first person consulted after we accepted this challenge. She graciously gave us advice and words of encouragement throughout, and she generously let us use her annotated working copy of *Behind the Birches* and the many notes she kept through the years. A special thanks goes to Bob Sunkel for the artwork on the title page and the book cover. We also welcome this opportunity to thank Mary Keith, Frank Grube, Vida Dunbar, Jane Kemp, Jim Reed, Monica Zirfas, Shirley Gray, Mary Jane Sunkel, Barbara Bernard, Bob Mallory, Bruce Wake, and Bill Bateman who each helped us in different and specific ways—in ways uniquely their own. Their help went far beyond the dutiful. Our task was made easier, too, by the staff members in the offices of the President, the Vice President for Academic Affairs, the Missouri State Teachers Association, News and Information, the Registrar, Student Activities, the Graduate School, Placement, Alumni, and Personnel and Payroll who assisted us from time to time in the collection of information. Wells Library, the Maryville Public Safety Department, and Rush Printing Company were also helpful. We interviewed eighty people whose links to Northwest—either past or present—are invaluable, and their recollections have helped us better understand the history of Northwest. They gave generously of their time, not only in two, three, or four hour interviews, but in conducting tours of their various offices and buildings and by pleasingly responding to spur of the moment telephone calls for answers to questions. They have made our task a bit more pleasant. We will always be grateful for Dorothy Weigand, Kathryn McKee, and Bob Henry. They have been especially helpful through a critical reading of the manuscript and the galley proofs. Dorothy took a further step and read the page proofs. Although Dorothy, Kathryn, and Bob have been guiding lights, they are not responsible for the content.

Finally, we wish to thank all people ever affiliated with Northwest Missouri State University who, in one way or another, helped us write this interpretive history.

Maryville, Missouri
July 31, 1980

Virgil Albertini
Dolores Albertini

TOWERS IN THE NORTHWEST

President J. W. Jones
1945-1964

1

Serenity, 1956-1959

And the one bird singing alone to his nest,
And the one star over the tower.

—Owen Meredith

The mid and late fifties for America was an age of television, tract houses, garish automobiles, industrial automation, population mobility, and long skirts. Arthur Godfrey and Elvis Presley were the biggest attractions in show business. Norman Vincent Peale was the country's most popular ordained moralist. Oral Roberts and Billy Graham were gaining momentum. Charcoal gray suits were worn with pink shirts and black ties. Men wore short hair, except for many young men whose long sideburns met at the back. Students were not politically involved and were known for their sporadic "panty raids" where men marched to women's dormitories and enticed women to throw out their underwear. The country's political hopes rested upon Dwight Eisenhower, a sixty-four-year-old human being who in 1955 had suffered a heart attack. America, too, was experiencing a social upsurge. More than half of the country's people had reached the status of "white collar." Colleges were beginning to recruit students regardless of family background. And problems following the 1954 Supreme Court decision ordering the desegregation of schools were plentiful. From abroad headlines were prevalent. Russia, our constant worry, was "coexisting" but Chinese Communism was making threatening noises. The Hungarian Revolution reminded us that Communists could be utterly ruthless. The Middle East, as always, was turbulent, made even more so by the rabid nationalism of Egypt's leader, Nasser.

The successful launching on October 5, 1957, of sputnik, Russia's artificial earth satellite, challenged America's supremacy of technical know-how. The shock in America was profound.

Americans in the mid and late fifties were middle road. Of course, they occasionally worried over national and international problems, but prosperity—although not universal by any means—was evident in the way people lived and played. If people could not buy things or rent them, they used credit.

3

The intellectuals insisted that there were numerous dangers in prosperity and that we could easily turn into an obese, numb civilization, unconcerned with the value that stoked progress—individualism. Of course, the general public did not listen.

America at this time had more of practically everything. Life, it seemed, became more impersonal. A dominant literary theme centered on man's struggle against the impersonal forces of society and his attempt to have an individual identity. Conformity seemed to be a virtue, and most did not wish to be bold and different. Colleges expanded and became more and more bureaucratic, and, in so doing, reduced the effectiveness of association among individuals.

Northwest Missouri State College, with varying degrees of emphasis, usually followed traditional collegiate patterns and interests in 1956. The main educational concerns for students centered on obtaining grades, earning degrees, and finding "good jobs" after they left their alma mater. The students here then were no different from anyone else in society. College degrees were important for their future welfare and security. Students, like students anywhere, were concerned about difficult examinations, excellent teachers, poor teachers, good courses, athletics, and social activities. President J. W. Jones, who accepted the presidency in December 1945, had successfully guided the College for ten years, but in January of 1956 he revealed that Northwest "has gone on too long on too little." Huge increases in enrollments were causing classroom spaces and on-campus housing facilities to almost burst, as President Jones said, at the seams. Jones cited the need for a new dormitory and additional classroom facilities. The Administration Building needed repairs; plumbing and heating lines badly needed maintenance. The percentage of enrollment increase in 1954 and 1955 exceeded that of any other state-supported school in Missouri, and a natural expansion of the student body certainly could not be expected unless the cramp on classroom space was alleviated and additional dormitory facilities for some 250 men and women added. The above was worrisome and could result in a more limited curriculum and possibly a restriction on the size of the student body. President Jones had reasons to be anxious because population trends indicated that the enrollment in the next ten years would climb to 2,400, more than double the now over-crowded enrollment. Dr. Jones was a planner. He developed plans for a new dormitory and more classroom facilities. But the plans involved large amounts of money and the Missouri General Assembly turned them down. Education always seems to have its best of times and its worst of times. Expanded enrollment certainly was a good sign for Northwest but poor facilities were not!

But in 1956 the good news was that Northwest was maturing as an institution of higher learning. Education was flourishing, and activities on campus were proliferating from honoring notable faculty members to holding author autograph parties. March 18-24 was designated as Missouri Home Economics Week, and tribute was paid to Miss Hettie Anthony, who started Northwest's home economics department in 1908 and diligently served it for forty-eight years. April 19 marked a momentous day for Maryville, for that was distribution day for *Behind the Birches,* the history of Northwest's first fifty years and authored by Mattie Dykes, a woman who knew the College intimately as a high school student, college student, alumna, and English faculty member for thirty-five years. The history was published as the capstone of the Golden Anniversary celebration of the College. Her research, too, was obviously painstaking, especially so with the early story of the school, a fascinating one of near-success, followed by defeat, of doubts, politics, scheming, and bitter rivalry. She shows the long struggle bearing fruit and how the school finally is established. *Behind the Birches,* to be sure, brings to the present new meaning and greater understanding.

Commencement was an especial and notable one, for it officially marked the end of Northwest's Golden Anniversary. The College was conceived, born, and developed during those years. Now it was well into the maturing process. Commencements, too, are memorable not for lengthy, inspirational messages to the graduates, but for significant awards, tributes, or other surprising features, such as the naming of buildings or stadiums—names that will carry on forever, like Rickenbrode, Wells, Roberta, and Hudson. This Commencement was etched into participants' memories when Judge M. E. Ford, chairman of the Board of Regents, announced the naming of the J. W. Jones Union Building in honor of President Jones and the gymnasium, the Uel W. Lamkin Gymnasium for Northwest's fifth president, Jones' predecessor. New York has its Yankee Stadium, often referred to as "The House That Ruth Built," because of the Babe's prodigious feats, but Northwest has its "House That Jack Built," for Jones worked tirelessly in the field of legislative lobbying to obtain funds. As Miss Dykes points out in *Behind the Birches,* he wanted a building on campus where one could experience "gracious living."

Sports, an integral part of any institution of higher learning for healthy competition, camaraderie, and student interest, be it intercollegiate or intramural, were healthy. An invitational track meet was held, the Sigma Phi Dolphin Swim Club presented its eighth annual show, and baseball reentered, after an absence of fifteen years, when the legendary E. A. "Lefty" Davis was coach, as a spring sport with

Bob Gregory as coach. Spring sports on campus consisted of track, golf, and tennis; and baseball added a needed activity for men who loved the national pastime. There obviously was a need to restore this traditional sport to its rightful niche of Northwest tradition. Games were played at the local city park (Beal). A new playing field would have to wait another year.

Aesthetics, like sports, link the college community together. The campus, then as now, was known for its beauty and rightfully claimed its title "The most beautiful campus in Missouri." Helping to enhance that image was the Chinese Golden Rain Tree on the east side of the front walk of the Administration Building. This ornamental tree, now more than eighteen-years-old, was a gift of Walter Williams, former president of the University of Missouri. College Park, not to be over-shadowed by the beauty offered by the campus proper, had its image enhanced by the addition of a large new shelter house and a brick oven plus the renovation of many tables and outdoor ovens.

Administrators, past and present, were in the news. Dr. W. A. Brandenburg, dean of faculty, announced his resignation to become president of Wayne State Teachers College at Wayne, Nebraska, where he served until 1973. Dr. Charles Koerble succeeded him. Branden-burg's predecessor was the affable and gregarious M. C. "Pete" Cunningham, who in 1949 left his duties here to become president of Kansas State Teachers College at Hays, where he reigned admirably for twenty years. President Jones always pointed with pride at the two and so did the College because obviously presidential timber was hewn here. Sadness also enveloped the College at this time for President Emeritus Uel Lamkin, who headed Northwest from 1921 until 1945, died at his home on September 16. And Mr. William a Rickenbrode, former registrar, business manager, secretary to the Board of Regents, a member of the business office staff, and secretary to the president, died on November 29 at the age of 87. One might note that the present football field and stadium are named after him, a fitting tribute to a man who could rightfully be called the first "Mr. Bearcat," for was there ever so avid a Bearcat fan? Miss Dykes points out that he never received a letter nor a sweater, but that he certainly left his imprint. The 1956 M Club, composed of men who lettered in some varsity sport, however, with admirable acumen, awarded the M Club blanket and a life membership in the organization to Mr. Rickenbrode in February for his long-time support. The blanket was traditionally awarded to senior lettermen. Mr. Rickenbrode, who served under six presidents, "played" many minutes for that blanket during his fifty years of distinguished and devoted service. Even in death his love for

Northwest was evident as he and Mrs. Rickenbrode, who died on May 23, 1958, bequeathed $10,000 in scholarships and $750 to the M Club for furnishings in the Bearcat Den. And the blanket? Mrs. Rickenbrode, after her husband's death, gave it to the M Club, and it graced one of the walls of the Club as a testament to the grand old patron of the athletic arts.

Walkout Day, long a tradition on campus and celebrated every fall, marked the end of "frosh hazing." Of course, the day was always highlighted by upperclassmen parading the freshmen uptown to the courthouse where members of the Student Senate conducted a "Kangaroo Court." The freshmen always seemed happy to see this day, for it officially stopped the five-week initiation period of such rituals as their wearing green beanies. The upperclassmen also eagerly anticipated Walkout Day. It definitely was a release from the coming and going routine of classes and study, because students were afforded the opportunity to have a fine lunch, participate in a variety show, see a movie, and finally dance in the J. W. Jones Union Building until the band culminated the finely structured day by playing its traditional "Goodnight Sweetheart." Now students could anticipate further events like the November Sadie Hawkins Week, a rage that was prevalent on campuses in the 1940s and 1950s, and the annual Christmas Ball.

Traditions, as one sees, were important not only on campus but in American life as well. The late 70s, as witnessed by movies, books, and television programs like "Happy Days" emerged with a plethora of nostalgia, memorabilia centering on the 50s. But the 50s, especially the mid to late periods, were not looking back in retrospect. Traditions, like the "Hanging of the Greens," were important and real to campus life. This ceremony on December 17, performed annually by the Residence Hall women, included a processional, carol singing, and dancing. Also included was an explanation of the traditions of the yule log, evergreen, mistletoe, and lighted candles in windows at Christmas. During the "Hanging of the Greens," the identity of the "Spirit of Christmas," always a senior honoree, was revealed. Reigning over the yuletide ritual in 1956 before 250 of the women students' relatives and friends was Sue Wright, a young lady from Graham, who twenty-one years later would become Northwest's first lady, as the wife of President B. D. Owens. This event was not only a symbol of the yuletide season but was a reminder that classes were about to disperse for the holidays. People who watched this ceremony were happy and grateful, too, because the audience was a select and privileged one.

On the national scene in the waning days of the year, responsible men in Washington were talking nervously, as they would be early in

1980, about the coming of World War III. The Middle East was again turbulent. Alarms, missile-rattling, and intimations of nuclear doomsday ran rampant throughout the world, but somehow it all settled down. The United States, believing in Herodotus' philosophy that anyone who would choose war over peace is a fool, threw its full weight behind restoring peace in the Middle East. Early in 1957, President Jones was applying a peace of his own to the serious problem of housing and classroom space when he disclosed plans for a new physical education building, two dormitories, and one classroom building. With an enrollment over 1,500 and 250 more expected in the fall, the situation was crucial. Sports enthusiasts, especially the baseball team, were happy, for President Jones also announced that work on a new baseball diamond and football practice field would soon start. Already approved were sites and plans for the new physical education building, the men's dormitory and women's dormitory, the men's to be at the Quad and the women's adjacent to Residence Hall. Included in the $3,000,000 expansion program was the extensive remodeling program of the Administration Building and the present gymnasium for use by the department of women's physical education.

Campus life obviously was flourishing: administrators were administrating; instructors were instructing; students were learning and working toward the day when they could make their mark—however significant in the world. But again social life was important, be it with the Greeks or the Independents. Six fraternities and sororities existed: Sig Taus, Phi Sigs, TKEs, Tri Sigs, Delta Zetas, and Phi Mus. The Tri Sigs and the Sig Taus made news for both celebrated anniversaries of their own, having the honor of being the oldest Greeks at Northwest. Tri Sigma, however, was born fifteen days earlier, March 18, 1927. Honorary fraternities, important for scholarship and recognition, were also in the news as the one-year-old Gamma Alpha chapter of Kappa Pi art fraternity was honored by seeing itself written up in the *Sketch Book,* a national art magazine.

The talk at Commencement centered on women. The first two master's degrees at Northwest were conferred upon two recipients from St. Joseph, Mrs. Winifred H. Paddelford and Miss Darline Roedecker. Commencement participants also discovered that two stalwarts of Dr. Frank Grube's English department, Miss Mattie Dykes and Miss Estella Bowman, were to retire effective at the end of the ensuing summer session. Both women's tenure totaled 69 years: Miss Dykes' thirty-five, Miss Bowman's thirty-four. The college faculty and administrators recognized these two and their outstanding achievements at a reception in their honor.

Five expansions in twenty years are a record that is hard to surpass. Enrollment, however, continued to mount in the industrial arts department, and a new addition was planned for a new general shop laboratory, an electrical laboratory, and storage rooms. Mr. Donald Valk, department chairman since 1932, and instrumental in all of his department's building accomplishments, felt that no other state school in Missouri could approach his department in area (25,000 square feet), equipment and, most important, number of students. His department, thanks to himself and Mr. Howard Ringold, Mr. Kenneth Thompson, and Mr. David Crozier, three long-time key members, boasted of courses in mechanical and architectural drawing, bench work, power woodworking, general shop, welding, crafts, elementary industrial arts, shop mathematics, metal machine work, and electricity. Of course, since Northwest at this time was primarily interested in training would-be teachers, industrial education was the mainstay. The department, however, prided itself in teaching pre-engineering students and, in addition, those interested in taking the department offerings for their own general use.

The "fifties" was labeled by many historians as the "silent generation," but a group of male students, led by Savannah's Francis "Bugsy" Williams, who would achieve fame a year later for serving as B. D. Owens' campaign manager in Owens' successful quest for the Student Senate leadership, and sponsored by the omnipresent and dedicated dean of men, Lon Wilson, decided to generate their own noise at pep assemblies, bonfires, and home games. Their name, The Ambassadors, obviously patterned after popular male singing groups of the time, like "The Four Preps" and "The Crew-Cuts," was a catchy one and this all-male cheering section appeared at said functions wearing green ivy league hats and green ties. The cane was their trademark and, since their purpose was to instill school spirit, they sat, much like the Bearcat Boosters at home football games today, in a reserved seating section. One of their prideful projects was soliciting a nickel per name from the student body in order to send a winning message by telegram to the Bearcat football team playing St. Joseph's College at Rensselaer, Indiana, a site long known for the training camp of the NFL Chicago Bears. Approximately 800 students signed the telegram, and an excess of twenty-one dollars was donated to the Student Loan Fund, a seemingly miniscule amount by today's standards, but eventful, nevertheless, because student loans were not as plentiful nor federally subsidized as they are in current times. The football Bearcats, incidentally, probably thought they were playing the Bears as they absorbed a 44-0 loss.

The telegram surely must have offered some balm to the athletes' gall of being soundly trounced.

Vets' Village, originated in 1947 and located immediately north of the Administration Building to accommodate married veterans and their families, bulged with 134 residents in the forty-four low-rent federal housing units. It was bigger than some of Maryville's surrounding smaller communities, like Arkoe, Bedison, and Wilcox. Vets' Village, to be sure, was not incorporated, but it did have a mayor, a constable, three councilmen, and a postman. Lon Wilson was their patron saint and looked after their needs. Two of Northwest's current staff members, Don Robertson, associate professor of art, and George Barratt, associate professor of mathematical sciences, are proud graduates of that community.

As 1957 drew to a close, America strolled down the middle road, worried occasionally about things like military spending, but mostly happily absorbed in its private affairs. Waves of prosperity seemed to keep rolling in, overwhelming any concerns about the world. Inflation always one's great enemy, slowly continued, but most Americans were enjoying more income than ever before. It was a time of relative tranquility and words like "suburbia," "conformity," and "automation" became a part of our vocabulary—words that reflected a concern with comfort. The campus community at Northwest was absorbed in its own private affairs like increasing enrollments, building expansion, quality staff, and quality education for its students. When Russia sent sputnik aloft, the shock here, as everywhere in America, was profound, for there was no doubt concerning the practical consequences of Russia's success. We were urged to achieve what was always called excellence, and the mandate for us in foreign affairs was again for dominance. American affluence, it seemed, had been exposed for the enfeebling thing it was.

As the frantic weeks continued nationally, Northwest heaved a sigh of relief, for President Jones announced that construction on the classroom building, designed to seat almost 2,000 students, would probably begin in August. For the visual aspects, construction had already begun on the addition to Residence Hall with the fine thought that it would be ready for occupancy in late 1958 and, hopefully, for the beginning of the fall semester. And by late spring the four-building construction program was well under way: two dorms, a classroom building, and a physical education building. To be sure, sputnik was a symbol showing America was second best in the technological field, and the unending crises abroad worried and frightened people about their future, but Northwest was planning efficiently for its future. While news was being made on the national and international scene, Northwest's student paper, the *Northwest Missourian,* was making national news of its own. Led by Miss Violette Hunter, adviser, and Bill Morse, the 1957 editor, the paper received its seventh consecutive first-place certificate by the Columbia Scholastic Press Association at Columbia University, New York City.

Northwest in 1957 and 1958 was a campus of eighty acres and numerous buildings, highlighted by the stately and grand Administration Building. It boasted a College Farm of some 180 acres, and for tradition lovers there was a kissing bridge where a young lady had to be kissed before the first snowfall in order to become a bona fide coed. It contained a community of varied people concerned with education in Northwest Missouri. Its rows of stately trees and shrubs helped make the campus the most beautiful in Missouri. It was growing fast; at the beginning of the decade it had 750 students and now there were 1,700. One-third of the students lived on campus, a third in approved housing in Maryville, which had a 6,834 population, and a third commuted from within a radius of sixty miles. Three-fourths of the students were Missourians. Others came from twenty-two states, but the majority came from Iowa. Ten percent were married and 287 veterans were enrolled. A total of 4,925 degrees in Bachelor of Arts, Bachelor of Science, Bachelor of Science in Education, and Master of Science in Education had been granted in the school's history. Northwest, in fulfilling its primary objective of educating men and women, offered full four-year courses in the several divisions of the liberal arts and sciences, as well as agriculture, home economics, industrial arts, and other subject matter in fields of elementary and secondary school instruction. Pre-professional programs were numerous, among them medicine, dentistry, law, nursing, and engineering. Northwest also had an arrangement with the University of Missouri at Columbia and with the Rolla School of Mines whereby a student who studied three years at Maryville and two years at Rolla received a Bachelor of Arts degree from Northwest and a Bachelor of Science in Engineering degree from Rolla. If a student chose law for his profession, he could spend three years at Northwest and then move on to the University of Missouri for three years and receive the combined degrees in law—Bachelor of Arts and Bachelor of Law. Cooperation among state schools was evident and not that difficult to perceive or arrange.

Eighty-one instructors, the most viable element in any classroom, represented the faculty, and seventy percent of the students were in teacher education. Prospective teachers garnered practical experience at the College's Horace Mann Laboratory School, which, in 1957, had 300 pupils from nursery through high school.

President and Mrs. Jones were feted by faculty and staff in May of 1958 for the twenty years that the couple had been at the College—seven-and-one-half of which President Jones was dean and twelve-and-one-half as president. One of the gifts given them was a portable TV, which President Jones used in his study to watch his favorite sports events until his death in 1979 on New Year's Day. Two months after the celebration they were asked to move from their gracious and dignified mansion to South Hall, a large white house on the campus at the entrance of College Drive housing several women students. No, they were not being praised in one month and denigrated in another, but houses of presidents, like other buildings on campus, need major repairs, too. So move they did from July until October when they returned to see their home replastered and redecorated and their heating system modernized. The two next bought new lighting fixtures to grace their residence, and then, with a fine generous touch, proceeded to donate their selections to Northwest.

Bedford, Iowa's Carl Barnes, a senior art and English major, did not run the hundred-yard dash in nine seconds, nor did he pitch a no-hitter, but he indelibly etched his name into Northwest's fifty-two year history by becoming the 1800th fall enrollee. His registration set an all-time record. Yes, students enrolling for a college education were extremely important and the campus was expanding.

It was obvious that provision of higher educational facilities for the large number of youngsters in elementary and secondary schools in 1958 would be a serious problem. President Jones, a man who obviously could look down the road, suggested that the state of Missouri have a coordinating or planning board which would help the several colleges of the state function better and more uniformly. Another progressive step—a far-reaching one—offered by Jones was for Northwest to extend its services and open a junior college unit in St. Joseph. It would have entailed the operation of the then municipally supported St. Joseph Junior College, and, if approved and put into operation, the Junior College would have become a branch of Northwest whereby a student from the St. Joseph area could take his first two years' work at St. Joseph with credit given under the name of Northwest. Jones' interest was not topical, for he felt that the state of Missouri needed to meet the problem of tremendous enrollment increases by establishing and supporting branch junior colleges of the state-supported four-year colleges in strategic localities as determined by a coordinating board for higher education. It was a fine situation for both Maryville and St.

Joseph. The accessibility to both institutions was easy, and agreement by both sides was not difficult since approval was given by the St. Joseph Board of Education. The proposal by Jones, as expected, was not one that was cursorily treated, for he and George Blackwell, St. Joseph superintendent of schools, studied long and hard, and both men also took into consideration the use of buildings and personnel of the educational facilities. Of course, anything worthwhile is usually difficult to attain. The Missouri Assembly turned thumbs down on the $200,000 request of annual funds for operation of such a unit which would have been the first in the state. Today's taxpayers would probably not disagree that the above represented low-cost education and, considering Northwest's reputation and heritage, quality.

President Jones was not a man easily deterred. He, backed by his Board, asked the General Assembly for an additional $30,000 to train teachers to work with the physically and mentally handicapped. These future teachers would be trained in St. Joseph at the Myrtle E. Miller School for Exceptional Children, a school nationally famous for its advanced work in this field. Superintendent Blackwell felt that the plan had great merit, and members of the St. Joseph School Board, the *St. Joseph News-Press,* and people vitally interested in education all agreed. It, too, would give Northwest's student teaching program more breadth since it already had student teachers working in St. Joseph's public schools, in addition to its own Horace Mann and the Maryville public schools.

Student Senate President B. D. Owens was making his own news at the time. He had married the former Miss Sue Wright, a very active leader herself as a student and now an alumna who was teaching music in the public schools. Sponsored by the Vets' Club—he was a member of the TKEs and the Vets—Owens had conducted a very spirited presidential campaign the previous spring under the capable hands of Francis "Bugsy" Williams. At the height of his campaign, and possibly as a foreshadowing of Northwest's future years in the late 70s and early 80s, three National Guard jets "buzzed" the campus. His slogan obviously was "We are now in the jet age here at Northwest." Considering what Jones was originating and accomplishing and what Owens was imagining and doing on campus, the slogan was an apt one.

Obviously Northwest was growing and maturing and carving its niche in the escutcheons of higher education. Proper and mature concept of the academic tradition, however, was not always followed, nor did some members of the faculty or administration consider it necessary. The most evident aberration was the absence of rank and tenure for teachers in the academic structure. During its first fifty-two years,

Northwest's instructors had no title or rank: they were simply called instructors. Now, no longer a normal school but a college since 1949, it was trying to shed its teachers' college image. Among the faculty, people like Dr. John Harr, president of the local AAUP, and Dr. Sterling Surrey, chairman of the division of business and quite ubiquitous and a ringleader in the College's internal affairs, were largely responsible for implanting the rank establishment. They talked to a receptive President Jones about their concerns. Jones then delegated Dr. Frank Grube, chairman of the language and literature division, to head a committee to formulate the recommended procedures initiating and maintaining the faculty ranking plans. This Grube did, and he submitted his committee's proposal to President Jones on December 5. On December 15, at a meeting called by Jones, the faculty, by a slight majority, voted down faculty ranking. Jones told his Board of Regents that he disapproved of the vote and then told his faculty that he favored Grube's committee report and said "We will have ranking at this college." He then selected Surrey, Dr. Joseph Dreps, department of foreign languages chairman, Dr. Irene Mueller of the biology department, Dr. J. Gordon Strong, chairman of the division of science and mathematics, and Harr to serve on the Faculty Rank Committee, the first of its kind in Northwest's history. These five were selected, based on their degrees and years of service, as an advisory committee to the president. Their task was not an enviable one, for they were being asked to recommend from their own peers who should be the professors, associate professors, assistant professors, and instructors. Even today, although one is elected by his peers, serving on rank committees is not easy. That first group certainly must have had its moments of anguish, teeth gnashing, and hand wringing, for it is never easy to try to judge one's colleagues. Their torturous task was made a bit easier, however, for the members could depend on suggestions or recommendations for promotion by division chairmen or the dean of the college, and, too, the ranking policy criteria were basically the same that were drawn by the original committee. The criteria certainly had merit because their basic makeup—albeit skeletal by today's standards—has not been greatly altered. Yes, the Committee's work was long, tedious, and arduous, but it also served as a standard-bearer for the following rank committees. Most of the faculty, who were definitely divided over the ranking issue, recognized the need to provide for their own protection.

An unexpected bonus, which was really a Christmas present to students and staff alike, was added to the hubbub of building expansion when the Board of Regents approved an addition to the six-year-old J. W. Jones Union. Construction was to start by March and to be completed for the 1959 fall semester. Classroom and living space, to be sure, are extremely important, but students need to eat and play, too.

Being able to see and hear national figures and participate in cultural events are also extremely important to the well-being of the individual. Northwest's populace in the past had the opportunity to see notables like Dorothy Thompson, William O. Douglas, and the Boston Pops Symphony. But now Mrs. Eleanor Roosevelt, America's perpetual first lady, was coming, and on the eve of Valentine's Day she spoke to an overflowing auditorium of 1,250 students and staff members. Perhaps the person with the most responsibility for Mrs. Roosevelt's welfare on campus was Student Senate President B. D. Owens. The young man filled his role with aplomb as he chauffeured her from the Union Passenger Station in St. Joseph and introduced her around campus and to the afternoon assembly in the Auditorium. Always gracious, Mrs. Roosevelt spoke extemporaneously on America's role as a world leader.

Earlier Mrs. Roosevelt was a luncheon guest of Mrs. Jones at the Jones' home. It was a propitious and almost prophetic moment for Northwest as three "first ladies" were present: Mrs. Roosevelt, Mrs. Jones, and Mrs. Sue Owens, future first lady of Northwest.

Mrs. Roosevelt obviously was delighted with her reception at Northwest, for in her perennial "My Day" syndicated newspaper column, on February 17, 1959, she devoted half of her column to the graciousness of her hosts, the delightful luncheon, and the audience's reception. President Jones always lamented the fact that he was not part of the reception, but obtaining money from the General Assembly for the College's expansion program was the priority, and he had to be in Jefferson City looking after Northwest's welfare.

Dances dotted the calendar in the early months of 1959, and the J. W. Jones Union—where dancing now is almost non-existent—was the place to dance. The big winter event, now defunct, was the Tower Dance, and this year people could whirl to Woody Herman and his stomping herd and watch Smithville's Barbara Burgess crowned Tower Queen. The fraternities and sororities were busy making plans for their spring formals.

The Bearcat basketball team had a respectable 12-8 season, the wrestling team led by Amazonia's senior Larry Schweizer was thriving, and Dr. Frank Grube's tennis team won the MIAA conference championship.

Theatergoers could see Dr. Ralph Fulsom's able thespians perform in two productions: *Hedda Gabler* and *Seven Keys to Baldpate,* and the music and speech departments collaborated and presented *La Bohème.*

On May 1 it happened! The long-awaited move by members of the departments of history, education, psychology, language and literature, social science, and business to the new Classroom Building had finally fructified. The building, originally intended for science and the fine arts but not really feasible to those disciplines' needs, lovingly opened its arms and embraced its tenants. The attraction was not an unrequited one, for its 73,728 total square footage brought much-needed instructional "breathing room" and a capacity of 3,000 students per hour. Some of the staff, to be sure, were cramped with two people to an office but that condition was later rectified, and the building—which in 1961 was named after the first president of the Board of Regents, Mr. Charles J. Colden—became the academic hub of the campus.

The 1959 May graduates set a precedent for following commencements because they received their diplomas in the new health and physical education building. Of course people who attended had to watch their step since the building was not yet completed, and females had to stray from the usual fashion code and wear low heels because of pratfalls that any unfinished building could present.

Phi Lambda Chi was the new social fraternity on the campus block and it, like the TKEs, the Phi Sigs, and the Sig Taus, was the fourth to buy and operate its own home. The group's colonization ended in 1961 when it was recognized as Iota chapter of Phi Lambda Chi fraternity, but, in the fall of 1964, the chapter dropped its formal national commitments and became a local fraternity. Then, through an annexation process in the fall of 1965, this fraternity became known as Delta Sigma Phi, a national organization with 122 chapters. In 1959, Northwest numbered the above mentioned four fraternities plus three sororities: Alpha Sigma Alpha, thirty-one years on campus; Delta Zeta, in its third year; and Sigma Sigma Sigma, beginning its thirty-third year. The following year the sororities would add another one to their group. On October 6, 1960, Zeta Lambda, local sorority, with forty-seven young women, officially became the Zeta Lambda chapter of Phi Mu national social sorority.

Other organizations abounded at Northwest, some honorary and some sponsored by various academic departments. Others, like Union Board and Alpha Phi Omega, were strong. Union Board sponsored, as it does now, activities of social, educational, and recreational value. Its thrust was to provide a diversified calendar for the interest of all students. APO, a service fraternity, had as its main goal service. It tried to do its bit in making the campus "one of the most beautiful in

Missouri" by refinishing the identification signs in front of the buildings and placing signs in front of the new Classroom Building. Sponsored by Myrl Long and Bob Seipel, they certainly were not a discriminatory group for they, led by Sergeant-at-Arms and President-Elect
and presently Director of Housing Bruce Wake, placed plaques for all
the fraternities and sororities in the Bearcat Den. They dipped into their
treasury to purchase plastic magazine covers for the magazines in the
lounge of the J. W. Jones Student Union. Facilities, as in so many
places in 1959, were not geared to the handicapped. New Hampton's
Betty McCaig was especially grateful to this group, for when she was a
student in a wheelchair at Northwest members of APO, and later
Gamma Sigma Sigma, helped her to and from classes. The following
year would be a capstone one for APO because it initiated the infamous
Ugly Man Contest, and the group donated the proceeds to the Student
Loan Fund. And 1960 would see APO have a sister service organization—Gamma Sigma Sigma, a fifty-four woman group that would
publish a student directory, adopt a family at Christmas, provide a
babysitting service, usher at concerts, and guide visiting guests of
Northwest. Mrs. Dorothy Walker of the women's physical education
department was the group's first sponsor.

Even though the Collegiate Radio Club was in its first year of
operation, it bears mention here because of its future impact on Northwest's broadcasting station. Originated and sponsored by Myles
Grabau, the Club was an amateur ham radio operation and was housed
in a tiny "broom closet" in Colbert Hall. It was nationally sanctioned
by the Federal Communications Commission and was officially licensed
KOUDL. It helped students by sending and receiving their messages.
This fledgling group was indeed proud of its two new radio transmitters
and one new communications receiver.

Although Northwest dropped "Teachers" from its title in 1949,
preparing future teachers was still one of the College's most important
functions, for 216 of the 1959 spring graduates were placed in teaching
positions. One strong group on campus that was the organ for elementary and secondary majors who were planning to teach was the John
Dewey chapter of Future Teachers of America, commonly known as
FTA. Dr. Wanda Walker of the education department was chief
sponsor since its 1955 inception, when she started the group and
watched it grow from the nucleus of twenty-eight members to an
astonishing 137.

Because of the large increase in enrollment, approximately 300
percent since 1953, President Jones reorganized his administrative staff
beginning with the fall semester. This reorganization was a forerunner

for several more in Northwest's future and was one of the recommendations made by the North Central Association and the National Council for Accreditation of Teacher Education, both strong accrediting agencies, at one of their visits to the campus. The new alignment had Dr. Charles E. Koerble as dean of students; Harry Bowes as his assistant; Dr. Robert P. Foster, dean of administration; Luther Belcher, business manager; the ubiquitous Everett W. Brown in the triad position of director of placement, extension correspondence, and alumni services; Mrs. L. G. Bladt, dean of women; Mr. Lon Wilson in the dual role of dean of men and director of residence facilities for men; and, finally, Mrs. Elizabeth Luer as director of residence facilities for women.

In 1959, Missouri still had no state-wide plan to help care for its state colleges. President Jones was still asking for a coordinating board for higher education, a plan he outlined as early as 1952. It seemed a mystery why our sister colleges kept opposing it because a concentrated effort by all the state institutions of higher learning would present a more orderly method of presenting requests and would result in a more effective demand for appropriations each year. Such a board would be able to accomplish much in the way of eliminating unnecessary duplication of high-cost specialized programs, especially when some of the state colleges were relatively close to each other, like today's Northwest and Missouri Western. Although the state did not deem it necessary to have a coordinating board, Governor James Blair, on November 14, did appoint Robert P. Foster, dean of administration, to study the selective admission practices and retention policies of the state-supported institutions. The coordinating commission was the result of a Governors Conference urging the state colleges and universities to work together on some of the problems of higher education in Missouri. At last it seemed that somebody in Jefferson City was listening to Jones' pleas.

Talk on campus at this time was that of "doubling." Projected enrollment figures showed that Northwest could have over 4,000 students by 1975, more than doubling the 1959 fall enrollment. To handle such an enrollment, plans were being laid for more on-campus housing, new buildings, and other additions. Jones explained that one of Northwest's biggest existing problems was again the lack of physical facilities needed to care for the expected enrollment. Work needed to be finished on the existing facilities: the old gymnasium was being renovated for use as a women's gymnasium, the new gymnasium required some additional finishing work—even though it was to be used for its first Bearcat basketball game against Graceland College on December 4

and was dressed enough for its impending dedication on January 16—
and the Administration Building was in the process of renovation to
better serve the College's science program. According to Jones, there
was also a definite need for a fine arts building, a new home management house, recreational areas for women, and parking facilities.
Roads and traffic-ways, always a perennial problem, needed constant
attention. A critical problem in relation to future development was
housing, but plans were being made because Jones and his Board
inaugurated a far-reaching housing program that would provide
dwellings for approximately 1,400 additional students. Added to the
existing 780 units, the plan would provide campus housing for approximately 2,200 students by 1970. Jones envisioned the total project to
cost $8,000,000. He felt that the housing program could be placed west
of College Park on land owned by Northwest.

Tennis buffs were happy also, for now they could play indoors
because a full-size tennis court had been placed in the north end of the
new health and physical education building, and a second would soon
be added. Planning for the future is undoubtedly important but the
present is ongoing, too, and theatergoers from November 18-20 were
thrilled and delighted with the speech and music departments' brilliant
presentation of *Brigadoon,* featuring the singing and dancing of the
future New York stage performer Maryville's Dan DeMott and the
tantalizing voice of Westside, Iowa's Shirley Noelck.

Growth was evident in almost all sectors of the institution, and
improvement in instruction facilities was apparent. On the surface it
appeared that Americans in the 50s were in a state of repose. Yes, the
1950s seemed placid on the surface and in an age of relative consensus,
but much of that placidity was on the surface because juvenile delin-
quency, inflation, radioactive fallout, segregation in the schools, and
beatnik protests were signs of a coming storm. Late in 1959, Charles
Van Doren, a Columbia University instructor and the son of a famous
intellectual family, finally confessed to an act of thoroughgoing fraudu-
lence. For fourteen consecutive weeks Van Doren, on the extraordinary
popular big money TV quiz show called *Twenty-one,* captivated
millions of the show's watchers. Many felt that he was an idol for the
young and counteracted Elvis Presley, that he had proved that studying
was not to be frowned upon. Yes, they thought, maybe an intellectual
could be as scintillating as a Clark Gable or a Willie Mays. Van Doren
was aware of his dishonesty and had knowingly entered into a total
deception and received huge sums of money for it. Although Columbia
University accepted Van Doren's resignation and NBC fired him and
newspapers and ministers commented on the state of American moral-

ity, the general public was unhappy with Van Doren's release, and a large group of Columbia students rallied in his behalf. The Van Doren incident was obviously one that served as a trigger for the turbulent sixties, for many people were saying that they would have done what Van Doren did for the money and fame. Tolerance of wrongdoing was more readily accepted. And a morality that put few restraints on the individual was beginning to emerge. This new code of ethics prompted John Steinbeck to write, "I am troubled by the cynical immorality of my country. It cannot survive on this basis."

2

Muted Rumblings, 1960-1964

Things always seem fairer when we look back at them, and it is out of that inaccessible tower of the past that Longing leans and beckons.

—James Russell Lowell

With the inception of the seventh decade of the twentieth century, America would enter one of its most tumultuous eras. The sixties was a time of enormous change in America's life style. People had more leisure time, places grew more crowded, and life, it seemed, was becoming more impersonal. One sensed in the early part of the decade, however, a feeling of hope and optimism. It then grew into a swell of demands for radical and immediate change and finally exploded into the variegated giant splinters of race, youth, violence, education, and the war in Vietnam. From the time of the sudden and violent 1965 Watts Riot in Los Angeles, which set the tone of open revolt, college administrators, parents, coaches, policemen were defied. "Irrelevance" and "unresponsiveness" were the key words thrown at people of authority. The sixties was, to be sure, an era of deep social turmoil.

There were some difficult moments at Northwest because there was no way to avoid some of the friction and internal debates which appear, when, after fifty-five years, a college comes of age. Along with the rise of faculty and student independence, there developed a growing inter-dependence of Northwest with the world outside. Northwest, as any true college, was bound closely with national and even world problems. The outside world during the 1960s was part of Northwest and with it the College began another ten years of growth.

Prior to 1960, Northwest's students, like most college students, were concerned about receiving degrees and finding good positions after leaving here. The emphasis occasionally varied, although the same educational concerns still largely existed, but a few came to please their relatives, or to keep money flowing from home, or to find a mate. Profound concern with the nation's basic social conditions did not seem to trouble any sizable group of either students or faculty for a while, but significant changes were taking place at Northwest. The school

21

increased in size, the faculty and staff were larger, and more subjects were being offered.

With the steady increase in enrollment, the change from a small to a medium-sized college was noticeable. Seventeen academic departments, headed by Dean of Instruction Leon Miller, were in existence at this time. Robert Foster was dean of administration; Jim Johnson was librarian. On April 11, however, came the impending and sad news: Horace Mann Senior High School, long a solid bedrock in the foundation of secondary education at Northwest, would be closed. Declining enrollment, according to Principal Herb Dieterich, was the culprit. Now in its last year, the senior high had an enrollment of 150 students and if it stayed open another year would probably dwindle to 125 students. Eight years later Principal Dieterich would also have to announce the closing of Horace Mann Junior High School.

In May for the first time the faculty discovered either the sweet or the bitter taste of the fruits of the ranking system, for the letters from the administration were sent out disclosing who were the professors, the associate professors, the assistant professors, and the instructors. Happiness was mixed with unhappiness, never a delightful combination.

Student organizations continued to thrive, and one more was added to the fold. Blue Key, a male honorary fraternity, established on the national scale in 1925 and concerned almost exclusively with campus interests, was installed on Saturday, May 21. Dr. Frank Grube, a life member of Blue Key, was named sponsor and senior Jack Freese, a student leader from Council Bluffs, was elected president. Since Blue Key's inception on campus, selection to the organization on the basis of leadership, extracurricular activities, and scholarship has been considered an especially high honor. The comparable organization for women known as Cardinal Key was formed on campus three years later with Librarian Carolyn Peterson as faculty adviser and Westboro's Jerilyn Irwin as president.

Tradition is definitely a keepsake in the world of academe, and people at Northwest were delighted when a piece of that tradition, a gift of ornate cast iron fence from the Ralph E. Martin family, was returned in May. What was so exciting about a piece of fence? The answer to that was the fence was cast here in Maryville and originally adorned the Thomas W. Gaunt home and nursery and homes of former Northwest presidents. President Jones, a staunch believer in tradition, was especially happy, for it was erected in front of "The House That Jack Built."

Student housing was again a problem with the fall enrollment at 1,971 with greater increases to come in the near future. Such increases would tax student housing since desirable housing off campus was limited, and on-campus dormitories were filled to capacity. President Jones was doing his bit by pointing out the need for rooms, and he was asking for two more dormitories. He continued to feel the need for a fine arts building, a new home management house, and more additions to the existing health and physical education building. As always, the head was planning. His announcement that he desired a fine arts building was timely, for five months later, during the week of April 24-28, Northwest would celebrate its first "Festival of the Arts," featuring various activities in the arts such as an organ recital by Glen C. Stewart of the music department, a lecture on art history by Dr. J. Kelley Sowards—formerly of Northwest—a presentation of *The Mikado* by the music and drama departments, directed by music man Gilbert Whitney and drama man Ralph Fulsom, and a viola-piano recital by the marital musical duo, Dr. and Mrs. Donald Sandford, accompanied by a college-community orchestra directed by the music department's Ward Rounds. Art exhibits were prevalent, too, and Charles Johnson, chairman of the Festival, was pleased and announced that the celebration would be an annual affair. Jones, of course, realized that a building for the fine arts was a necessity, for the arts serve not only to entertain but also to enrich people's daily lives. Students recognized the arts' redeeming values. The 1961 *Tower* devoted fifteen pages to drama and music and thirteen to all sports.

The 1960 fall term began quietly but, for the first time in thirty-seven years, without summer retiree Miss Mary Keith, long-time Horace Mann elementary teacher, and the end of the following spring term would complete the thirty-three year tenure of Miss Chloe Millikan, Horace Mann elementary school supervisor. Northwest's freshmen were causing a din, however, for they were seeking, it seems, to end the M Club's domination and, consequently, a long tradition on campus. They were tired of the M Club's tyranny. So they sawed loose and stole the clapper of the Victory Bell, traditionally the signal for the start of Walkout Day, which signified the end of freshmen hazing. They then sent an ultimatum to Student Body President Dale Cramer that the clapper would be returned when the indignities stopped. But the M Club, an organization with its own sense of tradition, said "No clapper—no Walkout Day." Since no student was willing to be an iconoclast and give up Walkout Day, the clapper was returned. In any revolt, however, the bold and the courageous will rise, and the freshmen had their undaunted group, for six freshmen kidnapped Cramer and kept him hostage overnight in a deserted farmhouse. The next morning the six locked him in a broom closet at the Nodaway County Courthouse before he was freed. Punitive measures always seem to be in store, or at least that is the way it was then, when one resists authority. Like Hawthorne's Hester in *The Scarlet Letter,* the six plus one unsuspecting student were branded, not with an "A" for their efforts, but with seven shaved heads that spelled out the word BEARCAT.

Intermixed with all of this activity was a freshmen-blamed food boycott—possibly a harbinger for the infamous food riot of 1964. Nearly 700 of the 900 diners who ate at the Student Union Cafeteria failed to appear at the noon meal. Dean of Students Charles Koerble viewed it as healthy because the students were making their feelings known about what they felt were insufficient food quantity and quality. The signs of independence and questioning of the status quo, signs of the sixties, were becoming obvious.

The freshmen's valiant efforts in the fall of 1960 did not go unnoticed nor were they in vain, for the time-honored custom of hazing freshmen was abolished the following fall semester. Future Northwest freshmen did not have to worry themselves anymore over kangaroo courts, duck walking, unwanted swims in the pond, strange haircuts, egg shampoos or whatever other deviltry was concocted for them. Joe Merrigan, the 1961-62 president of the Student Senate and a young man who probably had no affinity for deserted farmhouses or locked broom closets, stated that he and his Senate and the Administration felt that the rapid growth of Northwest made the positive change imperative. These groups, however, were not tradition-breaking purists, for they retained two of the colorful and exciting customs: the wearing of green beanies by the freshmen and the annual Walkout Day. As the institution marched with its growth and maturity, the students seemed to be in step.

The Administration Building was celebrating its golden anniversary, as Northwest was moving into its fifty-sixth year. The campus abounded with fine buildings, most of which had been built since Jones became president and there were more to come. Jones was not reticent in making recommendations or offering viable suggestions, for he told sixty campus-visiting Missouri legislators that their big job was "to loosen things too tight and tighten things too loose in handling appropriations." He told the listeners that higher education can never be cheap and should be thought of as an investment that promises rich returns and is indispensable to a free and explosively developing society. Northwest had its "explosively developing society," and Jones was telling them that Northwest needed new and replacement facilities. He also reminded them that the state of Missouri could save many tax dollars by establishing junior colleges under a state program in the state college districts under the supervision of the district colleges, a proposal Jones made two years previously, especially concerning Northwest and St. Joseph Junior College.

Jones was a man who lovingly looked after his College as a good parent would a child, and he liked to share his thoughts with others. He also liked to take pictures of his campus highlighted by the aesthetics, like the variety of flowers or the snowy winter landscape. With these slides, there was an idea. The slides, along with a letter and news of the College, were sent to the many graduates now living abroad. All the graduates, young and old, responded and wrote of their reacquaintance with once-familiar landmarks and recalled nostalgically their happy college days. The extra bit of thoughtfulness, ingenuity, and effort exerted by the President gave Northwest's international alumni in Iceland, Sweden, Holland, England, Norway, Germany, and France some fond memories of their alma mater.

Yes, Jones liked his campus, and it seemed to him that all parts contributed to the whole. He was genuinely interested in the sports program, as evidenced by his attendance. The Bearcat football team made him and the team's followers happy that fall because Coach Earl Baker, who moved in as the new mentor from Cameron, Missouri, High School where his team won thirty-eight consecutive games, guided his men to their best season in eighteen years. Basketball fans also got to see Captain Jerry Meznarich, LaSalle, Illinois, star, score 419 season points and watch the fluid movements of New York's Paul Lizzo, who is now Long Island University's head coach. Meznarich and Gene Jordan, a 505 point scorer from the year before, still rank in Northwest's top twenty scorers.

Locally, the town of New Hampton, Missouri, reveled, too, for Betty McCaig, a hometown senior was voted by her dorm-mates "The Spirit of Christmas" as the Residence Hall women once again celebrated their annual "Hanging of the Greens." Miss McCaig, stricken with polio in 1951, attended all of her classes in a wheelchair.

Closing his era, President Eisenhower gave his Farewell Address on January 17, 1961, and three days later President Kennedy gave his inaugural address and sounded his message with "Ask not what your country can do for you; ask what you can do for your country." Northwest was seeking to do more for its students, for talk on campus at the beginning of 1961 was the cooperative graduate program in education between Northwest and the University of Missouri, as five members of the latter school were on campus to discuss plans and policies. The visit must have been a profitable one, for the cooperative program was authorized in March and became effective with the beginning of the summer session. The summer session included courses in business, education, physical education, English, and history, and a student that summer could earn the maximum amount of nine hours. Northwest was now part of a trend in Missouri of developing cooperative graduate study, for similar programs existed between the University of Missouri and two of Northwest's sister schools: Southwest and Southeast Missouri State. The degree offered was the regular Master of Science degree granted by the University of Missouri but conferred by Northwest.

With the cooperative graduate program, Northwest was adding academic height to its growth, and a pre-Christmas announcement disclosed that Northwest would also grow physically. Both men and women students would be pleased because two new structures would be added to their existing dormitories during the next two years. The men's new L-shaped section, designed to house 248 men, would extend east and north from Colbert Hall, and would almost envelop the Quad buildings. The women's addition would host 260 additional women and extend from Residence Hall to the southeast along the College Drive entrance to the campus.

Because many of Northwest's students expressed the desire for a type of intellectual competition among themselves, the Student Senate, with the help of Union Board, created the "MSC Campus Bowl," a version of the popular Sunday afternoon nationally televised "College Bowl." The new competitive "sport," albeit non-athletic, provided an avid center of interest among student and even non-competing faculty groups. Dr. George Gayler, professor of history, was the quizmaster of this sixteen-team single elimination tournament, with a faculty member of every academic department involved in the official question committee. The Alpha Phi Omega-Gamma Sigma Sigma group—the two campus service organizations—had the distinction of winning the first match ever held at Northwest. Gayler, incidentally, continued to serve the "Campus Bowl" with distinction for its three-year stay on campus. In the second half of the 1970s and as the 1980s open, Gayler has spread his questioning talents elsewhere by serving as quizmaster for Shenandoah Radio Station KMA's "Brain Bowl" for Iowa high school history students and our own KXCV's "Brain Bowl" for Missouri students. KMA's contest format was borrowed from KXCV.

Bob Gregory, Frank Grube's successor as tennis coach, continued the netters' tradition of winning by coaching them to their fourth MIAA championship. Of course, it never hurts a coach to have a team led by such outstanding performers as Council Bluffs, Iowa's senior Jack Freese or St. Joseph's junior John Bregin.

Seeds are planted in the spring, but other kinds of seeds were being sown this spring, for heavy vibrations and forebodings of future events were sensed in the Northwest Missouri area. Since the state legislature rejected the proposal to turn the St. Joseph Junior College into a branch college of Northwest, petitions were circulating in St. Joseph for a four-year college, forty miles from Northwest. The petitions followed closely State Senator John Downs' proposal to have the University of Missouri establish a branch for third and fourth-year liberal arts study, an extension of the municipally supported Junior College. This, too, was at a time when Northwest was offering twenty hours of work in eight classes in St. Joseph.

Buildings were again in the news, but not for erecting. Thirteen existing buildings or halls now could be called by names that bore significant and animate identification of the individual structures. The names, upon long-overdue action, were finally approved by the Board of Regents after the group studied and considered all recommendations made by alumni committees and student groups. Known as Residence Hall since its birth in 1925, this women's dormitory would now appropriately and simply be known as Roberta Hall in honor of St. Joseph's Miss Roberta Steel, who died November 29, 1952, as a result of severe burn injuries when a St. Joseph Power and Light Company gas tank east of the Hall exploded during the night of April 28, 1951. The conflagration injured several girls and wrecked Residence Hall. Miss Steel spent many months in the hospital, and she seemingly had recovered sufficiently to enroll as a sophomore seventeen months later. Unfortunately, her injuries and burns were too much to overcome. She suffered a relapse and died on her twentieth birthday.

Freshman Hall, when completed, would be called Perrin Hall after Miss Alice Perrin, Northwest's first dean of women, and the College's first woman registrar, Nell Hudson, would always be remembered by generations of students through the naming of the new dormitory as Hudson Hall. Thus, Northwest's three women's dormitories, ready for occupancy for the fall 1962 semester, now bore the names of three women who played important roles in the evolution of Northwest.

Six names, five belonging to prominent former or present instructors or administrators and one former outstanding student athlete, would adorn the men's residences known as the Quadrangle: Hawkins, after C. A. Hawkins, Latin scholar and professor; Cauffield Hall, in honor of A. J. Cauffield, geography instructor; and Hake Hall, for J. W. Hake, professor of physics. Recognizing that sports are an integral part of any college's history, the Board bestowed a laurel wreath upon Jack McCracken, an outstanding basketball All-American for Northwest in the early 1930s, and named Quad 4 for him. Mr. Ryland Milner, who has seen many players in his fifty-one-year associa- tion with intercollegiate athletes, still calls McCracken one of the best players that he ever saw. McCracken, a former teammate of Milner's, played on that 1929-1930 unprecedented and—since then—unequaled team in Bearcat basketball lore that won thirty-one consecutive games. McCracken's mentor, the famous Henry Iba, would also have his head- line in August, for he was selected to Missouri's Sports Hall of Fame. The former director of field services A. H. "Bert" Cooper had the distinction of having his name on Quad 5. The men's hall was named Colbert Hall, after George H. Colbert, the first dean of faculty who was also a mathematics professor. The west wing became Wilson Hall for the popular Dean of Men Lon Wilson. Mr. Wilson died five weeks after the Hall was officially given his name, but he knew how North- west felt about his loyalty and dedication. The south wing was named for Ira Richardson, fourth president of the College, and the east wing was to be known as Cook after the late T. H. Cook, a long-time history instructor.

It was also time to name the place known as the Classroom Build- ing. Two years after its birth and still in its infancy, it was now to have the name of Colden Hall in memory of Charles J. Colden, first presi- dent of the Board of Regents and a diligent worker in securing the Normal School for Maryville. Mr. Colden, incidentally, was the one who chose what probably were and are the most read and quoted words on campus, "And the truth shall make you free." Those words, as alumni, students, staff, and guests readily know, are above the east door on the Administration Building. Other Coldens helped make an imprint later in the summer. Mr. Colden's two daughters, Mrs. Abbie Bell Colden Alexander and Mrs. Vi June Colden Hawthorne, con- tributed $2,700 to the Northwest State College Loan Fund, thereby helping make some students' financial loads lighter.

The naming of structures was again highlighted three months later at summer commencement when President Jones announced the names of the library and the women's gymnasium, two long-standing edifices on campus, and the athletic field and stadium. The library was named for the late C. E. Wells, who holds the record for being Northwest's longest-serving librarian—thirty-eight years—and the women's gym- nasium would now bear the name Martindale, after Nell Martindale Kuchs who chaired and taught in the women's department for seven years. The athletic field and stadium, President Jones proudly announced, would be henceforth called Rickenbrode, in honor of Northwest's immensely popular and avid Bearcat superfan, William

Rickenbrode, who at the time of his death in 1956 was the oldest active employee at the College.

Horace Mann Laboratory School opened its basement classrooms for the trainable, handicapped children of the Northwest area. The school, officially named The Missouri State School for Retarded Children, Training Center No. 26 and renamed the following year Training Center No. 26, was financed and controlled by the State Department of Education and taught by Mrs. Donald Peel. The school became functional in January, met in the basement of the Maryville First Christian Church, and was originally operated by a group of citizens called The Nodaway County Association for Retarded Children. The school proved its resiliency three years later when it energetically bounced back from a flood which virtually ruined all its equipment. People in the area also showed their mettle in a time of crisis and responded with donations of money and materials, and due to this display of strength the school became even better equipped.

Northwest, always a cooperative institution, added, beginning with the fall semester, to its number of degree programs by offering a program leading to the Bachelor of Science in Medical Technology. The program called for three academic years on Northwest's campus and a fourth year at Methodist Hospital and Medical Center in St. Joseph. Also launched and officially approved was the establishment of a Residence Center in St. Joseph, known as the Northwest Missouri State College Residence Center, and designed to offer senior college courses, thereby avoiding duplication—a fear that four-year colleges in the same general geographical area would have years later—of courses offered by the St. Joseph Junior College.

Also added to the academic program was a counselor-training program. Counselor training was recognized in 1961 as one of the greatest educational needs in the country, and Northwest recognized the need for high school guidance counselors and was in the position to provide this viable training necessary for one to be certified as a full-time guidance counselor in the public schools.

"Records are made to be broken" is a timeworn cliché that is usually heard in the sports world, and in the fall of 1961 Roger Maris of the New York Yankees hit his sixty-first home run and broke not only Babe Ruth's long-standing record of sixty home runs but the hearts of those who idolized the popular and flamboyant Babe. Northwest officials, however, were happy to meet a new record holder in the fall of 1961. Carol Long, a freshman from Grant City, set an enrollment record for Northwest by becoming its 2000th student. Although

Maris was disliked by many for his feat, Carol Long was feted for her timely and opportune accomplishment.

A growing college, academically and physically, always needs more than adequate funds, and 1961 ended very promisingly for "The House That Jack Built" and for dormitory expansion. The J. W. Jones Union would have its dining area enlarged, for the second-floor deck would be permanently enclosed, thus providing dining facilities for an additional 460 people. Because of the enclosure, students and staff could no longer dance on the roof when it was too stifling inside. There was a solution for that problem, to be sure. The whole Union, not just the dining areas, was going to be air conditioned! Now one could eat, dance, and play in relative comfort.

Four of Northwest's graduates were making their alma mater very proud early in 1962. Two of those four, Grant City's B. D. Owens and Bedford's Vane Basil Lucas, were studying for their Ph.D.s in insurance at the University of Pennsylvania. Each possessed the coveted and prestigious Huebner Foundation Fellowship. The third and fourth, Maitland's J. D. Hammond and Fairfax's George Green, also Huebner fellows, had already completed their doctorates. Owens, Lucas, Hammond, and Green, incidentally, received Northwest's Distinguished Alumni Award in 1972, 1974, 1976, and 1980 respectively.

The College and its division of business were especially happy, too, for more grants for graduate study by the Huebner Foundation during this time period were awarded to Northwest Missouri State College graduates than to those of any other college or university in the nation. The Huebner Foundation Fellowship continues to live on at Northwest. The fifth graduate from Northwest's department of business to receive the grant was Greenfield, Iowa's Norma Parrott in 1974. John Moore, a 1978 graduate from Kansas City, was yet another recipient. A driving force behind those fellowships was Dr. Sterling Surrey, a Huebner fellow himself and head of the division of business. Sadness enveloped Maryville in August, for the popular Surrey met an untimely death in Amherst, Massachusetts, where he had accepted a professorship of insurance and finance at the University of Massachusetts. He served the College well for twenty-four years, and he was applauded as a teacher, leader, adviser, organizer, writer, and as a man. Dr. Elwyn DeVore, professor of business and a former student of Surrey's, was appointed his successor to head the division of business, a post that DeVore still holds. Ironically, Dr. and Mrs. DeVore were house guests of the Surreys in Massachusetts hours before he died, and the DeVores did not learn of his death until they returned to Maryville three days later.

A definite testimony to what Surrey meant to Northwest was the immediate establishment of the Dr. Sterling Surrey Memorial Scholarship Fund. In a time before federally funded loans were available, the man was an avid believer in the College Student Loan Fund and did much to promote it. Seventeen years after his death the Surrey Memorial contained over $13,000 and continues to offer fine scholarships for students in the division of business.

Wilbur "Sparky" Stalcup, another Northwest alumnus and a native of Oregon, Missouri, was ending twenty-six years of collegiate coaching—sixteen at the University of Missouri and ten at Northwest. Stalcup was one of Mr. Iba's players, along with McCracken and Milner, when the team was making national headlines in the 30s, and he succeeded Mr. Iba as coach of the Bearcats. When Stalcup retired from active coaching, he was president of the National Basketball Coaches Association, and three months later was one of six distinguished coaches, along with five players with names like Wilt Chamberlain and Jerry West, elected to the Helms College Basketball Hall of Fame.

Back in 1958, B. D. Owens' bid for Student Senate president reached a new high on campus when three National Guard jets buzzed the campus, but subsequent election campaigning had its titillating moments, too. In the spring of 1961, when President Kennedy's Bay of Pigs fiasco was the big news nationally, Maryville's Richard Cornelison and Pontiac, Michigan's Oliver Cromwell advertised the candidacy of Corning's Larry Timmerman by floating in a canoe from Corning, Iowa, a hundred-mile trip down the Nodaway and 102 Rivers, and carrying with them a letter of best wishes from Dean Rogers, mayor of Corning, to President Jones. Yes, they were weary when they reached the Maryville water plant early on election morning. Excitement reigned, however, as the two boatmen were greeted by students, put in the lead car of a fifty-car caravan, and escorted to the campus where they gave the letter to Jones. They had fun and were treated as heroes, but their exploit was in vain. Timmerman, a member of Phi Sigma Epsilon, was defeated later that day by Stanberry's Joe Merrigan of the Tau Kappa Epsilon fraternity. Veterans, as was shown in the 1958 campaign, add a flair to attempted vote-getting. In the spring of 1962, one month after Lieutenant Colonel John H. Glenn flew around the world three times and became the first American to be put into orbit, Weston's Al Kyle, a former paratrooper, offered his own style of orbiting by jumping 1,000 feet from a campus-circling airplane. His stunt was to call attention to the desire of Stuart, Iowa's Ivan Lyddon to be Student Senate president, and his landing, not quite as heralded as Glenn's, was greeted by a brass band welcome and applauded by many gathering students. Backers of Rockwell City, Iowa's Earl Boyd, a Phi Sigma Epsilon candidate opposing independent Lyddon, borrowed a page from the Olympics and for two days marathoned through the campus with lighted torches. Independents jumped with ecstasy as Lyddon tallied the most votes, and the Phi Sigs received some satisfaction because Darlington, Missouri's Bob Cobb was elected vice president.

Social and political life are mainstays and so is the academic life. James Johnson, Northwest's librarian, estimated that students and staff were regularly using 75,000 books, reading 300 different magazines, and absorbing a dozen daily and four dozen weekly newspapers from many of the students' hometowns. The textbook library possessed 50,000 books for student use. NASA, probably because it helped reconcile Russia's lead in space, was showing its big space productions live on TV, and the public was exposed to thrills and dramatic moments. Yes, technology was important to Americans and it was important at Northwest, too. Officials were offering technological advancement to help relieve the hassles of student registration for both students and staff. Dean of Administration Robert P. Foster introduced new IBM machines, a remedy that would help alleviate the headaches at enrollment time and make it necessary for all students to be cleared for registration as far in advance of registration as possible. He and Registrar Ruth Nystrom, Gladys Raines, Monica Zirfas, and Martha Moles (Cooper), members of the office personnel, prepared themselves for these machines by participating in an IBM functional wiring and operating course at the IBM headquarters in Kansas City. Foster's staff continued to do all of the calculating and compiling of student grades, but new student registration would be easier because the student was not required to fill out registration booklets. With the help of his adviser, he made out his schedule, got it approved, pulled his class cards, and paid his fees. Of course, registration day still offered its problems; students still stood in line to see an adviser and worried whether their selected classes would close and if they would have to settle for an early morning or late afternoon class or an instructor they deemed less than desirable.

The Advisement Center and pre-registration, also remedies to help cure what ailed registration, were several years in the future.

The arts were thriving early in 1962 as evidenced by two major drama productions: *The Heiress,* based on novelist Henry James' *Washington Square,* and Lillian Hellman's *The Little Foxes.* The two were presented within two months of each other and were aptly directed by Dr. Ralph Fulsom. A poetry book featuring area high school and local college students' verses with the patriotic name of *Green and*

White, highlighting the College's colors, was introduced and edited by Dr. Frank Grube.

Twelve honorary fraternities and thirty-two student organizations now existed on campus, and one more was welcomed with the formal national installation of Delta Psi Kappa, professional fraternity for women physical education majors. Bethany senior Martha Gray was elected president of the seven charter members; Miss Bonnie Magill, head of the women's physical education department, was chosen adviser, and Dr. Kathryn Riddle and Mrs. Dorothy Walker, both members of the department, were accepted as associate members. Although intramural sports were as important to the Northwest women of 1962 as they were to the men, intercollegiate competition for the women was practically nil. This was not their fault, to be sure, because that was the way it generally was with women's athletics throughout the country.

Mrs. Dorothy Walker, however, did start a women's basketball team in 1962 and a volleyball team in 1967. Because of the trend in women's athletics, competition was limited, but the women's desire to play was evident. The emergence of Bearkitten organized and scheduled competition, however, had to wait until 1969 when Miss Sandra Mull's gymnastic unit became the first Northwest women's intercollegiate team to have an annual budget, marking the beginning for a comprehensive women's athletic program. Mrs. Walker, always attempting to develop interest in women's physical education, introduced a Career Day for interested area high school students. Career Day thrived in subsequent years as high school students came not only from Missouri but also from Nebraska, Iowa, and Kansas to see demonstrations by the Gymnastic Club, Dance Club, and Swim Club. They benefited, too, by talking to the department's majors and participating in gymnastics, dances, and games. They, in addition, had the chance to familiarize themselves with Northwest.

Miss Mabel Cook, chairman, and her staff and majors in the department of home economics were ecstatic when they learned late in the spring semester that they would be able to come back to a new home management house in the fall, a structure that was requested by President Jones in 1960. The three-level Colonial-style house, replacing the old one which had been in use since 1938, was designed by Mr. Donald Valk, head of the industrial arts department. The House offered, as it still does, the opportunity each semester for six home economics majors to live there and experience home management under the supervision of a member of the home economics faculty. Every Christmas season thereafter the young women displayed their learning by inviting several faculty members and guests for traditional Christmas enjoyment. The occasion, always a warm and memorable one, befits the young ladies and instructor, and, of course, the House. The House was simply called the Home Management House for ten years. But in 1972, one year after Miss Cook retired, the Board honored her by naming the domicile The Mabel Cook Home Management House. No one disputed this decision for Miss Cook had been, it seemed, associated with Northwest since its birth, for her father, T. H. Cook, and Northwest, then called Normal, began their collegiate careers together, and Mr. Cook, for whom Cook Hall is named, ended his here after thirty-nine years. The Cook mark is strong at Northwest. His daughter was a student and a charter member of Kappa Omicron Phi, a national honorary home economics fraternity founded on the Maryville campus by former chairman, Hettie Anthony. Miss Cook gave Northwest twenty-four years of dedicated work—nine as instructor and fifteen as chairman. The Kappa Omicron Phi fraternity, incidentally, presented gifts of candlesticks, china, crystal, and linens to the House when it opened that fall in 1962.

Traditionally, graduating classes of Northwest always give their College something to remember them by, and the seniors of 1962 certainly made their gift a visual one. They presented at the annual senior breakfast pictures of persons for whom the various buildings on campus are named. The pictures, enlarged and finished in brown tint, were selected by the honorees' families. The portraits hang in their respective buildings, honoring Uel W. Lamkin, Mrs. Albert Martindale Kuchs, Charles J. Colden, C. E. Wells, William Rickenbrode, Roberta Steel, Alice Perrin, George H. Colbert, Lon Wilson, A. H. "Bert" Cooper, C. A. Hawkins, A. J. Cauffield, J. W. Hake, and Jack McCracken. Of course, Rickenbrode's could not be hung anywhere in an outdoor stadium, or in the middle of a football field, but it did find a fitting home in the west lobby of the men's gymnasium. Lamkin's graces a wall of the east lobby. The fourteen pictures join the one of J. W. Jones in the Union and add a fine animate touch to their respective structures. Another picture was added on August 27, 1962, of Miss Nell Hudson to adorn the new women's dormitory named for her. It was presented at a tea in her honor at the dorm and was contributed by Chapter L, PEO members.

Saturday, May 26, four days after the graduating class gift announcement, brought more name disclosures when the Board designated that the new, yet unstarted, south unit of the new men's dormitory project would be known as Douglas Hall for the late attorney, R. L. Douglas of St. Joseph, who served on the Board of Regents for twenty-four years. The east-west wing of the project, as many people already knew, would be known as Cooper Hall. The original Cooper Hall, the name bestowed on it in 1961, was in the way of dormitory progress and was demolished. Construction started two days after the announcement, and students were able to occupy their "home away from home" in the fall of 1963. President Jones and the Board, looking ahead to future burgeoning enrollments, had expectations that one day another dormitory would be added extending from Cooper Hall to Wilson Hall, thus enclosing the men's dormitory region. Sometimes names for campus buildings come years after the building has been occupied and the honoree is dead, but E. A. "Lefty" Davis, former coach and director of athletics who retired in 1952 and died in 1965, knew that the future dormitory addition would be named for him because it was so designated at that May 26 meeting. But it was not to be; the dormitory region was never enclosed.

A big worry on any campus is where to put that automobile, and that problem was no less in 1962, for it seemed that almost every student had a car and not many instructors were into walking. Many college presidents were fond of quoting what has now become an aphorism, that the three main administrative problems on most campuses were parking for the faculty, athletics for the alumni, and sex for the students. Northwest, however, was doing its best to alleviate the first for it built a huge new parking lot south of the National Guard Armory. It was obviously important for the students, too, because the lot was highlighted in the 1963 *Tower* yearbook. The lot boded well for the future since it was located in the proximity of the site of the future high-rise dormitories.

President Jones, never shy about asking for what was needed for his College, told members of a legislative committee of the need for almost $3,000,000 in capital improvements to the educational facilities. The legislators knew that the College was in need when Jones asked, for his requests always seemed reasonable to them. His key request again was the fine arts building, one that was so sorely needed to enhance cultural opportunities. One definite benefit, however, awaited the fall returnee who was interested in his body. The basement in Lamkin Gym, the men's gymnasium, was now finished! One could find a variety of items there for the sports minded: an indoor asphalt track, a combination broad jump and high jump pit, a regulation pitcher's mound, a separate practice wrestling room, a separate area for Ping-Pong tables, and rooms for the sports that were becoming so popular—handball and racquetball. The day of the weight-lifting room was yet to come. For 1962, Lamkin Gymnasium was an equipped physical education fieldhouse.

It did not take eight people long to benefit from the Master of Education degree from the University of Missouri through the cooperative program, implemented in 1961, with Northwest. At the summer graduating exercises held at Rickenbrode Athletic Field, Maryville's Mrs. Velda May Walker Anderson, obviously because her married name began with an *A*, became the first to receive such a degree. The others waiting in line to receive their degrees from Dr. John Schwada, president of the University of Missouri, and to be hooded by Dr. Leon Miller, Northwest's dean of instruction, were Robert Eugene Glasford, Loree Edna Hogsett, Adam Bernard Moser, Ida Sue Lahr Paxton, James Phillip Ranck, Fred Reeves, and Lawrence Paul Wray, a biology instructor at Maryville High School. Moser had the "dubious" distinction of being the only one of the above who did not receive his bachelor's degree from Northwest.

Yes, the newly designed J. W. Jones Union was all dressed up and waiting for its old friends and the incoming fall freshmen. On September 20, the new Ballroom was used for the first time when the traditional faculty reception for freshmen was held. This affair gave the freshmen and the faculty a chance to wear their best clothes and an opportunity to chat informally in a social setting. This ringing affair, however, was beginning to sound its own death knell as freshmen classes got larger, thus offering minimal contact with the eager students and the receptive faculty.

The Ballroom, at that time and for several years following, witnessed many dance forms from the twist to the dominance of rock. The twist, a dance expression of the early 60s, was the dance craze, and it was remarkable because it came to dominate social dancing; it certainly prevailed in the Ballroom, although the band played an occasional two-step, as students, including some faculty sponsors, exercised their bodies with vigorous, exhibitionistic movements. The Ballroom readily accepted all these gyrations, probably knowing that the twist and its numerous descendants were really easy and safe. No one, however, who was either dancing or watching or denouncing these new movements, probably recognized the ideological impulse behind them because each person danced alone, "doing his own thing." The dancer in his ambience was surrounded by others doing their own thing in much the same fashion. The twist celebrated individuality, the right of everyone to be different in much the same way, a definite polarity to the conformity found in the 50s and a way of life in the near future, nationally and locally.

Many former students of Northwest have cherished memories of their school and of townspeople who befriended them and tried to make their stay away from home comfortable. Mrs. Clara Chick was one of those people and an exceptional one, for she certainly looked after many of Northwest's students through the years. This woman rented rooms to students for thirty-eight years and boarded them for twenty of those years, and she had as many as thirty-three boarders at one time. November 3, 1962, triggered the memories of those former roomers and diners. She died on that day at age eighty-nine.

Fall semester enrollees broke another enrollment record, but there was no picture celebration for any student record breaker. The freshmen were happy that fall because they discovered that the faculty reception was not such a stiffly formal affair after all. Some of them even found college instructors approachable and gregarious. The freshmen also instantly liked Student Body President Ivan Lyddon, for he was the one who said that the green beanies, the one traditional remnant left over from freshmen hazing days, "would not be worn on the Northwest Missouri State College campus this fall."

The Bearcat football team went 0-9; the Marion Moss coached basketball team finished at 12-11 and its leader, Austin, Minnesota's Roger Voss, became the leading single-season scorer in the College's history with 565 points, a record that was not eclipsed until thirteen years later when David Alvey scored 571 points. The swim team, headed by Dr. H. D. Peterson, enjoyed its third consecutive winning season in three years of varsity competition, and wrestling was quickly gaining its own hold as a major sport as its five-year record stood at 53-10. Coach Jerry Landwer's men, paced by Maquoketa, Iowa's Dave Moore and Tulsa's Harvey Hallum, definitely had established Northwest as the top wrestling college in the state. The team, incidentally, easily beat the University of Missouri. After the 1962 football season, Earl Baker decided to step down as Bearcat football coach, and President Jones hired Ivan Schottel, an alumnus and former all-MIAA and professional performer. Schottel was a highly successful football coach for the St. Benedict's Ravens at St. Benedict's College in Atchison, Kansas, where his team won the small college national championship in 1956. He had the distinction of being a successful coach without any more Ravens because the Atchison school eliminated football from its program late in 1962. But he could look forward to plenty of Bearcats, almost all of them enthusiastic underclassmen, including Jim Redd, the present Northwest coach, and four able coaches in number one assistant Baker, Bob Gregory, Burton Richey, and Gene Lasley.

After announcing the news concerning Schottel, Jones was making another disclosure—one that everyone interested in the College knew was eventually coming—about himself. He told over 200 people attending a session of the Knights of the Hickory Stick, a group of Northwest Missouri educators, in St. Joseph, Missouri, that he was retiring because of Missouri's retirement laws on July 1, 1964. Of course, a man of Jones' administrative stature does not retire the day he announces it, for he knew that the next year-and-a-half would still present much work and a multiplicity of problems. Announcements of such importance, whether expected or not, generally startle one and that seemed to be the general feeling on campus. Jones, not acting hastily, did want college officials and faculty to be thinking of his successor. The faculty, never slow in matters dealing with its welfare and governance, selected a committee to report to the Board of Regents on suggested qualifications for the future president of Northwest Missouri State College. This committee was the first sounding of a long series of discussions, official and unofficial, that culminated the following year when Jones' successor was finally chosen.

Jones gave another public talk the next month at a joint University of Missouri and Northwest Alumni meeting, the first time, Jones noted, that the "Bearcat" and the "Tiger" sat down together. It was a multi-pronged lecture that again strongly emphasized the need for coordination of Missouri's higher educational program, and he again urged his unrelenting support for a cultural center on Northwest's campus, a critical necessity for the College and the area.

Football had its news in February, and now it was basketball's turn in April. Dick Buckridge, former Bearcat all-MIAA performer and conference Sportsman of the Year winner, was coming home to coach the Bearcats, replacing Marion Moss. Buckridge must have felt a sense of family, for he was joining four other "grads" on the athletic staff: Schottel, Milner, Gregory, and Richey. Dean Charles Koerble was also feeling a sense of family by showing that an academic person could do well in city affairs. He was now serving his fourth year as Maryville's mayor. April, this forerunner of spring in Northwest Missouri, seemed to be the "welcome" month for the College because the eight Greek organizations on campus embraced yet another one—the Alpha Kappa Lambdas, known as the AKLs. Sigma Sigma Sigma sorority was celebrating something old—its thirty-sixth anniversary— but offering something new as they honored Miss Nell Hudson, the sorority's first charter member, with its first annual Steadfast Alumna Citation.

Spring also brings a newness and President and Mrs. Jones were suggesting something new as they were planning for their retirement from twenty-six years of dedicated and loyal service to Northwest. Wanting to remain where they spent so much of their lives, they asked the Board's permission to construct a house in the area known as the orchard south of Colden Hall to be used by the President Emeritus and his wife during their lifetimes. Upon their deaths, the house would become the exclusive property of Northwest and be utilized for any purpose so desired by the Board of Regents. The Board found the Jones' request an inviting one because all the College needed to do was set aside enough money from available funds to match the Jones' own personal money of $25,000. The offer was even more appealing because the couple was going to spend an additional $5,000 on furnishings which would be left, along with the house, by them to the College. The Board, after considerable study, felt that there would be no legal problems in combining college funds with private, accepted the proposal, but the generous and unselfish offer touched off considerable debate in Maryville. It is very difficult at times for some people to understand generosity and a good act of faith, and they consider such characteristics as either a nefarious or mysterious plot. The Jones, to be sure, did not anticipate the considerable controversy aroused by their offer, stoked heavily by Maryville's *Daily Forum,* which doubted the legality of mixing state and private funds and the wisdom of having a president emeritus living on campus. All the Jones really wanted was to have a place on campus where they could, hopefully, enjoy a long and happy retirement but it was not to be. Their bountiful and innocent request, which they hoped and originally felt would be a satisfactory and harmonious arrangement, was withdrawn, and President Jones asked the Board to rescind the offer. Jones felt that his request created an environment of doubt and distrust of his motives in desiring to build a house on the campus to be owned and operated by the College. He, with reason, was disturbed by the publicity given the matter, which he found detrimental to the best interests of Northwest. It had to hurt personally, too. He and Mrs. Jones felt that they were placed in an intolerable situation in regard to their enjoyment of retirement since they really were trying to help, and not hurt, Northwest. How one could really consider the offer as egregious or mercenary is quite difficult to understand because this was a man who occasionally turned down presidential salary raises so that his staff might benefit. The Jones soon ended any further discussion on this matter when they purchased their home on Ray Avenue, within walking distance of the campus.

In the summer, Governor John Dalton vetoed what was then called the Joplin-St. Joseph College Bill, one that would establish four-year colleges as branches of the University of Missouri at those two schools. The cacophonous cry for an undergraduate college in St. Joseph was still being heard by the hard-core supporters of the bill, but many, to be sure, felt that such a plan would dilute the state's educational system and water down state-supported college programs. Dalton's action was commended in the Maryville area. Governor Dalton was also giving and yet taking away. Yes, Northwest could have its cultural center—a fine arts building—but he reduced the $2,000,000 appropriation authorized by the legislature to $1,500,000. Dalton thought the lower figure would be sufficient, but he obviously did not consider that the cut would result in a loss in the theater's seating capacity and music recital hall.

Northwest was disappointed, but happy to receive its long-awaited, two-story circular modern building that would help enhance the arts and house its music and art departments and some theater. Officials, never slow when it came time to build, were ready, for the location— the square at the south edge of the campus—was already decided, and the architect's preliminary plans approved when Dalton made his announcement. It is ironic how fate swings its blows. Charles H. Johnson, acting chairman of the art department, who just began a year's leave, was felled by a stroke and died at age thirty-seven before the building would be completed. Approved also—but with a $250,000 Dalton cut—was the $500,000 remodeling and addition to Wells Library, for the thirty-four-year-old structure was beginning to complain that it really was not large enough now to handle all of the school's increased numbers of students. Since the two projects would take many months to complete, sidewalk spectators would be kept busy watching the progress on campus.

With the opening of two new sections in men's and women's dormitories and Cooper and Hudson occupied, Northwest was lauded for its being one of the few colleges in either Kansas or Missouri to have adequate housing for its fall semester students. Now 976 women and 972 men could stay on campus. Vets' Village for married veteran students was a help, along with the four fraternity houses off campus, plus a list of approved off-campus housing for both sexes.

It was still a year before Northwest would have its seventh president, but speculation existed on campus as to who would be Jones' successor. The Committee selected by the faculty to request its suggested qualifications for a new president had finished its work, after several meetings of considerable discussion and reflection, and submitted its report. The Committee, headed by Dr. John Harr, chairman of the social science division, represented a cross section of academic disciplines, with Dr. J. Gordon Strong from chemistry; Mr. H. R. Dieterich, education; Dr. Donald Sandford, music; Dr. H. D. Peterson, men's physical education; Mr. Donald Valk, industrial arts; Mrs. Elaine Mauzey, foreign languages; and Dr. Elwyn DeVore, business. Their report was in unanimous agreement among committee members and it was clear and succinct. The Committee's list of requirements for the new president read: (1) Have an earned doctoral degree; (2) should be preferably identified with the liberal arts area; (3) should have both considerable experience as a college classroom teacher and college academic administrator and be currently identified with higher education; (4) have leadership that is energetic, vigorous, and inspiring in relation to the College and community as well as the general public; (5) possess knowledge of present and possible future problems of higher education; (6) demonstrate fairness and good judgment; (7) show concern for student and faculty morale, harmony, and welfare. Several personal characteristics were listed, along with an age preference between forty and fifty-five years of age. The report, the Committee felt, would at least be an aid for a search committee and possibly quiet any faculty apprehension.

Northwest educators, led by Dr. Leon F. Miller, dean of instruction; Dr. Robert P. Foster, dean of administration; and Mr. Everett W. Brown, director of field services; were still working diligently and cooperatively with St. Joseph Superintendent of Schools George Blackwell and his assistant G. Max Coleman to assist St. Joseph in establishing a two-year residence center, offering senior college credit, in cooperation with Northwest. The above officials and a St. Joseph committee were mutually sincere in attempting to work out a harmonious program that would benefit St. Joseph and, of course, Northwest. Despite considerable agitation in Buchanan County regarding a four-year college, Northwest was trying for a third time to establish a center for St. Joseph, and its efforts had to be appreciated in many quarters, for numerous Northwest alumni lived in the St. Joseph area. In the fall of 1963, there were 404 teachers in the St. Joseph School System who attended or graduated from Northwest Missouri State College. Other forces within St. Joseph were at work, too. A large organization of St. Joseph citizens, purporting to represent a cross section of community interest, was attempting to finance and develop a branch of Tarkio College, a small private denominational school northwest of St. Joseph for the third and fourth year of college work in conjunction with the tax-supported St. Joseph Junior College program. Although St. Joseph was in near proximity of several four-year colleges, it was obvious that many of its people were desperate for their own four-year school, yet they were willing to woo the affections of other colleges, like Northwest and Tarkio, for a practical and acceptable solution to their long quest for a senior institution.

The nuclear arms race between Russia and the United States continued, but the threat of nuclear war was too remote to bother people much. Atmospheric testing was a concern, however, for fears of the fallout caused by the testing grew among American adults, mostly concerned over their children's future. President Kennedy addressed himself to these fears. Kennedy proposed a partial test ban to permit only underground tests and Premier Khrushchev agreed. It was a victory since it raised America's prestige abroad, for mankind, and for Kennedy in particular, and it showed that, although the United States conducted more underground tests after the treaty than before, America's citizens could be aroused and not apathetic about the future. Cuba and Vietnam were, at this time, other matters.

Although the College is a state institution, students still bring their religious faith, beliefs, and principles to the campus and, for many, religion is important. The 1963 fall term began with eight student religious organizations. The local churches have always been supportive of the student organizations, and in October the congregation of the First Baptist Church bought a home at 401 West Fourth Street to be used as a student center for Baptist youths attending Northwest. It was Northwest's first student center owned and operated by a religious group. The Catholics followed a year later when they purchased the home of former librarian C. E. Wells at the corner of College Avenue and Dunn Streets for their Newman Center. A year after the Catholic action, the Methodists broke ground for their Wesley Foundation on land at the southeast corner of the campus that was acquired in 1961. The Methodist Center was completed in 1965 and is a popular meeting place for student religious organizations. A Religious Emphasis Week offering varying views from outstanding speakers and thought-provoking discussions for students began on campus in 1938 and was generally presented the week before Easter until the Week was supplanted in 1970 by the Dildine Lecture Series, named for Dr. Harry Dildine, former missionary and professor of history at Northwest. The Week was an integral part of campus activities, and the student-faculty committee was chaired for twenty years by Dr. J. Gordon Strong, assisted by Dr. Irene Mueller. Dr. Kenneth Minter succeeded Strong as chairman of Religious Emphasis Week in 1965.

Along with the fence in front of the J. W. Jones Union, traditionalists could now point with pride to another piece of Northwest tradition. The historic sundial, presented to the College in 1928 by J. R. Brink, former superintendent of grounds, would become operable again. All that remained of the sundial in late 1963 were the pedestal and the base on which the original rested until the daughters of Mr. Brink, Mrs. R. P. Hosmer, Kotanah, New York, and Mrs. H. H. Bellows, Lake Forest, Illinois, had the sundial restored. The "new face," north of the President's Home, was an early Christmas present that delighted onlookers.

Everyone knows what happened in Dallas on November 22, 1963. The shock was felt so greatly at Northwest, as everywhere in the country, that classes were dismissed on that fateful day because Kennedy's assassination placed such an immense emotional burden on people. His death elicited remarkable expressions of grief, and at Northwest a large, somber crowd gathered its collective grief and met for a special memorial service in respect to the fallen President. Sad but impressive and with a touch of the majestic was the Tower Choir, directed by music's Gilbert Whitney, singing a farewell message to Kennedy, a man who created the possibilities of change and left behind the means of effecting it. Ellen Grube, 1964 *Tower* editor, and her staff printed a full-page portrait of the President and dedicated the yearbook to his memory.

Fourteen members of Tau Kappa Epsilon launched the New Year by journeying to the nation's capital to give large family Bibles, an idea conceived by Lineville, Iowa's Ron Zimmerman, to President Lyndon Johnson and Mrs. John F. Kennedy. Not many people were able to see either of the two in those hectic days, but the group did get to present the books to Mrs. Bess Abell, Johnson's social secretary. The New Year brought happy tidings for Horace Mann Laboratory School, one of the older buildings on campus; it was to be improved with new tile floors, new light fixtures, and fresh coats of paint. More good tidings went out to the gallant and the daring because Mrs. Dorothy Walker of the women's physical education department was forming a Fencing Club for individuals who cared about fencing and for area teachers who wanted to learn fencing techniques. The Radio Club continued to handle many student messages, ranging from birthday greetings to urgent "down slips" explanations to parents. The members held their own classes daily and on weekends to aid new members in obtaining their ham radio licenses. The group also supplied technical assistance to that "new kid" on campus, KDLX, a radio station set up by a group of enterprising students and sponsored by Mr. Robert Seipel, superintendent of buildings and grounds. KDLX transmitted from a small room, really a broom closet, in Colbert Hall, and early in 1964 the campus was wired so that students in any dormitory could listen from 5 p.m. until midnight to the latest campus news and music, hopefully to keep them informed and also to aid their studying with background music. "Teach Me Tiger," a recording by the popular and breathy April Stevens, was their sign-on, and the recording has been used as the sign-on after any disaster. Station Manager Gary Matthews from Kansas City hoped, too, that the small operation would grow into a regularly operated station. A few years later Matthews' hopes were more than realized.

In late January, R. T. "Dick" Wright, chairman of the College's department of agriculture, announced that he would retire the following July. The Agricultural Museum, located then on the first floor of the Administration Building, was started by Wright in the late 1930s and remained his main hobby. The Museum's prized possessions were an Indian ceremonial jug, dated 500 to 800 A.D.; a set of handmade working tools; a two-row corn planter, built and used in the early 1880s and one of the oldest implements of its type. Another outstanding display, one that is lauded by experts, is the Wright collection of different types of barbed wire. Artifacts from the Museum are now scattered over the campus and, hopefully, they will one day be gathered together again in a final resting spot. The College, in 1965, named its college farm the R. T. Wright College Farm. It was a tribute that certainly befitted the man.

After twenty-one years at Northwest another notable person was also retiring. Joining Wright and Jones was Dr. J. Gordon Strong, chairman of both the division of physical science and the division of science and mathematics. During Dr. Strong's tenure at Northwest, seven of his chemistry students received Ph.D. degrees. Three of those joined the faculty shortly after Strong's retirement: Dr. Sam Carpenter, Dr. Ed Farquhar, and Dr. Harlan Higginbotham. The first student from Northwest to receive a Ph.D. in chemistry was Dr. Richard Leet, one of Strong's earlier protégés and currently president of the Chemical Division of Amoco Oil Company. Still another of Dr. Strong's former students was Dr. Ted Weichinger, who succeeded Strong as chairman of the division.

On January 23, Harold Hull, Maryville attorney and president of the Board of Regents, was telling his fellow Rotarians that during his eleven-year tenure on the Board he had missed only one of eighty-eight meetings. That, however, was not the import of his talk. The Regents' president informed the group that in a day-long meeting of his Board three days earlier a total of forty-nine applicants for President Jones' successor had been screened to six candidates, and he hoped that the Board's business on this matter would be finished by March 1. Hull also made the "startling" revelation that one black educator from the University of Chicago had applied for the position of President of Northwest; he did not reveal whether the person was one of the six finalists.

From the time Jones made his retirement announcement, considerable speculation arose concerning his successor. Although the Faculty Committee defined the criteria, culled from the many suggestions from faculty, for selecting the new president, there is no indication that the Committee's work was heeded, nor was there ever a campus advisory committee composed of selected faculty, administration, members of the Board of Regents, alumni, and students to search out acceptable candidates for the Board to consider. The Board, to be sure, as Hull indicated, was arduously screening the credentials of those who had indicated an interest in the post.

On March 23, at a special meeting, the Board of Regents ended speculation and discussion and their five-month presidential search by naming Dr. Robert P. Foster, the forty-seven-year-old dean of administration, to succeed President Jones as Northwest Missouri State College's seventh president when Jones retired in July. Foster moved up the academic ladder along the following route: high school diploma from Warrensburg, Missouri; bachelor's and master's degrees at Central State College, Warrensburg; a doctor's degree from the University of Missouri in 1960; coach and principal at Carrollton, Missouri, High School; registrar at Northwest from 1948 to 1960; and dean of administration at Northwest from 1960-1964. Governor John Dalton lauded the new president as having the intelligence, the poise, the personality, and the forthrightness to make a great college president, citing several of the qualifications from the Faculty Committee on Qualifications. On March 24, although President Jones would still be in office over three months, the Board, attempting to apply a smooth transition in the presidential interchange, bestowed on Jones the title President Emeritus. Jones, like his predecessor, Lamkin, was also afforded an office in Wells Library.

Cultural events were very visible. The San Franciso Ballet troupe offered its usual exquisite performance and won new fans for ballet. April 23, 1964, William Shakespeare's 400th birthday, almost went unnoticed until Dr. Frank Grube's Shakespeare class gave a program of Shakespeare in Horace Mann Auditorium in observation of the bard's anniversary.

The threat of any type of student mob action was practically non-existent at Northwest in 1964, except for the usual spring fling when groups of college men would carry out panty raids at the women's dormitories, the perennial April outburst of youth, with possibly a slight protest against the zeal housemothers showed in protecting their girls' virtues. Some organizations were known for conducting general hell-raising, and in various ways, especially through the student newspaper, the *Northwest Missourian,* students occasionally expressed concern over what they considered inequities and injustices in the college community. But then it happened! On April 10, 1,600 clamoring students jammed the Rickenbrode Stadium bleachers at noon, when normally they would be having their lunch. They were not there as spectators at a football game or track and field event, but, like the ancient Romans in the Colosseum, they wanted action—definite action—for changes in the food served in Northwest's cafeteria. Chillicothe's Tom Kramer, Creston, Iowa's David Herring, and Lombard, Illinois' Edward Reeder were the student spokesmen, while Dr. Charles Koerble, dean of students; Mrs. M. T. Sheldon, dietitian; Luther Belcher, business manager; Dr. Leon Miller, dean of instruction; and Jack Lasley, dean of men; represented the administration. (Jones and Foster were both in out-of-town meetings.) Ringleaders Kramer, Herring, and Reeder said that all the students wanted was good food. They felt their complaints were not being heard, but Belcher told the students that quality food was being purchased for the cafeteria. This mass meeting, which ended with an uneasy calm, was preceded by a demonstration of approximately 850 students the previous night at the home of the dietitian, Mrs. M. T. Sheldon. Yelling for better food preparation and more variety, the students were noisy but, to the neighbors' relief, orderly and democratic at the Sheldon home. Concerned, however, that a mob was approaching his house, Dr. Sheldon, the dietitian's husband and a member of the education department, almost triggered an incident when he appeared on his porch with a shotgun in an attempt to scare away the intruders. Any untimely happening was averted, however, as a Maryville policeman, standing by and observing, took Sheldon back into his house. Lasley and Koerble, knowing that hundreds of students could not continue to stand and mill in the Sheldon's yard, neighbors' yards, or in the street, led them back to the campus and discussed with the students their grievances, which spilled over into the next day's meeting at the Stadium.

The weekend offered a lull but something else was spawning. On Sunday night the Maryville area, including the campus, resembled a disaster area, but the destruction was not created by any student action against monotonous and poorly cooked food. A tornado ripped through the west and northwest part of town littering streets with broken glass and tree limbs, toppling trees, sucking out windows, and ripping roofs from buildings and homes, causing $1,500,000 in damages. The campus was badly littered, and adding to the accumulated debris were hundreds of bluejays, sparrows, and starlings caught in the high winds and blown out of the evergreens and pine trees in front of the women's dorms.

Late Monday night, April 13, however, there were no high winds to deter student activity, and a large segment of the student body, numbering close to 700, created a whirlwind of its own by using the sit-down protest, a technique borrowed from February 1, 1960, when four black college students sat down at a whites-only lunch counter in Greensboro, North Carolina, and asked for service. Northwest's demonstrating students knew that the celebrated Greensboro incident captured the public imagination, and they were hoping that their sit-in would call attention to their dispute concerning food served in the cafeteria. They sat briefly in front of the Nodaway County Courthouse, and then moved approximately one mile south on Highway 71 and blocked traffic for an hour, attracting, to be sure, many curious onlookers. The human blockade backed up traffic for three miles, while Maryville policemen, officers from the sheriff's department, and members of the Missouri Highway Patrol talked to them in vain. Within a two-block perimeter of the sit-in were forty law enforcement officers equipped with tear gas, gas masks, riot sticks, guns, and a police dog. Finally St. Louis' Glenn Acksel, newly elected student body president, convinced some of the dissenters that the demonstration should be continued on campus and not on the highway. A considerable number stayed, however, and the police used one tear gas bomb, thrown into the middle of the crowd, to move them back to the campus. Coed attendance in this mass demonstration was light because of the women's 10 p.m. dorm hours, standard curfew in 1964. After twenty-five male students, returning from the scene on South 71, tried to break into Hudson Hall, with no avowed purpose in mind, Dean Koerble spoke to the group at 1 a.m. in front of the dorms. His message was that Jones would not meet with a mob but that administrative officials would meet with a student committee. This meeting with Koerble was over in five minutes with many proclaiming that there would be more to come. Jones, convinced that the agitators were in the minority and doing it for personal gain, recognized that the food problem was an annual one, but he felt that it could be resolved through proper student government procedure and through combined cooperative study and action. These were thoughts he made known the next day to the student body and faculty members.

A sharp contrast to the nocturnal student group activity was the student volunteer action on the campus the day after the tornadic storm. Many of the students, largely unidentified, worked unpaid between classes to help college personnel clean up the damage from the night before.

The students' chant from the night before that they would be back was not an idle boast. Tuesday night would mark their fourth mass demonstration in six days. It seemed as the day moved on that the unrest would stop. It was rumored the dietitian had resigned, and the students were informed of a meeting of fifteen men and fifteen women students with college officials to help settle the food differences. Dusk began, however, with turmoil on campus. In front of the men's dormitories, a large group of students appeared. Student leaders, like Acksel and Des Moines' Bob Dickey, Union Board chairman, attempted to convince them to stay on campus. The assemblage then departed for a dance, planned in the parking lot east of the men's dorms, but the dance never materialized because it is difficult to make rhythmic movements when there is no music. When a student shouted, "Let's go to town," the group moved, but slowly. Women, conspicuously absent the night before, made up forty percent of the pulsating group, numbering 1,500. As the mixed crowd assembled from the south edge of the campus to near the intersection of West Seventh and North Walnut Streets, they were met at the intersection by a fire truck and numerous police officers who had orders from their supervisors to keep the highways open. The fire truck, police dogs, and police officers advanced and herded the group back toward the campus while the fire truck unleashed its harmless water weapon at the students near the Wabash railroad tracks at the edge of the campus. Rocks began to fly, one slightly injuring a fireman, and that bit of warfare signaled the appearance of tear gas and more bombs hurled by the officers. The students, really defenseless against this type of weaponry, were easily herded along West Seventh Street and on toward the Student Union. As tear gas wafted across the campus, the students became disorganized and scattered, but, back on their home grounds, some of them regrouped near the men's dormitories. Fortunately, the encounter did not turn into a melee; no one was seriously hurt. Several students, however, did receive minor injuries from the tear gas. Four students were arrested on disorderly conduct charges for throwing rocks and bottles.

At 10 p.m. the women went back to their dorms and that significantly diminished the group. The rest heeded the requests of Jack Lasley, the imposing and strongly quiet dean of men, and trudged back to their rooms. The demonstrations were over except for some unrelated incidents the following night when some drinking non-students, obviously starved for entertainment, drove onto the campus and taunted students, trying to rouse them into demonstrating again. The few students did not care to listen to the overtures of the intruders, nor did Lasley, as he quickly dispersed them. Help was forthcoming the next couple of nights, however, for forty members of the State Highway Patrol were ordered by Governor Dalton to patrol the campus in order to restrict sightseers and to control troublemakers.

On Wednesday, April 15, the morning after the fourth concerted effort by the students, Mrs. Sheldon, who was the center of the student controversy, resigned. President Jones stated that her immediate resignation was for "the betterment of Northwest State College in view of existing circumstances." The large food committee of fifteen men and fifteen women, attempting to follow Jones' prescribed procedures in presenting complaints and having them resolved, was investigating the complaints and meeting with Mrs. Mary White, acting dietitian. The committee, after several meetings, presented the following proposal to President Jones: "Each student eating in the cafeteria be allowed two liquid drinks, either two milks or two juices or one of each." Jones approved it.

On Friday afternoon, following a hearing before the Faculty Discipline Committee, President Jones, heeding the recommendation of the Committee, dismissed both David Herring and Edward Reeder, accused of being the instigators of the demonstrations. The two were in their second semesters at Northwest, having transferred from other colleges. Jones, to be sure, was not happy with the two because they agitated against representative action through student government and brought adverse publicity to Northwest. The two, however, were allowed to take withdrawals rather than have their records shown as dismissals for cause.

Rumors were spreading and nerves were taut following the two men's dismissals, but nothing more really transpired because it was Friday, and the majority of the student body packed their suitcases and headed home for the weekend, along with the State Highway Patrol troopers. President Jones, after the dismissals of the two, was now optimistic that the situation was remedied and that there would be no more demonstrations. He liked the work of the thirty-student food committee, and it continued to work with the administration regarding the preparation and variety of food served to the students. The demonstrators never complained about the prices, but Jones stated that each meal at the cafeteria averaged fifty-four cents and that it was excellent food for the price. In an effort to improve the food service, he immediately hired Glen Vogt, a food service administrator who was food service director at Mercy Hospital, Denver, Colorado, and was formerly employed in food service at Wayne State College in Nebraska. Vogt, who actively sought the position, began his duties in August. The fall semester students, most of them spending the summer months at home and enjoying their mothers' cooking, could now look forward to food, albeit institutional, with more variety and abundance. In September, they would find a $6,000 food improvement program, offering new equipment for the preparation of special foods and a choice in meat and vegetables, and more milk.

Northwest, during those hectic and maddening days in April, had the dubious distinction of being the first college or university in the country that offered a mass demonstration in the 1960s. The University of California at Berkeley was the Bastille of the student revolution in the 1960s, but even that esteemed institution of higher learning did not have its first student uprising until October 1, 1964, when graduate student activist, Jack Weinberg, who said "You can't trust anyone over thirty," was arrested. Berkeley became a prototype of many subsequent student upheavals in colleges and universities throughout the country. Although student uprisings became commonplace, Northwest did not have another major one largely because the students discovered that many problems could be absolved by working through the proper channels, and they rediscovered that Northwest was not too big and impersonal and the faculty was not too remote. Dormitory curfews and certain dress codes, such as no slacks for females in the Library and no open shirt collars for men at Sunday dinner in the J. W. Jones Union Cafeteria, needed to end, but that would happen in time. A *Daily Forum* editorial, written by one who could dine in relatively fine splendor every evening, denounced the students who deigned to protest what they were served thrice a day. He lamented the bad publicity they gave the College and the town, and he was right. Considering, however, what happened later to scores of colleges and universities, where mass demonstrations turned into bloody riots and buildings were bombed and burned and people killed, Northwest and the town were fortunate. Measured by future events, the protest here was peaceful, damage was very minimal, and injuries minor.

While all this extracurricular group activity was taking place, other groups were quietly going about their business winning acclaim. Coach Gregory, assisted by Frank Grube, without the spectacular

John Bregin, but led by St. Joseph's Neil Reynolds, saw his team sweep all thirteen of its duals and extend its all-time dual record to seventy wins, six losses, and one tie. Dr. Burton Richey was coaching his baseball squad to its best season in Bearcat history with a 15-7 record.

Dr. J. W. Jones was president of Northwest Missouri State College for eighteen-and-one-half years, overseeing its strident growth and the education of its men and women and providing for them an environment toward success in the teaching profession and toward preparation for entrance into other suitable professions or vocations. The years of his administration also provided an impetus toward expanding educational concepts. His administration helped allay the skepticism that intellectual studies could also be utilitarian and that the academic realm could complement the practical.

As Jones neared retirement, he could look forward to the many festivities and honors planned for him and his first lady: the first official faculty retirement dinner at Northwest, including the two other retirees—Dr. J. Gordon Strong and Mr. Richard T. Wright—the Board of Regents party, the Alumni Banquet, and various staff and student parties and the dedication of the 1964 *Tower* to him. As this loyal and able man approached retirement age, he could look back at the tremendous changes during his tenure. No other president at Northwest had witnessed such growth and advancement in so many areas: his administration had experienced the most active physical and academic developments. Campus buildings were constructed during his tenure of office, including the J. W. Jones Union Building, Lamkin Gymnasium, Colden Hall, the Home Management House, the Rickenbrode Athletic Field and Stadium, the seven additions to both the men's and women's dormitories, two additions to the Industrial Arts Building and another one forthcoming, and an addition to Wells Library offering a doubled capacity for both books and people. Library holdings improved, although not sufficiently, as the expanding number of students needed more tools for their research. During the months following his official retirement day, he could watch his proud dream for a cultural center unfold; it was under construction and would be completed in 1965. He was instrumental in expanding the College Farm, improving the physical plant, and building campus roads and parking lots. In the spring commencement address, Governor Dalton told the graduating seniors that Missouri was proud of Northwest Missouri State College and that it had one of the best laid out, largest, and most beautiful campuses of any of Missouri's state colleges.

Giving careful attention to his staff additions, Jones made significant advancements in the personnel program by upgrading the faculty in quantity (numbering 129), quality, and qualifications, and by establishing the faculty ranking and tenure system. He was responsible, during his presidential stay, for refining the administrative structure to include a dean of instruction, a dean of administration, a dean of students, a director of placement and alumni, heads for the nine academic divisions, and chairmen for the various academic departments.

Jones could also look back to his continued efforts toward the creation of the Missouri Commission on Higher Education (renamed the Missouri Coordinating Board for Higher Education in 1974), a body that would control and support public higher education in Missouri and structure it on a well-designed state-wide cooperative and coordinated plan in the interest of economy and efficiency. The MCHE, at the time of his retirement, was still in its infancy, but Jones at least knew that the group was trying to accomplish some of the objectives that he thought higher education in the state sorely needed.

Further honors were extended to Jones by the college community and the city of Maryville. In spite of the growth of Northwest, there had been very little "town-gown" friction, even during the food riot crisis or the occasional brawls at the Catalina Club, one of the local night spots. Dinners for departing presidents can be dominated by perfunctory duties, but the ones held for Dr. and Mrs. Jones exuded genuine esteem which the various groups—be it the faculty, the Board of Regents, Jones' personnel staff, the support staff, Parent Teacher Associations, the Rotary, or the Chamber of Commerce—felt for them. Later in June, approximately eighty college employees, led by Robert Seipel, superintendent of buildings and grounds, and long-time employees, Maurice Randall, William Hill, and Mrs. Mildred Gorton, after their working hours, feted President and Mrs. Jones with a party and showed their dedication and appreciation to the two by presenting them with an 8 millimeter movie camera and projector. Human relationships were extremely important to Jones, and he was moved by their tribute as he lauded their friendship, help, and cooperation. Jones believed in family and the magnetic chain of humanity.

A commemorative activity, started many months before as individuals worked to start a J. W. Jones Scholarship Award, came to fruition at the annual Alumni Banquet. Mrs. Noma Sawyers, vice president of the Northwest Missouri State Alumni Association, presented Jones a check for $3,000 for the Scholarship. Jones, in happy response to the individuals' fine efforts, said that the gift would be matched by him and Mrs. Jones and that the interest would be used to provide an annual scholarship. That gift scholarship, given by those individuals and the Jones, is even stronger now than it was that June night in 1964 and is given annually as Jones requested. The Jones were never reticent with their money when they felt that it would benefit the College. At the annual Alumni Banquet the following year, when President Foster formally announced a fund drive for a bell tower, complete with carillon bells, the two were there with a $1,000 gift.

On Tuesday, June 30, Jones, as President, took his usual but final walk down the beautiful scenic path between the President's Home and the Administration Building and submitted his final report to the Board of Regents, marking his 125th meeting with the group. The report marked the close of his administration but offered capital improvements suggestions for the future of Northwest which included a science and mathematics building, an industrial arts building, an infirmary and health center, an extension of the women's physical education building, farm buildings and improvements, and an off-campus dormitory in North Kansas City. He paid tribute to his faculty, and he assured Dr. Foster that he would be of help at any time his assistance might be needed. The Jones were visible people for they were, during and after his presidency, usually in attendance at all college functions. He followed, to be sure, in Mr. Rickenbrode's footsteps as Northwest's number one Bearcat, and was affectionately known, especially in his retirement years, as "Mr. Bearcat." Every year he was the first to contribute to the Quarterback Club's annual drive to secure funds for scholarships for needy athletes. Most people readily agreed Jones was solid, reliable, and uncomplicated and that he was leaving Northwest a much better place than he had found it.

Orval Heywood

President Robert P. Foster
1964-1977

3

Forging Ahead, 1964-1969

Which of you, intending to build a tower, sitteth
not down first, and counteth the cost, whether he have
sufficient to finish it?

—Luke 14:28

The Jones era was now over, and July 1, 1964, officially marked the beginning of the Foster era. The date for President Foster's Inauguration was set for Tuesday, October 6, and plans for that gala event were being made. Sandwiched between those two dates were the flood that virtually destroyed State Training Center No. 26, summer commencement, a record fall enrollment of students, staff appointments, building supervision, and the various other myriad activities that help keep a college operable.

When Foster began his duties that first day of July, he was greeted by a violent cloudburst that rained down four inches in a short time. Fortunately the campus suffered no real damage, but the school to aid the trainable, handicapped children, located in a basement room in the Horace Mann Laboratory School, was virtually destroyed when the drainage facilities were unable to handle the four feet of water which covered the basement floor. The water either ruined or severely damaged appliances, books, food, records, and teaching materials. The school, in operation for four-and-one-half years, had been developing into a fine local institution to train handicapped children. Concerted efforts and contributions by local groups and Northwest officials and staff helped put the school in full-scale operation for the fall term. Since the state did not have a large budget for training centers or insure them, benefits had to be staged to raise money. One noteworthy event, sponsored by the American Legion, was a benefit baseball game between the "Old Timers" and the youths who played summer ball with the Junior American Legion and the Pony League teams. The "Old Timers" were outnumbered and "out-aged" by their opponents, but the former's big drawing card was Lefty Davis, their coach, known as the grand old man of Northwest Missouri sports. Retired since 1952, Davis headed and coached Northwest's athletics for twenty-five years and was coaching some of his former players: Ryland Milner, Ivan Schottel, and Bob Gregory, now "old timers," too. The reunion was a happy one. Six months after this event, which demonstrated the concern people had for the school, Lefty Davis died. Because of space limitations at Horace Mann, the school later moved to St. Gregory's Elementary School. With the closing of Mount Alverno High School, it has been relocated in recent years at Mount Alverno Convent and is headed by Mrs. Cleta Dowden.

The first major administrative appointment under President Foster's reign was the selection of Dr. Charles Thate as acting dean of administration. He would for several months assume a dual role as he continued with his leadership of the division of education, a post he began in 1960 when Dr. Leon Miller, education's former head, became dean of instruction. Dr. James Gleason, chairman of the department of elementary education, was later picked in April to be Thate's successor as head of education in order for Thate to devote full time to a position that was becoming increasingly more demanding because of Northwest's burgeoning enrollment.

The Bearçat Marching Band, under Director Ward Rounds, was gearing up for the coming football season, and Ivan Schottel's football charges were diligently practicing for what would be a 6-3 season. Homecoming committees were working, Fulsom's thespians were preparing for their highly successful fall production of Arthur Miller's *The Crucible,* and plans for President Foster's Inauguration were being finalized. It would be an all-day event consisting of the registration of guests, a coffee, a luncheon, an academic procession, the inaugural ceremony, and the reception. Governor Dalton would return to speak at the ceremony, with David Hopkins, a member of the Board of Regents presiding. Dr. Willis M. Tate, president of Southern Methodist University, would give the luncheon address, with Dean of Instruction Leon Miller presiding. It would be a busy, tiring but happy day for Foster, Mrs. Foster, their two sons, Bob and Kemp, and his mother, Mrs. R. P. Foster, Sr. The day's festivities officially began with a Maryville businessmen's breakfast as over 240 business and professional men, educators, and guests honored the new president. Everett W. Brown, director of field services and recipient of Alpha Phi Omega's 1964 Ugly Man Award, was selected to chair the gigantic task of Inauguration, and under his command were innumerable people like Miss Mabel Cook, Dr. Charles Koerble, F. B. Houghton, Sr., Clifford Kensinger, Myrl Long, Bonnie Magill, Elaine Mauzey, Leon Miller, Neva Ross, Charles Thate, and Dorothy Walker working, both on and behind the scenes, on plans for the luncheon, the housing and parking, the procession, the student services, and the reservations.

Glen Vogt, the new dietitian, proved that he and his staff were able. They served 460 special guests at the Inaugural Luncheon in the Ballroom of the J. W. Jones Union Hall, and, in addition, provided the usual noon meal for 1,900 students. His pressure was relieved, however, for Mabel Cook's Inaugural Luncheon Committee did its work well. The official inauguration of the new president came that afternoon in Lamkin Gymnasium, a dignified ceremony attended by approximately 5,000 people, while 400 faculty, officers of the student government, officers of the alumni association, representatives of learned societies and professional organizations, an unusual number of representatives from 188 United States colleges and universities including Harvard and Yale, and the Board of Regents assisted. The colorful academic parade extended in length four city blocks. Governor Dalton, introduced by Dr. M. C. "Pete" Cunningham, president of Fort Hays Kansas State College and former dean of faculty at Northwest, hailed the growth of Northwest Missouri State College and exclaimed that Northwest selected the right man to lead the College in the right direction and that it would continue to progress under his leadership. Foster, in his acceptance of the seal of office—presented to him by Harold Hull, president of the Board of Regents—cited the outstanding leadership of his predecessor, Dr. J. W. Jones, and pledged himself to the further development of Northwest Missouri State College. He said that he hoped to reflect only dignity and honor on a "great institution and the state which it serves." The new president seemed to have a firm grip on the helm of the Northwest Missouri Stateship of higher education in an age of great seriousness for all academe. Hopefully, President Lyndon B. Johnson could do the same for the nation.

When Mr. R. T. Wright, Dr. J. Gordon Strong, and President Emeritus J. W. Jones retired within one month of each other, they left seventy-six years of dedicated and active service to Northwest Missouri State College. Northwest still possessed, to be sure, its share of long-serving and devoted members, one being Mr. Herbert R. Dieterich, thirty-six-year member of the education department. Three days after the presidential inauguration, Mr. Dieterich was elected president of the Knights of the Hickory Stick, an association of schoolmen in the Northwest district, known for their continuous camaraderie among male administrators and teachers. Though the group had no charter, no constitution, and no dues, it numbered prominent educators, like Dieterich, who were seriously interested in the welfare of the College. The new president was a charter member of the group formed in 1920.

The year ended, as the previous year, on a high academic note, for the Missouri Commission on Higher Education was recommending for the College a new building of classrooms and laboratories for science and mathematics, progress was being made on the construction of the fine arts building, and Dr. Elwyn DeVore, head of the division of business, was announcing that his division would initiate a series of annual lectures by distinguished Midwest businessmen. Nationally, President Johnson was beginning the new year with his first full term as President. Almost no one could guess what lay ahead either for the nation or Northwest. The war in Vietnam was still small and distant, and President Johnson, as President Foster on the local level, was handling the presidency well. Johnson had handled the succession crisis brilliantly on that November day in 1963, suppressed the Goldwater rebellion, and squeezed a tax cut and a civil rights bill from Congress. He was celebrating a liberal majority and the majority here were behind Foster. They, for the most part, liked the accessibility of his "open door policy," his gregariousness, his willing handshake, and his leadership potential. Things would continue to go well with Foster, but not quite so with Johnson as the encounter in Vietnam would escalate and would mark what historians would call the beginnings of "The Desperate Years."

Although Charles Johnson would no longer be present to oversee the highly successful Spring Festival of the Arts, it was again celebrated, for the fifth and final time, in March 1965, highlighting the noted American poet John Ciardi, who embarrassed members of the English department when he failed to show up for a reception in his honor.

Martindale and Lamkin Gymnasiums were resounding with triumph. New coach Lewis Dyche's swimmers had a victorious season and, led by Maryville's Frank Fisher, who was undefeated for the season in the 100 and 200-yard freestyle events, set six new school records. Coach Jerry Landwer's grapplers were again making Northwest's wrestling program nationally known as his men completed their second consecutive undefeated season and extended their unbeaten record to thirty-six straight, while beating along the way university powers Kansas, Missouri, and Nebraska. Landwer's biggest winners were Chariton, Iowa's Ron James, Chenango Forks, New York's Allen Packer, and Cedar Rapids' Lonny Wieland, who were All-Americans. Landwer, after the wrestling season, initiated a new system for honoring outstanding wrestlers with a Northwest Wrestling Hall of Fame, designed only for the top quality matmen. Alumni Ralph Messerli, Doyle Thomas, and Ron Betts, all teaching and coaching the sport in Iowa, were chosen, along with spring graduate Lonnie Wieland.

April brought St. Joseph Junior College back into focus again with the *St. Joseph News-Press* attempting to distort the picture. The concerted plans to bring either Northwest or Tarkio College to serve as the third and fourth years of college in St. Joseph were apparently forgotten, and now Central Missouri State College at Warrensburg seemed to be the front runner, apparently a compromise move by the State Senate Education Committee since the Missouri House had passed a bill, recommended by Governor Warren E. Hearnes, to let St. Joseph Junior College be a branch of the University of Missouri. The *News-Press,* in an unsigned editorial dated April 28, related that state officials said that a compromise did result in their attempts to make St. Joseph an extension of Central. Senator John Downs from St. Joseph was the haranguing and vociferous workhorse in attempting to obtain a university branch in his city, but he reluctantly agreed to a branch of Central State in St. Joseph if one from the University of Missouri was not forthcoming. According to the plans made by the St. Joseph officials, the two-year addition was to be an interim operation until St. Joseph could secure in 1968—if approved by the Missouri Legislature— facilities and money for its own state school, Missouri Western State College. The *News-Press* further stated the reason for the proposed St. Joseph operation with Central was that there was "antipathy" toward a St. Joseph college. The *News-Press,* with its usual attempt to humorously demean a serious subject, satirically suggested that the simplest solution would be to attach St. Joseph's final two college years to the University of Alaska, the principal benefit being that it would not arouse the antipathy of college people at Maryville. The *News-Press* obviously did not do its historical homework, for Northwest officials had worked stringently for years with St. Joseph school officials to work out a cooperative plan and, after all that effort, why now Central State?

St. Joseph observers, longing to have a four-year college, seriously believed, and with reason, that their school would be a branch of the University of Missouri, and they were disappointed over the prospect of becoming a branch of a state college instead of belonging to a university system. Any plans to accept Northwest's cooperation were dropped when the University loomed into the picture, and to fall back now on Central when the university prize was almost won seemed like a Pyrrhic victory, for those same observers were admitting that the principal difference was really one of status. Yes, a diploma from the University of Missouri had to be more impressive than one from any state college, and to a large degree, they were saying, those state colleges are basically "teachers colleges" and somewhat limited. Student-faculty ratio, instructional quality, and individualized instruction in a friendly atmosphere at a traditional, quality institution, like Northwest Missouri State College, seemed to be forgotten with the dissenters' lament.

The above efforts to obtain either the University of Missouri or Central State College at Warrensburg, however, were all for naught because on Wednesday, April 28, the Missouri Senate Education Committee deferred action on the Missouri House-passed bill and listened as Carthage Senator Richard Webster, obviously with an eye centered on economy and accessibility, proposed that St. Joseph Junior College and Joplin Junior College be made branches of Northwest Missouri State and Southwest Missouri State College at Springfield. The Senate seemed in favor of the action, but the branch plan never materialized. Missouri Western Junior College evolved into Missouri Western State College. With the opening of the 1969-1970 academic year, Missouri Western State College began its existence as a four-year school offering baccalaureate degrees. President Foster, however, told the Senate Education Committee that Northwest would completely cooperate, as usual, to make the junior college an independent state college by helping in the development of its third and fourth-year program. Dean of Instruction Leon Miller, Foster's envoy, met with Missouri Western and University of Missouri officials innumerable times to help make the new college's transition smoother. A trouble spot did exist in 1965 for Missouri Western. It had no capital funds and no campus.

While people in Maryville, St. Joseph, and Jefferson City were being demonstrative over the political issue of the senior college at St. Joseph, nationwide opposition to the war in Vietnam started immediately upon its escalation. Organized by a handful of students and faculty, almost every large university, and many small ones, were holding teach-ins as a protest to the U.S. involvement in Vietnam, but, of course, they did not change the government's policy, nor stop the war. They did, however, make peaceful dissent respectable. Civil rights movements—nonviolent and integrated—were also fomenting, and Selma, Alabama, was in the public eye several days before the teach-ins occurred. Dr. Martin Luther King, Jr. was leading non-violent protest marches and, after tangling with the courts, obtained permission for a march from Selma to Montgomery. On March 21, the march began. When the marchers entered Montgomery four days later, 25,000 singing, cheering people joined them.

Fortunately, President Foster could now march home from Jefferson City for a while and attend to business on his own campus. The spring of 1965 was a marked departure from the previous one because building and moving plans, not food grievances, highlighted the campus. Some people did grieve, however, when they viewed an English acting troupe's bawdy performance of *The Beggar's Opera*. The fine arts building construction was on schedule, and viewers could see that it would be the first building on campus of truly contemporary design. The agricultural department, now under the direction of Dr. John Beeks, discovered, due to the expansion of campus buildings, that the farm buildings on the campus would have to be relocated and completely modernized. Northwest and Southeast State College at Cape Girardeau were the only state colleges having farm programs. The farm's largest enterprise was the dairy, where thirty producing cows of the Jersey and Holstein breeds were maintained, but hogs and poultry were also raised and emphasis was placed on field crops and pasture. The science and mathematics division was making plans for a new $3,000,000 building as faculty members were expanding the curriculum. A department of geology would be included. The staff learned that the new V-shaped structure was targeted for a 1968 completion date and would be located north of the Administration Building on the site of Vets' Village, the traditional housing for married veterans and their families.

President Foster, in a quest to increase campus beauty, desired a new structure to accompany the other campus buildings and the grounds. Early in May he announced a program to build a Bell Tower as a memorial to the College's war dead, deceased alumni, and former faculty. It would be a memorial to the past as well as an inspiration for peace to students in the future. Anticipating a completion day for the proposed $100,000 edifice, Foster announced that the Tower—with its set of carillon bells to be played daily and on special occasions— would be a 100-foot-tall brick structure designed in the style of the Administration Building towers. The site was to be the present bell mall, above the Bell of '48. Special name plaques honoring the war dead would grace the inner walls of the Memorial. The Bell Tower was definitely Foster's conception, and he formally and proudly announced its birth at the Alumni Banquet later in the month. Some people donated, as indicated by President Emeritus and Mrs. Jones' gesture, as much as $1,000. Mrs. Vera Moore Schmitt, the sister of Kenneth Allen Moore from New Hampton, Missouri, did as much.

Ensign Moore, a student at Northwest in the late 30s and early 40s was killed in 1942 when his naval plane crashed over the east coast. His sister found a name plaque a fitting tribute to her brother's memory. Frederic Lyman Parcher, a 1914 graduate of Northwest, liked Foster's idea and memorialized his grandfather, Captain Lyman Parcher, a man earlier area residents remembered as the state senator who introduced (in 1887) a state bill for a Normal School in Maryville.

Two fraternities were planning for their futures. On June 3, Sigma Tau Gamma, the first fraternity at Northwest to have its own house, sold its fraternity house at auction, and the members were now living in their large home at 631 Prather. Forty men lived there, nestled in with several faculty members' homes. The Alpha Kappa Lambda members would have their own house in September. Dean Savage of the elementary education department was constructing it for them at 622 North Walnut and leasing it on a per man basis to approximately thirty-eight men.

With an estimated 3,950 students in the fall and nearly 4,800 anticipated five years later, it was evident that greater physical expansion was needed. President Foster planned to meet the housing demand and—financed by government loans—two seven-story men's and women's air-conditioned dormitories, each to hold 330 occupants, were to be built northwest of the National Guard Armory. A dining unit and recreational center were also included. Land clearing would begin in the summer and occupancy was expected for the fall of 1966.

Foster was, at the same time, envisioning six more dormitories to accompany the first two, thus forming an octagon. Increasing student numbers would also necessitate more recreational and dining space and Foster was prepared for that, too. An addition to the J. W. Jones Union Building, doubling its present size, would be available in the winter of 1966.

The college librarians, especially the one in periodicals, and the department of chemistry were celebrating their own form of spring ecstasy, for Sam Carpenter, department of chemistry chairman, received word that fifty volumes of bound chemical journals would be given by the American Oil Company as a gift to the College. Chemistry students would find works like *Chemical Abstracts, Industrial and Engineering Chemistry,* and *Analytical Chemistry* invaluable.

The spring semester quickly reached its denouement with several events planned. Alpha Phi Omega's Ugly Man on Campus Contest netted $2,000 in the Student Loan Fund, and the winners of the Contest were Phi Sigma Epsilon's Roger Schlegel from Dubuque, Iowa, and the faculty's Bruce Wake, director of men's residence halls. The annual

Sigma Phi Dolphin Swim Show, with all the usual intricate swimming patterns, was again successful, and students attending the Spring Formal thrilled to the vibrations of the famed Count Basie and his band. It was a memorable spring, and the school year was capped on May 12 as 343 seniors, the largest graduating class in the history of Northwest, received their diplomas and heard Governor Warren E. Hearnes, in his first appearance in Maryville as a governor, give the address. Those same seniors, knowing that the fine arts building would soon be completed, gave a colorful mosaic mural for their traditional senior gift. The mural depicts the historical development of the fine arts from the primitive to the contemporary, and that class, on the building's opening, could find its gift adorning the stairway landing between the first and second floors.

The spring or summer of every school year has its bit of sadness on campus when vital faculty members retire. The previous year was no exception with Jones, Strong, and Wright leaving the campus, and the summer of 1965 was no different as biology's William Trago Garrett, a faculty member for thirty-eight years, was retiring. Approximately 180 people gathered for a farewell faculty dinner in tribute to Mr. and Mrs. Garrett. Five years after coming to Northwest, Mr. Garrett became chairman of the biology department when it was separated from the agriculture department, and during his stay in the chair the scope and function of the department greatly increased as three people—Dr. Irene Mueller, Dr. Bill Scott, and Dr. Kenneth Minter, chairman-elect—would verify.

The area that Northwest serves is fundamentally rural in nature. The fall semester enrollment showed that over half of Northwest's students came from Missouri, and forty-five percent of these were natives of the nineteen counties of Missouri making up the Northwest district. Iowa contributed 39.6 percent to the student body while other states sent 8.3 percent. Eighty-nine students were from New Jersey, New York, Pennsylvania, Rhode Island, and Michigan. Fifteen international students were attracted to Northwest. The College, as always, drew a sizable percentage from St. Joseph, Kansas City, Des Moines, Omaha, and Council Bluffs.

The fall semester would offer something different and something new and much of the same. For several years, and for several more to come, each fall enrollment was larger than the preceding one; this one was also a record enrollment-breaker. Most of the students, since it was an all-campus activity, began preparing for homecoming, as they still do, immediately upon their return for the fall semester. It was and is a fall highlight with its colorful pageantry, and October 23, 1965, would mark Northwest's nineteenth annual Homecoming. Every homecoming at Northwest has had its queen to reign over the festivities including the morning parade, the football game, and the dance, and students, alumni, staff, and townspeople reveled in her charm and happiness. But this year it would be different! Northwest had two queens: Storm Lake, Iowa's Dorothy Hardyman, Greek coalition candidate and Excelsior Springs, Missouri's Marlene Kelly, independent candidate. Homecoming queens are traditionally announced at the Variety Show, and the packed, hushed, standing-room-only Thursday night audience in the Administration Building Auditorium was stunned when co-queens were announced to share the royal duties. The student body vote did not end with a tie, but supporters for the two young women violated election campaign rules. When the transgressions were discovered, the members of the Student Senate collectively wrestled their minds and consciences for the right decision. After two long, wrenching closed-door sessions, the Senate, led by Indianola, Iowa's Jerry Taylor, had its decision: a duo of queens. Other colleges would later have their share of a different kind of collegiate history by crowning an occasional male candidate, but only Northwest had two charming and attractive queens! It was a beautiful and colorful day. The Alpha Kappa Lambdas and the Alpha Sigma Alphas won first place for their house decorations and the Alpha Kappa Lambdas, the Industrial Arts Club, the Phi Mus, and the Delta Zetas copped first prizes for their parade floats. Northwest partisans left the game happy, for the Bearcats were triumphant and on their way to another 6-3 season. Jim Redd, the present head football coach, was an all-MIAA performer on both offense and defense for that Bearcat team.

The fine arts building was completed and waiting for its formal dedication on Sunday, November 21. It and its theater already had names, for those were revealed three months earlier by President Foster at the summer commencement when he told the assemblage that the fine arts building would be named The Olive DeLuce Fine Arts Building in honor of Professor Emeritus Olive DeLuce, an artist and teacher who chaired the department of fine arts for forty years, and the 550-seat theater within the building would be called The Charles Johnson Theater in memory of the late Mr. Johnson, who was serving as acting chairman of the art department at his death in 1963. Professor Emeritus DeLuce, in academic regalia and part of the academic procession, and Mrs. Charles "Pete" Johnson and her three daughters were introduced by Foster as he made the announcements. An appreciative audience of 500 people came to the Sunday dedication ceremonies to honor Olive DeLuce and the late Charles Johnson. Dr.

Blanche Dow, national president of the American Association of University Women, president emeritus of Cottey College, former foreign language department chairman at Northwest, and a long-time friend of Miss DeLuce, delivered the dedicatory address, praising DeLuce's dedicated teaching and excellent artistry. Dr. Burton Richey, chairman of men's physical education and a friend of the late Johnson, paid a moving tribute to the memory of Johnson. Dr. Leon Miller, dean of instruction, presided at the program. After the dedicatory addresses, plaques commemorating DeLuce and Johnson were unveiled by President Emeritus Jones.

The campus was cloaked with sadness on January 5, 1966, for three members of the student body, Lyle Craig Clark, Thomas Webb Harvey, and Dorothy Ellen Ulmer Vulgamott, were killed when their car was broadsided by a truck, twelve miles from Maryville on South 71 as they were returning to their homes in Savannah after attending classes at the College. Their names adorn a large wall plaque in the Memorial Bell Tower in tribute to their memory.

The next month again brought a grip to the campus emotions, and students and faculty alike mourned as the campus flags flew at half-mast. On February 24, Mrs. Lula Mae Curfman Sheetz, a beloved member of the English faculty for twelve years, died quietly in her sleep. This dedicated lady had been ill for several days but she continued to meet her classes. On her last day, she taught her usual schedule and later that day met her freshman composition students in Wells Library to aid them in their research for their library papers.

Early in 1966 another type of dedication was taking place, not for a new building but for one ninety-six years of age, the home of Northwest's seventh president and where the previous six had lived. President and Mrs. Foster renovated the President's Home, that stately structure whose red bricks had been made by hand. The home was built for the horticulturist, Captain Thomas W. Gaunt, on land purchased for a nursery in 1857. The Fosters, because of the extensive work on this charming and dignified Victorian house, were inconvenienced, but their year's wait was now rewarded and they were comfortably settled. Hundreds of enthusiastic visitors were allowed to tour the lovely old home, steeped in campus tradition.

Northwest annually recognizes its top students by honoring them at an Honors Night in the spring. Now they would have their own academic program. For the first time in Northwest's history, an Honors Program was established to challenge superior students and to increase their educational opportunities. The Program, initiated by the Faculty Council, the faculty governing body, was administered and supervised by an Honors Council, composed of faculty members representing various phases of the academic and administrative curriculum. Dr. Sam Carpenter, chemistry department chairman, was appointed by President Foster to chair the Honors Committee. Students who qualified were offered advanced classes in twenty-four courses, plus independent study from ten departments. Other important changes were taking place in curriculum offerings. Psychology, sociology, and geography minors were expanded to majors, and fine arts was offering a secondary-elementary major. Interest in foreign language study was peaking and, for the first time in thirteen years, students could take courses in German again. Because it was not considered patriotic to be studying the enemy's language, the study of French supplanted that of German on campus during World War II. But in 1966 students could choose to minor in German, and in another year a major would be offered. A minor was being developed in philosophy. The speech department established a major in speech pathology, and the business division separated into the specialized fields of accounting, finance and insurance, management, marketing, and secretarial practice. An important addition was the agricultural-business major.

Students need such necessities as heat and water, and a greater number of students helps diminish such necessities. With the rapidly growing campus, a water shortage was realized. There would be an abundance of water, however, because a large water tower was being built behind the then existing farm buildings on campus. Besides serving the new dormitories and the Administration Building, this much-needed new 150,000-gallon capacity tank would supply better service and pressure to all the other buildings. The slender steel tower, with its large oval tank, looked like a NASA project and attracted much comment from its observers. The water situation on campus was vastly improved, and Coach Lewis Dyche's watermen could say the same as they won seven of ten matches and also garnered a second place in the MIAA conference.

Northwest Missouri State College, now in its sixty-first year, numbered 177 in its instructional staff. The ranking system was in its seventh year, and sixteen of those staff members were professors, eighteen associate professors, fifty-six assistant professors, seventy-four instructors, and thirteen had no ranking. Librarians, notorious for being discriminated against in academic matters, were then unranked.

The department of foreign languages, chaired by Dr. Joseph Dreps, began a program that allowed students to study a foreign language abroad. Maryville's David Bell and Trudy McCarthy, Excelsior Springs' Linda Sams, and Kansas City's Judy Thatch were the first group of Northwest students to participate in the Summer Study in Mexico program under the direction of Instructor Mary Jackson. For six weeks the quartet attended classes at the Technological Institute of Monterrey, Mexico, where they received six hours of college credit. They, in addition to the academic life, participated in the many cultural and social activities that the Mexican city offered. All the professors were native speakers, but Miss Jackson was invited to teach one of the courses. Others, too, were traveling to foreign countries that summer: Northwest for the first time participated in the Experiment in International Living by sending two student ambassadors to Mexico and Canada. Sidney, Iowa's Mary Potter and Marcus, Iowa's Nancy Boyd were selected by a student-faculty committee. Miss Potter's experiment was in Mexico, and Miss Boyd's in Canada. The Ambassador Program was a successful one for many years at Northwest.

Registration, always a strain for both students and faculty advisers, was eased somewhat in the fall because freshmen had pre-registered for their classes. Student leaders made it easier for those same freshmen as they organized an orientation program, designed to acquaint new students with the campus.

Something really was missing this fall, and it did not take long to find out what it was. No Walkout Day! A long-lasting tradition was changed because that great student event would occur in the spring and would not return to its traditional resting place—the fall of the year—until 1977.

The two seven-story dormitories, known as the high-rises, were finished, and students moved in on schedule for the fall semester. It was also obvious that Northwest soon would have two more of those high-rises. The money was already reserved by the Housing and Urban Development Department of the Department of Health, Education, and Welfare for a loan to Northwest, and the loans were ready to be offered after the plans for the new structures had been approved. What remained for the present, however, was naming the newest housing additions on campus. Everyone already knew, but President Foster officially announced at a public open house on Sunday, November 13, that the two constructs were to be called Franken Hall for the women's and Phillips Hall for the men's. Franken Hall was named in honor of the late Miss Katherine Franken, who was a member of the education department of Northwest from 1921 until her retirement in 1952. Phillips Hall was for the late educator, Homer T. Phillips, who started the Horace Mann Laboratory School and headed the education department for many years. He was also credited with organizing the Knights of the Hickory Stick in 1920. Greatly enhancing the Open House was the presence of the two special guests: Miss Margaret Franken, Katherine Franken's sister, and Mrs. Homer T. Phillips, the wife of Mr. Phillips. Margaret Franken was also a former faculty member, and the two sisters did much to aid Catholic students of Northwest. For a time they managed their own home as a Newman Club House, giving Catholic students a rooming house and the Club a meeting place.

In December of 1966, Wells Library had approximately 100,000 volumes in its collection and the Maryville Public Library possessed 13.000. The two libraries were headed respectively by a duo from one family, Mr. and Mrs. James Johnson. Sometime, very possibly over the dinner table, in their many discussions concerning their chosen professions, they devised a plan whereby cardholders at either library facility could check out books from the other library; thus students and townspeople had at their disposal a greater number and variety of significant works. It was, indeed, a program of inter-library cooperation.

The old and the new seemed to be thriving on campus and, as always, students were concerned about their futures as they were on most American campuses. The calendar year ended with 375,000 American troops in Vietnam. Escalation was in high gear and casualties on both sides were mounting. Draft-age students were troubled. The signs of the sixties were much in evidence. New styles were very popular. Miniskirts were common. Sideburns, beards, and moustaches sprouted and hair grew longer. Ties, collars, and cuffs widened; trouser legs flared and belled. Never had American men been so colorfully arrayed. Generally male fashions were following the women's lead. The nationwide rebellion against traditional fashion, largely due to the Beatles when they appeared in 1964 with their Prince Valiant hairdos, visored caps, and extravagant haberdashery, was quite evident on campus as many students and some instructors emphasized brilliant or peculiar fabrics and designs. Clothing also took another direction with surplus military garments and handcrafted ones. Army and navy surplus clothing were common for young people looking for a separate identity, and wearing them meant a certain flavor of nonconformity. They were favorites of dissenting youths. Occasionally, one could also see beads, bangles, leather goods, and fringes that fit in with the popular back-to-nature ethic, and faded blue jeans, army shirts, long stringy hair, and untrimmed beards were evident. There was a social conflict that was understood to be a function of age, vague and elastic, and the term "counter-culture" appeared. Supposedly counter-culture meant an attack on accepted views and styles, but it also came to mean all things to all men and embraced everything new from clothing to politics.

Along with the social change, Northwest was growing and adapting to change. The science and math building was under construction. The two new dormitories, Franken and Phillips, were thriving and expecting company with the addition of two more high-rises. The new and modern Olive DeLuce Fine Arts Building was making its inhabitants happy. The picturesque Administration Building provided a striking contrast to the newer buildings, and the traditional "Kissing Bridge" was getting comfortable with seven-year-old Colden Hall. Trees and shrubs of 150 different species graced the spacious grounds. The campus offered a pleasant blend of the old and the new, and most of its inhabitants retained confidence in society's norms.

The Bearcat cheerleaders, after basketball season officially ended, really felt a part of the athletic syndrome since they received athletic letters and awards, presented to them by Mr. Herbert Dieterich, chairman of the Athletic Committee, and Miss Bonnie Magill, head of women's physical education and the cheerleaders' sponsor. These nine young women, captained by Maryville's Elaine Sherman and Rock Port's Pat Noah, spent an exhilarating week the previous summer in Dallas where they competed against thirty-five colleges and received a third place ranking. Having tasted the victory of national competition in 1966, the group, led by captains Linda Snell and Dottie Wilson, liked the national taste much better the following summer. This time they jumped over second and landed with the number one ranking. Another success, the Bearcat golfing team, coached by Ryland Milner, kept its competitive juices flowing as it finished with an 11-2 dual meet record, the best in the school's history.

Although not a cheerleader or a golfer, but also one who owned crowd-pleasing talents, Council Bluffs' Gloria Kachulis drew national attention by being selected as one of the top ten baton twirlers in the country.

A constant reminder of competitive athletic spirit at Northwest is the "Bearcat," and at athletic events the "Bearcat" can be seen strolling and exulting and cheering his team on to victory. This Bearcat was always a student and ranged from the portly Vinnie Vaccaro, now executive secretary of alumni affairs at Northwest, to the very slight Steve Scroggins, who achieved national fame in 1977 by placing third in a university mascot contest at the University of Notre Dame. Both were crowd pleasers and instilers of spirit. When students and staff walked along the west side of the J. W. Jones Union in 1966, they could see a thirteen-foot mosaic Bearcat in varying shades of the traditional green and white adorning the main west entrance. Conceived by architect Ray Hershman and designed by artist Jan Roderick Carroll, who also designed the mural in the Olive DeLuce Fine Arts Building, it was a welcome bit of visual art for passers-by. Using this main west entrance of the J. W. Jones Union, one could walk under the Bearcat into the vastly expanded Union completed the previous summer. With the $1,500,000 addition, which increased the overall size by sixty percent, were a new games area—including a six-lane bowling alley—larger cafeteria facilities, a modern self-service book-store, a three-chair barber shop, conference and meeting rooms, plus complete remodeling and redecorating of the older areas. Something else was additional and new, too, for Bob Dickey, a 1965 graduate, became the new union director.

The spring semester began early in January with the expected visit of representatives from the North Central Association, an accrediting agency for colleges and secondary schools. When NCA last visited in 1958, Northwest's undergraduate program was reaccredited and its graduate program fully accredited. Since the 1958 visitation, Northwest phased out its own Master of Science in Education program and entered a cooperative arrangement with the University of Missouri for the graduate degree. The NCA visits are approximately every ten years; however, Northwest wanted to return to its own graduate program in time for the summer session of 1967 but with plans to continue work with the University of Missouri in some graduate areas of study. Extensive preliminary study had to be done, and Dr. Leon Miller, dean of instruction, was, after two years of careful study and preparation, prepared for their visit. He assigned faculty members and administrative staff to various study committees to secure data and to prepare written material, and he organized their results into two self-survey comprehensive reports. One of those reports was prepared for NCA's perusal of Northwest's graduate program and the other for the National Council for Accreditation of Teacher Education. NCATE also visited and studied the College's teacher education program. In April, the results of the visits by the two accrediting agencies were known. Official notice was given to President Foster that the College was granted preliminary approval for its graduate program and full accreditation for the teacher education program. Staff members, led by Dr. Miller, could reap the fruits of their hard efforts.

On March 7, 1967, Northwest lost a fifty-four-year-old building. On that day the original Dairy Barn, west of the Administration Building, was destroyed by fire, along with a silo and a calf barn. Members of the agriculture department were especially dismayed because nineteen small heifer calves—the beginning of a Holstein herd—plus several Jersey cattle and a flock of chickens lost their lives in the fire. Their loss was, to be sure, a disabling one. Equipment and irreplaceable records on the registered Jersey cattle were also destroyed. The fire, believed to be caused by defective wiring, sent shock waves throughout the campus and the community. President Foster, who was extremely prideful of Northwest's agricultural program, was particularly disturbed, and he immediately called for legislative help from the state. The Missouri Legislature acted promptly and gave Northwest emergency appropriations to help reactivate Northwest's farm operations.

Coach Burton Richey's baseball men brought recognition to Northwest and a boost to the baseball program as they won the MIAA Northern Divisional Championship with a commendable 14-5 record.

Campus radio station KDLX was in its second season in its new location at the east end of the Power Plant. Anyone affiliated with the station was also a member of the Radio Club, a group of students interested in ham radio who provided technical assistance for KDLX by building and working with electronic equipment in the station. The station, for the first time, did sports broadcasts from Lamkin Gymnasium, a beginning, however small, for bigger and brighter events in the near future.

When the fall semester opened, another long-time member of Northwest's faculty would not be present. Dr. Joseph Dreps, chairman of the foreign language department for twenty-four years, retired in May and was succeeded by Mrs. Elaine Mauzey, a member of the department for twenty-two years. Dreps and Mauzey were a two-people department from 1945-1962, and at Dreps' retirement there were ten members in the department of foreign languages.

At Northwest's sixty-first Commencement on May 27, the largest graduating class in the College's history received degrees. The 415 graduates heard comments from guest speaker Dr. Morton C. "Pete" Cunningham, president of Fort Hays Kansas State College of Hays and former Northwest dean of faculty.

Immediately after this commencement, Dr. Leon Miller was busy and eagerly anticipating the new graduate program. He was not disappointed as 259 full-time graduate students successfully initiated the College's new program, a definite forward step. Ninety graduate students continued in the cooperative graduate program with the University of Missouri. Miller was beginning to smile because the fall semester brought more than 200 graduate students studying for a Master of Science in Biology, a Master of Arts in Business, English, or History, or a Master of Science in Education in fourteen different areas. The following spring commencement would already show results. Mrs. Natalie Tackett was the first from Northwest's new graduate program to walk across the stage with a diploma—a Master of Arts in English.

One and two-year secretarial programs, after a five-year absence, were back on campus. Dr. Elwyn DeVore saw a definite need for them and was not reticent about reinstating the programs. Like many of the one and two-year programs on campus, especially in agriculture and industrial arts and technology, courses included college academic credits, which could be applied toward a degree should the student wish to continue.

The Memorial Bell Tower was not yet under construction although two-thirds of the funds were contributed. People on campus and in Maryville, however, could hear various musical pieces from the carillon bells—to be played later from the Tower—morning, noon, and night. Three different concerts a day and one on Sunday, orchestrated by Mrs. Monica Zirfas, administrative assistant to President Foster, were played these summer months. Hearing and delighting in the sounds of those bells were more than 200 delegates from fifty-one chapters of the Gamma Sigma Sigma national college women's service sorority. The members, all former Girl Scouts, were congregated on campus for their biennial national convention and were hosted by the local chapter, sponsored by Mrs. Dorothy Walker of the women's physical education department, Miss Barbara Palling and Mrs. Dolores Albertini, both of the library staff.

Missouri Western College, on schedule for its four-year school, caused a trickle of news when it had a ground breaking ceremony on August 22, marking the site of the new college on East Mitchell. The shoveling took place on the ground where the library—later to be called The Warren E. Hearnes Learning Resource Center—was to be constructed. President Foster, true to his word about cooperation, attended the festivities.

The Maryville Chamber of Commerce, the previous fall, wanted to do something to acquaint Northwest's students and faculty with the merchants of Maryville. As a means of welcoming people back to school, the Chamber sponsored a "Night on the Town" in the downtown area of Maryville. Stores stayed open that night to enable students to register for free prizes to be given away by the merchants; then the students attended a scheduled street dance designed for their fun. It was a good move by the Chamber and an honest attempt to acquaint the merchants with their prospective buyers, and it was a good way to help squelch gripes that the two might have about each other. Since the first one was so successful, the "Night on the Town" was offered again on September 12, the day before classes commenced, and most of Northwest's over 4,000 record enrollment were in attendance.

Faculty members at the beginning of the new semester were talking about the proposed Chair of Bible at Northwest. Some considered it desirable to offer instruction in religious education because there was interest among some students, and many religious organizations serving the student body desired to see religious instruction on campus. The Chair of Bible never materialized, but a more practical offering for a state school, a nursing program, along with a technical training program in industrial arts, was also being proposed by President Foster and would develop later. Other programs federally funded were also discussed that fall. Project Communicate, a three-year program under Title III of the Elementary and Secondary Education Act of 1965, was now in its first year on campus. Its purpose was to assist schools in the nineteen counties of Northwest Missouri by initiating the action approach to the teaching of communication skills and by devoting major attention to the resources available for teaching reading, writing, and speaking. Dr. Bennat C. Mullen headed a staff of sixteen specialists, and forty graduate students, all involved in education, attended the first summer session and received eight hours graduate credit. Another Northwest Missouri nineteen-county project, Upward Development of Rural Youth, was devised as a three-year program to encourage innovative practices in teaching disadvantaged children. This new educational service was co-directed by Dr. Roy Walker and Dr. David Dial of Northwest's education department. What they wanted to do was to help teachers plan and organize innovative programs designed to cope with individual school districts' problems.

At the end of the semester most people affiliated with Northwest seemed to be talking about an individual faculty member from the English department. On Thursday, November 30, 1967, they were reading a newspaper article stating that an assistant professor in the department since September 1966, Dr. Tommie A. Chandler, was granted a leave of absence for the 1968-1969 school year to pursue postdoctoral research in Europe under a Fulbright Fellowship and a Ford Foundation grant. The article, obviously written by Chandler, went on to enumerate his accomplishments; readers discovered that he was a former Woodrow Wilson Fellow, a National Merit Scholar, and a Phi Beta Kappa. Having previously studied abroad in several foreign countries, he, during his twelve-month study period abroad, would be working toward a second Ph.D. degree that emphasized contemporary European literature with a minor field in classical literature. All this study and research were to take him to different universities and countries as the seasons changed: in the fall, the University of Heidelberg, Germany; winter, the University of Vienna, Austria; spring, the Sorbonne, Paris. His cyclic sojourn would be completed in the summer at England's Cambridge University. Quite an academic coup! Chandler admitted, however, that he did not expect to complete his second doctorate in the one year but would return to Europe for two summer sessions. He had more news about himself. University Paperbacks was publishing his doctoral dissertation, "Transcendentalism in American Literature," and he was telling colleagues that his contract with the publisher was over $12,000.

On December 15, the *Daily Forum,* although not possessing all the facts, startled readers by publishing an article with the headline "MSC Prof a Phoney." It stated that Chandler was no longer on the college staff and that he left because of ill health the previous Friday, eight days after the published article about his accomplishments. Who was this man who seemingly possessed all these academic qualifications and whose teaching was so highly praised by high level administrators? He was not the real Tommie A. Chandler, a man who had not yet received a Ph.D. but had completed his course work and comprehensive examinations at Emory University in Atlanta, Georgia, and who, in 1967, was on the English faculty at Georgia State College in Atlanta; he was Ralph Stregles, an academic fraud posing as Tommie Chandler, a man Stregles knew and roomed with as an undergraduate at Berry College, Mount Berry, Georgia. Because of Stregles' varied stories about himself and the published laudatory article, Northwest officials became suspicious and began a check with Emory University, his purported alma mater, and subsequently discovered that there were two Tommie Chandlers, one in Georgia and one in Maryville. The real Tommie Chandler told the Emory University Placement Office in August, 1966, that he had suspected someone was using his name in applying for positions. Chandler's file was then marked with a special notation and bore Chandler's signature. Chandler's action was much too late for Northwest because Stregles was hired on January 12, 1966, with employment starting in the fall. Employment was offered to him after Northwest officials obtained and perused his credentials from a teachers' agency in Kansas City, Missouri, and after he was personally interviewed on campus. Emory officials in early December 1967 notified Northwest officials that the man on their faculty was not Tommie A. Chandler, and Northwest's only recourse was to release this man posing as Chandler with as little fanfare as possible. Stregles was gone, but there was lingering suspicion among some members of the English faculty that he could well use one of their names at some future time, and, alas, the man did in 1970. His act, however, was foiled because of a university placement office's careful attention to possible misrepresentations.

How could one hire an academic interloper? Although, in retrospect, there seemed to be inaccuracies concerning the man's file and word, Northwest officials really did not have any reason to doubt this man's qualifications, nor that he was duping Emory University, his teachers' agency, and Northwest. Chandler looked good on paper and, in 1966 in a twenty-two people English department, only two possessed doctorates, and one of those was the chairman. An additional doctorate certainly would help boost the department's image, which in 1980 does not need any boosting since thirteen of the twenty-one members possess doctorates.

Ralph Stregles, alias Tommie A. Chandler, apparently did not, in almost three semesters and one summer session, cause any academic damage to his students nor set any of them academically or emotionally adrift. Students liked him, his classes were overflowing, and he prepared well and diligently and with an enervating vitality. The man at times was exhausted because, lacking the academic qualifications of Chandler, he had to work extremely hard to stay abreast of his material. Although they could not use him for future recommendations, students who had Stregles' classes were allowed to keep their credits after his demise, and most of them did appreciate his interest and concern in their welfare and rated him as a fine instructor. Ralph Stregles' masquerade really was not anyone's great loss.

Members of the Tower Choir and the College Chorus, directed by Mr. Byron Mitchell, displayed their vocal skills by performing in concert with the Kansas City Philharmonic Orchestra on December 7.

Students in religious organizations at Northwest Christmas-caroled for various groups on campus and in town the week of the 10th and they, like the rest of the student body, left for their various homes on Friday, the 15th, the beginning of Christmas recess. The Newman Club members, of course, were no exception, but when they returned from Christmas vacation on January 2 they were grievously saddened. They found the Newman Center, their spiritual and recreational house, severely crippled by fire damage. They learned that the fire began early on Saturday morning, December 16, so no one was in the house to detect anything amiss, because they, and their chaplain, Reverend Thomas Wiederholt, were gone for the Christmas holidays. The second floor was gutted, and water and smoke damages were heavy throughout the building. The Center, however, was repaired with extensive work and effective effort.

Beginning the previous spring, many individuals connected with the campus, present and past, were being singled out or promoted for their worthy service and valid contributions. Bob Cotter became director of alumni affairs, a post he would hold until 1977, and Bruce Wake, the director of men's residence halls, became dean of men on July 1. Also in July, Dr. Harry P. Bowes, a 1957 graduate and former assistant dean of students at Northwest, was named president of General Beadle College in South Dakota, making him one of the youngest college presidents in the nation. In the fall, Major Alverado H. Kysar, originally from Hopkins, Missouri, and a 1954 Northwest graduate, received the Soldier's Medal, the Bronze Star, and the first Oak Leaf Cluster of the Army Commendation Medal with "V" for his many heroic actions in Vietnam. While Dr. B. D. Owens became assistant to the president of Ohio's Bowling Green University, Mr. Everett Brown, director of field services, received the same title in Northwest's administrative hierarchy. During the first week of January in 1968, Mr. Herbert Dieterich was cited by the Missouri High School Activities Association for his contributions to high school athletics. For thirty-six years he served on the Missouri High School Activities Board of Control and he, in addition, played an active role in college athletics by chairing Northwest's Athletic Committee and serving as the College's faculty representative to the MIAA conference. The department of agriculture was reveling in the accomplishments of one of its members who was being nationally recognized. Floyd B. Houghton, Sr., an agricultural instructor at Northwest for twenty-two years and a renowned specialist in Angus cattle, was awarded the 1967-1968 Outstanding Teacher Award of the National Association of Colleges and Teachers of Agriculture. Colleagues of Miss Mabel Cook, chairman of home economics, were happy for her, too, as the Maryville Soroptimists honored her for distinguished service to home economics and the community. Foreign language instructors were proud of Miss Lavera Malone, a French major from St. Louis. The senior coed was awarded the prestigious Danforth Foundation Fellowship to study at the University of Wisconsin, beginning with the 1968 summer session.

A majority of faculties and officials at colleges and universities, along with the general public, continued quietly on, unaware that they were directly in the path of an approaching storm. Before long that peace was challenged, and political and social unrest was beginning to emerge over America by the mid 1960s—a condition which should have forewarned administrations that college students wanted to be heard. There were, to be sure, serious protests against the social and political problems of the day, and many Americans found themselves in a deep crisis. Universities and colleges were now becoming central institutions in American society as major catalysts for articulating the need for reform. Prevalent at this time were many young insurgent groups, like the Students for a Democratic Society. Mostly protesting the war in Vietnam, demonstrators abounded over the country. The previous October, in a celebrated "Stop the Draft Week," draft cards were collected and sent to the Department of Justice. Many youths burned their cards, and the "Week" was heightened by the infamous March on the Pentagon. At the Democratic National Convention in Chicago during the summer of 1968, the Youth International Party proposed a cultural revolution to substitute for the political rebellion that other rebellious radicals envisioned. A subversion of the counter-culture, the yippies, the name by which its members were known, desired to overthrow the state by using dirty language and offering defiantly theatrical acts. Thousand of yippies, many with American flags sewn on the seats of their jeans, and many "straights" demonstratively participated those hot days in Chicago and in other cities, but there was no cultural revolution.

Between January 1 and June 15, 1968, there were 221 major demonstrations at 101 colleges and universities involving nearly 40,000 students. Northwest Missouri State was not one of those. Its student body was not apathetic or unconcerned about social, political, or cultural issues, but students here with their strongly rural and religious backgrounds did not see violent or disruptive demonstrations as a means of repairing society. President Foster's open door policy was comforting and so was Dr. Charles Thate's firm and steady hand in making decisions. Of course, faculty members always seemed available for conferences with students, too. Discontent with the Selective Service Act and its implementation was evident at Northwest as it was on every campus in America, but college students had a better chance for deferment than those individuals not enrolled. There were times, too, when there were protests against military recruitment officers in the J. W. Jones Union Building. A few extremists clamored for listeners, but they, for the most part, were left unheard.

Northwest did have, in late 1968 and early 1969, an "underground" or "off campus" magazine, *The Academic Analyst*. It was free from college control but could be purchased for a quarter at Northwest's bookstore. Edited by student Reginald Turnbull, the monthly magazine listed itself as one of literary, academic, and issue-oriented expression providing a sounding board for public opinion. Students and faculty alike contributed articles, poems, and stories. It was popular, too, at a time when the College had no literary magazine.

Many student groups, to be sure, confined themselves to doing good deeds locally, and they contributed significantly in their own subtle or peacefully active manners. One example was the Delta Sigma Phi fraternity. In cooperation with the "Support Our Servicemen" project of the American Red Cross, forty-seven members of the fraternity conducted a 260-mile marathon from Maryville to Jefferson City on March 24-26. Carrying a petition signed by over 1,000 Northwest students voicing their support for the embattled American soldiers in Vietnam, each of the men ran more than five miles as they covered the distance in forty-eight hours. The run, not to be construed as an affirmative nod for the War, was a tribute to those fighting in a war that could not be won. Seven days after this marathon run, President Johnson, with the ashes of defeat strewn all around, made the startling announcement that he would not run for re-election.

Other runners were performing that spring, too, but these were more concerned with competition and individual times for their events. Coach Earl Baker's track squad won all its dual and triangular meets, and one of the men, Pete Hager, broke a thirty-year-old 220-yard dash record set by Herschel Neil, an almost legendary figure in Bearcat track history for whom the present outdoor track is named.

A reminder of the old—the one-room country schoolhouse—would soon mingle and contrast with the newest addition on campus, the mathematics and science building. The Hickory Grove country schoolhouse, a pioneer building constructed in 1883 in the mid-portion of Nodaway County, northeast of Clearmont, Missouri, was to be relocated in the summer on the Northwest campus east of the Administration Building, Northwest's oldest and most historical building. Mr. and Mrs. Eldon Milbank, owners of the building, donated the old schoolhouse to the Nodaway County Historical Society, which, in turn, gave it to Northwest. Mrs. Neva Rhodes, Mr. Milbank's former high school teacher and chairman of the Society's Finance Committee, had the awesome task of directing a fund-raising program to cover moving expenses and future upkeep, and, of course, the Society, under Stephen LaMar's leadership, was in charge of the moving, renovation, and preservation. Many people, like the movers Mr. and Mrs. Ross Scott, Jr. and the preparers of the building and foundation Tom Devine, Keith Gleeson, James Lowe, Myrl Long, John Ed Fuhrman, Paul Pruitt, Alan Trueblood, and LaMar, gave much of their time and effort to make this move possible. Capturing a bit of the bygone in education, the building, today, is comfortable in its surroundings. It functions well as a small museum, and it offers the public a view of how education was formerly facilitated.

The new $3,000,000 mathematics and science building was ready and waiting to be dedicated on Friday, May 31, 1968, in the Administration Building, and it would also on that day embrace its well-wishers with an open house, overseen by Dr. Ted Weichinger, head of the division. The name of the building was known, for it had been previously announced, as was the custom, by President Foster at the Alumni Banquet, now held in conjunction with the homecoming celebration in October. The sparkling new science facility was to be called the Garrett-Strong Hall of Science in honor of two long-time members of the division of science and mathematics, Mr. William T. Garrett and Dr. J. Gordon Strong. It was a fitting gesture since both men made innumerable contributions to the College and to their respective fields of science. Now the departments of biology, chemistry, geology, physical science, physics, mathematics, and science education would be centrally housed in a construct of more than 100,000 square feet, making it the most spacious classroom facility on campus. The department of geography moved to the building in 1978. A pleasant feature and a horticultural aid for botany students was a greenhouse on the west end of the roof. The dedication and open house participants delighted in having an intimate glimpse of the edifice.

With the old and the new now added to the campus proper, the Missouri Legislature was telling Northwest officials in June that they would receive funds for a new industrial arts building. Registrar Ruth Nystrom and Dean of Administration Charles Thate were telling state officials the same month that 1,936 students, including 536 graduate students, were enrolled in summer school. The record number was a 490-student incréase over the previous record summer enrollment. Part of the increase was attributed to the growth of Northwest's own graduate program, and this summer enrollment figure was actually larger than the 1960 fall semester when 1,848 students were registered. Northwest in the summer of 1968 offered 300 classes in thirty-one subject matter areas. And, in addition, it provided a program of seventeen workshops and clinics ranging from basketball for high school athletics to an aerospace education workshop.

There would be no more Junior High School at Horace Mann Laboratory School. A decision based upon several factors was made by the Board of Regents to discontinue operation for the seventh and eighth grade years. The parents were advised that an enrollment of twenty-six pupils in the two grades was too few to provide adequate programs in instrumental music and athletics and too small to provide the most desirable or economical situation for observation and student teaching. It was a necessary move, to be sure, but it, like the 1960 closing of the Senior High School, struck a discordant note in the harmony of traditional academic instruction.

Recognizing that students in the late 60s really wanted a voice and some independence concerning their academic lives, President Foster and the Board of Regents initiated a first by inviting the student leaders to the Board's opening meeting of the 1968-1969 school year. They dined together and shared thoughts. As Foster pointed out, the meeting gave the Regents and the students an opportunity to become acquainted and to better understand each other's problems. The students could better visualize decisions made by the governing body. Also the Regents could see that their young luncheon guests were not insurgents but were concerned about themselves and the welfare of society. The students represented a cross section of campus life and those present were Mike Wilson, student body president; John Price, Union Board chairman; Mike Miller, *Tower* editor; Fred Beavers, *Northwest Missourian* editor; Rollie Stadlman, president of Radio KDLX; David Wasserfallen, Alpha Phi Omega president; Jeane Everett, Gamma Sigma Sigma president; Barry Monaghan, Inter-Fraternity Council president; and Jan Ellis, Panhellenic Council president.

Many new organizations and programs, conceived much earlier, were born in the fall of 1968. The Pre-Medical Professions Club, the first because it met in September, was for students preparing for careers in pharmacy, dentistry, medicine, veterinary medicine, nursing, medical technology, zoology, or chemistry. Mike Speece, David Hill, and Alma Morgan, now a physician in Fort Collins, Colorado, were the Club's first officers, and its sponsors were Dr. David Smith, Dr. Gerald Kirk, and Dr. Dale Rosenburg, one of its current sponsors. The members, then as now, conducted fund-raising projects to finance trips in their various professional areas to such places as the University of Kansas Medical Center, St. Luke's Hospital in Kansas City, the University of Missouri Veterinary School, and Topeka's psychiatric Menninger Clinic. The Club also distinguished itself as the only one on campus broad enough to include for membership all students interested in the medical sciences.

The following month Pi Delta Epsilon, national honorary college journalism fraternity, through the efforts of Mrs. Opal Eckert, adviser to the *Northwest Missourian,* was officially activated at Northwest. She and Dr. Frank Grube served as sponsors to the Northwest chapter, and Dr. Peter Jackson of the industrial arts department was an honorary member. Charter members were Fred Beavers, Kay Weidenhaft, John Ford, David Horsman, and Mrs. Gail Wiederholt; Jan Kieser, Mike Miller, and Dale Gorsuch were accepted as pledges. The organization is now known as the Society for Collegiate Journalists.

Something different was being added in programs the same month. Northwest's home economics department established a child development laboratory for pre-school children, ages three and four, for the primary purpose of serving as an observation and study center for the department's majors. Sponsored by the State Department of Education-Vocational Home Economics Division, the Child Development Laboratory, located at 528 West Ninth Street, was housed in a neatly landscaped white house with its interior scaled down to child size and fully equipped to meet the mental, physical, and emotional needs of its young occupants. Miss Catherine Moore, the instructor, and Mrs. Virginia Bouska, the director, were there to greet ten of the three-year-olds every morning and ten of the four-year-olds every afternoon. The laboratory developed into a two-year program and is designed for twenty new children each year. Headed by Miss Peggy Miller, it serves, besides home economics, the areas of child psychology and elementary education. The professionally supervised program also offers a much needed service to society because of working mothers. Young women can garner professional training in the care of children and be licensed and equipped to have their own day care centers, and the program is so designed that the students can continue on to complete a four-year degree in some area of child development.

The year 1968 was not labeled "The Year of the Child," but Northwest was trying to help children, this often neglected segment of society. In November, nineteen four-year-old preschoolers were arriving every morning at the Maryville Head Start Center in a large room on the first floor of the Administration Building. Vacated by the science department upon completion of the Garrett-Strong Science Building, the room offered these children many activities enabling them to expand their educational and social backgrounds in preparation for kindergarten. Most of the children in the Head Start program, taught by Mrs. Donald Armstrong and conducted by the Economic Opportunity Corporation, were from low-income families whose parents were not able to supply the materials or experiences that the program offered. An extra bonus was that Head Start did help each child make the transition from home to classroom easier, and it increased each youngster's competence in managing himself and his school tasks.

Immaculate white uniforms now occasionally dotted the campus. No, the Pre-Nursing students were not conducting dress rehearsals for their future professional careers, nor was Northwest establishing its own medical school. Those crisp white uniforms and pert nurse's caps belonged to nursing instructors who were part of the latest terminal vocational programs offered on the campus—the Northwest Missouri State College School of Practical Nursing. Northwest, Maryville's St. Francis Hospital, and local people saw the dire need for such a program in health care, and the College accepted the responsibility for establishing it and working with the local hospital to provide the necessary clinical facilities and experiences for the students. The weeks of planning and work, before the fall classes could commence in the two large second-floor classrooms of Horace Mann Laboratory School, were busy ones for the administrator, Mrs. Jane Morgan, who worked closely with Dr. Charles Thate, dean of administration, and Dr. Leon Miller, dean of instruction. Of course, Mrs. Morgan could not be expected to handle all the administrating and the teaching, too. Mrs. Gwen Lynch was hired as an instructor to work with Mrs. Morgan. Both women possessed strong backgrounds of training and experience as registered nurses, and they were ready for the first class of fifteen students, some who drove 100 miles a day to attend classes and who represented eight communities in Northwest Missouri. Upon satisfactory completion of all requirements at the end of the year's program, the students received pins and diplomas, but they had yet one more hurdle to face in order to become licensed practical nurses— passing the State Board Examination. Those first students were successful as have been all the graduates from Northwest's School of Practical Nursing.

The mathematics and science division members were comfortably settled in their fine home, and it was time to look after the oldest building on campus, the Administration Building. It had just undergone a checkup, and specialists and officials felt that it was necessary for the grand lady to undergo surgery. Extensive remodeling to continue for several months started in December, and she was gracious enough after her operation to welcome permanent tenants to the 77,508 square feet of newly renovated floor space. A new guidance center was accepted in the east wing of the second floor, and the agricultural department was relocated on the second floor because of more space and classroom offerings. Agriculture's neighbors were the offices of placement and field services, and room was made on the first floor for the president, his assistant, the dean of administration, the dean of instruction, and the business, public relations, and alumni offices. Home economics found its quarters on the third floor enlarged, and the grand lady was eagerly awaiting the arrival of KDLX, the campus radio station. Soundproof studios, instructional space, offices, and improved transmitting cables would be ready in the west wing of the third floor. Theatergoers, too, would revel in all the Building's splendor because the Auditorium's seats were upholstered and the aisles were carpeted.

Student Senate, under the leadership of President Mike Wilson, Vice President Barry Monaghan, and Secretary-Treasurer Betsy Thompson, and sponsored by Dr. Peter Jackson, was having a good year. It was incorporating many reforms in an attempt to keep up with the times and to alleviate student hassles. Negative credit, a timeworn student millstone and administrative burden for the faculty and the registrar, was placed in its grave and buried, hopefully forever, by the student governing group with the aid of President Foster and the Board of Regents. This practice of a student losing a credit for every unexcused day missed before or after a vacation recess was one policy that no one really missed. The Senate was also responsible for the relaxation of dress codes for men and women in the Cafeteria and in Wells Library. Librarians were especially happy with the Student Senate because they really were growing rather weary of telling ladies—young and old—that slacks were not proper attire in the confines of their building until after five o'clock. Open housing for upper division students and less strict residence hall regulations for women were other important breakthroughs established by the student governing body for the students. Lingering by couples on the doorsteps of the women's dormitories could be extended rather than their dashing up the steps to make the ten o'clock curfew. Campus attire and freedom of action were no longer cramped by the staid and conservative customs of the fifties and early to mid sixties.

New Left insurgent groups never gained a toehold on campus. Northwest, however, had a group of concerned, rational, and informed students, who were genuinely respected for their valid contributions. This was Dialogue, a student involvement group that made big steps in attaining better campus relations. They meaningfully focused, too, on how the nation's happenings, like Vietnam and New Left movements, were affecting Northwest and its students. They also conducted programs centered around the black student on campus, including a panel discussion by the Depth Involvement Group from the Wesley and Newman Centers composed of black and white students to help understand each other's feelings and attitudes. Although Northwest was not split along racial lines, some improvement of conditions for blacks was needed on campus and certainly in town. In the late sixties, national events worked against a peaceful settlement of college problems, but

Dialogue was something the campus needed then, for the group was a chisel that helped chip away pieces of potential unrest and, consequently, trouble.

Minority groups were recognized in a way they had not been even a few years earlier, and consultation with students over courses and teachers was no longer the exception. Along with the rise of more student and faculty independence, there had developed, as evidenced by the previous fall's activities on campus, a growing inter-dependence of Northwest with the world outside. By 1968-1969 the campus was less provincial. It was not that Northwest was listening to what dissenters were preaching to student rallies at Berkeley, Columbia University, or Madison; it was that Northwest Missouri State College, as in any true institution of higher learning, was bound closely with national and world problems. The Foster administration seemed to understand this, and, in turn, contrary to some faculty and student beliefs, encouraged controversial speakers to visit the campus. One good example was the week of October 14-18 when the campus was reverberating with the call "Give a Damn," which is what the week was called. During those five October days, the Student Union Program Council sponsored a series of events directed toward an exposure for the students of the most glaring problems of the day. The purpose, as stated by the Council, was "to enlighten the students to those inequalities and help to propagate a less permissive attitude on the part of everyone involved." "Give a Damn" provided the opportunity for students to encounter speakers like Julian Bond, black leader from Georgia; Andrew Hatcher, civil rights leader; Ilus Davis, mayor of Kansas City; and Ray Munjo, New Left dissident. Films, panel discussions, coffee houses, and art exhibitions were prevalent and enhanced the many speakers' visits. A capstone was "Hunger Day," when many students abstained from eating for a day and contributed what they would have spent on food to a worthwhile cause. Of course, some ventured away from campus to eat because three drive-ins reported increased profits for that day. But one thing was really obvious in October of 1968—plenty of Northwest students really did seem to "give a damn."

On the lighter—but still caring—social side, Associated Women Students was having its usual big year with its Fall Style Show and Spring Then and Now Bridal Show. AWS also produced, but sponsored by Mrs. Opal Eckert's journalism department, the Top Ten Coed Contest, won by Charlene Rush, and the group was busy selecting its Woman of the Year, Kay Hamilton; its Mother of the Year, Mrs. Eva

Thompson, mother of Betsy; and its Father of the Year, Mr. Joe Beavers, father of Fred.

Mr. John Ed Fuhrman of the division of field services was saying early in 1969 that "every day is high school day on campus," meaning that individuals or groups were welcome and guided by Fuhrman or his staff whenever they visited the campus. A new twist, however, was added in 1966 by President Foster and implemented by field services when the High School Ambassador Program began, and in February Fuhrman, the director of the program, and his people were preparing for the fourth annual program. Between February 13 and March 22, 300 students from public and parochial high schools in Northwest Missouri visited the campus. Each high school in the nineteen-county district was invited by field services to send representative seniors for one of the six Thursday through Saturday visits to the campus. The ambassadors were to "act" as college students. Living on campus, attending classes and social events, touring buildings, and visiting informally with faculty and administrative personnel were what the high school students did and seemingly enjoyed because it helped them break away from their own everyday routines during the twilight of their senior years. It was a free excursion into a phase of college life and, although not heavily advertised as such, an excellent recruitment device.

Many faculty members were demonstrating in February, not for better pay or lighter teaching loads, but by displaying their "talents" on stage. On February 6, eleven instructors in single or double acts, and a chorus line of thirteen male members of the faculty and administration in various female attire—directed by Dr. Kathryn Riddle of the women's physical education department—showed their acting and dancing abilities to an enthusiastic and overflowing audience in the Administration Building Auditorium. The entertainment was presented as a means of raising money for the College's Experiment in International Living, coordinated by Miss Mary Jackson, to help send students for summer stays in foreign countries. The event, the first of its kind at Northwest and spearheaded by geography's Don Hagan, was called "Faculty Frolics." It was successful enough to be put into operation again the following February. Sufficient money was raised from the second "Frolics," a faculty benefit basketball game, and a rummage sale to send five students abroad instead of three.

February should have been called International Month on the Northwest campus. Mrs. Lela Bell, the community's coordinator for the Experiment in International Living, organized the second International Festival, featuring foreign cuisine, thus raising funds to send a high school student to one of the Experiment in Living summer programs in a European country. A cosmopolitan atmosphere was still in evidence later in the month when Northwest's international students, representing thirteen foreign countries, decided they would show what they could do by preparing their own countries' foods. It is not that they were homesick for home cooking, but they wanted Northwest to share with them. This annual function of the International Students Organization also helped the group raise funds for field trips and activities that would enlarge the foreign students' knowledge and understanding of the United States.

February brought the news that Northwest would get twin high-rise dormitories to complement Franken and Phillips. Housing and Urban Development authorized the loan of $2,800,000 for the construction of one dwelling to house 312 women, and one to house 312 men. The money had been reserved for Northwest by HUD in late 1966 but was released over two years later. Occupancy was expected for the fall of 1970. President Foster was rightfully happy over the dormitory developments and Northwest's expanding enrollment and facilities, but he was worried about where his forty-five new faculty members, whom he hired to meet the student demand, were going to live in the fall. The housing shortage was critical, and Foster was asking aid from the Chamber of Commerce to secure local additional housing. He felt that without help Northwest would be forced to construct duplex apartments on state property to house its personnel. Fortunately, duplexes on campus never materialized. Ironically, despite construction of multi-unit complexes in Maryville, the housing shortage was largely due to an increase in married students. Live-in arrangements were becoming popular throughout the country, but Northwest's married students accounted for more than twenty percent of the enrollment.

Many students in the spring semester of 1969 were thinking of teaching as a career. During this semester, 400 Northwest seniors, working under the supervision of cooperative teachers in the field, were placed in forty-six public and parochial schools in the nineteen-county district of Northwest Missouri and in Iowa. Fifteen staff members in the elementary and the secondary education departments worked with those student teachers as their college supervisors. Dr. Frank Grispino, director of student teaching and a staunch believer in the visual aspects of education, was delighted with the recent innovation in the student-teacher program, the use of portable TV equipment whereby students were able to evaluate themselves and better understand their supervisors' evaluation of them.

Graduate assistantships would be offered in Northwest's enlarged graduate program in the fall, and the cooperative graduate program with the University of Missouri was to be phased out completely in the summer, but another cooperative graduate program between Northwest and the University leading toward the Certificate of Specialization in Educational Administration was to begin in the summer. Any educator with a master's degree who aspired to be a school superintendent or principal could partake in the program for two summers at Northwest and two summers at the University of Missouri and finish with the Certificate.

Again, it was time to pay homage to revered faculty members who were leaving their classrooms for the last time. In tribute to Mr. Herbert Dieterich and Miss Laura Frances Jackson, the J. W. Jones Union Ballroom was filled with faculty, administrators, friends of the honorees, and their families. Praise was given to them by their colleagues with Dr. Leon Miller serving as the master of ceremonies. Mr. Dieterich was leaving forty-one years behind at Northwest, and he was one witness of Northwest's growth. There were 556 students when he arrived in 1928 and three campus buildings: Residence Hall, the Gymnasium, and the Administration Building. His good friend and colleague Ryland Milner, a man whose career as a student athlete and faculty member nearly equaled Dieterich's, reminisced at the Banquet over Mr. Dieterich's accomplishments as principal of Horace Mann Laboratory School, instructor in the division of education, and chairman of secondary education. Although some people called him "Herb," most called him Mr. Dieterich because he and the name generated respect. Milner culminated his discussion by telling the throng of well-wishers that he always—and the two were close associates for thirty-six years—called him Mr. Dieterich. Even though Miss Jackson spent twenty-nine fewer years on Northwest's faculty than Mr. Dieterich, she was retiring with forty years of dedication to the teaching of English. She and her students had a mutual respect. She liked her students, worked with them, and helped them.

Countdown time was here this spring of 1969, for students were studying for final examinations and packing to leave for home. Organizations, too, were hard pressed to wind down their activities, and some were helping Gamma Sigma Sigma, Northwest's service sorority, finish one of its innumerable projects, this one international. The group, led by Redding, Iowa's Kay Saville and St. Joseph's Gail Didlo, was busy sorting and packing twenty large boxes of materials and books for the Peace Corps school in Addis Ababa, Ethiopia. The young women solicited the educational materials in Maryville and St. Joseph and from their sister sororities in the Midwest. They culled what was not appropriate, sold the culls, and bought more books. With the $200 in donations the women received, they bought more necessary materials. The Ethiopian children were helped in their educational endeavors with at least some varied reading that hopefully would enlarge their knowledge of the world and expand their minds beyond their own limited environment. The sorority was also restating the general hopeful tone of the campus by promoting what the coeds called the "Kwitchyerbichin" theme. Proposed by Sponsor Barbara Palling, the theme advocated doing something positive instead of complaining about world, national, and local conditions.

Alpha Phi Omega, their brother organization, was again highly involved raising money at the annual carnival and with the Ugly Man on Campus Contest. Mr. Jim Redd of the men's physical education department claimed the honor as he delighted his audiences with his imitation leopard skin jungle costume.

Orchesis, the modern dance club, culminated its year's work of rehearsals with its annual recital, consisting of solo and ensemble dance numbers. The then all-female dancers, sponsored and directed by Mrs. Ann Brekke, were composed of some members of Mrs. Brekke's modern dance class, some physical education majors, and others who were interested in modern and interpretive dance, as well as jazz and ballet. Besides hearing the Bearcat Concert and Marching Bands, the Tower Choir and Chamber Choir concerts, music aficionados saw that Maryville was not too remote for either a visiting group of artists or a single artist. The Norman Luboff Choir excited them, and Vlademir Horzowski, noted classical pianist, captured his audience's attention.

The Bearcat basketball team generated excitement for its fans, something they really needed since the fall football squad was winless. Coach Dick Buckridge's men finished second in the MIAA conference and had their best league record in nineteen years. The swimmers were having another good year, and number one golfer Larry Maiorano was achieving Bearcat golfing fame by extending his cumulative college record to 42-6.

One more national honorary fraternity was added to the fold of academic recognition at Northwest. On Saturday, May 17, the Maryville chapter of Alpha Beta Alpha, professional library science fraternity, was installed as a member of the national organization. The chapter was to be formally recognized as Alpha Mu chapter and was, in reality, organized the previous year by James Johnson. Library science was a thriving academic discipline with its share of majors and minors, and twenty-four women and one man were accepted as charter members of Alpha Mu. Since the group was organized months before the installation, ten women and one man became alumni members of the chapter.

A graduating class of 700 seniors, the largest in the College's history, would see something decidedly different on May 29, Commencement Day. Size is important and many colleges like to generate numbers, but sometimes numbers help diminish individual identity. In order to quickly facilitate those numbers, Northwest was departing from a traditional procedure by collectively conferring degrees upon the candidates according to their degree classifications. Honor students and candidates for master's degrees, however, were the exceptions. In recent years the tradition of recognizing each graduate was restored to its rightful corner of academic tradition.

On January 18, 1968, Frank K. Ulman, a farmer southwest of Maryville most of his life, died at his retirement home in Hot Springs, Arkansas. Not too many at Northwest would have noted his passing, but a later development etched this man's name forever in the future history of Northwest. When his will was read, the following words were heard: "I bequeath to the scholarship fund of Northwest State College the sum of $30,000, to be known as the F. K. Ulman Scholarship Fund and to be administered by the appropriate committee under the direction of the Board of Regents of said Northwest State College, Maryville." Mr. Ulman was a man who was not able to complete his own education beyond the fifth grade, but he was sincerely interested in helping educate young college people, thoughts he shared before his death with President Foster. The gift was presented to the College in June 1969, and the Ulman Scholarship has been a very viable one since its inception in 1971 when Betty Jane Christopher from Gilman City, Missouri, was the first recipient. Nine years later, the young lady's brother William won it and became the third member of his family to receive the award. Their sister Joyce was the winner in 1978, and the Christophers' cousin Linda Herring claimed the honor in 1972. The Ulman Scholarship is offered, after an extensive, competitive examination, to an entering freshman with a superior academic record. The $500 per year scholarship is renewable every year if the honoree maintains at least a 3.5 grade point average on Northwest's 4 point scale.

The early summer of 1969 was a relatively quiet one. Project Communicate was entering its last year on campus. Miss Karen Licklider, dean of women, was concerned. All the on-campus accommodations for women were already filled for the fall, and she was trying to find approved housing in town for 100 women students. The first Northwest summer French institute was in its final stages as six North-

west coeds, directed by Mrs. Elaine Mauzey and assisted by Miss Pam
Sayler, were preparing to fly home. Northwest Alumni Director Bob
Cotter took forty-two alumni and friends the previous summer on a
seven-day vacation to Nassau. This first trip was such a success that
Cotter decided to make it an annual event. His decision was a good
one, for sixty-nine people participated in the 1969 two-week excursion
to England and the Continent. An aviation course with two hours credit
was offered by Dr. Bob Bush, director of admissions. Construction on
the two new high-rise dormitories began, and the Administration Building, with its first major surgery since its birth, was recovering nicely
and was almost ready for visitors. And, hopefully, the Memorial Bell
Tower would soon begin to project its 100-foot frame.

It was not quiet, however, over the nation or the Northwest campus on July 20, 1969. A quarter of the world's population watched
live TV broadcasts of Neil Armstrong become the first man to walk on
the moon. It was a thrilling and mesmerizing moment, the climax then
of man's technological progress. We tend to mark happenings in our
lives with historic events, and this moon shot was marked by most
people in front of a TV set, observing the primary mission of beating
Russia to the moon. Although the event, as many do, faded in a relatively short time, it was one of the most talked about subjects on
campus in July.

Northwest's hierarchy was subtly being restructured that same
month of July. Effective July 1, Dr. Dwain E. Small became the dean
of faculties, formerly known as dean of instruction, the post held by
Dr. Miller. Holding a dual role by overseeing both undergraduate and
graduate instruction, Miller, because of the successful and growing
graduate program, could now devote his full-time energies to the
graduate school as dean of graduate studies. Dr. Charles Thate, with
his expanding duties as dean of administration, acquired an assistant.
Dr. Don Petry, a 1962 Northwest graduate, became associate dean of
administration with his major responsibilities as administrator of the
campus physical plant and planner for the future growth of the campus. The face of the rest of the hierarchy looked the same: Everett
Brown, as assistant to the president and director of field services;
Luther Belcher, business manager; Ruth Nystrom, registrar; Bob Bush,
director of admissions; Charles Koerble, dean of students; Bruce Wake,
dean of men; and Louann Lewright, new dean of women. The academic division structure was now defunct and twenty-six chairmen
headed their respective departments. James Johnson was librarian and
Luke Boone, the director of the instructional materials bureau, and, of
course, Foster was president. Two other people, beneficial to North-

west's future, came that summer: Mr. Marvin Silliman, the new J. W. Jones Union director, arrived in time to watch Armstrong striding the moon, and Mr. Bob Henry left his position as assistant professor of journalism at Wichita State University to become news/information director in August.

Twenty-eight high school students were on campus to attend a second two-week art camp, sponsored by the art department and directed by Art Instructor Lee Hageman. Highly individualized instruction, where each student's artwork was supervised by a faculty member, impressed the camp participants, and Hageman was promising a longer camp with more intensive training in drawing, ceramics, jewelry, design, painting, sculpture, silversmithing, and printmaking for the third camp.

Although student registration, because of technological advances, was not as onerous and time-consuming as in some past years, there was still evidence, due to Northwest's record enrollments and more academic offerings, of vestiges of the traditional enrollment procedures like long lines, frustrated students, and distraught faculty advisers. The Academic Advisement Center, a new pre-registration system, directed by John Mobley and manned by six academic advisers, was implemented for the fall semester. It was felt that the Center would allow students, especially freshmen and sophomores, to receive more complete advisement in place of the hurried process under the old system. The Center was operating at a time when Northwest exceeded 5,000 students for a total fall enrollment of 5,136.

The magic number for Northwest officials seemed to be 5,000, and they were dutifully looking for that student who would surpass 4,999. The student who broke that number was Gary F. Coy, a freshman from Barnard, Missouri. Coy was a twenty-one-year-old Vietnam veteran, who was awarded the Silver Star for gallantry in action, the Bronze Star for valor in action, and the Purple Heart for wounds received in combat. Coy was one of 1,851 freshmen, and there were 1,062 sophomores, 747 juniors, 966 seniors, and 488 graduate students. Twenty-two students were not certain what they were and remained unclassified. Included in the above enrollment total were 2,794 men and 2,342 women.

Effective also with this 1969 fall semester was the establishment of a graduate course center geared to the Master of Science in Education degree in St. Joseph. Again, Northwest was following its traditional concept of cooperating, and Foster announced at a September news conference in St. Joseph that the program made it possible for graduate students in elementary teaching to complete twenty-four semester hours of a thirty-two semester hour Master of Science degree at the Center. The remaining eight hours were to be taken at Northwest. St. Joseph area public school teaching personnel liked the accessible arrangements of earning three quarters of their higher degree work there in the city. They could take a maximum of six hours a semester, offered by the traveling graduate faculty members from Northwest. Lafayette High School, site of the Center, welcomed 102 graduate students, guaranteeing the program's success and bringing an expansive smile to the face of Dean Leon Miller. Stimulated by the Center, graduate enrollment at Northwest jumped to 495, a 57 percent increase over the fall of 1968. Northwest, attempting to be as accessible as possible, arranged to have library resources from its own library housed at the St. Joseph Public Library for use by the students, and Northwest's graduate instructors helped by carrying and supplying many of their own additional references and supplementary readings. One semester later, Northwest introduced courses at the St. Joseph Graduate Center leading to the Master of Arts in Business Administration.

For twenty years Northwest was known as Northwest Missouri State College, having dropped "Teachers" from its name in 1949. Officials at Northwest, watching closely the enrollment figures, more and better course offerings, more degree offerings, and an expanded graduate program, were no longer thinking of the College as a one-purpose institution. And they were right. Northwest was serving many different purposes as displayed by what the varied academic and vocational disciplines were accomplishing. In a special meeting for staff and students, President Foster explained the change in the role of the College and called it a multi-purpose one. Of course, the assemblage was waiting for his next word—university. Yes, he said that it was time for the College to become Northwest Missouri State University. That name change would take time and work as the many subsequent months would show.

Al Capp, noted humorist and creator of the Li'l Abner comic strip, made a fall appearance with a "canned" speech for the Northwest District Teachers Meeting, held every October on campus. Most of his comments centered around the Democratic National Convention in Chicago, and his remarks gratified the law and order people and inflamed the few idealistic students in attendance.

The Administration Building, fully recovered from her repair work, was again comfortable, and on Sunday, November 2, she was watching her newest occupant, Radio Station KDLX, finish moving to its new quarters in the southwest wing of the third floor, an area vacated by the chemistry department when it moved across the parking lot to the Garrett-Strong Building. Certainly a different breed of occupants were these radio people, but anyone who knew their nine-year history of struggle, toil, and financial hardship was happy to see them comfortably settled in more than 3,000 square feet of space, air-conditioned and soundproofed for acoustical control. Their story is one of a rise from "rags to riches" and part of it is worth retelling.

Originally housed in a broom closet in Colbert Hall, KDLX evolved from an amateur ham radio club with homemade and borrowed equipment. Stories about that tiny room in the early days of the Radio Club have taken on mythical proportions. Sponsored by Myles Grabau, and later Bob Seipel, club members worked long hours without course credit or college support. They, however, wanted a station on campus, but, without financial support and administrative recognition, they were doomed to stay in that closet with their meager facilities.

Those first seven years were really tough; with Alpha Phi Omega offering some financial assistance and Grabau supplying technical help, the group, with President Jones' permission, went on the air April 1, 1960, by broadcasting to the men's dormitories. They had one microphone, two homemade portable turntables, a homemade control board, a homemade transmitter, and a minimal number of records. What few they had were either borrowed or provided from the members' own record libraries. In 1962, the women's dormitories were added to the listening audience. The 1963 school year drew a blank on radio and not because of financial troubles or the lack of equipment. Playing their sign-on record April Stevens' "Teach Me Tiger" thirty-three consecutive times, making indiscreet and irresponsible comments, and telling racial and dirty jokes were not part of President Jones' attitude toward "gracious living" on campus, and the radio group discovered Jones' ire as he unceremoniously canceled broadcasting activities. Grabau, too, rightfully wanted no part of the melange. The year 1964 brought a new purpose. The intent of broadcasting on campus was reevaluated, and permission to be back on the air was granted. The following year was a foothold one for radio on campus. The Club, now known as KDLX Radio, received $500 in funds from the administration, more help from APO and its sponsor Myrl Long, and mechanical aid from Bob Seipel, who was really instrumental in bringing radio back from its year of oblivion. As superintendent of buildings and grounds, he was instrumental in the Club's leaving its miniscule quarters for roomier ones in the Power Plant although the new ones were still crowded and without rest rooms. Administrative funds were raised to $750 in 1966. The money and a credit course in broadcasting gave KDLX members a bit of prestige on campus. Hardly causing a ripple at the time, Rollie Stadlman, as a freshman, joined the Club early in 1966. Two weeks later, however, he was program director. President Foster had plans for this group, partly evidenced by the two years of financial aid from the College. His plans, however, were beginning to take on some substance in 1967. That was the year he hired Mrs. Cathran Cushman, an important thrust in the future of radio at Northwest. Mrs. Cushman knew of the station's past problems, and Foster told her that she would have administrative support. To prepare herself for her new marriage to radio and television, Cushman assiduously spent two summers in completing twenty hours of specialized postgraduate study in broadcasting at the University of Wyoming and the University of Missouri at Kansas City. She knew what lay ahead in developing the area. To have decent radio properties plus an important communications study was Foster's dream, and she was there to implement that dream. The first day of school that fall in 1967, Rollie Stadlman, now president of the KDLX Radio Club, was asked by its members to "check out" this "new lady on the block." Something new had been added and the members, wary of impingement on their territory, wanted to know what was going to become of their domain. So this tall, bespectacled blond trudged the four flights to Cushman's office in the Administration Building and intrepidly investigated her. Cushman talked to Stadlman of receiving all new equipment and eventually an FM station. He listened politely, not really believing what he was hearing. Chortling to himself as he descended the stairs, he felt that the Club would retain its status quo because this woman was talking about very expensive equipment, and this Club was used to little financial support and no quality equipment. He dutifully returned to the group and said, "She's crazy! Don't worry about her!" No, they did not have to worry about her, for the station came into its own that year as a full practical laboratory that supplemented additional courses in radio and television broadcasting, and Cushman developed the curriculum and the station as a recognized and important area of communications study. She, as a one-person staff in 1967, was director of broadcasting, director of programming, curriculum coordinator, and a full-time instructor. And broadcasting majors and minors began to come. Students interested in radio were nebulous about their future, and Mrs. Cushman faced thirty negative faces in her classroom, including Stadlman, currently the director of broadcasting services, and Larry Lewellen, presently production technician, and they remained unconvinced and perplexed until the day that big, beautiful control board arrived, replacing the little homemade board held together, as Mrs.

Cushman describes it, with "baling wire, spit, and a prayer." As the group huddled around the unveiling of the control board, any doubts, negativism, or hostility over any impending changes seemed to vanish. They sensed that the operation, with the administration's financial backing and Cushman's pushing toward quality, would be a first-class one. The $8,000 allotted to radio from Northwest's budget in 1967 enabled Cushman to replace much of that "baling wire, spit, and a prayer" material with new and modern equipment and, of course, records. A definite redeeming feature for KDLX Radio and the broadcasting curriculum was that Cushman was never reticent about asking for help from specialists. Sam Scott, founder of the first collegiate station in Missouri and head of broadcasting at the University of Missouri in Kansas City, and Bill Honnacutt, Scott's chief engineer, helped advise and set up equipment. John McMullen, broadcasting director at the University of Wyoming, aided, too. Cushman, along with students like Stadlman and Lewellen, also visited and solicited any station in the Midwest that would open its doors for them.

In 1968, the radio area was solid financially. Grant money from the Corporation for Public Broadcasting started arriving that year and has never stopped. That same year saw the addition of a broadcasting technician, John Perkins, to oversee the station's new complex equipment and to provide students with the necessary technical training. His hiring was timely; the Federal Communications Commission demanded that all students on the air pass the third-class radio operator's license test, the same one required by all commercial stations. So the following spring Cushman and Perkins took twenty-one broadcasting majors to the FCC offices in Kansas City to take tests for licenses, and they were successful. The FCC officials stated that they never expected or even saw such a large group from one school, nor did they ever have so many from one institution pass the technical professional examination.

Now comfortable in new quarters and with adversity seemingly left behind, this rapidly expanding field of study finally had a decent home of its own with solid financial support from the College and from federal grants. It boasted, too, a solid nucleus of majors and minors in radio and television broadcasting, and KDLX was on the air nineteen-and-one-half hours a day, reaching the dormitories, the dining facilities, the J. W. Jones Union Building, President Foster's home, and the Wesley Foundation. Television, however, was the tardy member in joining its radio companion in the embraceable arms of the Administration Building and would not do so until the seventies when room there was made for television and film expansion. Radio's companion, television, did not become overwrought and maudlin because of the physical distance now existing between the two. It seemed content to stay for the present with the audio-visual personnel, headed by Luke Boone, in Wells Library, using their camera, television, and taping equipment to produce a show a week over Cable TV, Channel 8.

KDLX learned to thrive on adversity, but because of its dedicated and tireless workers those days were left behind. With the excitement of the move waning, another chapter, guaranteed to generate more excitement, would soon be etched—the creation of an FM station of 100,000 watt strength.

AWS was continuing its tradition of honoring the "Father and Son of the Year," and for the fourth consecutive year sponsored Dad's Day at Northwest. Seventeen nominees were submitted by campus organizations, and Mr. Harold Wagner from Grant, Iowa, and his son Alan, a junior at Northwest, were selected by a faculty committee on the basis of the father's community activities and his son's leadership on campus. The two were honored at half-time ceremonies of the Bearcats and Rolla Miners football game and were presented plaques and a key to the College by Dr. Charles Thate.

Though few in number, hippies had a great effect on middle-class youth, and, even though in 1969 the hippie movement was dead, the hippie style of life was not. The great popularity of ex-hippie rock groups was one sign of the cultural diffusion taking place; marijuana and hard drugs were others. The hippies survived in many locales. They liked isolated farms, and they also thrived on the fringes of colleges, certainly not in abundance but in evidence at Northwest. Drugs, as anywhere in America, were available here, too. Drug trips were described by users, attempting to prove their superior morality, as beautiful experiences. Those suffering from bad drug trips, however, were experiencing something quite short of beautiful experiences. Excruciatingly repetitive drug patterns are difficult to break, and Mr. Gus Rischer was the man to turn to when one was demonized by drug or alcohol problems. A fortunate turn for Northwest regarding America's drug culture came when Rischer was hired to teach psychology in 1968. He had been a teacher and administrator for several years in the California public school system, but, when the drug culture became prevalent in the California high schools, he knew that it was time to return to his native Missouri, preferably the rural sector. What he found early in the fall of 1968 was what he first saw as a California high school administrator in 1961. He detected marijuana, and unsuspecting people were not conscious of its presence. Subsequently, he began, with his departmental chairman Richard Quinn backing him, to address the problem as academic in his adolescent psychology classes.

Not only did he take on the one controversial subject—drug education—but he added another one—sex education—and he was the first instructor on campus to do so. Considering him approachable and understanding of the cultural diffusion, students sought him out for help, and they found him willing to offer succor to their well-being. Rischer also started an information center in the J. W. Jones Union and had it manned by students he had helped, and they, in turn, helped other students by talking and by distributing government pamphlets and brochures which were factual and truthful. Help in the center was voluntary, and the students were knowledgeable. Although Rischer had been hired to teach psychology, the administration was positive to what he was doing and recognized his genuine and sincere contributions to a group of students who needed and were willing to be helped. Rischer, a man who thought he was leaving young people's drug problems behind when he left California, made 150 speeches concerning drug abuse during his first year in Maryville. He talked to anyone who would listen—people in high schools, colleges, and civic organizations. His work did not stop there, for he was a liaison between the student who was "busted" for using drugs and the local police department. He later formalized a three-hour credit class in drug education that he continues to teach, and has, since 1974, offered an annual drug workshop. Rischer has gained respect from state officials as shown by his membership on the State and Regional Advisory Council on Alcohol and Drugs.

Opposition to the war in Vietnam continued, but it lacked focus. On October 15, 1969, however, giant peace rallies, called a Vietnam Moratorium, were organized. Millions of people responded in America's large cities and in hundreds of smaller places, making the first nationwide Moratorium the greatest organized expression of pacific sentiment in American history. In November, the country's second Vietnam Moratorium focused on the nation's capital, where a half million people in a "March Against Death" represented the largest demonstration of any sort ever held in Washington, D.C. The November Moratorium was observed at Northwest for two days, November 13 and 14. Involved were two groups: the Northwest Union Board, and an organization called Delta, sponsored by two new English instructors, Mr. John Samsel and Mr. Charles Aycock. On Thursday, Delta, which professed nonmilitancy and nonviolence, conducted a door-to-door Maryville canvas to determine the number of the silent majority as well as the verbal peace seekers. The purpose of Delta's canvas was to determine how many people accepted President Nixon's proposals for gradual withdrawal of troops from Vietnam as opposed to a quick expedition of troop withdrawals. On Friday, Delta sponsored a teach-in, involving students and selected faculty members, to explain the Moratorium's purpose. The Union Board, under the direction of Kansas City's Bill Musgrave and Rhonda Finney, observed a version of the Moratorium with a variety of activities that reflected many points of view. Running throughout Thursday was a thirty-minute film on Vietnam, described, by Musgrave, as an objective one in its portrayal of the war in Vietnam. Students in the afternoon discussed the war from their points of view, and fathers with draft-age sons highlighted discussions in the evening. On Thursday night Dr. Berndt Angman of the political science department and Samsel discussed their opposing views. Samsel, of course, supported the Moratorium, while Angman was in favor of America's involvement in Vietnam. Since Thursday really was Moratorium Day, Friday's activities were slight. Students were polled by the Union Board to see which of six alternatives they thought the United States might take in Vietnam.

Northwest students participating in the Moratorium felt involved and found the Moratorium to be a learning experience. Although Northwest's participation was a valid one, none of the activities taking place over the country on November 13 had much effect. President Nixon continued to offer pre-game and sometimes half-time advice to selected university and professional football coaches, and Vice President Agnew denounced anti-war supporters as "effete snobs," or "supercilious sophisticates," and sometimes he chose rather caco-phonous and bawdy descriptions.

Several academic departments were undergoing changes, being added, or receiving honors before the end of 1969. Foreign language was thriving with nine faculty members and 450 students enrolled in foreign language classes. Advocating and practicing a certain amount of individualized instruction, the department would soon have a new forty-eight station laboratory. Chairman Elaine Mauzey disclosed that the thirty-five station laboratory and its old equipment were strained with age and wear. With the new laboratory, students in the back row would no longer pick up the local radio station, as they did in the old one, rather than their recorded foreign language lesson. Mr. John Dougherty of the department did much of the planning for the new facility, and Mr. Luke Boone, director of the instructional materials bureau, and Mr. Richard Houston, Boone's assistant, helped with technical advice and with the implementation. Although Dr. David Cargo and Dr. Bob Mallory had been offering courses in earth science, they were now officially members of the department of earth science, the College's newest academic unit. The two set up major and minor requirements for students interested in the field, and both men would in the future write their own textbooks. A department of statistics and data processing was also created and developed under the direction of Dr. Ron Moss. Joining 328 other universities, colleges, and conservatories holding memberships in the National Association of Music, Northwest, along with thirteen other schools, was elected to membership in November. Dr. John Smay, music department chairman, felt that it was noteworthy to be included and important for Northwest because the Association played an important part in music education trends.

The ubiquitous dress designers were doing it again. They decreed that skirts must be lengthened, and, very obediently, female trendsetters fell in line. The most striking fashion development, and so popular with Northwest coeds in the 1960s, really had not been so much the miniskirt itself as the new freedom it represented. A variety of skirt lengths from knee to thigh prevailed, and the range of acceptable costumes extended from sculptured elegance at the one end to military surplus garments on the other. Young women in due time would adapt their hemlines from knee to calf to fit their individual needs, but the miniskirt would be missed, and the free spirit it symbolized.

The decade of the 1960s saw the physical condition of America's people improve. Real income increased substantially and so did educational levels. Universities and colleges grew as never before, but many students began treating what had previously been thought a privilege as an execration. Institutions of higher learning were damned as racist and authoritarian. Irritated adults turned against them because of their failure to put down student complaints. Civil rights and liberties increased and poverty diminished, but not too many people mourned the decade's ending. Conservatives thought of it as an age of riot and a license for unbounded freedom. It could not pass into history quickly enough for them. Radicals saw it as a moment when the system broke down, and it was partly because they had overreached themselves with their dissident activities that the decade ended so badly. The student movement was transient and disappointing. One moment curriculum reform was applauded, and in the next instance distinguished universities became battlegrounds while some students dropped out or "turned on." For the students who gave up study for agitation, the more anti-intellectual they became, the more perceptive they thought themselves to be. Throughout this time of turmoil, most Americans were quiescent. Even the young often exhibited contempt for any disturbing social upheaval. Late in 1969, fifty percent of noncollege youth considered themselves temperate in their views and twenty-one percent cautious; only ten percent of the nation's college students classified themselves as radical dissidents and three percent as revolutionaries. Almost all of Northwest's people were in the first two categories and hardly any in the last. As is often the way in American life, a shift in outlook or attention led to overreaction, and at home the decade was one of unusual unrest and considerable tension. Illogical lengths in Southeast Asia seemed to be the central source of contamination for what was ailing America. In the end those lengths convinced most people that limits exist to what any nation can do. And, as our youth were quick to tell us, some tasks cost too much; some demand too great a sacrifice. With the winding down of the Vietnam failure, the general protest lost some of its reason for existence; the majority could again assert its power and make its voice heard above the tumult.

4

Good Times and Bad Times, 1970-1977

Stand like a firm tower that never shakes its top
for blast of wind.

—Dante

Most kinds of pollution were increasing as the decade of the seventies began. Environmental reform was becoming a popular mania, but, between rising living standards and population growth, it seemed a lost cause. To save a threatened beach or wildlife sanctuary involved struggles with powerfully motivated interests which were more often lost than won. It did seem as if the American way of life was threatened, and more individuals paid lip service to ecology while maintaining their old habits. But there was a rallying point. Nearly everyone could agree on saving the environment, and students and faculty members from diverse academic departments at Northwest were banding together early in 1970 as a group called LIFE—Let's Improve Future Environments. Initiated by student concern and utilizing interested faculty members in advisory roles, they were taking part in the expanding war on pollution and destruction of natural resources. The group planned to attack specific pollution problems, such as wastes poured into area rivers, and to send out speakers to tell area people about the local dangers of pollution and to involve them in the battle. The group also played a part in the April 22 nationwide "Teach-In" concerning pollution by having selected Northwest faculty members devote part of their class time on that day to discussions of the problem. LIFE members were backing their words with action. On Saturday, March 21, 250 of the group swooped down on the campus and the Maryville area and picked up people's litter. Plattsburg's Lloyd Logan, chairman of the clean-up committee and spokesman for LIFE, stated that one of the most noticeable ways to improve the local environment was to pick up the accumulated trash. That same spring, LIFE coordinated a county wide pick-up day involving college students, civic clubs, Boy Scout troops, and interested citizens. This group, helped by geography's Byron Augustin, biology's Myles Grabau, and fifty members of the AKL fraternity, gathered twenty-three truckloads of debris.

Many later efforts showed that Northwest students were concerned with what was happening to their environment. One of those efforts was the 102 River Club.

One tradition was absent this spring semester. Religious Emphasis Week, with its array of outstanding speakers, would no longer be there to offer students a spiritual and inspirational uplift. A quality substitute, however, called the Dildine Lecture Series, brought fine speakers to the campus. Named in honor of the late Dr. Harry Dildine, professor of history at Northwest from 1928 until his retirement in 1962, the Lecture Series had as its first speaker, Dr. Marcus Beck, director of the Foundation for Spiritual Advancement in Palos Verdes, California.

Early in March the city of Maryville was selected as one of eleven All-American Cities in a national contest in which several hundred cities competed. Sponsored by the National Municipal League and *Look* magazine, the contest and Maryville's crown bear mention here because many college people like agriculture's Dr. John Beeks, journalism's Opal Eckert, sociology's Dr. James Lowe, administration's Everett W. Brown, art's Don Robertson, and industrial arts' Dr. LeRoy Crist worked with Maryville citizens Mrs. Lela Bell, Craig Stephenson, Ray Cushman, Wayne Swanson, and City Manager Dean Maiben to accomplish the winning goal. And, of course, the College played no small part in the city's success.

Northwest, since its inception, has always had a quality reputation for preparing its student teachers, and it always seemed to be looking for different and better ways to prepare those future teachers. The spring semester of 1970 was no exception as Northwest launched a new program that was aimed at providing better trained teachers. Dr. Frank Grispino, director of student teaching, introduced the Teacher Assistance Program, an experience designed to provide education students an opportunity to participate in live situations in either the elementary or secondary schools before they began their student teaching. The Teacher Assistance Program, also directed by Grispino, was appropriately named for that was what the students were expected to do— assist the full-time certified teacher in preparing bulletin boards, working with special students, tutoring individuals, recording attendance, and operating audio-visual equipment. Simplistic in design, it offered a dual purpose: it allowed the teacher more time to teach and to evaluate students, and it offered the assistant a realistic professional experience. Participating students gained satisfaction and a better insight, and two of the students in that first program, Mrs. Carole Funston and Mrs. Susan Goff, felt that it helped prepare them for student teaching. The two, incidentally, are successful secondary teachers of French and English: Funston at Maryville High School and Goff at Fort Osage High School.

Another group was born and added to the long organizational list on campus. This was the Samothrace Club for college women undergraduates interested in business. It was organized by the Maryville Business and Professional Women's Club and offered the college women a chance to associate with outstanding business and professional women.

A department known for its additions in the history of Northwest Missouri State was enjoying another one. When the spring semester started on February 2, another building was getting its first start—the newly completed Donald N. Valk Industrial Arts Education and Technology Building. Located east of Wells Library, the Valk Building, encompassing 51,000 square feet, was welcomed fondly by the older Industrial Arts Building for its needed space and areas for the teaching of the newer aspects and expanding technology in the industrial arts and technology field. The modernistic one-story brick structure was so constructed that, if the need arose, it could be expanded to a two-story building. Valk, who retired at the end of the spring semester and died six years later, was head of the department for thirty-eight years. He came in 1932 as a one-man teaching staff in industrial arts. During those years, the affable and gentle Valk engineered seven additions to the older building and saw enrollment in the department's courses grow from twenty to 1,110 students in 1970, under the auspices of eleven faculty members. Valk, an architect, designed 100 buildings, including the Mabel Cook Home Management House and the Wesley Foundation Center, and he helped design Wells Library and the additions to the old Industrial Arts Building. He was also the official supervisor of construction on the building carrying his name. Valk was honored on Sunday, March 15, when the newest academic building on campus was officially dedicated in recognition of his service. A 1939 graduate of Northwest and Valk's former student, Dr. Walter C. Brown, professor of industrial education at Arizona State at Tempe, paid tribute to Valk and the gleaming structure. Following the dedicatory ceremonies in the Administration Building where 750 people were in attendance, an open house was held in the new building. Over 1,000 people, including dignitaries from many colleges and many Northwest alumni who had studied under Valk, stood in line and braved the cold and late winter winds for an opportunity to tour the structure and to listen to instructors and student guides explain the various laboratories and equipment. The Valk Building began in a mantle of cleanliness, established its reputation, and has maintained that reputation of being the cleanest building on campus. Mr. Valk wanted it as such; his successor Dr. Peter Jackson, now associate dean of faculties, wanted and kept it so; and Jackson's successor, Dr. Herman Collins, is maintaining the cleanliness tradition. Of course, with men like Custodian Leo Growney, presently coordinator of academic buildings, watching the birth of the Valk Building and caring lovingly for the structure, there really was no worry.

Some changes in campus life had taken place by the spring of 1970. There, however, were still restrictions. All women students living in the dormitories were required to be in their domiciles by 11:30 p.m. Sunday through Thursday nights. On Fridays and Saturdays, they had somewhat of a reprieve since they could stay out until one in the morning. At this time 125 females lived off campus in approved housing with adult supervision, and they had to keep the same disciplinary regulations as the ones living in the dormitories. The men had no restricted hours, and all male students under twenty-one years of age, except freshmen, could live in outside quarters with adult supervision. Open housing was permissible to those twenty-one and over.

April and May were months that would be long remembered by Northwest students and staff. Union Board was not fooling when it announced on April Fools' Day that headline speakers would be on campus for five days and nights beginning on Monday, April 6. It was quite a week in the annals of Northwest history, and Union Board officials called it "People Week." It was an outstanding effort by Union Board to give students an opportunity to hear speakers like Ralph Nader, Father James Groppi, Peter Weaver, Karl Hess, and several others discuss the many problems in society. Designed to emphasize the need for expanded understanding and cooperation of people, "People Week" was the child of multiple parents: Marvin Silliman, director of the J. W. Jones Union and adviser to Union Board; Stan Wright, a senior student and president of Union Board; Bill Musgrave, chairman of "People Week" and president-elect of Union Board; and Vicki Snell, chairman of "Starvation Day," the capstone of "People Week."

Father Groppi, the Jesuit priest who was a headliner throughout the 60s and into the early 70s, failed to shock his packed audience with language aberrations or his claims that he did not know the name of the college or town. Realizing this, he then offered a lucid, extemporaneous talk on the poisons of segregation and his advocation of civil rights. Groppi, however, was a man who did more than simply talk about civil rights. He campaigned actively, sometimes much to his superiors' chagrin. He participated in the famous 1963 March on Washington, the Selma-Montgomery March of 1965, and the Poor People's Campaign of 1968, and he did not mind localizing his activity. Groppi led a protest against membership of public officials in the segregated Eagles' Club in his native Milwaukee, where he also led open housing demonstrations. Groppi obviously was one of the energies loosed by civil rights churning on.

Peter Weaver, a top business and consumer magazine writer, took direct aim at disreputable and unethical practices and instructed his audience on how to distinguish between fact and empty promises in product claims.

Karl Hess, Barry Goldwater's former speech writer, was in the late 60s and early 70s a staunch supporter of the Black Panther Party, one of many black nationalist groups. He told his audience, predictably so, that the real tide of interest in fighting for liberty in America had flowed away from the political parties and into the activism of the New Left.

Yes, they came to hear Ralph Nader. Because so many came, the crusading attorney was moved from the Union to the Auditorium. Nader was one of the age's most remarkable men, a man who wanted to make a career of defending the public interest. There was no one like him at the time. No one had ever thought of making a practice from representing the public. He created his own financial support. *Unsafe at Any Speed,* a 1965 book that charged the automobile industries with failing to insure safety in their products, made a lot of money, and he used it to further his work. In addition to automobile safety, Nader and his army of young lawyers, college students, and aroused citizens—"Nader's Raiders"—investigated working conditions in the mines, the difficulties of Indians, meatpacking practices, and pollution. Nader, in explaining the many wrongs he was trying to right in his gigantic undertakings, offered no hints of discouragement. He would continue, he promised, to investigate abuses and outrages. He lashed out at the automobile industry, the food industry, and manufacturing companies in general for their unsafe and unclean products, and most of his listeners were left with the feeling that if the country could be saved it would be by people like him, for his career reflected the substantial changes occurring in America. Nader's talk was the finale for "People Week" speakers.

The "Week" focused on speakers, but other choices were offered by Union Board. Films centering on religion, the New Left, the Black Arts, and the environment ran continuously every day and every evening. Wednesday, the pivotal day of the "Week," was selected as "Starvation Day." Many Northwest students opted to fast all day and to use the cost of the meals they missed to help combat drug addiction in youth in Missouri. As a result of the students' caring efforts, $1,564 was collected, and the check was presented to Paul Williams, Governor Hearnes' secretary. Hearnes, who was ill, assured President Foster, Wright, Musgrave, and Snell that the donation would be used effectively to help rehabilitate drug addicts. Northwest students were gaining a state-wide reputation for their ready willingness to aid worthy causes. "Starvation Day" was not the first time they raised money by forbearance. The previous October they sacrificed their meals on "Hunger Day," a project during Union Board's "Give a Damn Week," and donated $2,102 to help feed needy children in St. Louis. "People Week" was positive and effective, and, after such a stimulating week, Friday night was devoted to recreation time in Lamkin Gymnasium. Union Board sponsored its final event of "People Week," a dance played by the "Rising Suns," a hard-rock group.

The Ugly Man Contest was back again and offered a lull from the worries of academic life and crises in the nation and the world. This week-long contest was a noteworthy one for Alpha Phi Omega, sponsoring its eleventh annual event, because $7,000 was raised for scholarships. The figure made a shambles of all existing records, and geography's Byron Augustin, with his bright red devil's outfit and horns and staff, soundly beat many other contestants for the title—the Ugliest Man on Campus.

The new, very modern foreign language laboratory was eagerly awaiting the test of a spirited and young group descending on campus the middle of April. Its caretakers, the faculty of the department, were sponsoring the first annual Foreign Language Day at Northwest Missouri State College. Representing twenty Northwest Missouri high schools, 350 students attended. Of course, the major purpose of the Day was to acquaint area foreign language teachers and their students with the department and its facilities. Attending seniors also competed for three scholarships, one each in French, German, and Spanish. That event, spawned in 1970, continues.

Black enrollment was increasing and black students on campus were unified and, although they represented a small percentage of the total student body, they were making themselves heard. In November, 1969, the students held their first "Black Week." The activities of the "Week" served as a means to educate white people to the black people's culture. The black students prepared a soul dinner for the public. This well-attended function teased many people's palates, and chitterlings and greens were some of the many varieties of food served. Regarding the blacks' culture, courses were added to the department of history, to the department of humanities, and to the department of English. History offered The Negro in American History, which explored in depth the experience of the American blacks from the African background to their residency in American ghettos; humanities' contribution was Afro-American Culture, a course surveying selected contributions from the art, music, literature, philosophy, and history of Afro-Americans; the English offering was Black American Literature and focused on the twentieth-century black American expression in fiction and poetry. The classes were taught by whites because Northwest had no black instructors. These courses were popular; approximately forty students enrolled in each. Many white students were also enrolled, not merely for curiosity but as a means of learning about the black culture. The courses remained popular, for students found them practicable and genuinely academic, not a combination of propaganda and activism. Although The Negro in American History is no longer offered, Afro-American Culture and Black American Literature are still thriving and substantial courses. The Afro-American Culture is taught by a black and generates many students, and Black American Literature draws a moderate number. The three courses introduced in the spring of 1970 were not given out of fear or enthusiasm as so many black studies were in colleges and universities throughout the country. Neither President Foster nor Dr. Charles Thate was insensitive to the rights of black students, an issue, along with the antiwar movement, that was causing campus unrest and outbursts at various colleges and universities. They listened seriously to blacks who called for recognition of their basic human rights, and so did Mr. Bruce Wake, dean of men.

Still, at Northwest, as on almost all campuses, some uneasiness hung over the spring of 1970, as more and more news of Vietnam, violence, and drugs surfaced. This unrest reached a new height on May 2 when President Nixon expanded the Vietnam conflict by sending American forces into Cambodia. After years of official misrepresentation, the depth of the muddling morass of an undeclared war, considered by many as unjust and immoral, was not widely understood by Americans that spring when disaster hit Ohio's Kent State University. On May 4, two days after Nixon's orders to send troops into Cambodia, an antiwar protest at Kent State ended in tragedy as National Guardsmen fired into a band of demonstrators and killed four young people. Protests against the Kent State shootings were held on many campuses throughout the week. On May 6, several

Northwest student demonstrators erected a pole in front of Colden Hall and hung the American flag at half-mast, symbolizing their reaction to the Kent State deaths. Their deep sorrow and spontaneity, according to observers, were counteracted by their thoughtfully bringing a photographer to record their action. For the more genuinely sincere, a student-initiated memorial service in memory of the four dead students was held on Friday, May 8, in Northwest's Rickenbrode Stadium. Although the week was cluttered with media headlines concerning the student killings and the subsequent student protests, no violence threatened, and the service, directed by Robert Nagle, philosophy instructor, was an orderly and venerable one, showing student concern for the fallen four. President Foster, convinced that the greatest percentage of the students at Northwest were serious and dependable members of the college community, cooperated with plans for the May 8 memorial service. On Sunday, two days later, 100,000 people held a peaceful demonstration in Washington D.C. At that time 448 colleges and universities were on strike or closed down by antiwar furor. Yet most of the nation's 2,200 institutions of higher learning were untouched by any flagrant attacks, violent protests, or parading people using obscenity as a weapon in public. For their students, riots, smoke bombs, angry words, and ugly confrontations happened elsewhere. Fortunately, this was the way it was at Northwest.

It was a good time for Henry Iba, the craggy-voiced living legend who had just retired as head basketball coach at Oklahoma State University, to come home. Speaking at the All-Sports Banquet in the Ballroom of the J. W. Jones Union, Mr. Iba, who recorded 816 career basketball coaching victories, was back where his tremendous coaching career began in 1929, and he left the 400 in attendance with a message applicable both to the arena of sports and society in general. Mr. Iba, in a reference to some of the ills of society, stated that people needed self-discipline "more now than at any time in our lives," and he called for families to grow closer together as one ingredient in solving the problems of society. Iba was pleased to see some of his former Bearcat athletes at the Banquet, and Kirby Bovard, C. T. Baldwin, Iba's brother Howard, Bernard Cowden, R. C. New, C. F. Russell, and Ryland Milner, were pleased to be reunited with their former coach.

Later in May, students and faculty and staff were paying tribute and eulogizing Mr. Donald Valk for his thirty-eight years of service as head of the department of industrial arts and technology. Valk would be remembered, too, for having a building named after him before he retired. Valk left his position happy, knowing that the demands of the chairmanship of the ten-person department would be left with the capable and qualified Dr. Peter Jackson. Tribute was also paid to a departmental colleague of both Valk and Jackson. He was not leaving the College but retiring from a task that required much extra time. Special recognition was given to Mr. Howard Ringold by the *Tower* staff. The 1970 yearbook was dedicated to him for his many years of meritorious service as *Tower* adviser. His successor as *Tower* adviser was Mrs. Muriel Alcott, an English-journalism instructor. Others, too, were honored in May, and the 1970 spring Commencement was the time and place because Northwest was initiating a tradition that would annually honor outstanding alumni for their contributions to the academic and the nonacademic world. Since the following were the first in this eleven-year-old tradition, they bear mention. The honorees were Dr. Mildred Sandison Fenner (now Reid), a 1931 graduate, and Mr. George H. Adams, a 1931 graduate. Both people could have full-length biographies written about them. Fenner in 1970 was the editor of the world's largest circulation professional magazine—the *Journal of the National Education Association*—and participated in numerous White House conferences on education. She and her husband, H. Wolcott Fenner, vice president of Ringling Brothers, Barnum and Bailey Circus, also compiled and edited an anthology: *The Circus: Lure and Legend.* Adams was director of parks in Santa Barbara, California, but was known nationally for his service to youth. He won the prestigious Pop Warner National Award and was chosen as Santa Barbara's sportsman of the year. The two were present, gave short talks, and received their Distinguished Alumni Awards from President Foster.

It seemed that Northwest was active in giving and recognizing, but now it was time for Northwest to receive. At this same Commencement, a valuable collection of 19th and early 20th century paintings, 18th and 19th century furniture, and other objects of art from the same periods were given to Northwest. The gifts were known as the Percival DeLuce Memorial Collection and were presented to President Foster by Dr. Blanche Dow, the executrix of the estate of Miss Olive DeLuce, who died in February and was the daughter of the famed artist. In accepting the treasures, Northwest agreed to maintain and exhibit the Collection, and Mr. Robert Sunkel was appointed permanent curator. Foster also announced the establishment of the Percival DeLuce Memorial Fund for the creation of a suitable, permanent exhibition for the Collection. The Maryville branch of the American Association of University Women heeded his words and contributed a $500 gift to the Fund. Sunkel did his work well. The opening of the

Percival DeLuce Memorial Collection was on Sunday, October 31, 1971, in the Gallery of the Olive DeLuce Fine Arts Building.

On Saturday, June 13, over 200 people were walking around and into a building on campus. No, they were not demonstrating for a cause, but they were there to see and dedicate the Hickory Grove School. Now students and the public could see firsthand the physical features of the early public education system and also view a historical monument to the early era of one-room rural school education in Nodaway County.

Construction of the two new high-rise dormitories was delayed because of a workers' strike. Consequently, the buildings would not be ready for their original planned opening, the fall of 1970. To alleviate the pinch in women's student housing, some of Northwest's coeds were asked to live in College Park. Northwest housing officials were not desperate enough, however, to have the young ladies live in tents. They managed to press into service twenty-five mobile home units. Eight women students lived in each of the four-bedroom, two-bathroom units. Counselors were present, and a resident housemother was also there to oversee the entire complex. The young ladies were not unhappy with their living quarters. College Park was especially beautiful in the fall and spring, but their living arrangements there had to end after a year because Millikan Hall was inviting them over in the fall of 1971. Those twenty-five units, however, would not be moved nor would they remain empty. The units were converted into apartments for married students, a surrogate for Vets' Village, housing units that were removed for the Garrett-Strong Science Building.

The social fraternities at Northwest numbered six in 1970. The newest was Delta Chi, established November 28, 1968, and colonized in 1969. Now, like its five brother fraternities, it would have its own house. The Delta Chi group purchased a house formerly owned by Bohm Townsend, at 219 West Second Street, and forty of its members were moving in for the fall semester.

Summer Commencement saw the naming of the two new high-rise dormitories and the happy and proud reunion of a father and son. The two new buildings were still being constructed, slowed by a workers' strike, but Foster announced to the assemblage the long-awaited news that the women's dormitory would be named for the late Miss Chloe E. Millikan. Miss Millikan came to Northwest in 1928 as a member of the elementary education department where she taught courses in early childhood education. She started the kindergarten in 1929 and was supervisor of the entire elementary school from 1955 until her retirement in 1961. The men's dormitory was dedicated to

Mr. Herbert R. Dieterich, professor emeritus of education, who joined the Northwest staff in 1928 and retired in 1969, serving the College first as principal of Horace Mann High School, and later as associate professor of education and chairman of the department of secondary education. Students living in Dieterich Hall today sometimes have occasion to meet the man for whom their structure is named. Many cannot contain their zeal, never anticipating that they would have such a splendid opportunity. Of course, the chance meetings between the students and Dieterich delight him, too. Prior to Foster's announcement, Mr. and Mrs. Dieterich's son, Dr. H. R. Dieterich, Jr., delivered the commencement address to the 313 undergraduate and graduate degree recipients. Young Dieterich, a professor of history and American studies at the University of Wyoming, in a stirring talk, offered a message that was probably formed years before in the Dieterich household: "Man once having surrendered his reason has no remaining guard against the absurdities of life."

Millikan and Dieterich Halls were ready for occupancy and filled for the 1971 fall semester. An October Open House was held to enable the public to inspect the two new seven-story residence halls. Many of Miss Millikan's former colleagues, such as Professor Emeritus Neva Ross, who succeeded Miss Millikan as supervisor of the elementary school, Associate Professor Kathryn McKee, former student and later elementary colleague of Miss Millikan, and Miss Anna Gorsuch, assistant professor of education, were in attendance. Both Mr. and Mrs. Dieterich were honored in the Dieterich Building, where they were on hand to greet people. Their son John and his wife Mary, the daughter of Mr. and Mrs. William Garrett and whose father's name adorns the Garrett-Strong Science Building, were there to help his parents celebrate.

Many loans and scholarships were becoming available to the college student, making it possible for most to finance a college education. Financial aid in the past to students at Northwest existed, but only to the extent of a few scholarships, some short-term loans, and part-time work available on campus. In the fall of 1970, however, help given to Northwest students totaled nearly $2,000,000 in scholarships and grants, loans, and work aid, and in the ensuing years the amount would continue to multiply because of inflation and the continuing increased costs of education.

A radically changed academic calendar was adopted for the 1970-1971 school year. In the earliest fall semester start in Northwest's history, students registered on Saturday, August 29, and began classes on Monday, August 31. The new calendar also showed the fall term ending on December 22, followed by a lengthy break until January 9, when it was time for spring semester registration. Students were relishing the thought of going home for Christmas minus the worry of writing fall semester research papers and studying for post-vacation final examinations. All of that would be finished on December 22! Once the shock of simultaneously finishing their academic work and shopping for Christmas gifts wore off, students found the change a welcome and easily adjustable one. The faculty, slower to readily accept change, eventually found it easier to begin a new semester in January, rather than to complete an old one by grading long papers and administering final exams. The calendar also offered a two-week spring vacation, and the term concluded with commencement exercises on May 14, fifteen days earlier than the 1969 graduation date. The decision to revise the calendar was not a flippant one because officials, headed by Dr. Dwain Small, dean of faculties, studied the plan for some time and allowed the student body and faculty to vote on the change. Their answer was overwhelmingly positive, and the calendar today still follows that 1970 plan but with two exceptions—spring vacation is only one week and the spring semester ends early in May.

General registration no longer required two days; only one day was necessary, and Dr. Bob Bush, director of admissions was ecstatic because the fall registration seemed to be the smoothest and most painless one remembered. Having 4,000 of the 5,530 record number pre-registered was certainly a help, but to aid the others who needed to register Bush smoothed their ordeal by implementing special telephone and television equipment and computer tabulators.

Those returning students also discovered some new physical alterations on campus. Two immediately noticeable changes were the establishment of a one-way traffic pattern on campus and a recreation area south of Phillips Hall that included tennis, basketball, and handball courts. Biology's Myles Grabau and his landscaping and nursery department staff further beautified the campus by planting shrubs and trees, many of those maples and oaks to replace diseased elm trees. Students also saw a fountain at the east entrance of the Administration Building. It was new for them but old for Maryville's senior citizens. The fountain once watered animals and humans from its various levels when it was located in the distant past at Fourth and Market Streets in Maryville. It was later moved in 1925 to a new park center at Northwest's entrance, remaining there for many years. Mike Cole, a Maryville art major, and Mr. Bob Sunkel and Mr. Tom Sayre, both of the art department, restored the marble structure and recast the missing ornamental pieces. The fountain was originally created by the John Swenson Granite Company of Concord, New Hampshire, in 1911. Only ten of the fountains were made, and Northwest's possession is one of four still known to exist. Because of the shortened summer caused by the revised academic calendar, painters, headed by Maurice Randall, had to scurry as they painted and redecorated Colbert, Wilson, Richardson, Perrin, and Hudson Residence Halls. They completely redecorated the four quads: McCracken, Hawkins, Hake, and Cauffield Halls. In the Administration Building, home economics students found a new food laboratory that was completed for them over the summer. Something else was noticed that fall of 1970. Ground was finally broken for the Memorial Bell Tower, a project that had been in the active planning stage for five years.

Students found something new academically, too. An educational innovation—microteaching—was introduced to the fall education students who were preparing to do their student teaching. Dr. William Hinckley, coordinator of the microteaching program, introduced the new technique at Northwest. It was, however, first used by Hinckley in the summer of 1967 as part of the training program for elementary and secondary teachers in Project Communicate, and again in 1969 for a new education program called Student Teaching for Experienced Teachers. Since the method proved successful, Hinckley decided to incorporate it into a secondary education course where students could practice particular teaching skills and then view their strengths and weaknesses on video tape. Seeing themselves as other saw them was a unique way to develop and build a repertoire of teaching skills before the students even entered an actual classroom. It remains an effective program.

In the spring, there was much dissent over the country concerning Vietnam, Cambodia, and the Kent State shootings, but many students in agriculture's animal science program were localizing a protest to something they found lacking in their curriculum. They discovered that a major livestock family—horses—was being overlooked. They, of course, made their displeasure known to the right people, and Dr. John Beeks, chairman of the agricultural department, agreed. He, like the students, thought a course in horse science would be a valuable elective for agricultural majors and of interest to students in other areas of study. The head of Northwest's psychology department, Dr. Richard Quinn, was enlisted to teach the two-hour course. Why someone from psychology? Beeks did not have someone readily available and Quinn, a long-time horse enthusiast, probably knew more about those large-hoofed mammals than anyone else on campus. The twenty-six men and women enrolled in that first class were introduced to a multidimensional world of horses. Their classroom instruction covered everything from physiology to feeding and from palominos to parasites, or as the catalog describes the course, "a study of the anatomy, behavior, genetics, nutrition, physiology, and reproduction of the horse." The students were able to apply their classroom knowledge in a weekly lab at the 120-acre Faustiana Farms, located on the southwest edge of Maryville. Northwest leased Faustiana Farms in February so that the agricultural department could use the land, stables, barns, and show-ring. No livestock except the horses owned and leased by the College were kept there. Northwest in 1970 was one of thirteen colleges to include a separate horse course in its agricultural program. Quinn has since left Northwest but the horse science course has not. It is an integral part of the animal science program and is taught by Mr. Joe Garrett, now head of the division of applied science and agriculture.

Horses were not the only livestock gaining attention. Hogs and cows were receiving their share of the limelight also. On a portion of the R. T. Wright College Farm was the newly-created Northwest Missouri Swine Testing Station, a non-profit, self-supporting project where area farmers could learn successful swine production methods. Northwest's students especially liked the cows because most of those students consumed milk and dairy products. The 160-cow herd, supervised by Dr. Dennis Padgitt, dairy specialist, produced a yearly average of 13,500 pounds of milk per cow, much of which was consumed in the form of milk, ice cream, and cottage cheese in the college cafeteria. The cows, made up primarily of Holsteins, some Jerseys, and Guernseys, had plenty of space to roam, for the agricultural department in 1970 possessed 340 acres. Not all of it, however, was pasture land, for alfalfa, corn, and small grains were grown. A technical program involving the dairy cows and the complex business of production and processing of milk from the time it left the cows until it was placed on the table was called Dairy Processing. In this two-year and later one-year course of study, students studied under Richard Knudsen, dairy technician, in the new dairy production and processing plant. Northwest's agricultural department was the first in the country to offer this program in 1968, for it recognized that processing plants were in need of operators skilled in operation, maintenance, and repair of the machinery, and in dire need of those persons trained in sanitation and laboratory procedures necessary for food handling. The cafeteria was happy to have such a plant and so was the staff of Northwest. They could buy quality dairy products at the plant for reasonable prices.

In the fall of 1970, several of Northwest's alumni were recognized both on the local and the national scenes. One stayed, one left, one would return, and one remained briefly. Ryland Milner, the one who stayed, found the November 7 Homecoming an especially warm one. Milner, at that time a member of the Bearcat athletic staff for thirty-three years, saw the return that Homecoming Day of two of his former players: George Nathan of Mountain View, California, and Vic Farrell, San Luis Obispo, California. They were representing a great throng of M Club members in honoring the long-time athletic director, coach, and former four-sport star. At half time of the Northwest-Southeast Missouri State football game, the California duo presented Milner with a plaque in appreciation of his years of dedicated service. They did not travel the great distance from California, however, to stand in the middle of Rickenbrode Athletic Field to present an award to the man whose coaching duties during his tenure spanned almost every sport— football, basketball, baseball, tennis, track, cross-country, and golf. They were there for another reason, and that reason was unveiled at the Alumni Banquet later that evening. There they presented a $2,700 check for a Ryland Milner Scholarship. Nathan, an avid Bearcat and a loyal alumnus who returns every fall for Homecoming, secretly launched the scholarship fund drive and expressed his personal thanks to both Mr. and Mrs. Milner for their many acts of kindness to Northwest students and alumni. No time was wasted in establishing the Milner scholarship. Mike Kennedy, a sophomore student athlete from Iowa City, Iowa, was the first recipient. Thirty-two of Milner's former athletes were at that Banquet to pay homage to "Coach," an appellation that fits him as well as it does DePaul's Ray Meyer or UCLA's retired John Wooden. Northwest's 1971 Homecoming was another pleasant reunion for Milner, Nathan, other M Club alumni, and present members. The Lettermen's Club at that time celebrated its Golden Anniversary and was recognized and duly honored by Northwest. Dr. Joe Merrigan, known simply as "Joe" back in the early sixties, while he was leading Northwest's student body, was the one who left. He now was applying the latest scientific techniques and theories to the solution of practical problems as head of Silver Halide Chemistry Laboratory at Eastman Kodak Company. When Merrigan was a freshman at Northwest, B. D. Owens was a senior and president of the student body. Dr. Owens was the one who would be back, but on November 9, 1970, he was named the sixth president of the University of Tampa, making him the youngest president in that school's history. At the time of his appointment, Dr. Owens was vice president for research and financial affairs at Ohio's Bowling Green State University, the youngest person ever to be named to such a top level administrative post at that institution. One who did manage to linger a while as assistant dean was Harry Bowes. After climbing the administrative ladder from dean of students to administrative assistant to the president, and then as president at South Dakota State College (formerly General Beadle College), Dr. Bowes accepted the presidency of Southern Colorado State College at Pueblo. When he became president of the Dakota school in 1967, he had the distinction of being the youngest college president in the nation. Raymond Watson, a member of the first four-year graduating class of 1910 at Northwest, had his name forever imprinted in Nebraska history that fall. On October 18, a new elementary school at his home in Hastings, Nebraska, was named in his honor. Fifty-one years this man served public education, thirty-three of them at Hastings.

Although the middle of December was a hectic time, students returning for the spring semester seemed to have no regrets in not facing final examinations, and their instructors liked the idea of starting new classes instead of finishing old ones as they did in past years.

Other changes were noticeable, too, and those were reserved for Bearcat sport fans. January returnees discovered that eight-year head football coach Ivan Schottel had resigned in December, and that administrative officials had dipped into the high school ranks to hire Gladden Dye, Jr., the highly successful young coach at Oak Park in North Kansas City. Schottel left to accept the dual position of athletic director and head football coach at Butler County Community College at El Dorado, Kansas. Schottel's Bearcat team recorded twenty-seven wins, forty-five losses, and one tie; his 1964 and 1965 teams were his best, both with six wins and three losses. George Worley became the new Bearcat wrestling coach, falling heir to a richly winning tradition by succeeding Gary Collins, who had succeeded Jerry Landwer in 1967. The program, inherited by Worley, began in 1957 under Dr. H. D. Peterson, and his and Landwer's and Collins' wrestlers combined for a total of 118 wins, 28 losses, and 2 ties; Landwer's men accounted for only six of those losses. Collins could boast, however, of two NCAA College Division National Champions: Paul Stehman won the 137-pound title in 1969, and Stan Zeamer seized the 134-pound title the following year. In accepting the wrestling position, Worley publicly stated that his goals were to improve the previous year's record and to win the MIAA championship. He must have been a prophet! He did both and also won for himself the 1971 Conference Coach of the Year honors. After coaching for eight years and compiling an 82 win, 40 loss, and 1 tie record, Worley decided to return to coaching high school football and wrestling. Only four men have ever coached wrestling at Northwest. Gary Collins, who in the long interim obtained a doctorate and coached at Iowa's Graceland College, succeeded Worley. Football and wrestling were not alone in their coaching moves; basketball was not to be slighted. After eight years of coaching basketball at his alma mater and putting together a 76-108 won-loss column, Dick Buckridge decided on the administrative route by becoming director of admissions at Northwest. Taking over for Buckridge was his six-year assistant Bob Iglehart. Buckridge's decision, nonetheless, was a surprise. Bearcat basketball was definitely on the upswing since his last two teams won 31 and lost 18 and had back to back second-place finishes in the MIAA. His 1969-1970 team, with seventeen victories, won more games than any other Bearcat team in twenty-seven years, when the 1942-1943 Stalcup coached team recorded eighteen victories. A former Bearcat star, Buckridge remains one of the top six scorers in Northwest basketball history, and so does one of his former players Don Sears. Both men, incidentally, won the MIAA Sportsman of the Year Award during their playing days, proving that fine talent, teamwork, and fair play can be blended together. First-year tennis coach, Dr. John Byrd, not to be outdone by Worley's accomplishments, was also a success story. His team captured the MIAA championship, thus eliminating the eight-year winning grip held by Northeast Missouri State. Pleasing to Byrd and the team was seeing freshmen Ed Douglas and Phil White beat the previously undefeated number one doubles team from Northeast Missouri State in the finals. The two netmen, along with senior John Gardner, won the singles titles, and Douglas and White posted individual records of 19 wins and 4 losses over the season. Two doubles teams composed of John Gardner, Phil White, Larry Wank, and John VanCleave, and singles players Phil White and Fred Seger totaled seven points and placed eighth in the national tournament at Indiana's DePauw University.

What Rollie Stadlman thought was one of Mrs. Cathran Cushman's pipe dreams back in 1967 was now a reality. That dream come true was KXCV, the new educational FM radio station of Northwest Missouri State College. It officially began broadcasting on Saturday, January 14, 1971. What Stadlman also did not know at the time he visited Cushman was that President Foster had FM in mind when he hired her, and what was in Foster's mind began as a dream. When Foster heard quality FM programming from campus stations like the ones at Kansas State University, the University of Kansas, or Iowa State University, he dreamed about Northwest having one, too. Foster did not dream long; for, like many others, he deplored the cultural

FM void on the area airwaves because it was impossible to enjoy fine music, intermixed with news programs, unless one installed a high antenna tower. To fulfill that dream involved quite a battle, but Northwest was ready for the fight. Both Foster and Cushman agreed that they wanted to bring in an FM station because the area had none; therefore, an FM outlet providing educational and cultural programming would eliminate that paucity. Of course, the two had academics in mind. Actual broadcasting experience certainly would not hinder students studying in that area. Foster and Cushman were not alone in wanting the FM station. The faculty, administrative staff, community leaders, and local government officials recognized the need for such a quality program. Now, however, came the excruciatingly arduous, and sometimes grim task of convincing the Federal Communications Commission that Northwest should operate an FM station. Cushman proved to be a battler, and, with Foster landing solid punches and Technician John Perkins aiding with adept jabs, Northwest was granted a construction permit from FCC in the spring of 1970. Of course, federal help was needed. In 1968, Cushman applied for a grant from the Department of Health, Education, and Welfare, and HEW in June of 1970 granted Northwest $75,000 for constructing and equipping a 100,000 watt educational FM station. Those three years of hard work and discouraging setbacks were minimized by the actuality of the HEW grant and the FCC license. FCC did offer a restriction with its license approval, however. Northwest could continue to use the call letters KDLX for its campus-confined AM station, but not for the FM because those letters were already in use by a ship at sea. The call letters KXCV were accepted and so was the 90.5 frequency. KDLX continued to be an elementary training ground for the beginning students of broadcasting and was staffed by students under the guidance of the official staff. It was and is operated similarly to small commercial stations. Much work needed to be done in the intervening time before FM on campus finally became a reality. Equipment had to be ordered and installed, and the November appearance of the 500-foot tower and transmitter in a field on the R. T. Wright College Farm, north of the Administration Building, made that new station real and certain. The red tower lights blinking at night were proof that a dream could come true. Larry Lewellen, a student technician in 1970 and presently a full-time production technician, felt the dream and fully recognized the reality for he helped install the tower. KXCV, when it went on the airwaves that January, was ready to broadcast the best possible programs. Even though Rollie Stadlman had never appeared before on "real" radio, Cushman obviously used care in selecting him to sign on. He certainly had served his apprenticeship since that day when he decided to join the KDLX Radio Club. Now a graduate of the broadcasting program, he had been station manager for nine months, a job he began on April 1, 1970, exactly ten years after KDLX had its inception in Colbert Hall's "broom closet," April 1, 1960.

But there was no fooling in the rise from a ham radio club to a 100,000 watt FM radio station. Since that 1971 January day, not one broadcasting day has been missed! The voice of KXCV has been heard every day of the year. True to its objectives KXCV offered fine classical music, good jazz, country music, festivals and concerts from the music centers of the world. Interesting and informative talk programs were chosen for quality with news offered several times daily, emphasizing editorials, commentary, and reports from around the world. Preparing for a career in broadcasting, advanced radio students coordinated the various programs, and they and the professional personnel were heard by their listeners. Many people labored, to be sure, to make KXCV a fine station, and there were many who did this without remuneration. One of those unsung heroes was Dr. Donald Sandford, professor of music. For several years he worked with thousands of the station's classical records as he sat hunched over huge stacks of albums with pen in hand painstakingly and clearly marking the correct phonetic pronunciations on every classical record. Student broadcasters without a classical music background sorely needed his help, and Sandford graciously volunteered countless hours of his time at nights and on weekends to contribute to KXCV's constant striving for fine quality. Three months after Stadlman signed on, this 100,000 watt reality— reaching people in a 125-mile radius with 116 hours of educational, informational, and culturally-enriching programs each week—was cited by the Corporation for Public Broadcasting for its excellence in pro- gramming and operation. CPB also notified Cushman that KXCV would receive a $9,000 grant and more on a yearly basis for as long as the station maintained its standards of programming and operation. The grant enabled Cushman to hire a production manager as the fourth full-time staff member. CPB has never faltered in bestowing grant money on KXCV. In 1979, it presented a $67,000 check to Stadlman, who succeeded Cushman as director of broadcasting upon her retire- ment in 1977, enabling him to pay salaries of two of his seven full-time staff members and to buy needed equipment. Since 1970, over $300,000 in grants has been supplied to KXCV. Many students, both men and women, profited from that dream. In 1970, broadcasting had fifty majors and minors, and when the decade ended there were 150.

Countless listeners called and wrote to KXCV personnel to tell them of their appreciation of the programming and the stereo sounds of the new station. A few, however, were writing not to praise but to vilify. Some area residents were experiencing visual discomfitures because KXCV was causing interference with their television reception. Because of the adverse effect on their home viewing, they complained to Foster. Not wanting his come-alive dream to dip into the realms of a nightmare, Foster recognized the problem and helped the aggrieved parties by supplying them with FM rejection filters, especially designed for the local problem. They prevented unwanted radio frequency energy from entering television sets' receiving system circuits, and his action helped alleviate strained relationships.

Because several KXCV personnel, including Cathran Cushman, visited the University of Kansas FM station in the summer of 1970, Northwest was able to acquire in late January an electronic pipe organ, a much needed instrument since the College had been without one for a number of years. The University of Kansas was seeking a new home for theirs and mentioned it to the visitors. Later there was an official offer, and Mr. Ward Rounds, Mrs. Elizabeth Rounds, and Miss Ruth Miller, all of the department of music, visited the Lawrence campus and accepted the offer. It was a fine act of generosity by the University of Kansas for the organ was valued at $40,000, and Northwest's only cost was a $2,500 tab for transportation and installation expenses. The organ, composed of some 1,000 pipes, was dedicated on April 15. The occasion signaled the return of Gerhard Krapf, former Northwest music instructor and then head of the organ department in the school of music at the University of Iowa. Krapf, who presently chairs the organ department at the University of Alberta at Edmonton, Canada, gave a recital in the Charles Johnson Theater and emitted from the newly acquired organ sounds of almost unlimited variety and volume. Assisting him in giving the audience a pleasurable music afternoon was a member of Northwest's music department Peggy Ann Bush.

When Mr. Tom Carneal of the history department arrived on campus in 1968, he, along with three fellow historians, Dr. Bill Fleming and Mr. and Mrs. James DeMarce, noticed that there was no collection of the history of Northwest, the area, or even the state. Their collective thoughts were "We should do something about collecting material on Missouri—specifically Northwest Missouri—and having a depository here." The quartet formed a committee with objectives and goals and presented them to President Foster, who was amenable to their plans of preserving history. Late in 1970, Carneal's, Fleming's, and the two DeMarces' kernels of ideas, with Foster's and Librarian James Johnson's help, popped into fruition because a research center was established on campus to serve as a depository for manuscripts and other primary materials relevant to area history. Carneal became, and still is, the director, and Johnson helped him get settled in three rooms on the second floor of Wells Library. Although the collection would be housed in three rooms, the center was called the Missouriana Room, and by 1973 a tour of the Missouriana Room was a journey into many facets of Missouri's history, ranging from information on and pictures of the famous race-horse trainer, Ben Jones, a native of Parnell, Missouri, a town fifteen miles northeast of Maryville, to artifacts from Albert P. Morehouse, a former Missouri governor from Maryville. Included are Morehouse's bound and indexed letters from 1868 to 1910. A permanent display that entrances visitors is the stained glass window that graces the entrance to the Missouriana Room. Taken from the First Baptist Church in Maryville when it was razed in 1970, the beautiful decorative glass was bought by Mr. Garvin Williams, a member of Northwest's Board of Regents whose term expired in 1971, and given to the Missouriana Room where two 12 by 3-foot panels and one 4-foot-square panel were installed by Northwest's carpenters. Carneal is proud to have the complete set of the *Yearbook of Agriculture,* donated by the late R. T. Wright and the only complete one in the Midwest. One part of the Missouriana Room contains a collection of personal letters, correspondence, and photographs. A prized item in that collection is a Civil War diary from a Union soldier who was captured by the Confederates and held in the infamous Andersonville prison, made even more infamous in modern times by MacKinlay Kantor's novel. Many family papers, diaries, documents, personal and professional papers, records, newspapers, pieces of clothing, and military items, plus a variety of artifacts covering twenty-three Missouri counties are there to be seen in the Missouriana Room. The collection has not grown recently to any extent; only true history materials, like books, are being added. There is a strong desire by historians, traditionalists, and interested people to see the Missouriana Room expand and have a full-time archivist, for, as Carneal says, it is "our responsibility to future generations to save some of the best parts of our generation to pass on to them." Carneal has always had a student help him maintain a semblance of Northwest's and the area's heritage. The selected student, who is usually a history major and dedicated to learning and research, not only has the privilege of assisting Carneal but is also awarded the Mahala Saville Scholarship. One of his current helpers Maryville's Catherine Miller had no trouble meeting the qualifications, and she could easily serve as the prototype of all the Saville winners.

Early in February 1971, the second annual Black Week was celebrated on campus. Activities illustrating phases of black pride and identity occurred every night, beginning on February 7, and culminated on Valentine's Day with a "soul dinner."

New industry, like Union Carbide and Uniroyal, began to appear in Maryville during the 1970s, and the industrial arts and technology department at Northwest played an important role in helping those industries in their early and later development. When Union Carbide opened its doors for employment in February of 1971, its officials asked Northwest's industrial arts and technology department to establish a program to help train the employees in welding, electricity, and machine shop. Dr. Peter Jackson agreeably responded, and in April announced plans for a seven-week training program in the department's laboratories for newly hired Union Carbide maintenance employees. Dr. John Rhoades, Dr. Bruce Parmelee, Mr. Howard Ringold, and Mr. Kenneth Thompson, instructors in the department, worked out detailed courses of study and taught the classes. A year later Northwest's department of industrial arts and technology was giving the same service to Maryville's second newest plant—Uniroyal. This program, however, was extended to ten weeks and focused on machine shop, sheet metal, hydraulics, and electricity. John Rhoades taught the first three courses and Bruce Parmelee the last. These programs have continued throughout the years whenever a Maryville industry has needed help in training its employees, and the industries have reciprocated with scholarships for students in need.

Student and administrative changes occurred in March. With the students, it was housing. Northwest, in its maturity, was becoming flexible. Now among the male students only the freshmen were required to live in the campus residence halls. It was, to be sure, a major housing breakthrough, for all male students, except those freshmen, were eligible to live in housing of their own choosing. That long-sought student freedom was finally won, but, like so many victories, anticipation is sometimes greater than the end result. Many of the "freed" students stayed, and some of those who opted to leave finally gravitated back to the campus. Through the years Northwest's academic and administrative structure experienced some reorganization and would undergo major changes in the future. In March, however, three new vice president positions were created in the administration and those were really name changes. Named to those new positions were Dr. Charles Thate, formerly dean of administration, vice president for student affairs; Dr. Dwain Small, formerly dean of faculties, vice president for academic affairs; and Dr. Don Petry, formerly associate dean of administration, vice president for business affairs. Earlier, Foster, with the Board of Regents' approval, had consolidated the academic divisional structure of nine divisions into three divisions—education, arts and sciences, and vocations and professions with the title "School of" before each division. The existing problem in 1971 was that the deanship for each of the three schools had not been filled, and it would be a year before that chore was partially finished. The existing administration, however, carried on the duties of deans of the three divisions, and the above three men, plus Everett W. Brown, Foster's assistant, constituted a presidential council headed, of course, by President Foster.

March was a busy month of approving changes for Northwest's Board of Regents. One change came not in reorganizing academic or administrative structures but in acquiring land. Northwest's latest acquisition was 310 acres of farmland, nearly doubling in size the acreage of the existing campus. Situated one-and-one-half miles north of the R. T. Wright College Farm, the additional farmland, owned by the late Mr. and Mrs. M. O. Anderson, added to the College's potential for future growth and was a valuable possession for the agriculture department's instructional purposes. It certainly helped enhance the department's 1966 acquisition of ninety acres of land immediately west of the campus, previously owned by Margaret Roney, which is primarily pasture but hosts the astronomy laboratory, horse arena, and boar testing station. The north farm is known for its crops, but also has herds of beef cattle, sheep, and swine. It, in addition, holds a farm manager's house, a large machinery barn, and barns for each of the herds.

A less significant change but a change, nevertheless, was replacing the name Horace Mann Laboratory School with Horace Mann Learning Center. It was time for a name change because the word laboratory had really outlived its usefulness. With the new name no one could make comments about the school being a place equipped for scientific experimentation on children. The new title for the school better fit the fine learning processes that were taking place there. Old names seem to die hard, however. In 1979 well designed, new directional signs were strategically placed over the campus proper, and the elementary school's signs were labeled Horace Mann Lab School, obviously disconcerting Dr. Dean Savage, head of the education division and the one responsible for the name change in 1971 when he was director of the Learning Center.

Happiness abounded in the department of home economics in April. Its honor society, Kappa Omicron Phi, founded on campus in

1922 by Hettie Anthony, then the department chairman, presented a color television and two suites of bedroom furniture to the Mabel Cook Home Management House. The furniture was a welcome addition to the House's decor, but probably as welcome was President Foster's invitation to Kappa Omicron Phi's forty-eight campus chapters to hold their national convention and golden anniversary celebration on campus. Everyone agreed that it was rather appropriate for Northwest to bring the national members back to the organization's birthplace. In June of 1972, approximately 170 of the national honor society's members came to the spot where it all started and were thrilled to meet Mabel Cook, who as a student gave Miss Anthony the idea for founding Kappa Omicron Phi and served as the local chapter's first president in 1922-1923.

Another organization on campus was busy in April 1971. On April 17-18, Alpha Omicron Pi international social sorority installed Lambda Omega, with its twenty-five young ladies, as its newest collegiate chapter. With the installation of the sorority's ninety-fourth chapter, Northwest's social sororities now numbered five. The month of May welcomed another honorary organization to the campus. Sigma Alpha Iota, professional music fraternity, established a new chapter, Epsilon Phi, and nineteen college people were initiated as members.

Lewis Dyche's watermen and Earl Baker's cindermen were crowded with activities. Diver Vic Konecny, a Cedar Rapids junior, competed in the NCAA College Division Championship and placed 14th in the one-meter competition and 18th in three-meter diving. Placing 18th might not carry much media attention, but Konecny's competitors were awed by his performances. They knew that the young man did not have the advantage of practicing on a three-meter board because Northwest did not have one. The trackmen broke twelve school records during their season, and one was the thirty-seven-year-old Herschel Neil long jump record, broken by freshman Joe Bowser. Neil, who died in 1961, was inducted posthumously into the Missouri Hall of Fame six months after Bowser's jump.

The happy spring mood coming from the Mabel Cook Home Management House was tempered somewhat because the department's leader was retiring. The education department, especially the people in the Horace Mann Learning Center, felt a twinge of sadness, too, for Miss Neva Ross was also ending her teaching career at Northwest. Together, they served the College fifty-three years, and Miss Cook, too, was associated with the school since its birth. Her father, Mr. T. H. Cook, was Northwest's first history instructor and taught the subject here for thirty-nine years.

In the spring of 1971, people in the geology and the earth science departments were not very happy with their Museum, a first floor storeroom in the Garrett-Strong Science Building. They were pleased, however, with their skeleton of a sea-going reptile that is approximately 150 million years old. The archeological find came from western Kansas and is the proud dig of Myles Grabau, Bob Mallory, David Cargo, and several of their students. Another student was painstakingly putting it together for people to observe. Later this unusual reptile, a twenty-two foot Mosasaur, was moved to a larger room in the building and properly displayed in a glass and wood case. The Mosasaur, the only one of its kind in Missouri, also has the company of rocks and minerals that are labeled and lighted in their own display cases in the more spacious quarters. Many of the specimens are indigenous to Northwest Missouri. The Geology Museum presently serves as a source of educational material for elementary, high school, and university students, and some people enjoy it for their own personal entertainment.

In 1971, Americans at large could usually view the Vietnam issue philosophically and at a safe distance, but they could not so view issues much closer to home such as civil rights and urban welfare policies. In April 1971, the Supreme Court declared busing to be constitutional. Busing, a scheme designed to achieve racial balance in school systems by transporting students to facilities at some distances from their homes, was an issue that festered in the early 1970s. Neither the Maryville Public Schools nor the Horace Mann Learning Center, to be sure, had busing problems, but something else was rankling many of the students of Northwest, and the cause of their displeasure was the 1971 edition of the school's yearbook, the *Tower*. It was an artistic creation, edited by art major Lynn Ridenour, but it was the absence of pictures, most notably those of sororities and fraternities, not the visually pleasing yearbook, that inflamed the Greeks. Many members of Northwest's sororities and fraternities charged the *Tower* with being "anti Greek," and Mrs. Muriel Alcott, the *Tower* adviser, responded by saying that the 1971 album was "an attempt to present life on campus." She was also quoted as saying that "about one-fourth" of the *Tower* staff was composed of fraternity and sorority members. The staff, incidentally, did have seven student members and four of those were art majors. The Greeks obviously did not feel that the *Tower* fully represented campus life, and neither did many independent organizations whose pictures were overlooked. It was difficult for many of these students to comprehend why the book contained two full pictures centering on two relatively obscure comedians calling themselves Tim and Tom, two pages of two local

bars including a 6½" by 4" insert of a partially drunk glass of beer—
a very uncommon sight in most student haunts—and two pages focusing on pillars and cornices of the President's House. Displaying their
displeasure at seeing omissions of their student life, 200 of the students
marched to the President's Home and then to the fountain in front of
the Olive DeLuce Fine Arts Building. There many of them initiated
their *Towers* by throwing them into the water. The books may have
been cleansed, but the "symbolic" application of water did not restore
to the yearbooks what their predecessors and successors contained—
pictures of the Greeks and all the independent organizations. Several
students took a pickup truck containing yearbooks up and down
College Avenue and displayed their burning emotions further by nailing
the albums to light posts and igniting them. Usually protesters expect
some form of punishment, but no disciplinary action was taken against
any of the students, a position that was interpreted as a silent nod of
affirmation by the administration for the aggrieved students.

Many of Northwest's faculty are devoted to research and publication, but they do not exist in the "publish or perish" vacuum so
common in many institutions. Quality instruction is emphasized at
Northwest, and most faculty members teach twelve to fourteen credit
hours and are involved in committee work. Some instructors, like Dr.
David Cargo and Dr. Bob Mallory, write their own textbooks; some
write scholarly articles in national and regional journals; and a few,
like Dr. Leland May, do much free-lance writing. History's Dr.
Harmon Mothershead in the summer of 1971 received acclaim for
authoring a book called *The Swan Land and Cattle Co., LTD.*, a story
of that Scotland-born company's contribution to the development of
the American West. Mothershead's book, published by the University
of Oklahoma Press, received fine reviews, and when James Michener
visited the Colorado Swan Ranch in 1972 he read Mothershead's book.
Before writing *Centennial,* Michener read 124 books dealing with the
West, but it is evident in comparing Mothershead's book and
Michener's 1974 work that the Swan Land story served Michener as a
source book because he used subjects, characters, or issues found in
Mothershead's book.

The summer of 1971 was a rather uneventful one except for enrollment figures, which reached a new summer high of 2,089, corresponding to the 2,041 enrolled in the 1970 summer session. In 1971, however,
753 graduate students came for classes, an increase of 101 from 1970.
President Foster told the summer graduating seniors that hopefully
when they returned to their alma mater in the near future they would
be stepping onto the campus of a university.

The beginning of the fall semester initiated some changes, especially for 250 industrial arts and technology majors. The older of Northwest's two industrial arts buildings had a new look, and was ready, after undergoing a renovation and remodeling operation, for the fall influx of students. A gleaming one-hundred-foot white tower, twenty-five feet in diameter, greeted the fall returnees, and it was not hard to see since the pre-cast concrete structure rose loftily from the center of the campus. Yes, it was the Memorial Bell Tower, the completion of a dream started during Foster's initial year as president. Originally planned as a brick structure designed in the style of the Administration Building towers, the imposing Bell Tower had undergone certain modifications due to inflation. Sounds emanating from the Tower also greeted the returnees. From an electronic console located in the J. W. Jones Union Building, music was transmitted through speakers from the top of the Tower. The rising structure so impressed Mr. Alan Peterson, a 1970 graduate and the 1971-1972 director of the Academic Advisement Center on campus, that he asked his future bride Miss LaRay Carlson to marry him under the open-air arches of the Memorial Bell Tower. She agreed, and they were married September 7, 1973, in the first such ceremony ever conducted there, indelibly marking the site in their memories. The Art Gallery in the Olive DeLuce Fine Arts Building was beautifully redone and ready, due to extensive efforts of Curator Bob Sunkel, for its November 1 showing of the year's first exhibit—the Percival DeLuce Art Collection.

The 1971 fall enrollment reached a historical pinnacle with 5,632 students, surpassing 1970's previous peak of 5,530. Never again in the 1970s would Northwest's enrollment reach that height. Tinging the ebullience of admission officials over the record number and perhaps reflecting the economic hardships felt across the nation was the slight dip in graduate school matriculation to 549 compared to 1970's 591. One of the many departments doing quite well with increases in majors was the art department. In nine years the department's enrollment increased in majors from 48 to a total of 226, and art students could major in any one of four basic programs of study. The department of chemistry that same fall received full accreditation from the American Chemical Society, making Northwest one of only three institutions in the state with such accreditation offering undergraduate degrees in chemistry.

Northwest's black students were not preparing for a fall black week but they were engaged in other activities, like preparing a grievance list and presenting that list to administrative officials. The black delegation, headed by Greg McDade, a member of the Student

Senate from St. Louis, cited a lack of communication between the campus blacks and Northwest's administration. To air those complaints, an open meeting was held the night of November 3 in the Administration Building Auditorium with more than 900 students in attendance. McDade, spokesman for the more than 100 black students on campus, informed President Foster and Dr. Thate that several disturbing incidents were particularly upsetting to his group and they wanted to see them rectified. What the black students wanted was the reopening of Hawkins Hall as the blacks' cultural center, adding at least five black faculty members by 1972, placing a black on the football and basketball coaching staff by 1972, relaxing dormitory hours for women, and ending discrimination against blacks by certain instructors and administrators. Dr. Thate, then and as he would in the near future, served as an intermediary and tried to offer solutions for what the black students were asking. Initially, the grievances were voiced to the Student Senate by the Brothers and Sisters Together, the campus black organization. The issues received the Senate's support and were then brought to the open meeting. The Student Senate, representing the blacks as well as the rest of the student body, asked for a monetary allotment that was equal to the percentage of black students on campus. The Senate suggested that the money be taken from the Student Union Activity Fund and used for black activities. Thate agreed and advised that blacks were part of the Union activities, and he urged them to join a special Union committee to insure black representation. They did exactly that, and Thate proceeded to work immediately toward mutually agreeable solutions to the issues. He met with student leaders and then made decisions. The Black Culture Center in Hawkins Hall would continue to operate for the needs of both black students and white students, and there would be a redoubling of Northwest's efforts to hire qualified black teachers, coaches, and administrators. Many, incidentally, had been offered employment in the past and elected not to accept. Regarding discriminatory practices by teachers and administration, Thate informed the black students that any charges would be fielded by the newly formed Human Relations Committee, which would conduct investigations if needed. Women's housing was another matter because the Inter-Residence Hall Council had jurisdiction over the policies concerning women's hours, but Thate said the administration would be receptive to a recommendation from IRC to extend key privileges to all women living in the residence halls subject to the written approval of their parents. It was obvious that women's liberation on campus had some barriers to break. Many students, as well as faculty, find it difficult to believe that as late as November

1971 there were still "closing" hours for women students in campus housing.

When the black students confronted the administration with their issues, Northwest employed only one black, a member of the Student Advisement Center. It has, to be sure, not been easy to hire black instructors and administrators at Northwest. Some would come for interviews and decide they did not, for a variety of reasons, want to be here. Some felt that the town would not be receptive to them. The summer of 1973, however, brought Charles Lee, a highly successful black coach in the Kansas City area. Lee played an integral part in Coach Dye's successful 1973 football season. Lee then went from here to the University of Arizona, Purdue University, and finally the University of Texas as an assistant coach in those "big time" university programs.

The black students, once they received the affirmative nod from Thate, proceeded to make Hawkins Hall into a black cultural center called Harambee House, the Swahili word for "coming together." The Center featured a reception area, a guest lounge, an art gallery, offices, meeting rooms, a library, a study room, and a classroom where Black American Literature and Afro-American Culture were taught. Because black culture has been better assimilated into the mainstream of North-west and white students better understand black culture, Harambee House today no longer exists, but black students use an office in the J. W. Jones Union Building and one of the conference rooms there for their meetings. Administrative officers listened to those complaints that the black students were raising in November 1971, and, because they did and since Thate was such a staunch supporter of their beliefs, possible inflammatory confrontations were thwarted and a peaceful settlement ensued.

Many students in the late 60s and early 70s in colleges throughout the country reacted rather strongly against the military, treating rather shabbily armed-forces recruiters on campus or attacking verbally, if their campuses had them, the ROTC and its cadets. Northwest did not have ROTC then, but it had its Vets' Club, an organization with definite military ties but one that coexisted quite handsomely and harmoniously with the rest of the student body. In this era of growing concern over public responsibility and social consciousness, the Vets' Club, composed of members who served their country in a branch of the armed forces, involved itself rather heavily in serving both the community and College. In 1971, the Club also turned its attention to providing loan funds for veterans, to contributing assistance to needy families, to giving support and financial aid to the United Fund campaign, and to acting as an information center for veterans concerning G.I. matters. Founded in 1954, when many of the Vets were living in the Village, and sponsored by Dr. Leon Miller, dean of graduate studies, the Vets' Club was one of the most service-oriented clubs on campus, and it found time, in addition to academics, to be active socially, politically, and athletically. Their annual multipage homecoming brochure is almost legendary to the campus, for at every homecoming one can obtain the Vets' homecoming program, which lists the parade lineup, homecoming queen candidates, house decorations, and the times of special homecoming events. The organization could very easily call Miller "Mr. Vet." He still serves as the members' guiding force.

When the College's 5,136 students returned early in January for the spring semester, most of them had trouble finding the student personnel offices. Traditionally housed in the venerable Administration Building, Student Personnel Services, headed by Dean of Students Phil Hayes, who joined the administrative staff in the summer of 1970, desired a place outside the lanes of the Administration Building traffic. The Services were then moved between semesters to Cauffield Hall, one of the original four men's dormitory buildings. Of course, higher administrative officials would be easier to find. Drs. Dwain Small, Leon Miller, Robert Ontjes, and John Paul Mees now occupied the places left vacant by the Student Personnel Services' move, and their secretaries were kept busy informing students as to the whereabouts of personnel people like Hayes and Bruce Wake. Ontjes was Northwest's newly acquired director of institutional research, a short-lived office, and Mees arrived in the fall of 1971 as Small's assistant. Dr. Thate and Dr. Petry then moved into the area previously occupied by Small and Miller. Moving from the Administration Building to one of the original Quads was a dramatic move and, although it was traumatic at first for students, they liked seeing the offices that governed their personal lives off "the beaten track."

New organizations began on campus during the 1972 spring semester and older ones endured. Speech pathology, under Mr. Jerry LaVoi's direction, was fast becoming a very thriving academic discipline, and in February Eta Beta Chapter of Sigma Alpha Eta Fraternity, the honorary society for speech pathology and audiology majors, was installed on campus. The oldest organization at Northwest, the Art Club, founded in 1921, had thirty-six members and was showing no signs of the strain of longevity. An organization that did not number any students among its members but one that was important to the development and the future of Northwest was the Northwest

Missouri State Educational Foundation, Inc. It was incorporated April 1971, but in March 1972 it was beginning to make itself known when 10,000 brochures announcing the details of the workings of the Foundation were mailed to Northwest's alumni. Chartered in Missouri to promote the welfare, goals, and programs at Northwest, the Foundation was incorporated "to receive, hold and administer gifts for charitable and educational purposes." Since state schools do not have a tradition of alumni giving, it is difficult to convince alumni to give back to their school. Many think it is not necessary because of the state's financial support. And, too, Northwest graduates were not as affluent as those of institutions with a high percentage of alumni in medicine, banking, industry, business, and the law. The hard facts were simply that Northwest's alumni and friends were not in the habit of making significant financial contributions to the College. In this respect traditional attachments were lacking. Foster's idea, however, to form a private corporation was unique and basically sound. He and Everett W. Brown, Foster's assistant, called that first meeting which resulted in the incorporation of the Educational Foundation. He asked alumni to serve on the initial Foundation Board of Directors and each contributed $1,000. The Foundation was attempting to fill the gap in areas not covered by legislative appropriations, and funds received through the Foundation would help Northwest grow in excellence. What the Foundation was asking of the alumni in those first years was money for student scholarships, National Defense Student Loan matching funds, and library acquisitions. J. Norvel Sayler, Maryville industrialist, was the Foundation's first president, and he served on the Foundation's Board of Directors until 1979 when he was selected by Governor Joseph P. Teasdale to be on Northwest's Board of Regents. Don Carlile, who assumed the position of director of placement at Northwest in January, immediately assisted the newly formed organization and became secretary in 1976. One year later, because alumni and friends listened to the Foundation's appeals, scholarships were provided, and $8,000 was earmarked for library acquisitions. That same year the Foundation owned eighty acres of land in a planned recreation area with the intent of establishing some form of outdoor biological nature area and field laboratory, men's and women's physical education facilities, agricultural development, and recreational facilities for students and faculty. Following the Foundation's purchase of the land, Northwest entered into a lease-purchase agreement with the Foundation for use and eventual ownership of the land. The tract of land east of Maryville is in a location which will be fronted eventually, it is hoped, by a 1,000-acre reservoir to be created by the proposed Mozingo Watershed. The land is presently used for hay production and pasture by Northwest's agriculture department for its dairy herd. In 1975, at the Foundation's third annual meeting, Treasurer Harold Voggesser, a Maryville CPA, offered a report that reflected dramatic financial growth. In one year, the Foundation experienced a fund balance of $88,029.48. Besides money for scholarships, over $15,000 was provided Wells Library for acquisitions. This non-profit organization now numbered nineteen directors. Of course, a small splash, but a splash, nevertheless, helped the Foundation's report every year because Northwest's faculty and staff started a holiday tradition in 1972 by contributing, in lieu of exchanging Christmas cards, to the Foundation's general fund. Collections from two of those years enabled the new library director, Charles Koch, to purchase $2,600 more in library acquisitions. At their 1976 meeting Board Member Charles R. Bell, a Maryville attorney, reported that the Foundation would realize a bequest in excess of $90,000 from the estate of the late Beatrix Winn Ford, who died the previous December. Mrs. Ford chaired the department of English from 1913 to 1924 at Northwest, and her husband M. E. Ford was a long-time member of the Board of Regents. Scholarships and library additions in the Ford name were the results of this generous gift. When the Foundation was first established, some eyebrows were lifted, but these skeptical people did not see that Northwest was still breaking ground in the matter of private fund raising. Serving without a full-time director, the Foundation members generously contributed their time and money, and their pioneer work paid dividends for Northwest. Their principal task is to act as custodians of gift funds to Northwest, and they are obviously doing that job well. The Foundation's fund balance at the end of June 30, 1979, was $429,658.77, an increase of $66,780.75 from 1978.

Although women's basketball at Northwest has been played sporadically since 1908, the sport did not really approach prominence here until the 1971-1972 season. Intercollegiate women's basketball seemed to dribble in and out of Northwest's history, but the "modern era" for the women really started in 1966 with Dorothy Walker of the women's physical education department. She sponsored practices, organized transportation, and chaperoned the young women. Sandra Butler, the player-coach, guided the team for her four seasons as a student. There were no funds for varsity female teams until 1970. When the team traveled, it went because of generous instructors and students who drove cars and donated gas. On those rare occasions when a bus was chartered, team members, the sponsor, and the coach divided the cost and paid their dues before the driver would pull the bus away from Martindale Gymnasium. Walker would walk down the aisle of the bus with palms extended until she had enough to insure the transportation cost. After Butler graduated, Don Lock coached for two seasons and saw the primarily half-court game changed to full court five-player conditions. The women's basketball teams in Northwest's past were known in the 1920s as the "Kittycats," but the modern young women chose to be identified as the "Bearkittens," a fine companion name to their male counterparts. The Bearkitten program in 1971-1972, under Coach Sherri Reeves, now assistant athletic director, started fast and never stopped until the women won the MAIAW conference, the first time in Northwest history that its women ever belonged to a conference. Compared to today the team did not play many games and finished with a 9-2 record. Reeves, however, found more opponents and increased the number of games in subsequent years. When she passed on her coaching duties to Debbie Jones three years later, Reeves possessed a 61 won and 15 loss record. Jones' team won the MAIAW conference, as Reeves' first team did, and finished with 20 wins and 8 losses. In 1976, John Poulson, a highly successful Iowa prep and college women's coach, was hired and his teams in three years garnered 53 wins and 29 losses. Wayne Winstead, a twenty-year veteran of Missouri high school basketball coaching, took over, after Poulson's resignation, as Bearkitten coach in 1979 and ushered the team into the 1980s with 20 wins and 11 losses. Aiding him was graduate assistant Janet Cooksey, the Bearkittens' all-time career and single season scorer, until current Bearkitten, Patty Painter, a junior from Lawson, Missouri, broke Cooksey's career scoring record early in 1980. Northwest's 1971 decision to have its basketball women enter a conference and participate on an intercollegiate level was a judicious one. The women's basketball program now has a solid past, possesses a tradition, and is thriving.

With the beginning of the calendar year, people on campus began to anticipate the omission of the word College and the addition of the word University to Northwest's title. They were watching the piece of legislation—called House Bill No. 1136 and Senate Bill No. 427—slowly wind through the Missouri Senate and then the House of Representatives. After passing through those two bodies, the Bill, early in April, was awaiting the signature of Governor Warren E. Hearnes. While Northwest was listening for official word and anticipating its status change, other events and happenings, some from within and some from without the campus, were newsworthy. The North Central Association announced in March that Northwest had received accreditation for its graduate programs. NCA's announcement included

approval for a new Master of Science in Education and a Master of
Arts in Teaching Programs in Mathematics and a new Master of Science in Agriculture. The continued accreditation of the undergraduate
program was also included. Northwest now offered either a Master
of Arts degree or a Master of Science degree in twenty-two academic
disciplines; the College seemed ready for a name change.

Triggered by the black students' charges during the 1971 fall
semester, a change in regulations for residents of the women's residence
halls at Northwest was announced by Dean of Students Phil Hayes
late in March. All women residents on campus were eligible for pass
key privileges—the right to come and go as they pleased. Excitement
reigned for both female and male students, but women under twenty-
one years of age still had to have parental permission before they could
enjoy the open hours' privileges. A bonus was also included in the
relaxed freedom package for the women: open house hours for visitation in the women's quarters were extended to include 1 to 5 p.m. on
Sundays and 8 to 12 p.m. on Fridays and Saturdays.

Northwest has been fortunate in having relatively few publicized
cases of dismissals of staff members. On December 23, 1971, Clifford
E. Bruce was dropped from the department of speech and theater, and
subsequent happenings stirred up controversy, both on and beyond the
campus. Bruce had come to the department as an instructor in 1966,
holding a Bachelor of Science degree from Indiana University and a
Master of Science degree from St. Francis College at Fort Wayne,
Indiana, and was promoted to an assistant professorship in 1970. When
Dr. Ralph Fulsom stepped down from the chairmanship of the speech
and theater department in 1969 to devote more time to his theater
duties, Bruce was appointed acting chairman until Dr. Bob Bohlken
was hired to head the department beginning with the fall semester of
1970. Since Bruce was employed by Northwest for five years and
possessed the necessary graduate hours above his master's to then attain
tenure, one of Bohlken's first duties was to poll the two members in
the department who had tenure. Bohlken received favorable votes, and
he endorsed their recommendations, along with a recommendation for
a sabbatical leave the following year so Bruce could pursue doctoral
studies. One day later, on September 22, 1970, Bohlken called a
departmental meeting to discuss teaching assignments for the spring
semester. At that meeting Bohlken had to make a decision concerning
a course called "Articulation Disorders." Bruce, a speech pathologist,
was teaching it, but Bohlken offered it to Mr. Jerry LaVoi, another
speech pathologist who came to the department as an instructor in
1969. Bohlken's judgment seemed sound enough since he was attempt-

ing to lighten Bruce's tentative teaching load of fifteen hours and increase LaVoi's teaching schedule from eight to eleven hours. Bruce, who was not present for the meeting, was not at all happy that "his" course was offered to someone else, and he made his unhappiness known both to Bohlken and to the dean of faculties, Dwain Small. Feeling that LaVoi was not qualified to teach the course, Bruce threatened before both men to resign as of January 1971, claiming that his letter of resignation was in his typewriter at home. That threat, it seems, did not cement any endearing relationships. A week later Small informed Bruce in writing to conform and that if he could not work in these the prescribed boundaries of his department that he should formalize his ultimatum for resignation. During a meeting with Bohlken and Small, Bruce declared that he had planned to resign but was now so enraged he would not. After consulting with one of his tenured members (the other was now on sabbatical), Bohlken withdrew the recommendation for tenure and requested from Small on November 12 the termination of Bruce's employment—citing his incompatibility to work within the department's framework, his unwillingness to accept administrative policies, and his threats of insubordination. Small concurred with Bohlken and recommended to President Foster that Bruce be terminated, and, following Northwest's employment practices, given a one-year notice. Foster agreed with the requests, and on January 7, 1971, officially notified Bruce of his termination, beginning at the end of the 1971 fall semester. His sabbatical was also rescinded.

On March 30, 1972, Northwest administrative officials and some of the faculty were jarred by an Associated Press release stating that Bruce filed suit in federal court against Northwest because of alleged violations of his civil rights. No official notice previous to what people read in the newspaper was received by Small or anyone connected with the suit, but Northwest was soon officially informed that Bruce sought damages for alleged denial of his procedural and due-process rights and that he had named the Board of Regents, Foster, Bohlken, Small, and the five members of the Faculty Hearing Committee, composed of elected members of the faculty, in the suit. Bruce's former peers were included because the members of the Faculty Hearing Committee decreed two months before Bruce took court action that his contract appeared to be legally terminated under the conditions outlined in the 1970-1971 *Administrative Handbook* and that there appeared to be no intent or design on the part of Northwest to abrogate its complete responsibilities. The Committee had further ruled that in giving Bruce a one-year notice the College had completely fulfilled its obligations to him.

Obviously Bruce did not agree, and that is why he filed charges. Four long years later, on June 11, 1976, Judge John W. Oliver of the United States District Court ruled, in a seventeen-page opinion, that Bruce was denied due process when he was released from his duties. The Judge also decided that Northwest was liable for financial loss suffered by the former member of the speech and theater department. The earlier granting of a sabbatical to Bruce seemed to be the thorn in Northwest's side because Judge Oliver felt that, even though Bruce was denied tenure, he was still under contract with Northwest because of the sabbatical—an agreement granted, Oliver thought, at a different time and under different circumstances. Attorneys for Bruce and Northwest met with Judge Oliver and decided what damages, if any, would be paid him. What Bruce finally received on December 9, 1976, for his "financial loss" was not $825,000 but the smaller sum of $18,000 covering pay for his sabbatical, upkeep for two houses, and personal anguish.

Besides trying to equalize his instructors' teaching schedules in that momentous departmental meeting on September 22, 1970, Bohlken must have recognized an essential attribute in LaVoi when he asked him to teach the "Articulation Disorders" course. LaVoi, until he left Northwest in the fall of 1979 to teach at St. Cloud State College in Minnesota, continued to teach the course, became a leader in the speech pathology field, and attracted many majors to the rapidly growing program.

On April 21, 1972, Governor Warren E. Hearnes did sign House Bill 1136 and Senate Bill 427, and a ten-letter word replaced a seven-letter word in Northwest's title. State Representative Jerold Drake from Grant City told the Board of Regents that it had the authority to do the name changing but would have to wait until the bill became a law in August. Other state colleges that would soon be calling themselves universities, along with Northwest, were Northeast Missouri State, Kirksville; Southeast Missouri State, Cape Girardeau; Central Missouri State, Warrensburg; and Southwest Missouri State, Springfield. Hearnes' signing resulted in the third name change for the Maryville school since it was founded in 1905 as a Normal school. In 1919 it was changed to Northwest Missouri State Teachers College, and it remained that until 1949 when Teachers was omitted. The legislation by the House and Senate obviously recognized Northwest's position as a multi-purpose institution. The pen used by Hearnes to sign the Bill signifying the name change became a historic memento for Northwest. Representative Drake, who co-authored the University Status Bill and was extremely instrumental in seeing that Northwest became a university, presented Foster, with Hearnes' permission, the pen, which Foster immediately gave to the Missouriana Room, much to Director Tom Carneal's glee, for display.

Two very tangible objects were different on campus in May, and both were welcomed by students, faculty, and staff. South of Colden Hall, one could count twenty flowering crab apple trees bursting into full flower for the first time and offering to passers-by their many vivid colors. Adding additional beauty to the campus, the trees were a memorial gift to Northwest in memory of the late Mrs. R. P. Foster, mother of President Foster, who died in December 1969. During the summer droughts of 1970 and 1971, Foster could be seen watering those four varieties of the crab apple. His efforts certainly helped the trees flower into a delicate spring beauty. It is not an unusual sight now to see them in bloom in early spring, but it was uncommon to see Colden's back yard in such colorful array in 1972. Another display, although a human one, abounded with colors one evening during the middle of May. Northwest was having one of its rare outside commencements. Because of adverse weather conditions, so many planned outside commencements had to be transferred inside Lamkin Gymnasium. That decision to switch sometimes took place only minutes before the opening ceremony, but this year Mrs. Elaine Mauzey, who chaired commencement exercises for twenty-five years until her retirement in 1976, could relax for the day dawned clear and windless, and the weather remained as such for several days. Again Northwest was honoring two of its own with Distinguished Alumni Awards. Dr. Merrill Ostrus Staton, a 1940 graduate received an award for his vast accomplishments in music, and the other award was presented to Dr. B. D. Owens, class of 1959, for his significant contributions in education. Dr. Owens also delivered the commencement address. Little did President Foster know when he bestowed Northwest's highest honor upon Owens that he was shaking the hand of the College's future president, nor did any of the 870 graduates have any idea that their speaker would five years later become Foster's successor and the eighth president of their alma mater.

The war in Vietnam continued, Nixon was gearing up for another election campaign, and Henry Kissinger, the secretary of state, emerged from four days of talk with the North Vietnamese announcing that "peace is at hand." In June, the nation heard the news of the bizarre break-in at the national headquarters of the Democratic party in a Watergate office building.

In preparation for the university status which would become effective in August, Northwest's hierarchy was finally beginning to appoint deans for its three schools—education, arts and sciences, and vocations and professions. In May, education was the first School to be awarded a deanship, and its faculty members felt fortunate that their new dean, Dr. Fred Esser, was a person who had come through the academic ranks. Esser guided the areas of health and physical education, guidance and counseling, psychology, library science, elementary and secondary education, and student teaching. Three months later Dr. Robert Barnes, an associate dean of arts and sciences and former history professor at Western Washington State College, Bellingham, was hired to head the School of Arts and Sciences. Under his province were sixteen different academic disciplines. A dean was never hired for the School of Vocations and Professions. Dr. John Paul Mees, assistant to the dean of faculties, however, temporarily fulfilled the role. The other two positions proved to be temporary, too, principally because of another university reorganizational alignment early in 1974.

Several students from the art department, along with their instructor Tom Sayre, were kept extremely busy over the summer and were sculpting a fine relationship between themselves and the users of a park in Maryville. For three hours a day that summer, Sayre's Advanced Design art class, with the approval of the Maryville Parks and Recreation Department, renovated the East Third Street Park. The group arranged stumps for climbing and designed and built a wooden fort, a large sand box, an obstacle course, culverts, a wooden climbing apparatus, a wooden swing, tire swings, teeter-totters, and other items, all playground equipment that allowed children to play imaginatively. One summer later, Sayre's Advanced Design class was again making people happy. This time the students designed and constructed equipment for a new playground area in University Park; the playground was used primarily by the children of married students, but one could also view the children's parents occasionally using the playground toys.

Early in August, the 1972 summer graduating class gave its alma mater an appropriate gift that would help usher Northwest into official university status. Mrs. Maxine Hinshaw, spokesman for the group, announced the gift at a breakfast honoring all degree recipients. The present was a new entrance marker at Northwest's main entrance to be erected following August 13, the legal date upon which the College would become Northwest Missouri State University.

When the 1972 fall students, faculty, and staff returned to the campus on August 28, they may not have sensed any difference, but they were definitely beginning a new era. The site was the same but the name, of course, was new. President Foster described the reality of university status as "a natural development in the evolution of this institution." But Northwest had been a multi-purpose institution for some time, and one hardly noticed any change in the daily academic routine.

Student attendance in 1971 had reached a peak of 5,632, and Northwest had enjoyed a record enrollment year for eleven successive years. But 1972 broke that record string with 5,341 students and, thus, initiated the beginning of a decline. University or not, the decrease of 291 students was there. The number seemed small enough, but the enrollment drop came as the result of a reduction of 481 non-Missouri students. What happened to those non-Missouri residents? Their tuition, because of a budgetary necessity, was raised from $260 to $405 a semester, thus creating a major reason for the absence of so many out-of-state students, although there was a record number of Missouri students enrolled. Many state legislators, it seemed, were ascribing to the popular theory that Missouri institutions of higher learning were created for Missourians, a theory which was fine when early students at the Maryville Normal School were required to sign a pledge declaring their intent to teach in the schools of Missouri once they completed their degree requirements. Because of the legislative dictum that state schools should concentrate their educational efforts on Missouri students, Northwest had no recourse but to raise non-resident fees and in the process made no effort to recruit in Iowa. Acting on the advice of the Missouri Commission on Higher Education and some members of the Missouri legislature to place out-of-state fees at a level more commensurate with the students' ability to pay, Northwest's Board of Regents wasted no time in attempting to rectify the aggravating and worrisome tuition problem. In an October meeting, they decided to lower the non-resident student fees for the 1973-1974 academic year to $300, a drop of $105. Enrollment, nonetheless, did decline during the next several years, reaching a low of 4,207 in 1978. More out-of-state students returned, to be sure, in the ensuing years, and lower enrollments could not be attributed to fees. There were other varied reasons, as most universities in the country were discovering, like changes in the birth rate (the post World War II baby boom was over), a percentage of young people not desiring to enter college, financial depressions in some families, and unforeseen calamities beyond the control of the University. The war in Vietnam was beginning to wind down and was finally over in 1973, thus creating another factor not usually discussed concerning enrollment trends; universities lost those enrollment bodies who were in school to escape the draft. They represented a small percentage but a percentage, nevertheless.

The fall, because of traditional homecoming festivities, always marked the return of many alumni. Two 1961 graduates, however, came for a different reason. Mr. and Mrs. David Paul Hargrave were back home for the Show-Me Invitational Debate Tournament, sponsored by Northwest's Pi Kappa Delta, national honorary forensics fraternity. No, they did not return to help judge the entries in the Tournament but were here to honor Mr. Hargrave's former debate coach and Mrs. Hargrave's former instructor. What Hargrave, a native of Maryville and a Kansas City lawyer, and Mrs. Hargrave, the former Sonya Skoglund of Barnard, brought with them was a traveling silver trophy named for Dr. George Hinshaw, associate professor of speech and theater and a faculty member since 1956. It was a tangible tribute from the two because of Hinshaw's efforts in creating fine competitive forensics squads during his tenure as coach from 1957 to 1967 and for the keen interest he had in his students. The Show-Me Tournament, started by Hinshaw in 1957, is held annually on campus, and Kansas State College of Pittsburg, which captured championships in both varsity and novice competition, was the first school to carry the gleaming Hinshaw trophy home. When the Hargraves made their presentation to Hinshaw, he was dazed but titillated by the honor.

Over 22,000 people watched Northwest's Homecoming Parade, reigned over by Cameron's Margaret Frances Rooney, on November 4, and 12,000 came to see the Bearcats come from behind in the last quarter to defeat Southeast Missouri State, 22-13, a win that gave them the impetus to defeat Southwest Missouri State the following week and gain a share of the MIAA conference title with Lincoln University. Many alumni members were honored on this special day, including seventeen former student body presidents and fifteen members of the 1952 Bearcat football team. The presidents, along with some of their former Senate members and faculty advisers, were feted at a special Homecoming breakfast. Colonel H. L. Ungles from the Wentworth Military Academy in Lexington was the 1929 student leader, and he and Stan Barton, the most recently graduated president, reminisced over the similarities and differences of students, student government, and student freedoms during the years the two reigned. Dr. Joe Merrigan, Mr. Theodore Young, Mr. C. V. Green, Mr. Stan Ogden, and Dr. B. D. Owens came from New York, New Jersey, Tennessee, California, and Florida respectively, while Dr. Sam Carpenter, chemistry chairman at Northwest, only walked several yards from his office in Garrett-Strong to enjoy the camaraderie. Climaxing the

Homecoming festivities was the Alumni Banquet at which the former gridiron Bearcats were honored. These fifteen men of 1952, along with their coach, Ryland Milner, were praised at the Banquet because they played on the last Northwest football team to either share or win an MIAA championship. Bringing these men back for special recognition was timely because one week later the 1972 team would be, like them, co-champions also. An extra highlight at that Alumni Banquet was awarding the first annual Don Black Memorial Trophy to the most outstanding football player of the day. The trophy, in memory of the late Don Black, a teammate of the players of 1952, was established by George Nathan, and Mrs. Black was present for the trophy presentation. Jim Albin was selected by a seven-member press box panel as the first winner for his explosive running exploits.

Because 1972 was such a big year for sports on campus, academics were halted on November 28 as classes were canceled for an all-school assembly to honor the University's sports heroes. Not only was Dye's team being honored but so was Earl Baker's undefeated champion cross-country team, the first time that Northwest's harriers ever won the MIAA. Not to be forgotten were the MIAA Bearcat tennis champions and eighth place finishers in the NCAA College Division Tournament. And, of course, the Bearkitten basketball team was the MAIAW champion.

Dye, incidentally, when he came to Northwest as its eleventh football coach, was committed along with staff members Jim Redd, Richard Flanagan, and Phil Young to rescue the program from oblivion. The coaches committed themselves to a three-year building program, but they produced a championship in the second season with a 5-1 conference record—estimable numbers compared to the mediocrity of recent past seasons. A Dye coached team would go on to win another championship in 1974—this one unshared—before he left the confines of Northwest for a high school athletic directorship after the 1975 season.

With the advent of Dr. Charles W. Koch to the University Library as its director, people were asked to call the Library the Learning Resources Center because of its expansion of services. The name of the building, however, remained as Wells Library. James Johnson, the librarian from 1948 to 1972, directed Wells Library, headed the academic library science program, and supervised the burdensome rental textbook room. Budgets for maintaining an institution of higher learning are always a crucial matter, but library appropriations invariably seemed small until 1971. For his first fifteen years, for example, Johnson was allotted only $10,000 a year for library collections, and it was not until his last year as director that the administration began to take serious notice of the money slight toward library materials. The small amount spent on the library represented Northwest's most serious defect, and the extra burden placed on the professional librarians, who were also asked to teach library science courses, was an unneeded strain. North Central Association for Accreditation told Northwest early in the 70s that one person should not be divided among so many duties, that librarians should not be asked to hold two professional positions simultaneously, and that finances needed to be funneled into library holdings.

A school may become a university, they were saying, but the library has to keep pace, too. Officials listened to NCA and two library consultants. They hired Koch, gave him more money appropriations, and asked Johnson to head the library science department, a discipline he helped begin on campus, one that so steamrolled that by the 1950s Northwest was training more school librarians than any other state college in Missouri. He and Mrs. Ruth Killingsworth now comprised the library science department, and Koch, who added specialized reference librarians and 5,500 new books to the library his first year, directed everything in the confines of Wells Library. Besides the library proper, he oversaw in his "learning resources center" the Instructional Materials Bureau, Instructional Television, and the "Missouriana Collection," which remained under the direction of Tom Carneal.

Late in the fall semester Johnson discovered that several people in St. Joseph were interested in taking library science courses. He and Mrs. Killingsworth proceeded to offer eighteen students basic courses at night during the spring semester in St. Joseph. The courses they taught were those which would prove most useful in the professional or graduate careers of the students.

Over the holidays, many of Northwest's future teachers were either eagerly or worriedly anticipating that new experience in their lives—student teaching—which would begin for them early in January. Nine of those future educators were also thinking of traveling because their student teaching experience was to occur on Hopi and Navajo Indian reservations in Arizona and New Mexico. Dr. Frank Grispino felt that a number of Northwest's teaching candidates would profit from the different type of setting. Because some students wanted to serve where they were most needed and since there was a desire in the Southwest Indian communities to have teachers with diverse backgrounds, Grispino, with the help of Mr. Gerald Wright, who formerly taught in that area, set up the pilot program for the student teachers. This was the second innovative student teaching plan in recent years. In the fall of 1971, Grispino had initiated a program to give several student teachers firsthand experience in teaching in the inner cities of metropolitan areas.

Northwest's male students of draft age could breathe a long sigh of relief. Finally, in January 1973, Vietnamese and American representatives signed an armistice in Paris. This struggle had cost the United States 46,370 dead, an estimated $140 billion in arms and supplies, and untold social and human chaos at home. The end of the American venture was over, but not the war.

Late in January 1973, Northwest's Board of Regents passed an Affirmative Action Statement and officially became an equal employment opportunity and non-discriminating institution. Early in February, in conjunction with the national Black History Week, February 4-13, Brothers and Sisters Together held their third annual Black Week and called it "Soul Excursion." Attempting again to offer students and area residents an insight into black culture, black student leaders, like Tommy Walton, Steve Harrison, and Jefferson Edwards, offered a program of films, fashions, African dancing, panel discussions, and a "rap session" on alternate views of the black students. Extended newspaper coverage was given the Week, and the highlight article, written by Mrs. Amy Davis, was the presentation of the alternate views of the black student's experience, featuring Mr. Bill Session and Mr. Jefferson Edwards. Of course, the ubiquitous soul dinner was the capstone of the Week.

The "Soul Excursion" was a fine success, similar in achievement to the Black Homecoming Pageant the previous October when Miss Harolyn Swanson of St. Louis was crowned Miss Black Northwest Missouri State University. Now, however, in the middle of February Jefferson Edwards, nicknamed "Rainbow," a senior business administration major from Kansas City, was in trouble with the University. On February 15, fifty black students waited quietly in Cauffield Hall for the Student-Faculty Discipline Committee's verdict on whether Edwards was guilty of the charges leveled upon him for "persistent irresponsible behavior." The Committee, after deliberating almost eight hours, decided there was not enough evidence against Edwards. It did not take long, however, for Edwards to again incur the wrath of officials. Because Edwards was suspended from his classes on February 19, the second time in a week for "persistent irresponsible behavior," about 100 students, including blacks and whites, staged a peaceful sit-in on Tuesday, February 20, protesting Edwards' suspension. They occupied the J. W. Jones Student Union from midnight until 4 a.m., and some observers looked upon the peaceful demonstration as a publicity stunt. Others, of course, like Security, did not. It was a sleepless night for Union Director Marvin Silliman since he, a very responsible person, felt it his duty to be there. Later that night Dr. Charles Thate held a meeting in Harambee House with seventy students, mostly black, and announced that Edwards could report to three of four classes from which he had previously been suspended. Edwards' reinstatement to three of his classes was a short-lived one. Two weeks and two days after his partial suspension, Northwest's Board of Regents held a full and complete hearing of Edwards' case—a meeting that lasted for ten hours. Their decision? The Board unanimously voted to expel Jefferson Edwards for "persistent irresponsible behavior." No longer did Edwards have the Cauffield Hall or the Union demonstrators supporting him; he faced this final expulsion decision alone. Edwards, however, would not let his dismissal die. He reapplied for admission in December and was denied reentry. Then, in January 1974, he filed a federal court suit against Northwest for violating the 5th and 14th constitutional amendments. In July 1975, Edwards' injunction requesting his readmittance to Northwest was denied by Judge John Oliver of the United States District Court on grounds that Edwards' expulsion was not unconstitutional. Oliver, in dismissing the suit, managed to chide Northwest officials for not following their own procedural disciplinary rules.

The two demonstrations in February must have been infectious. Although they were not demonstrating, a small group of students were vociferously circulating a petition on Wednesday, March 7. Petitions are usually harmless, but this one was noticed by officials because it concerned food quality in the school's cafeteria, and the students were complaining about rubbery jello, cold food, soft ice cream, and chili served every Saturday. The petitioners felt that their grievances were being ignored by Glen Vogt, head of food services, who rescued the food services as the new director following the food riots of 1964. Ironically, in 1971 he was being lauded for keeping students smiling thrice daily. These students were not smiling, however, and they were asking fellow students not to eat in the cafeteria the following day. The boycott was not successful because it had little effect on the number of meals served, but a public display did occur during the Thursday evening meal. Resembling children conducting a snowball fight, forty male students egregiously participated in a food throwing demonstration. No damage was done except for Vogt's feelings and the time and effort for employees to clean up the mess. Cafeteria workers, who bore the brunt of cleaning up, did not carry home with them unfavorable thoughts about bestial eaters. If anything, they were left with a warm feeling because the non-throwers stayed and helped remove the disarray their peers fomented.

Richard Nixon and especially Spiro Agnew always seemed to be making unsavory front-page news for many months in 1973, but locally some of Northwest's past and present people were the focus of attention for their worthy contributions. Miss Mattie Dykes was named, late in February, as the 1972 Missouri Press Woman of the Year. A fascinating sidelight to Miss Dykes' honor was that another Maryville resident, Mrs. Beatrix Ford, was the 1971 winner. Miss Dykes was a past student of Mrs. Ford and both women formerly taught at Northwest. Donald J. Johnson, who once thrilled Bearcat basketball fans with his quickness and his stutter steps while performing for Dick Buckridge's 1969-1971 quintets, was returning to campus not to shoot or dribble basketballs but to talk. Now, in 1973, a coordinator for minority student affairs at the University of Missouri, where he was studying for his doctorate, Johnson was here to address the Conference for Black University, College, and High School Students for the State of Missouri. Northwest was losing fifty years of notable service as two people, Dr. Frank Grube, professor of English and former head of the division of language and literature and later chairman of the English department, and Mrs. Ruth Nystrom, registrar since 1959, were retiring at the end of the spring semester. Their contributions were not unnoticed, however, for 300 people came to pay homage to the pair at a merry banquet in the J. W. Jones Union Building. Before the celebration was over, the pair were given standing ovations.

Thanks to physics' Dr. Paul Temple, Northwest received a grant of $7,740 under the Cottrell Research Grants Program of the Research Corporation of New York to support a research project being conducted in the spring of 1973 by Temple. The first instructor at Northwest ever to receive a grant from the prestigious Research Corporation, Temple dealt with the study of surfaces. The grant donors felt that Temple's research could lead to a better understanding of surfaces and eventually to the cleaner utilization of fuels in motor vehicles and a better use of our natural resources. Charles O'Dell, a member of the English department for five years, developed an interest in the local writer, Homer Croy, who achieved national fame with his many novels. O'Dell, the previous fall, shared his research by delivering a talk on Croy for the English department's Colloquium Series. In so doing, O'Dell became the first Colloquium speaker and began for the department a successful semester event. The fruits of O'Dell's research were published in the March 9, 1973, issue of the *Kansas City Times* and later in the spring as a seventy-five page booklet in the *Northwest*

Missouri State University Studies, edited by Dr. Irene Mueller and presently by Mrs. Mary Goad of the English department.

Northwest was happy to announce in the spring a definitely needed acquisition for the welfare of its students and staff. Effective July 1, Northwest would have Dr. Desmion Dizney, its first full-time campus physician. Although local surgeons had furnished medical treatment for students in the past, Dizney's addition to the staff provided a service sorely needed on campus.

For the fourth consecutive spring, students who wished to leave campus and find solace and comfort in nature could easily do so by driving or hiking ten miles southeast of Maryville. Traversing through downtown Arkoe, across the 102 River, and a short distance on a gravel road, nature lovers could lose themselves in a forty-acre woodland of virgin timber. That peaceful and scenic place, called Dobbins' Woodland, is officially named a Nature Conservancy as the result of a campaign initiated by biology's Dr. David Easterla, Northwest's conservation specialist. One of the very-few sections of land in Northwest Missouri preserved in its primitive state, the Woodland serves, too, as a valuable study area for Northwest's biology and botany classes.

Mr. Gladden Dye astounded Bearcat football fans by leading his team to a championship in only his second year, but Mr. Jim Wasem was able to achieve that in his first year as coach of the university baseball team. His team won twenty-one games, and it was the first time a Bearcat baseball squad had won more than seventeen games in a season. This team was also the first Northwest baseball team to participate in NCAA post-season play. Dr. John Byrd's tennis team, led by Jukka Narakka, David Imonitie, and Phil White, surprised no one by finishing first in the conference and fifth nationally.

In the spring of 1971, the traditional Walkout Day on campus was eliminated because too many students were leaving the structured entertainment on campus to find their own entertainment, like pubs in Kansas that legally sold beer to eighteen-year-olds. Animal lovers were not happy either with part of the ordered entertainment on campus such as corpulent male students pouncing on a small greased pig, and country folk were not ecstatic about the amount of litter dropped on their roads that Day. Offered as a substitute for Walkout Day was Joe Toker Daze, still organized entertainment but presenting more variety intended for a weekend of diverting fun for the students. It appeared to be working well on its third anniversary, the weekend of May 4, for students could hear four different concerts and participate in varied events including a skateboard contest, a soapbox derby, a frisbee contest, a bicycle race, and a car-packing contest. University officials, students, the rural area people, and animal lovers were much happier with the new event, but the same, of course, could not be said for the tavern owners!

Mrs. Opal Eckert, an enterprising and energetic woman who came to the campus in 1965 to teach journalism and advise the University's student newspaper, the *Northwest Missourian,* had another idea for journalism students, and that was a high school journalism day on campus. Known as J-Day, the first one, hosted by Mrs. Eckert and her students with the help of Dr. Carrol Fry, serving in his first year as chairman of the English department, proved to be such a success for aspiring young journalists that it became an annual event and now highlights the year for Northwest's journalists. Panel discussions, lectures, and workshops by successful print media people, along with competition for scholarships in a competitive examination covering newspaper and yearbook publication, were what took place that first year. Eckert designed the event to give area high school and Northwest journalism students a better look at the various opportunities in the field and an opportunity to share philosophies with working journalists and teachers. J-Day in very recent years, through Fry's ability to obtain grants, has attracted journalists from the national and the international scene.

The University's largest graduating class in history possessed an unusual educational coterie. Four members of one family graduated together: Mrs. Charlotte Poe, Maryville; her daughter and son-in-law, Mr. and Mrs. John R. Stalling, Oregon, Missouri; and another son, The Reverend George Thomas Poe. Mrs. Poe and the Stallings were bachelor degree recipients, while Mr. Poe, who shortly after commencement became a campus minister and instructor of religion at Southwest Missouri State University, received his master's. Members of this class were the first in Northwest's history to have the word UNIVERSITY instead of COLLEGE appear on their diplomas.

Former and present university personnel were extremely saddened to learn of the May death of Dr. Blanche Dow, chairman of the foreign language department from 1919 until 1949, when she left to assume the presidency of Nevada, Missouri's Cottey College, a post she held for sixteen years. Dr. Dow was a nationally known educator, served as the national president of the American Association of University Women, and had been a member of the White House Commission on International Cooperation. Five colleges and universities had recognized her meritorious educational accomplishments and awarded her with honorary degrees.

Since Northwest was born into the educational world on the grounds of a nursery, established by nurseryman Thomas W. Gaunt, supervisors of campus beautification throughout the years took their jobs rather seriously, and Nursery Supervisor W. D. Driskell and his assistant Mr. Richard Hallenberg were no different from their predecessors. They were, however, giving the campus a new outdoor look the summer of 1973 by having a twenty-five woman corps from the student body working part time on their campus crew. Driskell, obviously a believer in equal employment opportunity, had his female employees mowing grass and doing anything else that involved working with the campus grounds. Mr. Edgar Friend, director of custodial services, and Mr. Maurice Randall, paint supervisor, for several years had hired women students for either janitoring or painting, but the female contingent now, like the males, had indoor-outdoor options. Judy Dowden of rural Barnard, who always worked outside, thought it fun and a good way to get an honest sun tan, and she received for her outside tasks a warm feeling of pride for helping to maintain campus beautification. The students' work kept both Driskell and Hallenberg happy.

Summer school 1973 offered both undergraduate and graduate students enrollment options that were more flexible than those of previous summers. In addition to the usual proliferation of short courses, students could, as now, choose their summer courses from three regular sessions. Two five-week sessions and one ten-week session were available instead of the normal full-time credit load of nine hours for an eight-week session. The reason for the change was a response to the increasing demands from graduate students for a session shorter than the existing eight-week session. There was also a greater demand from students for a ten-week session which would enable students to earn more than nine hours of credit during a summer enrollment. The normal full-time credit load for the ten-week session, as it is in 1980, was established from ten to twelve hours; in either of the two five-week sessions, students could gain a maximum of six hours credit. Some faculty members complained, feeling that meeting a three-hour credit class for one-hour-and-a-half a day in roughly twenty-three days would not allow enough time to cover their courses adequately. Students, unless too many tests and papers were required, did not seem to bear any ill will toward the change. Dr. Merle Lesher of the education department, wondering what effect the shortening and the lengthening of the summer session had on faculty and students, asked his fall research class and Dr. Robert Ontjes to survey the attitudes of both. Almost seventy percent of the faculty and ninety percent of the students were in favor of the five-week sessions. Students liked the course variety, and, of course, the opportunity to complete more hours; the faculty noticed improved teaching and appreciated the student appeal and liked the leisure time of teaching in only one five-week session. Over sixty percent of the faculty, however, still worried about the brevity of five-week sessions. Overall, both parties seemed to think the new academic structure was a decided improvement, and it does look as if it is here to stay.

Shortly before the ten-week summer session ended, Teresa Hilt, a young lady who received her degree in elementary music education in the spring and was planning on a graduate degree in guidance and counseling at Northwest, was found murdered in her apartment near the University. She was one of six music majors who performed in Phi Mu Alpha Sinfonia's first stage production, *You're a Good Man, Charlie Brown.* Her killing remains unsolved. Linda Webb, like Teresa Hilt, graduated in the spring with a degree in elementary education and she also died in August. Her teaching career was embryonic. After her first day of teaching, she came back to campus, climbed to the seventh floor of Millikan Hall, and jumped.

Institutions of higher education throughout the nation were suffering declining enrollments in 1973. Inflation and a decline in both federal and state support were working together in making money tight on college and university campuses for both the student and the institution. As a result, several private colleges had to close their doors. Many schools, and Northwest was no different, made cutbacks in their faculty and staff. Being the president of a state university in the late 1960s and early 1970s meant adding new instructors and facilities to handle enrollments that rapidly increased annually, but in 1973 President Foster had to find his job, at times, rather onerous since a growing number of lawmakers seemed to be showing a trace of enmity toward higher education by taking a hard-nosed stand toward budget increases. State legislators were worried because the cost of public higher education in Missouri had exploded from $31,000,000 in 1962 to $167,000,000 in 1972, and their next concern was that enrollments were leveling off. University presidents, and Foster was no exception, valued the autonomy to control their own institutions, and they realized that they had to do something like decreasing personnel, not hiring new people, eliminating needless duplication of programs, and attracting with special programs the working people in order to make up for the loss in state aid.

Northwest did its share of the above and entered into an educational partnership with Ft. Leavenworth's Army Education Center. In the fall of 1973, Northwest and the Army Education Center began to offer programs at Ft. Leavenworth that led to three degrees granted by Northwest: Associate of Arts, Bachelor of Science, and Master of Business Administration. The areas of interest within each degree were in business and business management. The program was a unique one since it was developed especially for active duty military personnel and their dependents at Ft. Leavenworth and was directed by an advisory group of three Ft. Leavenworth officials and three Northwest staff members, along with the University's on-post program coordinator, Mr. William Dizney. In this degree completion program, members of Northwest's faculty commuted to Leavenworth and taught all the courses. At the 1974 spring Commencement, Major John Hesse, assigned to the Fort's Command and General Staff College, had the distinction of being the program's first graduate, obtaining the Master of Business Administration degree.

In February 1973, Judge John Sirica sentenced the seven Watergate burglars to prison. Disturbed because some of these men had obvious White House ties and sensing there was more to the story, Sirica suggested that Congress pursue the matter. As a result, a special Senate committee was established to investigate Watergate and other alleged 1972 campaign abuses. Beginning in May, Americans were able to watch the fifty-three days of televised hearings, and with each passing week the question of presidential involvement became more crucial. The nation was staggering from one constitutional confrontation to another. Northwest, however, was fortunate that summer to have United States Congressman Jerry Litton, representative from Missouri's Sixth District, address its August 10 graduating class. He was one commencement speaker graduates really heard, as he, after taking notice of the Watergate problems, gave them advice that seemed inimical to the times, and that advice was to get involved in politics because, as he said, "The way things have been going, there's plenty of room at the top." Litton, who died three summers later in a plane crash, assured his perspiration-drenched Lamkin Gymnasium audience that politics were not dirty or crooked, but that the challenges at this time in history were tremendous.

Returning fall students did not immediately recognize any changes, and they were eager to proceed with their academic and social endeavors. Math students were interested to see that their department was now called mathematical sciences. They discovered that the former mathematics and computer science departments had merged. Twenty-seven college students, mostly elementary education majors, became immediately involved in a Big Brother-Big Sister program, coordinated by Eugene Field's Mrs. Virgina Brown. What these twenty-seven young people were doing was providing needed outside activities and offering helpful guidance to young children from one-parent homes. The program had its inception in 1968 when Miss Kathryn McKee, of the elementary education department, and the Association for Childhood Education (ACE) saw a definite need for such a program. Two years later, Sigma Society, a service organization sponsored by the Soroptimists, began to help Miss McKee and ACE by getting many college students assigned to the program and to help entertain the children during the holidays.

Homecoming is always a nostalgic time for alumni, staff, and many students, and the 1973 participants could see visions of the past in the floats, house decorations, bands, jalopies, clowns, and the variety show, all in keeping with the theme—"Historical Happenings." Many of the homecoming scenes triggered memories and elicited conversation concerning the past. Dr. Frank Grube was reminiscing about the past at a special breakfast that initiated Homecoming Day. The breakfast, in his honor, was sponsored by Blue Key, and President Foster used the occasion to announce the institution of the Frank Grube Scholarship, to be awarded annually to an English major, or a varsity tennis player, or a member of Blue Key, three of Grube's major interests. The scholarship was initiated with a gift of $1,000 from Mr. and Mrs. Frank E. Babb, former students of Grube. Babb, a prominent Chicago area attorney and a member of the Northwest Missouri State University Educational Foundation, wanted, along with Mrs. Babb, to perpetuate their former mentor's name for the considerable influence he had on their lives and to reward worthy students. Cinda Steele, an English major from Maryville, was the first recipient of the Frank Grube Scholarship in 1974. The breakfast was a fine kickoff for the morning. Members of the 1973 TKE fraternity, however, probably still discuss their float "Chicago Fire." Their float was a matter of the historical becoming actual again: in the middle of the parade it burned. The Marching Bearcats and the Tower Choir performed at the half time of the game between homecoming foes Northwest and Northeast, and before they completed their selections a deluge of hail and then rain sent them and the crowd scurrying for cover. Those who stayed through the cold showers saw the game end with Northwest winning in the final seconds, 7-6, thus enabling the Bearcats to retain possession of the historical Hickory Stick, the victory symbol kept by the winner each year. Since hard rock was not a historical happening in 1973, "Grass Roots" provided for its concert audience in Lamkin Gymnasium a quiet selection of its old but famous hit songs.

Governor Christopher S. Bond and the Missouri General Assembly were telling Northwest that allocations for 1974-1975 would result in a $450,000 budget reduction. The threatened budget cut was based upon falling enrollment which Northwest, like other universities in the country, had experienced. Because of the severe legislative budget restrictions placed upon Northwest and its sister institutions of higher learning, President Foster announced rather sweepingly to his faculty in a meeting which launched the spring semester that Northwest would undergo yet another reorganizational alignment in order to bring university spending into the guidelines dictated by the anticipated budget slash. He also told his faculty members that they could expect a series of staff reductions amounting to twelve administrative positions, twenty-four faculty posts, and thirteen support staff positions in order that the institution could live within the anticipated budgetary requirements. The reorganization included the appointment of Vice President for Student Affairs Charles Thate to the office of provost, a title that befuddled most of the faculty in attendance until they discovered it really meant chief officer or vice president for academic affairs and dean of faculties. Dr. Don Petry would no longer be called vice president for business affairs but vice president for administration, and Dr. Dwain Small, who had served as vice president for academic affairs since 1969, was now to be known as special assistant to the president. And the deans of the schools? Their titles were abolished, but Dr. Fred Esser assumed the short-lived one of dean of undergraduate studies, and Dr. Barnes' position was eliminated as was Dr. Robert Ontjes' status of director of institutional research. The third deanship, that of the School of Vocations and Professions, was never officially filled; so there was nothing here to dissolve. There was, however, another new title awarded: Dr. John Paul Mees, Small's assistant since 1971, was now Thate's top aide as assistant provost. Gone, too, was the Academic Advisement Center. Foster's news of Dr. Small's demotion or promotion, however one considered it, stunned many at that initial spring meeting. Foster explained that Small's reassignment as instructional supervisor of the Industry Services Program placed him in the position to supervise Northwest's "new" nationwide training program for persons in life insurance and equity funds sales management, and that program was, said Foster, with Elba Systems Corporation of Denver, Colorado. Elba was a word that university staff and students had been hearing for several months but really knew very little about. What Foster was saying to the group was that Northwest was becoming part of an emerging trend in higher education to bring the college to the individual. Some people called it an Open University, but whatever it was called it was a trend produced, in part, as a response to rough financial conditions and declining enrollments among the traditional eighteen to twenty-two-year-old students. For many adult students, alternative programs meant an opportunity to study while working, and for many universities it meant their budgets could once more be balanced. Recognizing an eagerness among many adults to continue their education and seeing a way to develop its own innovative program, Northwest contracted with Elba Systems Corporation early in August 1973 to provide alternative training programs to personnel in the insurance and equity fund industries. It was a marriage that began in Kansas City that August when the two established a Career Education Center to offer career education programs in life insurance sales management and equity funds sales management, and it would end in a bitter divorce four years later. Since the relationship had such an impact—both good and bad—upon the University, the story of its harmonious wedding, the children that grew mercurially and unshackled, and finally the bitter dissolution of the marriage partners needs to be told.

Elba was founded in 1954 by Elbert Barrett, a native of Maryville and a 1936 alumnus of Northwest, and he derived the corporation's name from the first two letters of his first and last names. As president of the corporation, Barrett branched it into the audio-visual systems business to such an extent that Elba had an international reputation in the development of a life insurance and mutual funds sales system. That system included an audio-visual selling and marketing program as well as recruitment and management training programs. Elba, in the early seventies, operated six regional sales offices in metropolitan areas, and its total net income for the fiscal year ending in April 1970 was $2,747,284. Barrett, known in the world of insurance for producing films for life insurance agents and packaging for them a complete sales training course designed for home study, was recognized in 1971 by his alma mater with a Distinguished Alumni Award, the one given annually to a person in a nonacademic profession. In 1972, he became a director of Northwest's Educational Foundation, a post he relinquished in 1977. It was obvious that Barrett was interested in his former school and the feeling was mutual. Indeed, they could even help each other as their August 1973 meeting indicated.

Northwest that August began administering the program—the first of its kind in the nation—in the Kansas City area with approximately 100 students. Elba had been operating the complete sales training course, approved for veterans by the Veterans Administration, on its own for many years, but now the classroom instruction would be conducted by Elba employees, while several Northwest State business instructors would periodically monitor the classes. The course was basically a system of programmed instruction with class meetings once a month. Enrollees, who were mostly veterans, could complete sixty hours of instruction and receive an associate degree in technology. Veterans liked the idea of being affiliated with a university, however minimal that affiliation might be, and they also liked qualifying for larger benefits because of that affiliation. Elba and Northwest, of course, were not adverse to veterans' enrollment in the program. It seemed to be a bona fide, solid nonacademic arrangement and received the sanction of the Carnegie Commission on Higher Education, the NCA, the Veterans Administration, and the Missouri Commission on Higher Education. A presaging signal, however, that no one seemed to recognize, was that it had no guidelines. The program kindled in Kansas City, Missouri, but, unfortunately for Northwest, it spread like a prairie fire on the windy high plains and developed into a multimillion dollar insurance correspondence course. Before the program, called Industry Services Program, was one year old, 10,000 students in 190 instructional centers in thirty-eight states were enrolled and were paying $2,107 in tuition fees, split between Northwest and Elba with Northwest receiving the normal student fee of $330, while Elba received the remaining $1,777 for teachers' salaries and educational materials. Part of Northwest's $330 fee paid the salaries of instructors monitoring or supervising the classes and their travel expenses to the centers. What Northwest did with its share of the profits, estimated by Foster at $500,000 through June 1974, was funnel much of it to the Learning Resources Center for library acquisitions and toward the $200,000 operating deficit that existed in the dormitory system because of the declining enrollments.

Northwest officials never dreamed that the Elba program would expand to such immense numbers and to so many centers. Because of the mushrooming, Elba created many problems for the University. It was difficult to control because the recruiting and instruction were done by Elba, and also Barrett had difficulty understanding that academe, even if a program like Elba's was nonacademic, has to maintain control and insure standards of quality or quality suffers or completely diminishes. Because of its proliferation and its extreme difficulty to control, the program came under the scrutiny of the Missouri Coordinating Board for Higher Education and the North Central Association. What concerned the agencies was academic credibility, finances, and the amount of time Elba's instructors were spending with their students. What also was of concern was Northwest's possible misrepresentation in gaining the program's approval and the impact on the university budget from the expected revenues since Northwest was anticipating $2,400,000 during the 1973-1974 fiscal year. Elba itself was expecting $17,000,000.

On November 7, 1974, Northwest began terminating its educational marriage with Elba, an arrangement that had rapidly soured. Initial thoughts of doing so were conceived in July when Elba refused to modify the contract in order to align the program with new guidelines issued by NCA. Provost Charles Thate told his faculty at a special meeting that Elba had been notified of the discontinuance of the program, and the effective date of termination of the contract was to be July 1, 1975. Students who were enrolled in the program before November 7 were allowed to complete the 1974 course of study. The problems, to be sure, were insurmountable in administering the program, and they could not be overcome with the explosive enrollment. The immense amount of paperwork was staggering, and, because of that abounding enrollment, a lack of quality academic control existed. The program's death knell really was sounded earlier by the Veterans Administration, when it, leery of the program's scope and scale and weary of the controversy surrounding it, stepped in and made "new" rules that essentially banned veterans' benefits from the Elba program. Residency requirements composed the principal portion of the VA's criticism. The VA maintained that a degree, even a nonacademic associate of technology degree, could not be granted without the benefit of some tenure on campus by the students. The VA also required personal contact between the students and regular staff members from the Northwest business department. Those conditions seldom exist in open universities or correspondence courses, and it was no different with the Elba arrangement. The controversy engendered by the Elba program surfaced on October 23, when an article raising questions about Elba appeared in the *Columbia Missourian,* the student newspaper at the University of Missouri. After that initial startling information, a plethora of print presented itself, including articles in the *Wall Street Journal* and the *Chronicle of Higher Education.*

Lingering like a migraine-headache hangover, the phaseout was not easy for it involved much time and energy. Feeling a moral obligation to offer a second year of courses in the Elba program to those students who wanted it, Northwest included a second year and a new phaseout time of July 1, 1977. There were few second-year students, however, since the Veterans Administration had withdrawn its approval. President Foster himself was placed in the unenviable position of defending Northwest's association with Elba Systems Corporation before the Missouri House-Senate Committee on Fiscal Affairs in late November.

Explaining to the Committee and to Jack Cross, the state commissioner on higher education, that the Elba program was now dead because it was too successful and that opponents of vocational education had leaked distorted news stories about the course of study to hasten its demise, Foster told the group that it would not be fair for Northwest to receive a smaller than usual state appropriation for its 1975-1976 general operating budget because it had made an independent effort to generate funds. Foster made many subsequent trips to Jefferson City to plead for Northwest's budget cause, but Governor Christopher Bond, with advice from Jack Cross, forced the University to subtract $444,000 from its general revenue request, making the budget plight traceable to the revenues from the Elba insurance program which were considered earnings generated by the school. It was money, too, that Northwest now did not have because it had been used for the Library and to pay off residence hall indebtedness.

When Elba was being phased out, President Foster stated that 1,200 to 1,500 students would have been enough for a successful program, and he admitted the University's lack of foresight in not setting enrollment limitations. Feeling that the program was years ahead of its time, he predicted that others would travel the same road and use the knowledge gained from Northwest's mistakes. Some institutions of higher learning in late 1979 and early 1980 obviously had not learned, however, for their efforts to offer courses in distant locations set storms swirling around them. Far-flung extension courses, to be sure, can and do get out of control. Northwest's involvement with Elba was a two-edged sword. It helped bring in revenues and added recognition, but the sword was cutting the University to pieces. With the institution's farewell to Elba, the sword was back in Northwest's hands.

Because Elba's association with Northwest was dying and the death rattle was quite evident, Dr. Dwain Small's position of supervising and coordinating the Industry Services Program became rather tenuous. He, consequently, resigned on July 17, 1974. His post, to be sure, was not filled. The dean of undergraduate studies position was eliminated also when Dr. Fred Esser resigned on August 30. Although those two offices were obviated, the administrative hierarchy, newly formed at the beginning of the spring semester, remained basically the same except that in June Mr. William Churchill, director of data processing, became Petry's aide and assumed the title of assistant to the vice president for administration.

Other state colleges and universities, besides Northwest, were busy talking to state legislators late in 1973 and early in 1974. Central Missouri State University at Warrensburg irritated the House Appropriations Committee and Governor Bond by reporting what the legislators said were incorrect enrollment figures. Auditors discovered that Central counted part-time adult education course students in its total figures and, thus, incorrectly received an overappropriation of $1,700,000 to $2,300,000 for the 1973-1974 academic year. At the insistence of the Appropriations Committee, Central was forced to return $903,000, and the controversy resulted in Central's losing its Continuing Education Center at Independence, Missouri, to the control of the University of Missouri system. Dr. M. O. Looney, president of Missouri Western State College at St. Joseph was, like Foster, making many trips to Jefferson City. He was pleading for the state to fully fund Missouri Western. Supporters of the College had tried several times to obtain full state funding for the school but the legislation failed each year. The state's continuing legislative action, not to provide funds for the third and fourth years for Missouri Western, was a major irritant for its advocates, and Trustee President Fred Eder was voicing his displeasure publicly. He contrasted Missouri Western with Northwest, and his disparaging remarks about Northwest were a foreshadowing of the same kind of comments made about the University by several Missouri Western supporters and St. Joseph leading citizens before the Missouri Coordinating Board for Higher Education in a public hearing held in Savannah, Missouri, in the fall of 1978. His leading comments were, "All we are asking is what is rightfully ours as taxpayers in the state of Missouri. I'm getting sick and tired of Jefferson City telling us about Northwest Missouri State University. If it can't stand on its own feet, it ought to close up." Desperate words from a disappointed man, but the following year saw his wants fulfilled because the 78th Missouri General Assembly, without the Coordinating Board's approval, passed the full funding measure. President Looney was calling it "quite a year" as he cited, along with the full funding, his school's final accreditation by the NCA, and the accreditation of the teacher education program. Referring to Northwest Missouri State University as a teacher education institution, Looney expressed the hope that his College could be labeled as a comprehensive one. He obviously had forgotten that seventy-year-old Northwest was a university with multi-course offerings.

President Foster's trips to Jefferson City were not just to defend the Elba program or to request needed appropriations, but he was also asking the budgetary committees to consider establishing a school of optometry on Northwest's campus. What prompted his request was the fact that the University lost over 1,000 students over a three-year period, and there was existing dormitory space to house such a school.

His arguments were persuasive and thoughtful, and he listed many valid reasons for such a school in Northwest Missouri. Startling yet obvious facts were that Missouri had no optometric school, and Northwest could save the state $5,000,000 by using existing facilities. Metropolitan areas wanted the school, and arguments were heard and rebutted from both sides. There were, however, too many barriers, like big lobbies and power blocs, for Northwest to overcome. Although Missouri even now cannot claim an optometry school, Northwest's fate was decided because of its so-called remoteness, but Foster could take some comfort since the original idea began with him.

Springtime has been known for bringing college youth out in flocks in quest of something different. The early days of March ushered in something different—a new fad called streaking—and the "bare running at high speed" syndrome hit most of the nation's college and university campuses. Streak week was launched on campus the night of March 4 when two male students, clad only in hats and shoes, streaked from the Wesley Center to the Library, and it happened again later that night when a dozen men, wearing only ski masks and shoes, streaked in front of Millikan Hall. Thirty-five males streaked the next night and attracted 250 onlookers. Isolated streaking incidents appeared for several nights afterward until the fad finally ran its course. Female photographers always seemed to be in abundance, but female streakers were not observed until Thursday night when two coeds briefly streaked in the area of the high-rise dormitories. It was such a short appearance that the few onlookers themselves were skeptical of what they saw. One male streaker bragged that one of the reasons for the streaks was to make Northwest comparable to big schools, but Northwest could not cavort with the University of Missouri, for 600 of its students danced in a nude congo line earlier in the week. Unseasonable, spring-like weather certainly helped activate the bare madness, but the streaking incidents were peaceful and no arrests were made.

For years, different members of Northwest's faculty either wrote or revised a new, workable faculty constitution. Finally, the faculty, at the end of 1973, voted its approval, and in January the Board of Regents also voiced acceptance. The document, which was the result of long deliberation between faculty and administration, outlined levels of faculty involvement in the University's government, and it resulted in a greater faculty voice in Northwest's decision making. The Constitution abolished the smaller Faculty Council and created the Faculty Senate, designed to give each academic department better representation. Two months after the Board approved the Faculty Constitution, the Faculty Senate was ready for the 1974-1975 academic year. Senators and their alternates were elected by their faculty peers, and the Senators, in turn, elected their officers and approved Senate committees. That First Faculty Senate quickly showed its acumen by electing Mr. Robert Sunkel as its chairman, a move that was never regretted; for his leadership, organization, and assiduousness were necessary requisites in pulling the group together to face the many challenges. Helping Sunkel, too, were the Senate officers and the chairmen of the various committees, all composing the Senate's Executive Committee.

It was a fine year for the visual arts on campus, and theatergoers could choose from a variety of university productions: *Of Mice and Men, Hamlet, The Importance of Being Earnest, Spoon River Anthology,* and *The Night Thoreau Spent in Jail.* In order to expose students, faculty, and area residents to a number of cultural perspectives, the Performing Arts and Lecture Series Committee, headed by Dr. Bradley Ewart, brought to campus such productions and performers as *A Thurber Carnival,* the Minnesota Dance Theatre, both the St. Louis Symphony and the Kansas City Philharmonic, pianist Leonard Hambro, author J. P. Donleavy, and consumer advocate Betty Furness.

Because they were retiring from their university duties, six faculty and staff members would not be back to answer the ring of the fall school bell. Mr. Floyd B. Houghton, Mrs. Opal Eckert, Mrs. Pauline Arthur, Mr. John Ed Fuhrman, Mr. Robert Seipel, and Mr. Vance Geiger were the honorees at the University's annual retirement dinner. These affairs could be stiffly formal, but the six were honored in a light but dignified manner. With verse, song, and remarks by their peers, the retirees smilingly listened to the tributes paid them. Houghton, Eckert, Arthur, Fuhrman, Seipel, and Geiger surely, as they were listening to all the accolades, must have been silently reminiscing over their combined ninety-seven years of respective service to agriculture, English/ journalism, Horace Mann Learning Center and secondary education, field services and continuing education, the physical plant, and secondary education.

At Northwest it has always been assumed that the primary duty of the faculty is to teach. Teaching has been construed to mean not only delivering lectures, conducting discussions, and directing laboratories, but also taking a personal interest in students, and giving significant time to advising them on problems of a personal nature as well as those connected with their classwork. Teachers attempting to fulfill such ideals realistically cannot be expected to do the scholarly research and publication demanded in the larger universities. The idea of research and publication, however, has not been entirely absent at

Northwest Missouri State University. Many members of the faculty have been able to do some research, and a few have done considerable amounts even with full teaching loads. A good resource for faculty and even student publications is Northwest's own *Northwest Missouri State University Studies,* a source used by many faculty writers and some students through the years. It is not uncommon, however, for Northwest's faculty to publish nationally. In the spring of 1974, Miss Mary Jackson, associate professor of Spanish, published a brochure entitled *What and How for Foreign Language Students,* a unique and much-needed informational guide on career opportunities for the foreign language student. She later would author two Spanish readers, published by Allyn and Bacon, entitled *¡Qué Fácil!* and *¡Qué Divertido!,* meaning *How Easy!* and *How Entertaining!* Earth science was experiencing a publishing bonanza, and two professors, Dr. David Cargo and Dr. Bob Mallory, were offering huge grins because they were the reasons for the publishing coup. They were the authors of a 548 page, illustrated textbook called *Man and His Geologic Environment,* a book focusing on environmental geology. The text, published by Addison-Wesley, deals with man, geology, and environment and gives the student a better understanding of how geology fits into his life and how our environment has come to be what it is today. A departure from the classical geology taught for many years and the first new approach in geology textbooks in twenty years, Cargo's and Mallory's book was used by many colleges and universities. Since their first edition was eminently successful and because the subject outdates quickly, the two changed one-third of the text and published a second edition in 1977. Their first book interested many publishers, and McGraw-Hill asked them to do a second textbook on the basis of how well *Man and His Geologic Environment* had done. Because their own students and other geology students in the country found the first book readable, informative, entertaining, and serving a definite educational purpose, the two professors accepted McGraw-Hill's offer and published *Physical Geology* in 1979. Now the two, whose faculty offices adjoin each other, are engaged in friendly competition with one another. Mallory is writing a text on earth science which interests McGraw-Hill, while Cargo is composing one on the same subject for Prentice-Hall.

President Foster was quickly approaching the end of a decade at the top of the hierarchy of Northwest Missouri State University. Mr. Bob Henry, director of news and information, decided it would be fitting to write a tenth-anniversary feature centering on Foster's accomplishments as president. Foster agreed, Henry wrote the article, checked it carefully, and released it to the wire services. Feeling good over his long article that reviewed Foster's presidential career, Henry relaxed. Sunday, June 23, however, was anything but relaxing for him. Henry was awakened quite early by the piercing ring of his telephone, and he despairingly listened to Dean of Admissions Bob Bush's excited voice telling him about Foster's retirement. Bush's source was a news story released by the Associated Press and printed in Sunday's *St. Joseph News-Press*. Henry dropped the phone, rushed out to his drive, tore open the paper, and found the headline "Foster to Retire as Northwest State Prexy." Clad only in his pajamas and bathrobe and with his heart pounding rapidly, Henry read the first paragraph that stated Foster would retire the following Sunday, June 30. Quickly dressing, Henry, now hearing the thumps from his heart, drove to his office and fearfully pulled out his story to make certain he had written it correctly. Yes, he had, and he could not understand how the Associated Press copy editor could interpret anything resembling "retirement" from the article. All Henry was trying to do was write an anniversary piece, and it certainly ruined his Sunday. His day was spent correcting someone else's mistake. And Foster's day? He and Mrs. Foster were informed of his "retirement" as they were leaving early church services. They were exasperated, and relatives and friends were irritated because they had not been "told." He, consequently, spent his day, like Henry, on the phone denying his departure. The *News-Press* repaired some of the damage the next day by saying that the report of Foster's leaving was premature and that Foster was looking forward to serving as Northwest's President for several more years. By the end of the week both Henry and Foster were smiling again. The *Daily Forum* published Henry's entire article on Saturday, June 29, and readers could see that it indeed was a fitting piece, marking the end of ten years of work since Foster assumed the presidency on July 1, 1964.

A president did resign later in the summer and the press did not misinterpret this resignation. On August 5, three new transcripts showed that Richard Nixon had personally ordered a coverup of the facts of Watergate within six days of the break-in. With his conviction on impeachment charges almost a certainty, the President appeared on television the evening of August 8 to announce that he would resign, effective at noon the next day.

Northwest Missouri State University and the Soil Conservation Service decided early in September to join forces to help hasten the development of the Mozingo Watershed. Mr. Leon Tillett, district conservationist for the SCS, enlisted several members of Northwest's staff to provide an assessment of the environmental setting of the

Watershed. As then planned, the project would eventually have a large earthen dam that would create a lake covering 1,000 acres, thus providing more water for Maryville, a rural water district, flood control, soil stabilization, and recreational use of the lake. Dr. Bob Mallory headed a research team to determine what the environmental impact would be on the area covered by the impending lake and on the surrounding region. In the specific study required by the Environmental Protection Agency, Mallory's staff had an assortment of functions: Dr. Bill Scott, the impact on plant life; Dr. Ken Minter, the impact on animal life; Mr. Christopher Kemp, archeological investigations; and Mallory, the water quality collection and analysis. Aiding the research staff was a select group of students. The men, after several months of study, submitted to the SCS their interpretative findings and suggestions for improving the Watershed design and concept.

Late in September, Northwest was expressing deep appreciation to the Quarterback Club. From 1959 to 1973 the Club raised $65,872 to aid 731 student athletes, and in 1974 the year's total reached $6,895, eclipsing all previous records. The Club's scholarship aid was not limited to just the men, and members were happy to see Northwest's women involved in sports and doing well. In its first year of intercollegiate competition, Coach Debbie Jones' women's cross-country team won the MAIAW championship and, competing with the country's best, finished eighth in the national championships. Jones' women's track team also captured first in the conference earlier in the spring. Erstwhile cross-country runners in the Club delighted in John Wellerding's feats. Placing first in most of his meets, he raced to a ninth-place finish in the nationals, and for his performance he was named All-American, Northwest's first ever in cross-country. Of course, the football Bearcats also pleased the Quarterback Club by capturing Northwest's first solo football title since 1939, when Coach Ryland Milner's squad registered a 9-0 season.

The Bearcat Marching Band, whose members obtained no scholarship aid but received credit for physical activity, was 140 strong in the fall. Directed by Dr. Henry Howey and led by Drum Major Bob Still, they were rewarded for their extensive practices of marching and playing that fall by performing, along with the twelve Bearcat Steppers and the flag bearers, in St. Louis' Busch Memorial Stadium. There was a gathering of 50,000 people to watch the St. Louis Cardinals and the Philadelphia Eagles play a professional football game and to exult in the Band's program called "Prescription for an Energy Crisis."

Preparations were again being made for a visit from the seven-member NCA team on November 25-27. They were coming for a routine visit to evaluate the University's graduate programs for final accreditation. Focusing on the involved progress of the graduate programs, Dr. Leon Miller and his accreditation committee had their latest "Self-Study" ready, after two years' preparation, for the team. The "Study" also considered the Elba program. Northwest could expect the members to look closely at this new program. That they did, for they questioned many people, including members of the newly formed Faculty Senate, and read many reports. In April NCA notified Northwest that its graduate programs had final accreditation. Since Northwest was severing its ties with Elba, NCA eliminated the danger of the University's loss of any accreditation. NCA commented, too, on the ongoing developments in Learning Resources, the capabilities of the professional librarians, and the financial efforts extended by alumni, the Educational Foundation, and the University for library acquisitions.

University administrators and Mr. Bob Brought, Bob Seipel's successor as director of the physical plant, were dismayed early in November when several cracks adjacent to the vertical columns around the perimeter of Lamkin Gymnasium began to appear. The damage was blamed on the loud noise and high frequencies produced by the electronic sounds of rock groups. One month later, after studying the consulting engineer's report, the Board of Regents voted to bar further rock and roll performances in Lamkin Gymnasium because of the problems caused by the high, sustained decibel level of rock music. The students, of course, were not titillated over the Board's decision. But the damage was done. Rock bands generate about 170 decibels, and the safe level for music in Lamkin in 1974 was 90 decibels. Repair of the supporting columns was immediately made, and Foster and the Board took steps to remedy the situation by having a company install suspended noise suppressors from the ceiling. It was a move that placated the students, and Lamkin Gymnasium was once again open to rock concerts two years after the Board's prohibition.

One accomplished technical program in existence in the fall of 1974 seemed to cause no furor and went quietly about its business. This program's smallness, as contrasted to the Elba program's thousands, would go unnoticed. On November 26, Library Technician Certificates were granted to eight St. Joseph residents. The certificates signified for the students their successful completion of Northwest's thirty-hour Library Technician Program, under the auspices of Mr. James Johnson and Mrs. Ruth Killingsworth. Mr. Everett Brown and Johnson conducted this initial awarding of certificates.

Northwest in the past did have counselors, but they divided their time between teaching and counseling. In 1974, however, Northwest had two full-time counselors, Mr. David Sundberg and Mr. Rick Long. Their abode was the Counseling Center in Cauffield Hall, and in the summer of 1979 the Center was relocated in Hake Hall. Sundberg, who serves as director of the Counseling Center, and Long always seemed prepared to talk about any student problem in their counseling sessions with individual students, but Sundberg perceived in his first year a reluctance among students for self-help. He thus conducted workshops and volunteered to train the residence halls' staff, and word of mouth among students helped, so that 350 students were counseled during his second year—almost twice as many as the previous year. Now, thanks mainly to what Sundberg and Long established during their early years here, students find it more acceptable to seek counseling. Faculty members and community people also consult with Sundberg, and 1978-1979 was his peak year when the Center served over 1,500 people! The Counseling Center has certainly reached an apex.

For the first time in Northwest's history, the spring semester enrollment was larger than that of the preceding fall semester. The increase was only thirteen, but it did help reverse the trend toward lower enrollments.

On January 19, 1975, Thomas Hart Benton, Missouri's famous artist, died. Although there is no evidence that Benton ever visited Maryville, his death served as a reminder to many people of an association that he once had with the University. Graduating classes of Northwest traditionally leave a gift to their school that will be useful and yet aesthetic. The class of 1939 approached Benton seeking to purchase one of his paintings to leave Northwest. Benton explained in a letter to Miss Olive DeLuce, class adviser, that the prices for his paintings were set by his New York agents and were really prohibitive. Benton, however, was pleased with the interest the members of the senior class showed in his work and presented them with one of his prints. The print which Benton gave the class for the University is "Cradling Wheat," a lithograph signed by the artist. Bob Sunkel, art curator, explained that the print is quite typical of how Benton concentrated on the Midwest for much of his subject matter.

Tradition lovers were chagrined in 1974 when the annual Tower Dance was discontinued. Tower Dance partisans again were disgruntled in the winter of 1975 when they discovered that the previous year's decision was final. No more would the Tower Queen's portrait grace the yearbook, no more would the following year's *Tower* editor be publicly announced, and nevermore would the students attend a Tower Dance and move their bodies to the rhythm of the band.

The spring semester seemed to belong to the agriculture department. It suffered a loss but made several gains. Dr. William Treese, a member of the department for over ten years, resigned at the end of the fall semester to accept a similar position with the University of Purdue at Vincennes. KXCV would especially miss him, and Rollie Stadlman did not allow Treese to leave unnoticed. KXCV recognized Treese, a regular on the station's Agri News and Views program, for his voluntary services to the station. For three years, Treese averaged four programs a week—a total of 624 hours—offering informative and entertaining agricultural tips, especially in horticulture. One of agriculture's gains, and also the Library's, that semester was an $8,200 bequest on behalf of a Kansas City philanthropic trust foundation for library acquisitions in the area of undergraduate and graduate agriculture books and journals. The gift was made by Joe Bixby, president of the Kansas City Life Insurance Company, and he indicated that part of the credit for the present was due to the interest of Wilbur Pollard, a Kansas City attorney and national president of Northwest's Alumni Association, and Trans World Airlines pilot Thomas E. Schaeffer, a former student who was also honored as "Professor for a Day" by Northwest's department of business. During the 1973-1974 academic year, Donald Carlile, Northwest's director of placement, received 119 requests for teachers of vocational agriculture. Because that discipline was absent on campus, he could not fill those requests. From 1971-1974, seventy high schools a year across the United States were dropping vocational agriculture for lack of teachers. The need for vocational agriculture teachers was growing, and it was obvious that the teachers were necessary and would be in demand in the future. Agriculture's Dr. Fred Oomens was not unaware of the teacher dearth in his area, and he initiated steps in 1973 which resulted in Northwest's newest discipline in the spring of 1975—the certification of vocational agriculture teachers. Because of his efforts, Northwest became the first non-land grant institution in Missouri to provide a program for the preparation of agriculture teachers. This newest academic program swelled Northwest's wide-ranging curriculum to 300 major and minor combinations. A student also could select from eight undergraduate degrees and five distinct master's degrees. Thanks to the efforts of a leading beef producer, Northwest was given the opportunity to build its own Polled Hereford herd from offspring belonging to the Felton Hereford Ranch. Partners Austin G. Felton and Frank A. Felton physically transferred fifty head of cows and heifers to the University's R. T. Wright College Farm, a transfer that made the herd readily available to the department's undergraduate and graduate students as well as to agriculture's faculty for laboratory work and research. Chairman John Beeks was scintillated by the arrangement and noted that the agreement between Northwest and the private beef cattle enterprise, owned by father and son, was a giant step in the department's long-range plans to develop a top beef cattle herd. In December, because of agriculture's Joe Garrett's efforts and salesmanship, seven head of Angus were given to the University, adding to the Northwest herds of Jersey, Guernsey, Holstein, and Polled Hereford.

In the winter of 1973, three major construction projects on campus were begun: an addition to Martindale Gymnasium, the renovation of the Administration Building's fourth floor, and the air conditioning of Colden Hall. For years the denizens of Colden Hall had heard about the cooling of their building, but it never seemed to get done. For those who taught and learned during the prickly heat summer seasons, their time for teaching and studying in relative comfort would start with the coming 1975 summer session. The gracious grandmother of all the campus buildings, the Administration Building, was again opening her arms and making more room for the University's students and faculty. The generous matriarch, after months of painful renovation to her structure, now offered the departments of home economics and speech and theater more room for their offices on her fourth floor and five new kitchens for home economics on the third floor. Women student athletes, concerned somewhat over receiving their share of the sport's scene and the sport's dollar, were relieved when they returned from their spring break in 1975 and, after months of waiting, received a firsthand look at the changes in the newly opened Martindale. The like-new edifice, the second oldest classroom building on campus, was proof that Northwest was not going to allow its women to have inadequate facilities. Martindale was, to be sure, remodeled but much of it was also new, and it displayed an airiness and a freer atmosphere. Northwest's women did have a structure that offered them the most modern and comfortable classrooms, laboratories, dressing rooms, and gymnasium. With the exception of the Donald Valk Industrial Arts and Technology Building, it is probably the cleanest building on campus. Bonnie Magill, head of women's physical education, expressed joy over the new facilities, and Sherri Reeves, Bearkitten basketball coach, aptly summarized the change, "We ought to put up a sign, 'Happiness is not being a senior.' "

Campus work crews were waiting late in March for the ground to thaw so that they could remove a wall between two North Complex ground floor rooms in order to install water and gas lines, drains, and laundry equipment. This spring "young men's fancies" turned to thoughts of clean clothing, and the residents of North Complex were upset because there were not enough machines to keep those clothes clean and dry. So they hung their dirty clothes from windows and displayed signs that vented their displeasure. The very visible objects caught the eye of the vice president for administration. Petry did help purify the soiled situation, but only after Mother Nature cooperated.

The Missouri Division of the American Association of University Women, an association of women college graduates, chose Northwest Missouri State University as the site for its biennial three-day convention, April 11-13. It was the appropriate place because the convention was dedicated to the memory of the late Dr. Blanche Dow, a past national AAUW president and former head of Northwest's department of foreign languages. Since contributions to the organization's prestigious Educational Foundation had been named in their honor, Miss Mary Keith and Mrs. Lela Bell, two local women, were also honored.

The University was deriving much satisfaction from the regional and national attention that Coach Jim Wasem's baseball men were bringing the school. It was the greatest year in Bearcat baseball history for the team won the MIAA, the Midwest Regional NCAA Division II Tournament, and placed fifth nationally. Their thirty-three wins were the most ever by a Northwest team, and Coach Wasem was selected not only the MIAA Coach of the Year, but, in addition, the NCAA District 5 Coach of the Year. Wrestling's George Worley was voted by his conference peers as MIAA Wrestling Coach of the Year based on his team's unexpected strong second place showing. Coach John Byrd's tennis team again did the expected and ran away with the MIAA tournament and placed fourth in the nationals for a fifth straight finish in the top ten teams of NCAA Division II. Coach Debbie Jones' Bearkitten softball team won its conference, and, like men's baseball and tennis, also went to the national tournament and placed sixth in the "College Women World Series." The Bearkittens' 22-7 season was a turnaround from a dreary 2-5 finish in 1974.

On the night of Study Day, May 7, the University's free day before final examinations, Northwest's largest number of retirees were honored at a traditional recognition dinner for their collective 362 years of service to their University. A partial reason for fourteen members, an unusual number, leaving their teaching duties was that the Board of Regents, several months before, decided that retirement was mandatory at age sixty-five instead of the traditional and accepted seventy. The fourteen—Mr. Ryland Milner, Mr. Kenneth Thompson, Dr. Irene Mueller, Miss Anna Gorsuch, Miss Avis Graham, Mr. Howard Ringold, Miss Violette Hunter, Dr. John Smay, Mr. Myrl Long, Miss

Vida Dunbar, Dr. Charles Rivers, Dr. Kathryn Riddle, Dr. William Tackett, and Mrs. Cathran Cushman—with their absence in the fall left an academic void. Provost Charles Thate summarized them best when he stated that the group represented a corps that kept the institution functioning during the lean years, and, because they came and stayed and worked, they left the University far better than they found it. This was one dinner that Miss Violette Hunter did not help plan. For many years she chaired the University's Faculty Social Committee and was responsible for special dinners like this one. Known for her attention to detail and the graciousness with which the duties were performed under her direction, Miss Hunter found herself the relaxed beneficiary of the dinner, coordinated by her successor Mrs. Esther Knittl. As for recognition dinners honoring Milner, it was only the beginning as the whole summer seemed to be dedicated to him. At the May 11 Commencement, held three days before final examinations were completed, Thompson, a member of the industrial arts and technology department for thirty-three years, and his colleague Ringold, a thirty-year member, learned that the North Industrial Arts Building (commonly known as the Old IA Building) was being renamed the Thompson-Ringold Industrial Arts and Technology Building.

Thompson and Ringold were pleased to have the building where they spent so much of their careers named for them. Dr. David Easterla was just as satisfied to have an insect with horny wings named for him. The biology professor discovered the new subgenus and species in Texas' Big Bend National Park in 1971. The official announcement of the naming was published in *The Coleopterists Bulletin* during the spring of 1975, and Easterla learned that his discovery would forever carry on his name in the insect world with the title *Eleodes Caverneleodes easterlai*. In the world of science, the likelihood of discovering a new species and then having the species named after the discoverer is very minute.

The 1975 senior class decided to use its gift for two different purposes. With a gift of $700, the class initiated a scholarship in the name of Dana Wray, a senior coed from Waterloo, Iowa, who was seriously injured in an automobile accident, and then presented their $700 balance to the University for library acquisitions. The class of 1976 followed suit in continuing the long tradition of giving to Wells Library; only this group offered its total coffer of $1,500 for new books and new periodicals.

Immediately after the 1975 spring graduation, President Foster flew to Russia for a ten-day visit. A member of a six-man American delegation, Foster, the national chairman of the American Legion's

Foreign Relations Commission, was invited by the Russians to join in their observance of the thirtieth anniversary of the allies' victory in Europe in World War II. It was a Russian summer for Foster. Three weeks after he returned from the Kremlin, his visit was repaid by five Russian World War II veterans. Foster was delighted because the visitors picked Northwest, Cape Kennedy, and both the American Legion and the Disabled American Veterans' national headquarters as their four choice spots to visit while in the United States.

Because of a summer auction, some of Northwest's married students were miffed and perplexed with an action taken by the Board of Regents. The mobile homes, the only married student housing, obtained by the University when a construction strike held up completion of needed dormitory space, were to be sold on August 16. University officials argued that they were too costly to maintain at $125 a month including all utilities. The students' lively rebuttal over losing inexpensive University Park housing with convenient and reasonable living conditions was not unheard, but the University was devoting itself to budget cuts and to finding minor sources of revenue. Losing married student housing was not the only blow. Eliminated, too, was the cafeteria service at the new cafeteria, which catered to the residents of the high-rise dormitories. Thus, some students grudgingly trekked to the Union Cafeteria for food. Dormitory residents were somewhat mollified, however, with a snack bar and a recreational center in their former cafeteria. The formulation, too, of several new and varied meal plans ranging from the twenty-meal-a-week plan to no meals a week helped assuage some of the pain. The budget paring was dictated by the declining occupancy in the dormitories, and the above two moves saved the University approximately $140,000. Also helping to save expenses was Northwest's decision to enlist the Library as a member of Ohio College Library Center (OCLC), a computerized library cataloging service. Expenses for cataloging in 1975, as estimated by Director Charles W. Koch, were $70,000 annually, but under this new program the cost was halved.

At the end of the summer session, Dr. Ken Minter, biology department chairman for ten years, decided to return to full-time teaching and to research. The quiet, scholarly professor, during his ten-year tenure, saw the number of biology majors grow from 125 to 225. During his first year as chairman he, along with Dr. Irene Mueller, introduced Beta Beta Beta, biology's national honor fraternity. Minter, former president of the Missouri Academy of Science, was not reticent in applying for and obtaining federal grants involving his specialty, aquatic ecology. With the University of Missouri at Rolla and the Army

Corps of Engineers, he was involved in a two-part, two-year environmental inventory and base-line inventory of the Missouri River. Biology colleague Myles Grabau assisted with the latter study, and the grants for the projects totaled $60,000 from which Northwest received, after the inventories were completed, equipment and supplies valued at approximately $10,000.

There were other decisions made in August that elicited more exclamatory comment than Minter's because they involved the top levels of Northwest's administrative ranks. President Foster told a summer commencement crowd that he, at a Board of Regents' meeting earlier in the day, had signed a three-year contract, and when that expired he would retire from the University's top post. Actually, Foster would retire on June 30, 1977, at the end of two years, the third year to be a sabbatical. The Board, Foster also announced, decided to advance Dr. Don Petry, vice president for administration, to the newly created position of executive vice president, thus making Petry the senior member of Foster's staff and giving him the coordination of the University's academic and nonacademic affairs and empowering him to act as president whenever Foster was absent from the University.

After losing approximately 1,000 students and seventy staff members in three years, Northwest seemed to reach the bounce-back point. The new policy of allowing either separate or varied contracts for room and board brought 147 more students back to dormitory living, and students were discovering it was more economical to live on campus. They also found Mr. Del Simmons, the new food director, approachable and his food rather delectable. The University also was launching a special effort to grow again by employing two full-time traveling recruiters and budgeting $25,000, exclusive of the recruiters' salaries, to advertise in the electronic and print media. The NWMSU Educational Foundation financed a summer advertising campaign on radio and in the newspapers. During the following academic year, the Student Senate, under Dwight Tompkins' leadership, committed itself to recruitment. Members of the Senate's recruitment committee, chaired by Leo Brooker, visited high schools and talked with prospective students. The Senate, in addition, sponsored what it called "Class of 80," a University weekend held for high school seniors. The weekend, the second consecutive one hosted by the Student Senate, was devoted to giving high school seniors a surface view of university life. The weekends helped recruit students, for two-thirds of the 250 participating high school seniors ultimately enrolled at Northwest. Since the 1976 fall enrollment showed an increase for the first time in five years, the student leaders' efforts were obviously worthwhile.

One does not forget that it is the academics that bring most of the students to campus, and Northwest was not negligent in offering quality programs by blending the traditional with the new. Northwest's medical-related offerings were helping to increase the University's academic offerings to benefit as many areas of health service as possible. Pre-professional programs in medicine, veterinary medicine, dentistry, pharmacy, physical therapy, dental hygiene, nursing, and optometry were thriving. In allied health programs, Northwest students could enter non-degree programs for dental hygienists, medical secretaries and record keepers, practical nurses, and a multitude of program options in health education. Northwest has an excellent reputation in placing its pre-professional students in professional schools. For example, in 1969 and in 1971, Alma Morgan and Percy Myers were graduated from Northwest, following completion of pre-medicine programs in the University's department of biology. In 1973, Morgan was graduated from the University of Missouri School of Medicine, and in the spring of 1975 Myers was graduated from the University of Kansas School of Medicine. The two became the first woman graduate and the first black graduate of Northwest to complete doctor of medicine degrees. Morgan today practices in Colorado and Myers in Kansas City and both have solid medical reputations. Professional schools know that Northwest students are good products, and they also know that the University's pre-medical committee meets with candidates and submits frank advice as early as possible to students who do not have the aptitude for a particular field. Committee members use this same honesty when writing recommendations in behalf of students desiring to enter professional schools. With well over 200 students now enrolled in pre-professional programs, it is obvious that Northwest's commitment to providing trained persons for the country's medical-related needs is quite sincere.

The state of Missouri will eventually adopt a comprehensive school health education act, which when finalized will require school districts to offer comprehensive health education at all levels—nursery through senior high school. In 1975, Northwest's department of physical education had already made giant strides in this area to provide trained teachers in health education. Students could either major or minor in health education, with the major meeting certification requirements of all states and allowing the graduate to teach extensively in health education. An eighteen-hour graduate emphasis, preparing students to coordinate school and public health programs is also available. Dr. Mike Morris began, implemented, and coordinated the program before he left to assume the chair of physical education, health and recreation at Idaho State University in 1976, but Dr. James Herauf, his successor, has maintained and further developed the quality of health education on campus.

Other course offerings at Northwest were quite viable, but the health-related fields in the fall were receiving much attention, partly because of their success and partly because some were new. The newest was the Bachelor of Science in Nursing program, supported by the Missouri State Board of Nursing. The program, after two years of planning, was announced in the spring and began the fall semester with six students. St. Joseph's Methodist Medical Center heightened Northwest's initial interest to begin work on the development of the Bachelor of Science degree, and the advice and counsel from officials of Methodist Medical Center over the two-year period proved to be a sustenance and a stimulant for Northwest. Especially helpful in implementing the program for Northwest was Mrs. Marilyn Meinert, director of the Center's school of nursing. Director of Nursing Sue Gille, who succeeded Mrs. Jane Morgan as coordinator of the School of Practical Nursing, received approval in 1973 and immediately began designing the program to provide an opportunity for registered nurses to further their educational and professional training and, in addition, to provide a basis for their future graduate education. The options open to degree-holding nurses include such areas as teaching, nursing service administration, and public health. The following spring saw two of the nursing program's students graduate, and the program has grown steadily from those original six students to twenty-four in the fall of 1979. The initiation of the program was timely because it corresponded to the trend towards continuing education; Northwest's entry in 1975 made it the first school in Missouri to offer a Bachelor of Science for registered nurses, and it gave the University another level, along with practical nursing and pre-professional nursing, for its training of nurses. The following fall the twelve new enrollees moved from the decentralized facilities in the Garrett-Strong Science Building to enlarged quarters in Wilson Hall, conveniently adjacent to Northwest's health offices. In the fall of 1978, Northwest's Bachelor of Science in Nursing degree was expanded because of a cooperative agreement between the University and the Methodist Medical Center. Because of the covenant, St. Joseph area registered nurses were able to take upper division nursing classes at the Medical Center, thus they had the opportunity to complete a significant portion of their degree requirements in their home area.

Student numbers in the department of business and economics, chaired by Dr. Elwyn DeVore, actually expanded during the University's period of declining enrollment. Many students, conscious of their futures, responded to the various departmental offerings that seemed to guarantee security for future graduates, and the department offered a variety of selections for those who wanted to major in accounting, economics, finance, management, marketing, and office administration. Business students could also choose to major in one of nine inter-disciplinary courses of study from agri-business to business-journalism. Immensely popular, too, were the one and two-year certificate programs and the two graduate degree programs: the Master of Business Administration and the Master of Science in Education.

The extracurricular programs, always a boon to academics, were thriving, and the Bearkitten cross-country team proved that its first season was no fluke by again winning the MAIAW conference. The Bearkittens were pleased to add two newcomers to their varsity sports agenda: tennis and volleyball. Not as successful as early as their sister sports—basketball, track, cross-country, gymnastics, and softball—the two now have emerged as strongholds.

Faculty members usually do not give mimeographed notes from their superiors their utmost attention because missives of that nature are sometimes vapid and offer information concerning meetings, absence reports, grade sheets, and the like. Provost Thate sent one of those mimeographed notes on Friday, September 26, and it was anything but insipid. Many faculty members held that Friday morning's communication tightly in their hands and read it several times, not really comprehending its contents even though the words and thoughts were uncomplicated:

> The Board took action removing me from the position of provost effective June 30, 1976, with the stipulation that I have the option of returning to a faculty position. I have not yet been given any reason for this action but I recognize the right of the Board to take such action as capricious and precipitous as it seems to me to be.
>
> In the event that I elect to accept the option to rejoin the faculty I certainly hope that I will be accepted as a contributing colleague. Any initial hesitancy to accept this option turns on some feeling of inadequacy to do justice to teaching having been away from it for 11 years.

Yes, Thate was to be terminated from his duties as provost, and the University would have a lame-duck high level administrator for the 1975-1976 academic year. No word was given why Thate was dismissed, a fact that did not succor faculty morale. Thate either did not know or he was not telling, and Mr. William Phares, president of the University's Board of Regents did nothing to relieve the tension by muzzling himself, and President Foster, probably not knowing himself the Board's reason for decapitating Thate from his administrative duties, remained silent at least for the time being. On the following Tuesday, however, Foster sent a mimeographed memo that, like Thate's, was read by his faculty. Foster stated that the Board of Regents' removal of Thate was made over Foster's "strenuous objections." Although objecting to one of his top administrator's removal, Foster added that it was his responsibility to carry out the Board's orders and that he would give Thate his full support if he desired to return to the teaching ranks. Thate proceeded to carry out his duties the following months with aplomb and élan, and, as was his usual wont, he did not hesitate to make necessary and hard decisions. On June 30, 1976, Thate, the man who since 1960 held most of the high level administrative positions in Northwest's governing body, surrendered his post and returned to teaching as a professor in the University's department of education, where he continues to serve in a professional and admirable manner. Even today Northwest's staff does not know why the Board acted so peremptorily. Many conjecture, however, that Thate was that group's sacrificial lamb for the now infamous Elba program. If the Board were using him as such, then to relieve him, when so many were involved and hurt because of this misadventure, was grossly unfair.

The selling of beer on campus was considered for several hours at the Board of Regents' November meeting. Proposed originally by Board member Raymond Speckman in order to have the students drinking in a controlled situation, it became a debated issue among the members for several weeks. Since half of Northwest's students were under twenty-one years of age, the Board realized that enforcement and control of beer sales would be extremely difficult. President Foster also warned that any action for beer sales on campus should come from the Missouri Legislature. Even Student Body President Dwight Tompkins recommended to the Board that, although beer sales might eventually be good for the school, it should not act precipitously on a policy until a careful study of student opinion had been made. The Regents were not too happy with the publicity, and they consented to Foster's wish not to sell beer on campus until the Missouri General Assembly lowered the legal drinking age to eighteen, something the Legislature has not done and probably will not do, if at all, for many years. At that same lengthy meeting, the Board, in a move that seemed almost anticlimactic, approved the request retirement of Everett W. Brown, Foster's assistant, with a six-month's sabbatical leave beginning July 1, 1977. A member of the administrative staff for thirty years and a man whose duties were innumerable, Brown asked for the early retirement so he would be free to be a candidate for the Democratic party's nomination to the 5th District seat in the Missouri House of Representatives, to which he was later elected.

In December 1975, the beautifully arrayed Northwest Missouri State University Madraliers, under the direction of Mr. Gilbert Whitney, produced a Feaste, an unusual and enjoyable evening of dining and entertainment for students, faculty, and area citizens. It was an evening reminiscent of the 16th century Elizabethan era with traditional feasting and the Madraliers' singing of familiar songs of Christmas cheer and of Elizabethan-era songs of Christmas cheer in the madrigal style. Musicians, jugglers, magicians, mimes, and clowns, in their colorful costumes, added to the festiveness, and the University's Orchesis Modern Dance Club added to the highlights with dance performances. The grand banquet processional, led by Whitney, set the tone for the evening, and the food and the performances initiated the Christmas season for the spectators. Since the first Feaste drew a capacity crowd, Whitney extended the occasion to two nights the following year and continued the format the next three years. Whitney did offer a variation from the first two celebrations by adding the Lord and the Lady of the Manor, played admirably by Dr. and Mrs. George Hinshaw. Since this five-year-old celebration has become a wonderful December tradition on campus, people need not fear losing it because of Whitney's 1980 spring retirement. Since the Feaste has been so successful, it will continue under someone else's direction, but, of course, Whitney and his singing and his ebullience will be missed.

In the midst of campaign rhetoric and the bitter memories of Vietnam and Watergate, the nation paused in 1976 to celebrate its Bicentennial. This in reality was a yearlong spectacular entertainment marked by parades, concerts, fireworks, speeches, art exhibitions, and similar commemorative events. Thousands sang and waved flags on the very ground where antiwar protesters and police had met in pitched battle only a few years before. The rancor and bitterness of the 1960s and early 1970s was much less evident. Northwest itself was officially designated a Bicentennial Campus and was proud to fly the Bicentennial Flag. State Senator Truman Wilson, a Northwest alumnus who was present for the official ceremony the previous November, probably expressed the changing values of the mid-seventies best when he stated that Americans should rededicate themselves to their rights and freedoms, choices inherited from the forefathers of 1776. One meaningful project which helped to commemorate the Bicentennial on campus was *1776*, the first play of the spring semester, which represented a joint effort of three departments: theater, music, and women's physical education. One of the official events of Northwest's Bicentennial year, the three-hour musical recollected, of course, the events leading to the signing of the Declaration of Independence and the emerging birth of the country. Also timed in conjunction with the Bicentennial, the department of art offered a night course in American art. Taught by Mr. Robert Sunkel, the students examined architecture, crafts, decorative arts, folk arts, painting, and sculpture from the 17th century through the first half of the 20th century. Sunkel used slide lectures and the resources of the Percival DeLuce Memorial Collection.

In 1976, Northwest's Pam Fish of the department of speech and theater was the only nationally certified audiologist in Missouri north of Kansas City. Because Dr. Bob Bohlken, her chairman, was adept at preparing and receiving grants, the Speech and Hearing Clinic was $41,000 richer in equipment. The $41,000, granted to the University on the basis of need, service, and qualifications of staff members, was received from Crippled (Handicapped) Children's Funds under Title V of the Social Security Act. The Clinic serves as a training ground for students studying to become speech-hearing therapists. In the spring of 1976, eighty students were preparing for their future by using the facilities in the Clinic, and in 1975 they, Fish, and Mr. Jerry LaVoi performed more than sixty speech-hearing diagnostic evaluations and provided speech and hearing therapy for the same number of children. The grant, to be sure, helped provide diagnostic and therapeutic equipment necessary for complete speech and hearing services, not only for children but for adults who needed assistance.

Alpha Phi Omega, known for its service-oriented activities and for sponsoring the traditional Ugly Man on Campus Contest, presented in January a $431 check to the community's Sheltered Workshop, an employment center for the handicapped. Each year APO worked industriously to generate student enthusiasm for the Ugly Man Week by promoting a carnival that guaranteed fun and games, yet made the group money for scholarships and needy organizations. The 1975 carnival was not to be, however. Student enthusiasm seemed to wane, and the only campus organization that really industriously cooperated with APO that year was the Phi Mu social sorority. Their candidates throughout the years had a remarkable habit of winning the Ugly Man Contest. Keeping Phi Mu's record intact, Dr. Virgil Albertini won the contest, and most of the above's $431 was produced by the young women's efforts. Unfortunately, 1975 marked the last year for Ugly Man on Campus, commonly known as UMOC.

Late in January Northwest's Board of Regents announced the

formation of a Presidential Search Committee. Raymond Speckman, a Board member, was appointed to chair the Committee, composed of seventeen other members from the ranks of the Regents, chairmen of the University's academic departments, faculty members, students, administration, and alumni. The Committee included, besides Speckman, Ed Geyer and Judge John Yeaman, representing the Board of Regents; Dr. Margaret Briggs, Dr. Peter Jackson, Dr. John Harr, and Dr. Burton Richey, the academic department chairmen; Robert Brown, Robert Sunkel, Dr. Merry McDonald, and Jane Costello, the faculty; Dr. Robert Bush and Dr. John Mees, the administration; Leo Brooker and Clarissa Smith, the student representatives; and Wilbur Pollard, John Dunlap, and Gerald Sprong, the alumni. The committee members, cognizant of the importance of their role and responsibility, had many months of study and meetings ahead of them. Specific, concrete guidelines for them to follow were that Northwest's new leader had to possess an earned doctorate plus higher education administrative and teaching experience. The candidate could also be either from within or without the University. The Committee set August 1, 1976, for deadline applications, and January 1, 1977, for the final selection of Northwest's eighth president.

Certain academic programs, both the traditional and the new, were causing much comment on campus during the March and April months. The Board of Regents in March, upon Foster's recommendation, voted unanimously to eliminate the major-minor sequence in philosophy from Northwest's 1976-1977 edition of the general catalog. Foster justified his recommendation by stating that there were too few philosophy majors and that the department did not generate enough student credit hours, a formula used by the Coordinating Board for Higher Education to recommend appropriations for individual schools. Its removal from the catalog would eliminate the program. The Board's move was a unilateral administrative recommendation that completely bypassed the Faculty Senate. Both students and faculty, however, voiced their displeasure over the Regents' decision to scuttle the philosophy major-minor sequence. Members of the Faculty Senate were nonplused because the Faculty Constitution clearly states that the Faculty Senate must be contacted before any action can be taken on curriculum matters. Fearful that the Board's decision would set a precedent in eliminating courses, senior Becki Kenton Selim rallied students and met with approximately 200 students and faculty members in an open forum in the Union Ballroom. Because of warm April showers, the Ballroom was extremely humid, but Selim's thoughts were not muggy as she explained how interested persons could help reinstate the philosophy major. The assemblage obviously was a concerned group, like the Faculty Senate, with a legitimate grievance. The Student Senate also joined forces with the Faculty Senate and Selim's group to rescue philosophy from its proposed grave. Foster proceeded to hold meetings with administrators and members of the Faculty Senate to discuss whether philosophy should be reinstated. Reaching a decision, he then recommended to his Board members during their April meeting that they reverse their earlier decision. They agreed to do so, and philosophy at Northwest was safe again.

Candace Barnes, Sharon Craig, Rae Cole, and Janet Brown were doing their studying of government on the national level. They were involved in "Field Problems in Public Administration," a semester-long senior level course, offered by the political science department and coordinated by the department's year-old Center for Public Adminstration and Public Affairs under the direction of Mr. Douglas Tucker. The students, like their predecessors in the program, were gaining from their job experience in the nation's capital by working as regular employees in Congressman Jerry Litton's and the United States Attorney's offices. Taking classes at night, researching problems, and attending congressional hearings, in addition to working, the students profited from their Washington educational experience.

In April, Miss Mattie Dykes was honored by the Maryville branch of American Association of University Women in recognition of the twentieth anniversary of her publication *Behind the Birches*. The organization, which had been such an important part of Miss Dykes' life since 1922, recognized her at a reception at the home of Mrs. Lela Bell. Visitors were exuberant, too, when they discovered that Miss Dykes would autograph copies of her history for them. Of interest, particularly to the women present, was the fact that Miss Dykes was wearing the same silk dress she wore at her first autograph party twenty years earlier. One month later the local AAUW announced the establishment of a scholarship in her honor for an upper-division Northwest student interested and proficient in creative writing.

For several years the student leaders from both Northwest and Missouri Western were chagrined because the two schools, only forty miles from each other, never engaged in competitive sports, especially football and basketball. The schools never played each other in football, and their basketball ties were severed, at Northwest's request, in 1974 after crowd incidents involving the two erupted at games both in Maryville and St. Joseph. Talk then, as now, seemed constant over resuming competition, not only for the friendly rivalry that proximity can generate but as a boon for their athletic budgets, since it is obviously less expensive for a team to travel forty miles than several hundred. Northwest's Student Body President Dwight Tompkins, with both institutions' best interests in mind, sent a resolution to Dr. M. O. Looney, Missouri Western's president, endorsing a proposal to renew competition in all sports and suggesting that scheduling begin as soon as possible. Looney said that Missouri Western was willing and Foster agreed. Northwest, incidentally, belongs to the National Collegiate Association of Athletics, while Missouri Western has membership in the National Association of Intercollegiate Athletics, an athletic governing body that allows its member schools more athletic scholarships than the NCAA schools. Foster pointed out the disparity but also thought that was hardly a barrier to delay competition. Northwest's Athletic Director Michael Hunter stated that competition between the two would undoubtedly resume but probably not for two years. Hunter, now gone from the scene, proved to be a bad prognosticator, because the two schools are still talking but not playing. Even Missouri's Coordinating Board for Higher Education suggested that renewed competition today would be healthy, and Missouri Western's Athletic Director Charles Burri clearly echoed many prevailing views in both St. Joseph and Maryville by stating in 1976, "The administration and coaches of both these institutions should speak with good will and show genuine enthusiasm towards a friendly rivalry and leave the competition on the playing courts and fields."

Again Northwest was honoring its own as over 300 faculty members, administrators, and staff members paid tribute at the annual retirement dinner on April 23 to four colleagues who were officially leaving their teaching and administrative duties at Northwest. The four were Miss Bonnie Magill, chairman of women's physical education, Mrs. Elaine Mauzey, chairman of the department of foreign languages, Dr. Ralph Fulsom, professor of speech and theater and former chairman, and Mr. Everett W. Brown, assistant to the president. Magill's, Mauzey's, Fulsom's, and Brown's service numbered respectively thirty-three, thirty-one, twenty-five, and thirty years. Magill, retiring three years before the mandatory date, led her department through many important changes and saw Northwest's women heavily engaged in intercollegiate competition; Mauzey, who was part of a two-person department when she arrived, not only chaired and taught but served in a wide variety of capacities, like chairing commencement activities for twenty-five years; Fulsom, who was honored in absentia during the dinner's activities, was leaving his heritage of fine theater at Northwest, and he did not disappoint his spring audience with his final production—*One Flew Over the Cuckoo's Nest*. Honored as Maryville's 1968 Chamber of Commerce Man of the Year, Brown, probably the most recognized man in Northwest Missouri because of his engaging personality and the myriad activities he performed for Northwest in his thirty years, was also highlighted in June at a special Northwest Alumni Association Banquet. A capacity audience of university and community people listened to the "roasts and toasts" to Brown by friends who supposedly knew him best. A serious moment did prevail when Brown himself took time to recognize and laud the patience and work of Miss Shirley Gray, his long-time secretary. Mr. Fred Handke, a member of the business department for fourteen years, succumbed to the lure of the Arkansas mountains and the mountains of Colorado and took an early retirement at the end of the summer session. He, consequently, missed all the spring festivities honoring retirees but was properly feted by his department and President Foster with a banquet and gifts.

Dr. E. L. Whitmore from Northwest's department of psychology saw his idea that had been germinating for six years come to fruition during the 1976 spring semester. The idea, in full flower that spring, was called "Country Cousins." Every Thursday afternoon and evening, five lower elementary school-age youngsters and five university volunteers from a course of study involving the exceptional child met at the Whitmore ranch to share, along with Dr. and Mrs. Whitmore, in a caring relationship. They devoted themselves to group activities like feeding the cattle herd, and one-to-one activities between the university student and the elementary student; then at 5:30, the third time period, the twelve sat down to a farm-style meal, prepared by Mrs. Whitmore. Working with Whitmore in selecting the younger cousins was Mrs. Virginia Brown, counselor at Maryville's Eugene Field Elementary School. The program was important because it offered the quintet of children the opportunity for physical, emotional, and mental growth and gave them the tangible and intangible benefits of a wholesome family life. The next year "Country Cousins" more than doubled in size with thirteen selected university students and twelve elementary school children, and the meeting times were extended to also include Saturday mornings. The Whitmores, incidentally, provided the food and paid most of the expenses for this innovative and genuine program. Unfortunately, when Dr. Whitmore died in the summer of 1978, the "Country Cousins" program died, too.

On May 9, Mrs. Elaine Mauzey was chairing her final commencement. As if blessing her for all her years of dedicated work on commencement, the day was sunny and calm, and no hasty decisions had to be made to move the affair indoors. Fortunate, too, was the administrative decision to break from the onerous, short-lived tradition of recognizing the graduates en masse. Undergraduate degree recipients once again would be recognized individually, a judgment that pleased both attending graduates and their picture-taking families. Northwest offered something else at the 1976 Commencement, not the predictable single guest speaker but three! The crowd heard J. Norvel Sayler tell the graduates "You have a choice;" they heard Wilbur Pollard call for "The understanding of integrity;" and they listened to Dr. J. D. Hammond exclaim "Think critically and continue to learn." Each of the speakers was Northwest's choice for the University's highest honor, the Distinguished Alumni Award. Dr. Hammond, professor of business administration at Pennsylvania State University, specifically pointed out the late Dr. Sterling Surrey for having a profound effect on his life, and he told the assemblage that he was wearing Dr. Surrey's academic regalia, a gift from Mrs. Surrey after her husband's death. Along with the 750 undergraduate and graduate degree candidates, there was a very special one in attendance—Miss Dana Wray. Miss Wray, paralyzed from the shoulders down in a 1974 automobile accident, received her Bachelor of Science degree in Elementary Education some seventeen months later than had been her intention. Various university groups and individuals—like Delta Sigma Phi with their 100-mile September run to Liberty, Missouri—plus area clubs and citizens conducted or assisted in fund drives to help defray some of Miss Wray's huge medical bills. After winning the fight for her life, she took aim at completing her degree. Miss Wray, waiting in her motorized wheelchair, was rewarded for her determined efforts with a standing ovation from the 4,000 people in the audience and with a kiss from President Foster when he stepped from the platform to personally deliver the young woman's diploma. Foster would do the same at the 1977 Commencement for the graduating Charlie Johnson, also in a motorized wheelchair, not with a kiss, however, but with a handshake.

In December, Northwest was greatly concerned when Governor Bond's 1976-1977 budget recommendation for the University was $200,000 less than the amount recommended by the Missouri Coordinating Board for Higher Education, the group that recommends how schools should be funded. Bond's action evoked much outcry throughout Northwest Missouri, and Foster told the Senate Appropriations Committee in January that he was asking for only enough money to operate his University, a 6.8 percent increase over the previous year. He found sympathetic audiences in both the Missouri Senate and House Appropriations Committees because the Governor recommended increases averaging 8.5 percent for the other regional universities and state colleges, while suggesting only a one percent boost for Northwest. In May, however, the Governor seemed more receptive to the University's needs and signed an appropriation bill totaling $7,195,071, a $702,537 increase and $400,000 more than Bond originally recommended. A month later Northwest also received $743,000 of a $54,600,000 capital improvements bill signed into law by Governor Bond. The University's share of the state funding was used for general physical plant improvements and for remodeling of the Administration Building, known as Phase One, the first of a three-phased renovation. Part of that money, too, was used to restore the running track with the installation of an all-weather, six-lane course for the Bearcat and Bear-kitten track and field teams, area high school teams, and any interested joggers. The department of agriculture was happy, too, for it was adding to its farm buildings with a new Agricultural Mechanics Lab on the R. T. Wright College Farm.

New appointments captured the Northwest spotlight in May and June. Director of Admissions Dick Buckridge was picked to succeed Everett W. Brown as assistant to the president; Charles Veatch, assistant director of admissions, stepped up to the director's slot; and Dr. John Paul Mees advanced a step from his assistant provost position to acting provost, succeeding the deposed Dr. Charles Thate. Dr. Margaret Briggs, chairman of the department of home economics, was given additional duties as acting administrative assistant to Provost John Paul Mees. In addition, new departmental chairmen were Barbara Bernard, women's physical education; Mary Jackson, foreign languages; and Dr. Harold Jackson, music. Earlier announcements were the appointment of James C. Redd as the new Bearcat head football coach to succeed Gladden Dye, and Sherri Reeves' elevation as assistant director of athletics and coordinator of Northwest's intercollegiate athletic program for women.

Summer entertainment on campus for several years, with the exception of an occasional movie, was practically nil. Summer undergraduates who found an abundance of amusement like Union Board's All-Nite Party, or Geraldo Rivera, Lily Tomlin, and Maynard Ferguson during the regular school year noticed the change and involved themselves with outdoor activities. David Shestak, from the department of speech and theater, worried, however, about the dearth of pleasure and acted to bring some diversion to summertime at Northwest. The first quarter of the twentieth century, reminiscent of hot and lazy summers in the Midwest, came to life again on the Northwest campus in late June and early July. It was a rebirth of the old "Chautauqua" as Northwest's department of speech and theater presented a return to the past with a "Maryville Chautauqua." The site of the 1976 production was the same site—the west edge of the campus and west of Rickenbrode Stadium in College Park—where the annual Chautauquas were held in Maryville from 1906-1924. Like its predecessors, this modern day Chautauqua entertained its audiences with old-time political speeches, temperance songs and orations, a melodrama, and a variety of other offerings. This was not the first time that Shestak brought outdoor fun to a summer campus almost starved for entertainment. In previous years he directed such spectacles as the Wild West tent show *Indians* and the outdoor melodrama *The Drunkard*.

In the spring, Dr. Carrol Fry, chairman of the English department, was inundated with 500 prose and poetry manuscripts from high school creative writers for the department's magazine *New Wine*. Late in June, however, he could sit in his office with the published copy in his hands and amiably read the sixty-six selections of poetry and prose in the second edition of this creative journal, which was first published in 1975. Now that the collection was published, his only concerns were sending each author a copy and preparing for the third edition. Fry continued to edit *New Wine* until 1978 when Mr. Craig Goad from the English department became editor. The magazine has gained such a reputation that it is not unusual for Goad now to receive over 1,000 manuscripts from contributors.

Physics Professor Jim Smeltzer traveled to California in July. Many people from the Midwest sojourn in California in July, but, even though he was having fun, he was not vacationing. Smeltzer was selected as one of 100 educators from throughout the United States to participate in a "Viking Education Conference" at the Jet Propulsion Laboratory at the California Institute of Technology in Pasadena in conjunction with the landing of Viking I on Mars. Smeltzer, well-known on campus for his astronomy classes and his racquetball prowess, participated in and listened to discussions concerning the history of planetary exploration and of the scientific projects to be completed by NASA in space exploration and also heard discussions of scientific findings during the Viking I mission. Smeltzer, no stranger to NASA, attended his first conference for a chosen number of educators in December 1974 when a space probe circumnavigated Jupiter. In the ensuing years, Smeltzer has become increasingly involved with NASA, and this responsive agency is not hesitant in inviting him to its momentous happenings. For the last several years Dr. Bob Mallory has accompanied Smeltzer and the two, a physicist and a geologist, nicely complement each other. Besides learning and mingling with national leaders and figures like author Carl Sagan, the two greatly enhance and inspire their classes with their newly acquired information from these meetings.

Members of the Quarterback Club discovered in August that their organization was defunct, and a new one called the Bearcat Boosters Club had taken its place. Really an outgrowth of the older Quarterback Club, the Boosters broadened their activities in order to get more people involved and to support more Bearcat and Bearkitten sports. Members of the Club receive monthly athletic department newsletters, attend award banquets, pre-game and post-game parties, special team previews, and members and their families get to know coaches and athletes personally. The usual early arrivals—the ones who like seats on the fifty-yard line—at the first Bearcat home football game against William Jewell in 1976 were disappointed that their traditional, choice seats were cordoned off. Yes, they were reserved for the Boosters, who could leave their pre-game party and arrive shortly before the kickoff, a definite advantage, to be sure, in being a member of the Booster Club. W. R. O'Riley, a local young businessman and alumnus of Northwest, served as the new organization's first president, a fitting move since this man rarely misses a Bearcat or Bearkitten sporting event, home or away.

Graduate students in the fall of 1976 had two more degrees from which to choose, one in business and the other in counseling. The degree in business was unusual and flexible because Dr. Elwyn DeVore, the chairman, was making it possible for qualified persons to earn a Master of Business Administration degree on weekends. Under this new arrangement, students were involved in classes scheduled on Friday evenings and during the day on Saturdays every other weekend, allowing the degree candidate to complete the MBA in a period from forty-four to forty-eight weeks. The new advanced degree in counseling led to the Master of Science in Counseling Psychology and prepared counselors to work in non-educational settings, such as mental health centers, psychological clinics, mental hospitals, various governmental agencies, and personnel departments in corporations. The following August, Mrs. Norma Jean King, a registered nurse at St. Joseph State Hospital, became the first recipient of the counseling degree. The home economics department was ready, too, to offer a Master of Science degree in Home Economics Education. The department's proposal was approved by the University's Graduate Council and the Board of Regents, but needed final approval from the Missouri Coordinating Board for Higher Education, which was finally given early in the spring, allowing the department to offer its first courses toward the thirty-two-hour requirement the following summer. Another academic move that fall was the combining of humanities and philosophy with history, under the auspices of Dr. John Harr. Dr. Gary Davis, chairman of the humanities and philosophy department, stimulated the action when he requested a release from his administrative duties to return to full-time teaching.

Coach Redd proved to be an able successor to Gladden Dye as he continued Northwest's winning tradition with an 8-2 record. A victory against Northeast in the final game of the season would have assured the Bearcats the MIAA championship, but it was not to be. The Bearkittens, under new coach Dr. Glenda Guilliams, won its third consecutive cross-country MAIAW title. Her job was made somewhat easier with the return of Ann Kimm, who finished first in the conference meet for the second straight year. Coach Earl Baker's men did not do as well as the women but finished third in the MIAA meet, their highest finish since 1972. Baker was happy, too, for Vernon Darling seemed to be the heir apparent of the graduated All-American John Wellerding. Coach Sandra Mull's gymnastics team aroused attention when it won its own invitational meet.

The International Students Organization, boasting 130 members, was not discontented but happy to display to others a different way of life. These students, from over thirty countries, transformed the Union Ballroom into a mass display of exhibitions and simulated life styles of their own countries during their International Weekend. They also prepared food and the crowd sampled their preparations. Part of International Weekend, too, was the first organized soccer game on campus as the foreign students displayed their skills. The Weekend did bring the foreign students, American students, and area residents together and helped create a better understanding among the groups.

The seventh annual Black Homecoming Queen Pageant, traditionally held the week before Homecoming, probably enjoyed its greatest success in 1976. "Black Essence" was the theme, and the students, alumni, and friends were enthralled with the talent and poise displayed by the contestants and the band that performed while the young women prepared for pageant events. Janetta Fulsom was elected queen by the coterie of judges, and the black students were delighted to see a record number of black alumni in the audience and members of Sigma Gamma Rho, a black sorority and the newest one on campus.

The Presidential Search Committee was quietly and efficiently doing its work, but Chairman Speckman announced in October that over 100 applicants had submitted their names, hoping to become Northwest's eighth president. The candidates represented twenty-nine states and one foreign country, and Speckman speculated that the final contestants would be selected and interviewed by mid-November. The faculty and staff, eagerly anticipating Foster's successor, learned from Speckman that the Committee would draw up recommendations on the finalists for the Board of Regents after the interviewing process was completed. The Board was then expected to make its final decision by January.

Members of the University's student affiliate chapter of the American Chemical Society and their professors were smiling over their test tubes in the chemistry laboratories before Christmas. For the second consecutive year, the group received an early Christmas gift. They were being honored again by the parent American Chemical Society as one of the outstanding chapters in the United States. Only forty-nine of the total 652 chapters were commended for such excellence in the 1975-1976 school year.

The Bearcat tennis team won its sixth straight MIAA crown in the spring, and, with their newly resurfaced courts, were the proud hosts of the NCAA Division II Championships where they finished eighth in a field of twenty-nine schools. That conference crown, however, was infested with thorns, for it was unceremoniously removed from Northwest's head in January. The Missouri Intercollegiate Athletic Association's Infractions Committee withdrew Northwest's championship because of what the Committee judged illegal scholarships offered by the coach, Dr. John Byrd, and also placed Northwest's tennis program on probation for a year. The Committee declared that foreign student scholarships offered by Byrd to tennis prospects were in reality athletic scholarships, thus causing Northwest to offer more than fifty-seven athletic scholarships to its athletes and to exceed the maximum number an MIAA institution could offer. Five of the six "Conference champions," incidentally, were from foreign countries. Northwest's administrative officials conducted their own investigation of the tennis program and reported their findings to the MIAA Committee. Northwest's athletic director, Dr. Mike Hunter, was calling the decision a fair one, but Byrd refused to discuss the verdict because he felt the issue was a dead one and that Northwest would not benefit from prolonged discussions. Byrd's men, however, rebounded fast and entered the MIAA throne room again in 1977 by capturing the championship with only one returning letterman and an all-foreign cast of players.

On January 20, 1977, Jimmy Carter was sworn in as the thirty-ninth President of the United States by Chief Justice Warren E. Burger, and at the same time speculation was running rampant on campus in late January concerning which of the four finalists would be Northwest's new leader. The Search Committee knew and, of course, the

Board of Regents knew. On Wednesday, January 26, the Board passed a resolution strongly commending the Committee's yearlong work. The praise was well deserved. This was a working committee that not only studied the applicants' credentials, selected the finalists, and conducted their interviews but permitted enough time and queries for faculty and students to respond to the final four. The Committee was not the usual type of screening committee so common in many institutions of higher learning but an authentic search committee that was totally involved in the decision making. The members took deep pride in what they had accomplished and experienced a unanimity of feeling concerning their work. Mr. Speckman, who conducted the twenty regular meetings during the search and visited the campuses of the final competitors, referred to serving on the Committee as his most rewarding experience ever. Provost Mees called it his single most challenging job. Dr. Burton Richey was skeptical in the beginning over the Committee's importance in the final selection, but he quickly changed his mind after observing the thoroughness, the sincerity, and the responsibility of his group.

On Monday, January 31, the faculty, staff, and general public stopped guessing and discovered at a press conference, held in the Ballroom of the J. W. Jones Union Building, that Northwest Missouri State University's next president was Dr. B. D. Owens, the president of the University of Tampa since 1971 and a man eminently experienced in classroom and administrative situations in higher education. Dr. Owens proved, contrary to Thomas Wolfe's adage "You Can't Go Home Again," that one indeed can come home again. A 1959 alumnus, Dr. Owens praised his alma mater before the bulging crowd, including Mrs. Owens and their two sons, Brent and Kevin, and said "I feel I am coming home and Sue [Mrs. Owens, a 1957 alumna] feels the same. I am deeply honored and privileged to be asked to assume the responsibility of leadership of this University. . . . It did a lot for Sue and me and I'm grateful for that. It is a University that equipped us for the world. . . ." Owens also added that he would not have considered accepting the Northwest presidency except for a sense of commitment to the school and the concentrated efforts of the University family and community during the search process. Stating that the quality of Northwest was great, he asked the community to join with him in a continued search for excellence, a word that would become a hallmark during his administration.

A university, like Northwest, is a small community and any community worries about debilitating and crippling fires. On November 13, 1973, fire caused $2,000 in damages to the furnishings and contents of the basement of the Child Development Laboratory, a space utilized primarily as a play area for the children. The fire began shortly after the children were dismissed for the day and was started by fumes igniting from a cleaning agent that was being used to clean the basement floor. In February 1977, Dr. John Beeks experienced his second fire as chairman of the agricultural area. Not nearly as destructive as the dairy barn fire in 1967, fire from an inadequate electrical extension cord caused damage to a hay barn and contents, and, one year and two days after the hay barn fire, another fire occurred in a sixth-floor room of Dieterich Hall, apparently started by an electrical short in a small refrigerator in a student's room. Fortunately, the fire, causing $6,000 damage, occurred in the afternoon when occupancy was limited and only a few residents had to be evacuated.

The spring semester seemed to be a time for press conferences. Another one was held in February, not to announce an appointment but two resignations. Usually the media is not that interested when faculty or staff members retire or resign from their duties, but this was a dual announcement involving a former Bearcat basketball coach and a present one: Dick Buckridge and Bob Iglehart. Buckridge, who succeeded Everett Brown as Foster's assistant, spoke for the pair when he stated that the press conference was called to squelch erroneous rumors and to prematurely announce their plans to enter into private business in Maryville. Iglehart, formerly Buckridge's basketball assistant at Northwest, added that the University needed to know his plans so that his successor would have the time to recruit players for the following year. Their resignations became effective July 1, but the Board of Regents was not hesitant in hiring a new coach. At the Board's March meeting, Larry Holley, Iglehart's assistant for two years, was named the Bearcats' fifteenth head basketball coach. Dr. Owens would later select Dr. Bob Bush, dean of admissions, as Buckridge's successor. Fans, on the night of the two men's meeting with the media, saw Iglehart coach his team for the last time, and for the last time, too, they were seeing Iglehart's ace David Alvey, the Bearcats' all-time leading career scorer with 1,747 points.

Although Dr. Owens was off campus and winding down his duties as president of the University of Tampa, his thoughts were also here at Northwest. One of those thoughts centered on who was to be his chief academic officer—or provost as the position was then called at Northwest. Dr. Virgil Albertini's office-hour reverie was broken one morning in February when Owens called him from Tampa with the request that Albertini head a Search and Screening Committee to find a vice president for academic affairs. Of course, Dr. John Mees had

filled the position as acting provost of the University since being
appointed to that post in the spring of 1976. After listening to
Albertini's startled response, Owens charged this Committee with conducting an extensive search both within and outside the University.
The responsibilities, he explained, were to define criteria, advertise the
position, screen the applicants, recommend four final candidates by
July 1, coordinate and help with the interview process, and assist in the
final choice. It was Owens' firm intention to have this academic head
on campus for the fall semester. The Committee began its work
immediately. It was a large committee, having seventeen members and
representing a cross section of the campus with seven chairmen, eight
members of the faculty, and two students. Representing the chairmen
were Dr. Elwyn DeVore, Dr. Sam Carpenter, Mary Jackson, Dr. Dean
Savage, Dr. David Smith, Dr. John Beeks, and Dr. Harold Jackson;
working for the faculty, besides Albertini, were Dr. Wayne Amsbury,
Rose Ann Wallace, Lee Hageman, Dr. Frances Shipley, Dr. Stanley
Wade, Dr. Dale Rosenburg, and Dr. Gary Davis; and serving for the
students were Rex Gwinn and John Moore. Sentiment among many
chairmen and faculty members immediately arose for retaining Dr.
John Paul Mees in that key position. Mees, as most university people
knew, moved up from his position as assistant provost to acting provost
at a most difficult time at Northwest. He formed a fine working
relationship with the University's chairmen and established a reputation
among the faculty as a dedicated and conscientious administrator who
possessed integrity. The Search and Screening Committee constantly
kept the faculty abreast of its work, and at the very beginning polled
the faculty members as to what they desired in a chief academic officer.
There were 160 faculty members wanting the Committee to retain Mees
and thirty-five desiring the Committee to conduct an extensive search.
Because the Committee was entrusted with a careful and wide-ranged
probe, the query was significant only in that it tested the faculty
temperament. Dr. Mees never applied for the position, and when Dr.
Owens visited the campus in April he told the Committee that he
needed a person in the critical area of student development. Knowing
that Mees had a variegated administrative life since coming to Northwest in 1971, Dr. Owens, citing Mees' excellent qualifications, informed
the group that he had asked Mees to be his vice president for student
development and that Mees had accepted. Owens termed Mees'
appointment as a "major step toward the University's full development
of a living and learning environment for our student body."

While Northwest was gearing itself for changes in the administrative hierarchy, students were proceeding as usual with their classes

and social life. Phase I work on the grandmother of all the campus edifices—the Administration Building—was completed late in the fall when the building's department of agriculture was remodeled, and more improvements were made in the home economics department. Again in the fall the grand lady allowed more surgery on herself so that various segments of the speech and theater department could be consolidated and the University's broadcasting facilities in radio and television centralized. Now in April, the second part of her operation, referred to as Phase II, was almost completed. With the finished renovation of her fourth floor, the Administration Building would greet the department's Speech and Hearing Clinic in its move from the Horace Mann Learning Center to its sophisticated new quarters. She also found room to transplant the department's main and faculty offices to the top floor from their third floor location. Occupying the vacated space on the third floor was KMSU-TV, the University's instructional television station, housed, since its inception, in Wells Library and commonly known as ITV (Instructional Television). The physical move of ITV from Wells Library to the Administration Building's third floor was a sensible one since it merged with radio for better utilization of professional staff and more efficient broadcasting services for Northwest's students. Dr. Bohlken worked many long and difficult hours to release ITV from the Library, and his applying for and receiving a total of $70,000 worth of equipment from grants with the prospect of even more federal money helped make the administrative decision to move ITV easier. Dr. Mees also worked diligently for the centralization to better coordinate the broadcast services, and he arranged the merger so ITV could be comfortable in its union with its communication's cousin. One area that construction surgeons could not eliminate from the lady's ailments was the bats in her hair. For years the Administration Building housed bats in her attic, and the resident bat expert, Dr. David Easterla, strenuously objected to exterminating them. For years theatergoers could occasionally see one of the bats circling the Auditorium. Pigeons, too, were known to inhabit the area as Dr. Bob Bohlken well knows since one of them helped disrupt his class one day. While teaching Introduction to Mass Media in the Building's fourth floor speech classroom, Bohlken heard one of his female students shout an expletive. Bohlken, thinking that she was commenting on his lecture, was ready to excoriate her but stopped suddenly when he saw the reason for her displeasure—fresh pigeon excrement on her class notes!

Neither the bats nor the pigeons deterred theatergoers, however, and they again were treated to fine performances from Northwest's drama students. An especial treat was *Tobacco Road,* based on Erskine Caldwell's 1932 novel of an oppressed and degraded Georgia sharecropper and his family. The drama once had a continuous run of 3,182 Broadway performances and was popular with Northwest's students. Technical Director Don Folkman designed the set for the university production, and his work was rated the best at the American College and University Festival at the University of Iowa.

Embers decided in the spring to return to what it was originally known as on campus—Cardinal Key. For several years the group was known as Embers, a local honor society, but now in April Northwest again would have a campus chapter of the national honor society. The chapter was officially installed on April 16. Initiated were twelve women students from Embers, along with eighteen new initiates who were not members of Embers. Four university men were among the new ones accepted into this heretofore all-women honorary society. Because Cardinal Key had recently revived its constitution to become coeducational, the Northwest chapter was one of the first in the nation to include men. Marty Pope was elected the chapter's president, and he also achieved instant renown by becoming the first male Cardinal Key chapter president in the nation. Their adviser, Mrs. Jean Kenner from mathematics, also was adviser to Embers. With the official installation of Cardinal Key, Embers became defunct. The University's Blue Key chapter, formerly known as Cardinal Key's brother organization, has remained traditional by honoring only men.

Although not an honorary society, another campus organization was celebrating in April. Its celebration, however, was not a rebirth but an anniversary. The Alpha Epsilon chapter of Sigma Sigma Sigma turned fifty years old on Sunday, April 24. It was a dual golden anniversary, for its alumnae chapter also became golden on that day. Both groups reveled in the thought that the sorority was the first national Greek organization on the Northwest campus.

For several years, Dr. Charles Koch, director of Northwest's Learning Resources Center, was the willing recipient of an energetic program of rapidly enlarging Wells Library's holdings. President Foster began then to respond to the growing emphasis being placed upon student research and the expanding graduate programs by directing his financial attention to the library acquisitions. Because of those efforts, books were flowing in at such a rate that the cataloging department was overwhelmed with volumes. The books, consequently, could not be cataloged quickly enough, and the result was a serious backlog. There were 8,000 of those volumes awaiting final cataloging in the winter of 1976. One year later the problem no longer existed. There was no backlog of books, and catalogers and library patrons were thanking the University's association with the Ohio College Library Center (OCLC), a computerized cataloging service that the University joined in the spring of 1976. Increased speed in cataloging was the major benefit of membership in OCLC, and, because of the computer hookup with OCLC, 1,600 books a month could be added to the library's stacks. Of course, the catalogers had to accept the philosophy of making changes in the method of cataloging books. Lola Nair, head of technical services in 1976 who has since assumed a library position at Oral Roberts University in Tulsa, and Head Cataloger Kathryn Murphy were praised by Koch for helping make OCLC on campus a reality when he said, "They could have dragged their heels and scuttled the whole effort." Miss Nair brought OCLC experience with her when she came to Northwest, but Mrs. Murphy willingly learned it, spent much time digesting its intricacies—even sacrificing a summer's leave from her own graduate study to help fulfill this much needed computer library network at Northwest—and has since trained numerous staff members in the new procedure.

In the spring of 1977, Wells Library was also the beneficiary of something else it badly needed—a display case complete with security gates. Mrs. Edward V. Condon of Maryville presented the gifts in memory of her late husband, Colonel Edward V. Condon. Her husband, former owner and operator of a popular drugstore, was for years an admirer and staunch supporter of Northwest. Condon was well-known for his generosity, and at least a dozen students and staff members benefited from his weekly largess by receiving free malts at his establishment. The display case became the bearer of the University's first rare book, also a gift to the Library. The book, bestowed on Northwest by Mr. and Mrs. George D. Triplett from Monterrey, Mexico, was an English language translation of *De Re Metallica,* a sixteenth century book on mining, mining history, and the history of metallurgy by Georgius Agricola. The edition, presented to Northwest by the Tripletts in memory of his father, who was the book's first owner, was translated into English from Latin by Mr. and Mrs. Herbert Hoover and autographed by the former President of the United States. The book's bequest signified Mr. Triplett's and President Foster's friendship. The following summer Wells Library was surprised to see yet another permanent gift; but this one came under the auspices of Tom Carneal, for it was to belong to Northwest's Missouriana Room Historical Collection. The gift, a rare collection of circus memorabilia concerning the famous Ringling Brothers and Barnum and Bailey Circus, was a thrill for both the young and old, the academe and the non-academe. The twenty-six piece collection, named the "Cotton Fenner Exhibit: The Circus and Nodaway County," was presented to the University by Dr. Mildred Sandison Fenner Reid, a Northwest alumna and the University's first Distinguished Alumni Award recipient, as a tribute to her late husband, Wolcott Fenner, who was the senior vice president of the Circus.

Celebrities were in abundance on campus during the spring semester. John Wooden, retired basketball coach from the many times UCLA national champions and a National Basketball Hall of Famer, offered his coaching philosophy and views on contemporary basketball to a packed Auditorium crowd. Northwest's drama people produced the award-winning play *Harvey,* the first dinner theater in the University's history. The husband and wife team of Peter Lind Hayes and Mary Healy, all-star performers of stage, screen, radio, and television, appeared in the title roles. Members of the Northwest Alpha Psi Omega Honorary Fraternity were Hayes' and Healy's supporting players in this five-night event, directed by David Shestak in the Union Ballroom. A second person, like Dr. Owens, proved that one indeed can come home again, and Sarah Caldwell, the first lady of American opera, did just that on April 20. Miss Caldwell, a native of Maryville who spent her early years here, returned to Northwest as guest conductor for the St. Louis Symphony Orchestra. It was, to be sure, her day; Governor Joseph Teasdale made it official by proclaiming April 20 as "Sarah Caldwell Day" in Missouri, but her presence did not need official sanction because Northwest welcomed her as one of its own. Caldwell, the founder and director of the Boston Opera Company, and her mother, Mrs. Carrie Margaret Alexander, a former piano instructor at Northwest, were honored at a university luncheon. President Foster presented Caldwell with a NWMSU Citation of Achievement, an award similar to what some universities offer as an honorary degree, and J. Norvel Sayler, chairman of Northwest's Educational Foundation, announced at that same luncheon that a Sarah Caldwell Scholarship would be offered on a permanent basis in the music department.

Retirement festivities in April featured an all-female cast. The four faculty and staff members who contributed eighty-nine years of service to Northwest were Mary Jackson, chairman of the foreign language department; Esther Knittl, assistant professor of elementary education; Ruth Miller, associate professor of music; and Leta Brown, circulation librarian. The four were honored at the annual Northwest retirement dinner on April 26. Because of a June banquet planned for him, President Foster was not singled out for retirement honors. The night's festivities belonged to the four, and they were thrilled to see not one but two presidents—one outgoing and the other incoming—at their recognition dinner.

Although Miss Jackson would not be around to teach Spanish classes and chair her department in the fall, she was not deterred from developing a new academic program during her year's tenure as department head. That new program was a major or minor in International Studies that led to a Bachelor of Arts degree. Interdisciplinary in nature, the program was offered, in cooperation with the departments of business and economics, history and humanities, geography, and political science, to give the student a concentration in the language and culture of French, German, or Spanish speaking countries. In addition to offering a broad academic background in the areas taught by the four other departments, the program was designed for those students who wanted to prepare themselves for careers in international affairs. Charles Slattery, Jackson's successor as chairman, implemented the program for her. Dr. Carrol Fry, chairman of the English department, showing that his department was certainly not deficient in development, announced a new English-journalism major, requiring course work in only journalism or journalism-related fields and, in addition, a minor area of concentration. And Northwest was yet to offer another Master of Science degree—this one in Communication Disorders. Planning three years for the new graduate degree, Dr. Bob Bohlken, chairman of the speech and theater department, indicated that the new program was a continuation of Northwest's development of programs in specialized educational areas including language and perceptual skills. The principal purpose of the degree was to provide graduates the academic requirements for the Certificate of Clinical Competence in Speech Pathology issued by the American Speech and Hearing Association. Another valuable addition to Northwest's academic courses came in the summer when Lee Hageman, the department of art's silversmithing, jewelry, and pewter specialist, offered an extensive pewtersmithing course to art teachers in order to develop their skills, so they, in turn, could pass those skills on to their students. To make room for his pewter students, Hageman opened an area in the basement of the Olive DeLuce Fine Arts Building. There his students could work quietly and undisturbed. The course was Hageman's brainchild and in 1977 was the only such course offered anywhere. The new additions were welcome, but, because of excessive expenses and dwindling students, the vocational dairy processing course was discontinued at the end of the spring semester. Instructional dairy programs continued, however, and the dairy herd was maintained.

Another 1959 Northwest graduate, like Owens, would assume the presidency of an institution of higher education in the summer of 1977. Dr. H. Rex Craig became president of Contra Costa College, a twenty-one-year-old San Franciso Bay area school with an enrollment over 9,000.

Northwest's seventy-first spring Commencement, held May 8, will be remembered by graduates, participants, and spectators for two things: heat and President Foster. Because of rain, Lamkin Gymnasium served as host, but its heat was stifling as temperatures hovered well over 100 degrees. It, however, was mostly remembered as the last time Foster presided over Commencement.

Early in June the Vice President for Academic Affairs Search and Screening Committee had narrowed its applicants to the final four. The finalists had been notified, and the Committee was ready to discuss, as originally directed by Dr. Owens, its selections with him on July 1, his first day in the President's Office. The four were ranked in order of the Committee's preference.

The month of June really belonged to Foster as he was honored throughout the dwindling days of his presidency. His staff had parties for him and Mrs. Foster, and his faculty did the same. The town feted him and proclaimed June 25 Robert Foster Day in Maryville, and he was honored by the University's Alumni Association that night with a tribute banquet. Many speakers, garnered from present and former colleagues, Northwest alumni, and city and governmental representatives, recounted Foster's contributions to education during his Northwest tenure. The speakers, too, showed no fear of levity as they gently "roasted" the retiring president. The program, too, was keyed by the humorous quips and retorts of Master of Ceremonies Rollie Stadlman, the University's director of broadcasting. Foster was especially pleased that his friend the former Northwest dean of faculty and President Emeritus of Fort Hays State University Dr. M. C. "Pete" Cunningham was there to recall their early days together at Northwest. But the real pleasure for President and Mrs. Foster was reserved for near the conclusion of the night's tribute when J. Norvel Sayler stood up before the 470 alumni, faculty and staff members, and friends to say "It is my pleasure to announce tonight the gift he wanted most of all." That gift was a $50,000 scholarship fund, created by contributions from members of the sponsoring alumni association, from current and former faculty and staff members, and from friends of the Fosters. Launched the previous fall by Alumni Association President Barbara Sprong, it was to commemorate the name of President Foster and assist academically superior junior, senior, and graduate students in the forthcoming years. That scholarship, announced by Sayler, was the largest scholarship fund created by such a campaign in Northwest's seventy-two year history, and it also displayed a fine pulling together by the Alumni Association for something this man seemed to want most. Both he and Mrs. Foster, to be sure, were genuinely moved by the concentrated effort. The two were also deeply affected earlier when they were presented with a bound volume of some 200 letters from alumni, friends, and colleagues expressing their appreciation of the Fosters' leadership and service to Northwest.

On Thursday afternoon June 30, 1977, President Foster walked out of his office for the last time as head of Northwest Missouri State University. Most people readily agreed that he, like his predecessor Dr. J. W. Jones, was leaving the University a much better place than he had found it. A significant share of the improvement, however, most likely would have come about under any capable administrator. In paying homage to his service, there was a tendency for extollers to exaggerate the accomplishments of the President while ignoring or minimizing the success of top assistants—like a Mees or a Thate—faculty, regents, leaders of the student body, the alumni, friends, and even the legislature. Foster publicly recognized the fact at numerous times. At his retirement dinner, he expressed his appreciation for the above's support, and the honoree praised Mrs. Foster's devotion and dedication and Mrs. Monica Zirfas, his administrative assistant, for her efficiency and control over the years as his aide.

Foster strengthened Northwest Missouri State University during his thirteen-year stay as President. He was instrumental in the nearly $15,000,000 in capital improvements and saw Northwest rise from college to university status. Many buildings, always an outward sign of progress, were added during those thirteen years, including the Garrett-Strong Science Building, the Donald N. Valk Industrial Arts and Technology Building, the four high-rise residence halls and their dining facility, the Memorial Bell Tower, the Agriculture Mechanics Laboratory, the Dairy Barn and numerous farm buildings, the J. W. Jones Union addition, as well as a complete renovation of Martindale Gymnasium and extensive remodeling of Lamkin Gymnasium and Colden Hall. Extensive improvements were also completed, and more were under way at his retirement on Northwest's favorite lady—the Administration Building. Most pleasant to Foster was Northwest's excellent art department, the development and expansion of the radio and television facilities, the evolution of the agriculture program, and the growth of the business department. Foster's and Cathran Cushman's long and hard efforts to secure funding, much of it from federal sources, for the creation of KXCV-FM were legendary on campus. In

1977 there were 135 students majoring in broadcasting, and the 100,000 watt station served the region with informational, educational, and culturally enriching programs nearly 130 hours a week. Agriculture, in addition to its various new buildings, increased its land holdings tremendously, acquired and increased its beef and dairy herds, and from 1964 to 1977 multiplied its student majors from twenty-three to 365 and received accreditation for vocational agriculture.

Because of his interest in academics—as evidenced by the many new undergraduate and degree offerings—Foster originated the NWMSU Educational Foundation. Due to his leadership in the Foundation, nearly $29,000 in scholarships was granted to university students, and, by reason of his efforts, over sixty restricted scholarships were available through the Foundation, which at the time of Foster's retirement had a total income of $345,245.

Foster, to be sure, witnessed much growth and advancement in many areas: his administration experienced most active physical and academic developments, and his adminstration confronted some of the most difficult times in the University's history. In the sixties and the seventies, there were many more problems than had been the case in Northwest's earlier history. Considering how central to our society our universities and colleges had become, Foster could draw a great deal of satisfaction from his thirteen-year presidency and his reputation was enhanced because of it. He demonstrated, during his tenure, qualities of adaptability and durability—the latter probably not possible without the former.

Orval Heywood

President B. D. Owens
1977-

5

A Continued Search for Excellence, 1977-1980

Its courts are ravaged; but the tower
Is standing with a voice of power . . .

—Wordsworth

Although serious problems persisted in the United States in the middle of 1977, a sense of well-being and community spirit seemed to pervade. Across the country, charities reported sharp increases in donations of all kinds. People seemed to feel confident and relaxed about the future. Certainly the wounds of Vietnam and Watergate were healing. For the future, there was the belief that America would mediate, not interfere in remote foreign fights. The issues of inflation, unemployment, energy, and taxes were worrisome to Americans, but concerns about far-off Russia or Africa were low on most people's worry list. Despite the damages of inflation, the American family's median income rose in 1977, and 92,000,000 Americans were working, up from 86,000,000 in 1974. Students continued to be concerned about grades and jobs. Corporate recruiters drew record crowds of students and had many job prospects for spring and summer graduates. Although marijuana was common, alcohol was the principal drug of abuse among the young. Student demonstrations were now a rarity. Political issues really did not seem to bother the students of 1977. It was as if they were saying, "We need a break. Let us go about without feeling a sense of remorse." The nation seemed to be experiencing a gentle, easy mood.

Friday, July 1, 1977, was a gentle and calm day as Northwest's eighth president, Dr. B. D. Owens, officially began his leadership duties. Adding a touch of Florida with his yellow slacks, blue blazer, and white shoes, he appeared as gentle and calm and relaxed as the Northwest Missouri weather. He seemed confident and ready to face Northwest's immediate and future priorities.

President Owens' highest priorities were in organizational planning and in filling the position of vice president for academic affairs, made vacant in the spring when Dr. John Paul Mees was appointed vice president for student development. The Vice President for Academic

Affairs Search and Screening Committee had its four finalists, as promised, and President Owens agreed with the Committee's top choices. Two candidates were immediately brought to campus for interviews, and, one of them, Dr. George English, was invited back a second time with his family. Between his two visits, however, selected members of the Committee visited the campus at Indiana's University of Evansville where English was dean of the School of Arts and Sciences for nine years and held the academic title of professor of political science. There the visitors studied the man in his ambience and talked with approximately forty campus people who could comment on English's work and character. Before the visits began, English had emerged as the Committee's first choice among the final four, and the visit to Evansville did nothing to diminish that choice. He possessed an abundance of administrative and teaching experience in higher education and certainly met the Committee's criteria. It was also evident that English was the man Owens wanted, and he was offered a contract upon his second visit to Northwest. Before July ended, President Owens had taken care of one of his first priorities.

And before Owens' first month as president was over, the initial steps in the planned $616,000 Phase III portion of remodeling the Administration Building were under way. Much scurrying about was taking place as various personnel offices were relocated. The major and final thrust of Phase III, the remodeling of the theater facilities, would soon begin. Fall semester students, to be sure, would at first have problems finding certain offices, like the registrar's, since it was moved to the second floor while the President's Office was moved across the hall to the rooms left vacant by Registrar Martha Cooper and her staff.

One structure that pleased the fall students, however, was Rickenbrode Stadium. The student section, called the east bleachers, was moved back from the track and elevated in July to allow fans a better view of the gridiron. No more would the spectators have to worry about splinters and chipped paint because the wooden boards were replaced by aluminum planks. The players also had the advantage of performing on lush grass as a result of the Stadium's underground irrigation system, also installed in July.

August is usually a quiet month on any campus, but several important changes dotted Northwest's calendar during the month. The announcement that Bob Cotter, the popular director of alumni affairs, was resigning to enter the field of bank management initiated August, and Dean of Admissions Bob Bush's appointment to the position of assistant to the president culminated it. On August 12, President Owens had his initial meeting with the Board of Regents and participated in his first commencement as president of Northwest. One decision that would definitely affect students' palates was made during the day's meeting. Northwest decided to end its traditional operation of food services and accepted a bid from SAGA Food Services, a national firm with professional food management techniques, to operate the campus dining areas. For an institution of higher learning, Northwest's move was not an unusual one. Universities and colleges throughout the country had been employing professional food vendors because they were more economically feasible. The arrangement with SAGA existed until the summer of 1980 when the University, after extensive study, replaced SAGA with ARA, one of the nation's largest food service companies. Northwest administrators found the ARA bid captivating, and students were anticipatory since ARA would offer a cornucopia of eleven entrées for the same price as the four entrées offered by most services. Enticing, too, was ARA's promise to establish a delicatessen and to assist in the renovation of the third floor cafeteria in the J. W. Jones Student Union. Pleasing to Owens was the new food company's commitment to student recruitment and retention.

Probably the most important announcement during Owens' second month in office was the agreement between Northwest Missouri State University and Missouri Western State College to open a Graduate Center on the Missouri Western campus in St. Joseph for the following spring semester. Northwest since 1969 had offered graduate work as "off-campus" classes at St. Joseph's Lafayette High School. The program was called the St. Joseph Graduate Center, but in 1974 state appropriations for off-campus courses ceased. That year the Missouri Legislature closed Central Missouri State's Residence Center in Independence and assigned it to the University of Missouri system. Because of Central's deleterious habit of including in its total enrollment those students taking classes at the Independence Center, the Missouri Legislature decided not to supply funds for off-campus courses. Northwest then received no state funding because its St. Joseph Center was regarded as an off-campus offering and, as a result of the move by the Legislature, was compelled to publicly drop the name St. Joseph Graduate Center and call the program NWMSU Graduate Classes at Lafayette High School in St. Joseph. Northwest and the St. Joseph Public Schools closely cooperated as the University offered St. Joseph area students graduate courses in both business and education. Northwest's graduate arrangement with Lafayette High School effectively ended, however, with the establishment of the University's Graduate Center on the Missouri Western campus. The momentous decision to launch the program to bring graduate education to St. Joseph was announced at a press conference on the Missouri Western campus on August 19, and both presidents, Owens and Looney, were there representing their respective institutions. President Looney announced that the "MWSC Graduate Studies Center, within whose framework the Northwest Missouri State University Graduate Center will operate, is being planned so we can better serve the community." President Owens commented that the Graduate Center would allow Northwest "to assist Missouri Western develop its library with graduate-level holdings and utilize college classroom and laboratory space not currently being used in the evenings." In the beginning, however, Northwest, as part of the agreement, furnished the library resources for the Graduate Center. Both presidents praised the action as an attempt to solve individual problems at both schools. The cooperative plan, to be sure, helped eliminate unnecessary duplication of educational programs and offered better utilization of facilities, in addition to educing greater cooperation between two institutions in such proximity with one another. The program was coordinated and administered by Northwest's Graduate Dean Leon Miller, and, as President Owens explained, persons in the St. Joseph area could expect the same high quality graduate work as that offered on the Northwest campus. The cooperative plan was especially gratifying to Owens because it was in keeping with his educational philosophy to bring quality education at less cost to the taxpayers. Approximately 200 students enrolled the first spring that the courses were offered on Missouri Western's campus, and the fall of 1979 saw the largest number to date with 235 students.

When the 1977 fall semester students returned, they found that the traditional street dance, sponsored by the Maryville merchants, no longer existed. The students did find, however, a new kind of welcome that was designed to help their budgets. Each Northwest enrollee received from members of the Greater Maryville Association of the Maryville Chamber of Commerce a coupon "get-acquainted-with-Maryville" booklet. Most students were pleased with each of their thirty coupons, which gave them a useful gift or a sizable discount on a purchase at one of the city's participating stores. The fine gesture by the Greater Maryville Association showed that a large part of Maryville, at least, recognized that the University's students are a vital part of the community, and, of course, a student who began his school year with a possible thirty acquisitions was very apt to return to the stores that welcomed him.

The University, like the city of Maryville, was offering a different kind of welcome, too, during the days and nights immediately preceding the beginning of classes. Students could find a myriad of activities, coordinated by Director of Student Activities Irene Huk. Recognizing that students would miss the popular street dance, Mrs. Huk initiated a street dance at the parking lot behind the high-rise residence halls. In past years a sure signal that the fall semester was ready to begin was the faculty-student picnic in University Park, but a faculty-student dinner in the Student Union Cafeteria now replaced the picnic. The new dining activity proved popular and will probably continue.

Since President Owens was ensconced in his position at the top of Northwest's hierarchy, plans were under way early in September for his inauguration as the University's eighth president. The event would be known as "Inauguration Week," and the activities which would begin on Sunday, November 13, were being planned by a broad-based inauguration committee, composed of faculty, staff, alumni, students, and area citizens. The "Week" was beginning to generate much talk and enthusiasm by university and community people because of the wide variety of activities that it promised to bring.

During the middle of September, various students could be observed studying moving vehicles on campus. From sixteen different watchpoints across campus, fraternity and sorority members of Alpha Kappa Lambda, Delta Chi, Delta Sigma Phi, Phi Sigma Epsilon, Sigma Tau Gamma, Tau Kappa Epsilon, and Phi Mu were noting the number of vehicles passing their stations and charting information about them. The members of the Greek organizations were not pledges involved in a "hell week," but they were conducting a traffic analysis for the University under the direction of the Bishop Engineering Company of Kansas City. The students became a familiar sight as they manned their stations for a week. Their survey aided Northwest in implementing a new campus traffic plan one year later. Driving patterns were altered drastically by rerouting much of the through traffic to the perimeters of the campus and by creating several one-way streets. The new plan, to be sure, protects pedestrians and minimizes traffic hazards since traffic through the campus is greatly reduced. Drivers, not accustomed to the new pattern, generally reacted negatively, as some still do, when confronted with their seemingly circuitous route. Another group of students, composed of both men and women, was highly visible in the fall. Circle K, born in September of 1977, was engaged in projects that helped both the campus and the community. Sponsored by Don Carlile, director of placement and career planning, and Perry Echelberger, KXCV-FM operations manager, the organization made such an imprint with its worthy contributions that in April, seven months after its birth on campus, it was honored with the Outstanding Club of the District Award.

Dr. Don Petry, executive vice president, offering no less a surprise than Bob Cotter's earlier decision, submitted his resignation to President Owens on September 19. Dr. Petry, a holder of several and variegated administrative positions while at Northwest, offered no specific reason for his resignation. Petry's office was duly eliminated, and his fiscal responsibilities were assumed by Business Manager Don Henry. Dr. George English, vice president for academic affairs, and Dr. John Paul Mees, vice president for student development, divided Petry's other areas of responsibilities. Mr. Bob Brought, director of the physical plant, followed Petry's resignation path in October, and President Owens' assistant, Dr. Bob Bush, assumed, along with his presidential aide duties, the administrative responsibility of the physical plant operation. Under Bush's direction, the physical plant organization underwent a streamlining. As a result, much more campus construction has been done by university personnel, thus helping Northwest economize. Other appointments, besides Bush's, were made in October. Vincent "Vinnie" Vaccaro was named to replace Bob Cotter. With his new position, Vaccaro, a 1973 Northwest alumnus who had been teaching English and speech at Lafayette High School in St. Joseph since his graduation, also assumed a new university title— executive secretary of alumni relations. Vaccaro's selection ended a two-month search which involved approximately thirty candidates. The affable Dr. Pete Jackson left his duties as chairman of industrial arts and technology to Dr. Herman Collins to become associate dean of faculties. Included with this position for Dr. Jackson was a quartet of directorships: summer school, vocational education, special workshops, and continuing education. Although Jackson relinquished his chair duties for the newly created position as Dr. English's assistant, he retains his professorship and continues to teach one class each semester. In another change, Mr. Don Henry, former business manager, was named university treasurer, overseeing all institutional financial matters.

A popular tradition was resurrected, and another tradition was born during the 1977 Homecoming weekend. President Owens and Student Body President Rex Gwinn from Des Moines, Iowa, rang the Victory Bell on Friday, October 21, precisely at the time when eight o'clock classes would have been convening. When Walkout Day existed on campus from 1915 to 1971, when it was replaced by Joe Toker Daze, students were not apprised of the date the holiday would occur. For several days they would exude with happy anticipation as they went to their first hour classes, and when they finally heard the pealing of the Bell they seemed to be captured by their verve. The two presidents' action actually joined two traditions: the former and older Walkout Day, and the more recent one of dismissing classes the day prior to homecoming to permit students time to prepare for the festivities. The anticipation and suspense of past walkout days are gone, but students are happy to use the day to work on homecoming decorations and parade entries and to have an early jump on the varied activities that the celebration usually brings. Walkout Day is secure again, and the day—the Friday preceding homecoming—is designated on the academic calendar. Miss Bernice Howard and Mr. Fred Street, both 1927 alumni, conceived one of the outstanding events for the 1977 Homecoming—a Golden Anniversary reunion of the class of 1927. Their idea fructified into Northwest's first fifty-year class reunion, and 1980 Homecoming officials are planning for the fourth such gathering, while members of the 1930 class anticipate their October return to Northwest.

The Victory Bell was quiet on Sunday, November 13, but the usual church bells were ringing, calling worshipers to services. Surprising some parishioners, the bells were tolled again at noon to signal the beginning of Inaugural Week at Northwest Missouri State University, climaxing with President Owens' inauguration during the Inaugural Convocation on Friday, November 18. It was an unbelievable and fascinating week of educational experiences for students, faculty, staff, alumni, and area residents that emphasized Northwest's rich heritage. Organized by a steering committee and its fifteen subcommittees under the general direction of Assistant to the President Bob Bush, the Week's activities included approximately sixty events, featuring lectures, seminars, concerts, theater productions, music clinics, art and historical exhibits, a communications festival, a marathon dance, the installation of the Missouri Epsilon chapter of Pi Mu Epsilon, national honorary mathematics fraternity, luncheons, receptions, and the capstone—the Inaugural Convocation. Many universally known people participated in Inauguration Week activities. Earth scientist Dr. Robert A. Dietz, one of the co-founders of the plate tectonics theory participated; United States Senator Thomas Eagleton served on a panel discussing the problems of farmers, and on the same panel was Oren Lee Staley, then president of the National Farmers Organization; Warren Lebeck, the retired president of the Chicago Board of Trade spoke at an Inaugural Week Farm-City Banquet. Colonel Harland Sanders, the eighty-seven-year-old fried chicken patriarch and a personal friend of President Owens, appeared in his familiar white suit and black tie to speak at a Boy Scout Leader dinner. In addition to the above, other leaders in education, business, and politics, including many of Northwest's alumni, like Dr. J. D. Hammond, shared their knowledge during the week.

The Week's functions, to be sure, were directed toward knowledge and entertainment for students, faculty, staff, and the general public. Following the theme, "The University's Heritage: Margin for Excellence," the activities helped stress Northwest's seventy-two-year heritage by calling attention to the past and to the present. Ceremonial objects are important in historical happenings, and Northwest would have its share of those because of the diligent work of three members of the art department: Chairman Bob Sunkel, Mr. Lee Hageman, and Mr. Phillip VanVoorst. As heavily involved in inauguration plans as anyone on campus, the three were engrossed with their own activities— the design and creation of a mace and a presidential chain-of-office. Once a weapon of the Middle Ages, the mace has developed into a symbol of authority for many academic institutions. It was time for tradition-conscious Northwest Missouri State University to have one of its own. Realizing this, the trio worked cooperatively on the mace for approximately three months. Their concerted efforts left Northwest with a concrete symbol of authority and an embodiment of aspects of the University's heritage. The forty-two-inch-long twenty-pound mace, made of modern pewter, silver, gold, and walnut, also symbolizes the torch of learning, for each of its three blades depicts an era in the growth of Northwest—one represents the Fifth District Normal School, 1905-1919; another, Northwest Missouri State Teachers College, 1919-1949; and the third, Northwest Missouri State College, 1949-1972. The design of the octagonal form in the center of the mace-head is derived from one of the turrets on the Administration Building. Completing the symbolic reference to the University's historic development is the official seal of Northwest in an appropriate setting on the top of that form. Because of Sunkel's, Hageman's, and VanVoorst's interest and creativity, the mace, seen at all formal, academic ceremonies, already has found its niche in Northwest's tradition.

Another effort by the three art professors produced a presidential chain-of-office, symbolizing the office of President of the institution. The medallion is similar to the center form of the university mace, for it contains the seal of the University in an octagonal frame obtained from the design of a turret on the Administration Building. On the rectangular links of the chain-of-office are engraved names of President Owens' seven presidential predecessors and the years they served. President Owens' name anchors the eight and indicates the year he assumed office.

The formal Inaugural Convocation in Lamkin Gymnasium on Friday, November 18, was a solemn and traditional one indelibly etched in Northwest's history. People came to pay their respects to the University's eighth president, and most of them went away with a renewed and strengthened pride in the institution. What they saw and what they heard that morning were not easily forgotten. Following the colors, Lee Hageman, carrying the mace he helped create, led the colorful and earnest procession of the representatives of learned and professional societies, the delegates of universities and colleges, the faculty and administration, the presidential party, the presidential chain-of-office bearer VanVoorst, and the President into the darkened gymnasium to the music of *Academic Procession,* played by the University Symphonic Band. A definite part of the colorful pageantry was the new academic regalia worn by the Regents and President Owens. Their green robes, hoods, and caps added a renaissance quality. Since the gymnasium was darkened to spotlight the mace and the colors, much of the colorful raiment in the procession was lost to observers.

This tradition-oriented Inauguration Convocation will be remembered for introducing the university mace and the presidential chain-of-office and for initiating the Distinguished Service Award, an honor which recognizes service to mankind, higher education, and the State of Missouri. Immediately preceding the President's oath of office, eleven persons were honored with the Awards, again designed and created by Sunkel, Hageman, and VanVoorst. President Emeritus J. W. Jones was presented Northwest's first Distinguished Service Award, and the long, appreciative applause from the audience was gratifying to the sixth president of the University and to Mrs. Jones. Ironically, Mr. E. D. Geyer, the 1977 president of the Board of Regents who presided at the Inaugural Convocation and helped present the Distinguished Service Awards, received one himself in 1980. Another tradition began on November 18, when Dr. Elwyn DeVore was selected as the grand marshal and Dr. Burton Richey, Dr. Frances Shipley, and Mr. Bob Sunkel as associate marshals, setting another precedent for future academic processions. After receiving the oath of office from Missouri Supreme Court Justice J. P. Morgan, a pledge written especially for the occasion by Morgan, President Owens responded by pledging his best teaching and leadership efforts to further the objectives of Northwest Missouri State University in its continued educational service as one of the country's finest universities. He challenged his faculty and staff by stating, "This University is moving forward. For those in our academic community who do not feel the momentum, I invite you to first carefully examine your own personal and professional goals. I invite you to discuss with your colleagues and students the challenges, ideas, and excitement left with us by the interaction of symposia participants and special guests this week." In addition to a packed gymnasium of area citizens, special guests, students, faculty, and administration, a special quartet, seated in the front row, were looking up admiringly and listening proudly as the President was speaking. Mrs. Sue Owens, Mrs. A. L. Owens, Brent and Kevin Owens were seeing him not only as the first alumnus of Northwest to serve as its president but as a husband, a son, and a father. It was obvious, too, that Owens wanted to rededicate Northwest to the challenges of the future as he further stated, "It will be the responsibility of all of us to build on the University's heritage for the future. We are starting with a margin of excellence." Observers were then treated to the University Chorale's singing of Howard Hanson's *Song of Democracy,* a composition personally selected by the President and presented at his inaugural at the University of Tampa. At the end of the recessional, participants were given memorial medallions as mementos of the occasion.

Following the Inaugural Convocation, 500 people attended a Luncheon in the Student Union Ballroom, and afterward over 1,000 persons came to greet President and Mrs. Owens at an Inaugural Reception in the lounge of the Union. That night many of the Inauguration Convocation participants attended the department of speech and theater's production of *Summertree* with seven student cast members and directed by Dr. Charles Schultz. Cast members were dumbfounded to see the President visit one of their rehearsals and were happy when he and Mrs. Owens attended Saturday night's performance.

Of course, Inauguration Week and the Convocation itself generated some complaints by the usual pessimists. They complained about the expense. Most of the doubters stopped grumbling when they discovered that the expenses for the Week were minimal and that the various committees assigned to the Inauguration were operating on shoestring budgets. Many of the speakers were obtained through the various academic departments' assembly budgets or through grants, and some speakers even refused to accept a fee. The media attention Northwest received made any Inauguration costs seem insignificant. The largest costs were the mace and the personal invitations sent to each of Northwest's students. The mace-head, covered by thin plates of silver and gold, is very valuable in 1980, and the students, receiving those invitations in the mail, felt as if they had been treated with the same rights and privileges as the dignitaries who were invited. The Inauguration was a vehicle for making people aware of the heritage, the strength, and the service role of Northwest as it focused on traditions, symbols, the alumni, and the element of ceremony so important in the world of academe. It, to be sure, set a guidepost of standards, a tone, and an example for Northwest's future.

The women of Millikan Residence Hall helped close Inauguration Week, one of the biggest weeks in the University's history, by sponsoring a twenty-four-hour marathon dance for muscular dystrophy on November 18-19. President Owens and Mrs. Owens, tired but happy, were there to initiate the endurance contest by dancing the first number. The dancers solicited pledges from sponsors for each hour they danced, and a dozen couples were still on their feet when the extravaganza was over. Occasional rest and eating breaks were programmed into the event for the dancers. The participants had an additional treat, for Steve Carpenter, a 1977 alumnus and music director of Radio Station KKJO, St. Joseph, donated his services to act as the disc jockey for the marathon. The marathon is now part of Northwest's lore, and Carpenter continues as part of that tradition. Because of the dancers' efforts and other groups' interest, over $6,000 was raised for the battle against muscular dystrophy. The local chapter of Blue Key, national honorary fraternity, was the largest contributor with $777.77. Offering their own version of a marathon by-walking thirty miles to Savannah, Missouri, eleven members received pledges from sponsors for each mile they walked. For the collective 315 miles the men walked on Sunday, October 30, they received from the women of Millikan Hall a large trophy that dwells in a display case in Colden Hall. For two of the men, the walkathon was their second consecutive venture. In 1976, eight of the fraternity made the same walk on Halloween Day and gained $444.44 for the Youth Association for Retarded Citizens (YARC). Steve Carpenter, incidentally, was a member of the 1976 travelers to Savannah.

As a participant in an inaugural week symposium, Leigh Wilson, president of the Maryville Industrial Development Corporation, discussed how the University benefited from Maryville's industries such as Uniroyal, Union Carbide, Riegel Textile, and Lloyd Chain. Late in November, an action by Union Carbide seemed to offer substance to Wilson's comments when the company presented a $2,500 gift to Northwest to be used for scholarships. Of course, industries here recognize that they also benefit from the University as evidenced by Northwest's Master of Business Administration degree and the programs for plant maintenance personnel offered by the department of industrial arts and technology.

In late November each year, Bearcat and Bearkitten basketball fans anticipate a tournament that began in 1976. Known as the Ryland

Milner Invitational Tournament, it features men's and women's collegiate competition in the game which Mr. Milner played and coached so admirably. In 1977, Coach Larry Holley, in his first year as Bearcat coach, directed his men to the tournament title, and Coach John Poulson followed suit with the Bearkittens. The titles were appealing to Mr. Milner, but almost as satisfying to him was the selection of Bearkitten Janet Cooksey, a senior mainstay, as the women's Most Valuable Player for the second consecutive year.

On December 13, the tournament spectators, along with the rest of the nation, were dispirited to learn that the fourteen-member basketball team from the University of Evansville, Indiana, and its coach, along with fourteen other passengers, were killed when their chartered airplane crashed in rain and fog upon takeoff on its way to a game. Another disaster involving students also occurred on the same day as the Evansville tragedy when seven students were killed in a fire on the top floor of a women's dormitory at Providence College in Rhode Island. Since the building had neither fire escapes nor a sprinkler system, the Providence College fire caused many university and college officials throughout the country to eliminate potential fire hazards in their student buildings.

Humans become old and die; computers become obsolete and are replaced. After months of preparation by the University's physical plant employees in installing cables and power sources, the PDP 11-70 replaced, in early 1978, the older IBM 360-30, the main computer used by Northwest since the mid 1960s. The two belong to the computer family, but the new acquisition left Dr. Jon Rickman, director of computing services and data processing, with the warm feeling that he had just acquired the talents of a Julius Erving in place of an uncoordinated junior high basketball player. The PDP 11-70 seems to match the wizardry and the versatility for which Erving is known. Located in the Administration Building, the PDP 11-70 was connected with terminals for student and faculty use in an adjacent room, in the Garrett-Strong Science Building, Colden Hall, the Learning Resources Center, the Valk Industrial Arts and Technology Building, and in the Horace Mann Learning Center. Sixty-three terminals can be hooked into the PDP 11-70 via telephone lines, and the computer can respond simultaneously to each of the terminals. Installed principally to serve the needs of the academic community, as well as others, the PDP 11-70 offers an unlimited number of practical uses, and because of this sophisticated equipment Northwest possesses one of the best academic computer network facilities in Missouri.

Top-name personalities continued to come to campus, and this seemed to be the year for women. Nikki Giovanni, noted black poet, aroused the emotions of participants in Black Culture Week on campus early in February, and Judy Carter, daughter-in-law of President Carter, discussed the Equal Rights Amendment in January to people who were both favorable and unfavorable to its adoption in Missouri. A video tape of her talk was played on March 14-16, as part of Awareness Week at Northwest, a program designed for both men and women to gain an understanding of the changing role of women in society. Positive changes for the two minorities—blacks and women—were the two women's major concern. In 1969, millions of television viewers watched the first man—Neil Armstrong—walk on the moon. Neil Armstrong did not arrive on campus, but another famous moon walker James Irwin, Apollo 15 astronaut, had no trouble finding the University. His talk, his display of moon rocks, and the film clips of his journey to the moon proved to be entertaining as well as informative. Members of the geology department, Drs. David Cargo, Bob Mallory, and Dwight Maxwell (the man instrumental in obtaining Irwin), found that their students were appreciative of Irwin's knowledge, experience, and the time he spent with them. The University's Performing Arts and Lecture Series, now chaired by mathematics' Dr. David Bahnemann, who recently succeeded Dr. Richard Fulton of the political science department, remains as the principal agency for bringing talented performers to Northwest.

North America experienced the worst weather extremes in the twentieth century during the winter of 1977-1978 as the North, East, and South suffered through a record cold winter, and the Far West underwent a drought that brought severe water rationing to much of Northern California. Buffalo, New York, experienced savage storms, and Northwest Missouri had its share of cold and snow. Because of the severe weather, something extraordinary happened at Northwest on Monday, February 13. School was dismissed! Classes had not been canceled at Northwest because of adverse weather conditions since 1912. A foot-deep snow that effectively immobilized the faculty and administration, however, made President Owens' early morning decision a plausible one. The residence hall students, obviously hearkening back to their childhood days, busied themselves not with books but with building snowmen, sledding, and participating in snowball fights. The city declared an emergency, and the town square of Maryville had a ghostly aura since only two shopkeepers were open for business that memorable morning.

When Dr. George English was being interviewed for the vice-president for academic affairs position the previous July, he stated to administrative officials, faculty, and students that if he assumed that top academic post he would begin immediately to reorganize Northwest's academic structure. Reorganization was indeed one of the president's urgent concerns, and both administrators felt that twenty-six academic organizations, with the same number of chairmen, were too unwieldy to operate in a university structure. Reorganization had its inception six weeks after Vice President English began his duties when a sixteen-member faculty and staff Reorganization Committee, chaired by Dr. Pete Jackson, was appointed by Owens to study the University's academic structure and to make recommendations concerning revisions. In appointing the Committee, Owens called for progress reports and asked the group to have its final report by February. The Reorganization Committee was ready, and it forwarded three plans and held hearings before the faculty and staff concerning those plans. The members of the Committee felt that there were too many structural changes in the academic area during the past ten years, and, because the various changes brought problems in monitoring and job definition, the University needed a more stable structure. The plan finally approved by Owens, English, and the Board of Regents on March 15 is a refinement of the Committee's three plans. No longer would top administrative officials, like Vice President English, have to contend with a many-headed academic construct. The ten created academic units that became operable on July 1, 1978, in addition to the graduate school, are the Division of Fine Arts (art, music, drama); College of Education (secondary and elementary education, student teaching, library science, and administration of the Horace Mann Learning Center); School of Business Administration (accounting, economics, finance. business management, office administration, and marketing); Division of Health, Physical Education and Recreation (men's and women's physical education); Division of History and Humanities (history, humanities, philosophy, foreign languages, and religious education); Division of Behavioral Science (psychology-sociology and political science); Division of Communications (English, speech, with their programs of journalism, radio, and television); College of Applied Science and Agriculture (agriculture, industrial arts education and technology, home economics, and nursing); Division of Mathematics and Computer Science; and the Division of Sciences (biology, chemistry, physics, geology and geography). Military science (ROTC), courted but not yet born on campus, would be added to the College of Applied Science and Agriculture in the summer. No academic disciplines were eliminated with the reorganization, but some found themselves designated as programs within a department or division. Most of the disciplines, like geology and geography, fit snugly into their new areas, but foreign languages seemed to be a strange bedfellow in joining the Division of History and Humanities. Foreign languages, formerly a department but now a program, adapted well, however, and appears to be flourishing in its ambience.

Another administrative matter was completed, but Dr. English was faced with the task of finding heads for those academic units. Not known for hesitation, English had most of the positions filled by early May. In the decision making, however, he asked the members of the existing twenty-six departments to aid him in the selection process. The departments were represented by their own individual committees whose members were elected by their peers, and, after many grueling meetings, they finally submitted their choices to Dr. English, who then made his decision on eight of the positions and submitted his candidates to President Owens and the Board of Regents. Both approved, and the following persons named to head their respective division, school, or college were at the time chairmen of academic departments: the Division of Fine Arts, Mr. Bob Sunkel; the College of Education, Dr. Dean Savage; the School of Business Administration, Dr. Elwyn DeVore; the Division of Health, Physical Education and Recreation, Dr. Burton Richey; the Division of History and Humanities, Dr. John Harr; the Division of Communications, Dr. Bob Bohlken; the Division of Mathematics and Computer Science, Dr. Morton Kenner; and the Division of Sciences, Dr. David Smith. The Division of Behavioral Science and the College of Applied Science and Agriculture appeared rudderless, unlike their academic cousins who possessed leaders, but Dr. English temporarily filled the void himself for the behavioral scientists until Dr. Eugene Galluscio arrived to assume the position at the beginning of the 1979 spring semester. Dr. Pete Jackson filled in for the College of Applied Science and Agriculture until Mr. Joe Garrett from agriculture was designated to lead it in 1980. Two sidelights emerged from the above selections: Dr. Galluscio was the only one who was chosen from outside the University, and Dr. Harr retired the following year, relinquishing his reins to former student Dr. Harmon Mothershead, professor of history. Department chairmen within the ten major units were to be selected by the new heads.

Reorganization and the selection of the heads of the ten academic units were the favorite topics of conversation among most members of the faculty and the administration during the spring semester, but Dean Leon Miller's preferred subject was the "Self-Study" and the North Central Association's impending visit again in March. He and Dr. Merle Lesher, a professor of secondary education, compiled the

"Self-Study" that gave an overall view of all aspects of the institution. Members of the NCA team carefully perused the study and talked with students, faculty, administrators, and staff during their three-day evaluation period on campus. Northwest, of course, received its continued accreditation, but the visitors were especially laudatory, an element lacking in the 1974 visit when the group scolded Northwest for its cooperative venture with the Elba Corporation. That 1974 visit, however, did elicit praise for Northwest's graduate program when it gained final NCA approval. The 1978 NCA evaluators commended the record of the Placement Service, the individual attention that faculty members gave students, and the new nursing program. The Library's progress in the last four years ranked high on the NCA commendatory list. The NCA members were impressed, too, with the favorable attitude of Northwest's students, but they felt that too many students showed a disinterest in the intercollegiate athletic program. And, like any valid evaluating team, the group did have some other concerns: a need for more clerical help, more research among the faculty, better maintenance of the older dormitories, and further remodeling of the Union.

Sports proved to be an intriguing interlude from the academic life late in the spring semester. It had been some time since Northwest named anything for one of its most illustrious members, but on April 1, 1978, the late Herschel Neil, Northwest's most famous track and field athlete, was honored by the University when its new all-weather track was officially named for him at the second annual Northwest Invitational Track and Field Meet. During his four-year track career at Northwest from 1934-1937, Neil won seventeen individual MIAA titles and set eight school records. Many national followers of track in 1936 knew about Northwest because of Neil's exploits in the Olympic Trials in New York. Competing in the triple jump against the legendary Jesse Owens, Neil finished fourth, but Owens, who later won five gold medals in the 1936 Olympics at Berlin, felt that Neil was really the better jumper that day. What Owens saw on Neil's first leap was a distance of almost fifty-one feet, a mark that would have won the event for the Bearcat All-American, who was the 1936 NCAA Champion in the triple jump. Owens was relieved when officials judged Neil's first attempt a foul and disallowed his jump. President Owens formally dedicated the track, The Herschel Neil Track, at a 7 p.m. ceremony in the Rickenbrode Stadium and Athletic Field. It was a poignant scene as Neil's mother Bessie, his daughter Mrs. Theresa Brennen, his brothers Don and Max, and his sister Dorothy Neil Ellis participated in the formalities. Members of the Bearcat and Bearkitten track teams quietly observed, offering, it seemed, collective thoughts of the finest track competitor in Northwest history. Blue Springs High School in Blue Springs, Missouri, where Neil was principal for six years until his death in 1961, obviously held the same affection for him as his alma mater did. In 1973, the new gymnasium at the school was named in his honor.

Although the Bearkitten basketball team was eliminated in regional play after completing a 20-8 regular season and finishing second in state tournament competition, the women proved they could compete against the nation's major basketball powers. In a close thriller, the Bearkittens lost 66-63 in the first round of regional play to the nationally ranked University of Kansas Lady Jayhawks. Glen Zenor, a senior from Cedar Rapids, Iowa, brought, during his four-year wrestling career, many smiles to George Worley's face, the usually stolid coach who was completing his last year as the wrestling mentor. Zenor finished sixth in the NCAA Division II rankings and earned All-American honors, the first wrestling All-American at Northwest since Stan Zeamer in 1970. Parnell, Missouri's junior Julie Schmitz, seemed to be Zenor's female counterpart in gaining honors. Schmitz, named the outstanding track individual at the Northwest Invitational Track and Field Meet on April 1, when The Herschel Neil Track was dedicated, won first place in the 400-meter hurdles at the thirty-one team AIAW Region VI Small College Division Meet and helped Coach Laurie Meyers Potter's team garner seventh place. Schmitz, incidentally, is well remembered in Bearkitten basketball history as the all-time assist leader.

Dr. John Harr, known on campus as the history professor and chairman who ran five miles daily, was quickly approaching the Northwest Jogging Club's record of 5,000 miles, a mark he reached in October. Harr, incidentally, will be inducted in the fall of 1980 to the Wisconsin Hall of Fame for his football and track exploits while an undergraduate at the University of Wisconsin at LaCrosse. He was not being singled out in late March or early April, however, for his running endeavors. Harr's department was hosting the twentieth annual Missouri Conference on History, and it was named in his honor. The Conference, coordinated by Dr. Roger Corley, associate professor of history, was designed to provide a forum for scholars in Missouri and neighboring states. Harr's fellow historian the noted Dr. John Hope Franklin, a professor of history at the University of Chicago and the country's most outstanding historian of Black America, was the Conference's principal speaker.

Sports Information Director Mike Kiser's 1977-1978 *Bearcat*

Basketball Guide was rated the best among the nationwide small college entries and seventh overall from more than 250 entries in the major university and small college category in the second annual *Basketball Press Guide Review*. The award was Kiser's twelfth national honor in compiling and editing Bearcat and Bearkitten brochures in his eight years at Northwest. The baseball team did not win its usual twenty or more games, but Coach Wasem's men won the MIAA championship again and finished second in regional play. Wasem, known for his leadership qualities and deft control of tight close-game situations, found that he could not control one facet of Bearcat baseball destiny— the weather. The 1978 schedule was limited as he and his team, the winners of eighteen games, lost twenty contests to adverse weather conditions. An unrecorded win for the team came early in May when the senior class offered its traditional class gift with funds designated to purchase a suitable baseball scoreboard. Golf Coach Bob Gregory, Swimming Coach Lewis Dyche, and Gymnastics Coach Sandra Mull would not have to be concerned about winning or inclement weather after 1978. Acting on a recommendation by Dr. John Paul Mees, vice president for student development, the Board of Regents voted to remove the three sports from Northwest's intercollegiate athletic program. Lack of facilities seemed to be the principal culprit for the demise of the three, but adding to gymnastics' problem was its limited budget and a dearth of competition within easy traveling distance. Of the three sports, swimming had the best chance of being rescued from its drowning, but that would occur only if the Martindale pool was renovated or if the University could acquire an aquatic center, certainly a very slim hope in 1978.

Not a sports activity but definitely related to the sports program was Athletic Director Mike Hunter's resignation. Administrative officials hesitated little in choosing Hunter's successor. They picked the craggy and candid Mr. Richard Flanagan, the hard-working track coach and football assistant. In accepting the administrative appointment, Flanagan, an alumnus and a member of the faculty since 1971, relinquished his football duties but refused to surrender coaching his tracksters.

The major portion of the $616,000 Phase III renovation of the University's matriarch of buildings, the Administration Building, began in June. Campus observers wondered in the spring about the mobile home parked northeast of the Administration Building and why President Owens and Dr. Bob Bush, the assistant to the president, could be seen entering and exiting the trailer several times a day. Their anxieties were allayed when they discovered that, because of Phase III, the

mobile structure was the spring and summer campus office for the two
until their Administration Building offices were refurbished.

The 1978 undergraduate and graduate degree recipients who were
unable to attend the Inauguration Convocation saw at their own commencement what they had missed the previous November. Of course
that November 18 day had set a traditional precedent for future
commencements. Marking its first use at graduation, the mace, the
ceremonial symbol of the University, was again prominently displayed
in the commencement processional and recessional. The grand marshal
and his associate marshals were very visible, but this spring ritual also
saw the establishment of a new tradition when the fathers of two graduating seniors Mr. Dale Boyer, Amity, Iowa; and Mr. Donald Guthrie,
Grandview, Missouri; participated in the commencement ceremony.
Boyer and Guthrie, the fathers of Rod Boyer and Beth Guthrie, members of the 1978 graduating class, respectively gave the invocation and
the benediction. The day was a homecoming for St. Joseph State
Senator Truman E. Wilson, an alumnus and a member of the Missouri General Assembly since 1968. He not only received both the
University's Distinguished Alumni and Distinguished Service Awards
but also delivered the commencement address. He did not summarize
his talk with ringing, resounding words of advice—so common with
many graduation speakers—but surprised his audience by singing
"You'll Never Walk Alone." The graduates, to whom the song was
sung, were enthralled with its message and with Wilson's appropriate
and beautiful rendition. For them, it was a memorable moment.

In the summer of 1978, the University initiated the annual summer
Honors Program for outstanding spring high school graduates. Coordinated by Dr. Gary Davis, associate professor of humanities, the new
freshmen are able to take four courses that meet Northwest's general
requirements: Honors Composition, American Civilization, General
Psychology, and Religion in Human Culture. This viable program
offers the participating students a close relationship with four faculty
members and the opportunity to be part of a group that studies and
enjoys social activities together.

July 1 marked President Owens' first anniversary, and Northwest
was striding forward as a residential institution where students could
thrive in a living and learning environment. President Owens made
changes and offered some surprises during his year in office, and his
second summer commencement proferred its own form of surprise. The
commencement ritual, to be sure, was as traditional as the Inauguration Convocation and the spring graduation, but the large audience,
including 260 undergraduate and graduate degree candidates, did not

hear the standard time-honored commencement address. The speaker, Mrs. Lela Bell, an outstanding Maryville citizen and a member of the Missouri Coordinating Board for Higher Education, appealed for the end of "wrong and devastating" competition between Northwest Missouri State University and Missouri Western State College, two institutions only forty miles from each other. Voicing her own opinions, Mrs. Bell, not one to mince words, called for the creation of "one excellent regional University with two campuses—a residential campus in Maryville—a commuter campus in St. Joseph." She held the audience's attention. She pleaded for Northwest and Missouri Western to work together in order to discontinue costly duplication of student recruitment, course offerings, and degree programs. Quoting from the Carnegie Higher Education Report, Mrs. Bell related that "a truly endangered species in higher education is the small, teacher-related four-year college with a similar four-year college within forty miles." Mrs. Bell, who received the University's Distinguished Service Award, commended the Northwest Graduate Center on the Missouri Western campus and the fall launching of the Army Reserve Officer Training Program, two recent cooperative efforts between the two schools. Mrs. Bell, however, concluded with the plea that more cooperation is essential, and she stated that the Coordinating Board's Master Plan III for Higher Education in Missouri, then in its draft stage, would concern itself in part with these problems. The response to Mrs. Bell's speech on the Northwest campus and in Maryville was, for the most part, quite favorable, but the reaction to her comments on the Missouri Western campus and with many St. Joseph citizens was that of disquietude as the subsequent fall furor between the two institutions would show.

Two new graduate degrees at Northwest were awarded for the first time at the 1978 summer Commencement. Angela and Frank Forcucci, speech therapists in the St. Joseph School System, became Northwest's first recipients of the Master of Science degree in Communication Disorders. Because of the uniqueness of having a husband and a wife simultaneously become the first to finish a new graduate degree program, the two caused much excitement locally as they were feted by members of the University's speech department. The department of home economics had its first, too, when Mrs. Charlotte Stiens, a resident of rural Maryville and home economics teacher at Northeast Nodaway High School in Ravenwood, Missouri, received the Master of Science degree in Home Economics Education. Her husband, Larry, was a member of the general audience as he had no desire, because of his successful farming career, to be part of a home economics degree!

The 1978 fall enrollment showed a decrease of 176 students from the previous fall. The figure was misleading, however, since Northwest, in its attempt to assault mediocrity, asked approximately 400 previous enrollees who did not care to be brushed by the fires of academe to leave.

Fall returnees would find no more Saturday night home football games. Because of a decision made by President Owens to conserve energy and to enable visiting teams to arrive home earlier, the games were played, as they are now, on Saturday afternoons. Owens' judgment proved to be good since fans found it much more pleasant to watch the Bearcats on a crisp, sunny afternoon in lieu of a cold autumn night, and with the removal of the light poles spectators could now have an unobstructed view of the game. It was, however, a frustrating season for the team, its coaches, and its fans since the Bearcats were winless.

Beginning with the fall semester, registered nurses desiring to receive the Bachelor of Science in Nursing degree at Northwest were given the opportunity to complete their clinical nursing courses in St. Joseph at Methodist Medical Center because of an agreement between the Medical Center and Northwest. For the first time in Northwest's seventy-three-year history, the Army Reserve Officer Training Corps (ROTC) was on campus. After experiencing an embryonic start in the summer, ROTC was fully launched in the fall of 1978 with forty-nine students. The program began as a cross-enrollment agreement between Northwest Missouri State University and Missouri Western State College to provide ROTC instruction to students at Northwest and was headed by Colonel Franklin Flesher, professor of military science at Missouri Western and head of the department of military science, and Major Robert Sauve, the ROTC executive officer. Because of the relatively large enrollment and pre-enrollment figures for the spring semester, the cross-enrollment arrangement was eliminated in November, and Northwest began operating as an extension unit of the program at Missouri Western. It meant that Northwest could now have its own Army personnel assigned to the campus to administer the program and teach the cadets, and it also meant that the equipment used by the Northwest unit was now appropriated solely for the University's ROTC cadets. Colonel Flesher remained as the commander of both units. He, however, would retire in the summer after twenty-seven years of army service to become Northwest's assistant to the vice president for academic affairs. Lt. Colonel John G. Coombs succeeded him as commander. The program's mission is to bring students into military service by providing for them either active duty in the Army or part-time careers through the Army Reserves or the National Guard. The ROTC program at Northwest also offers "Adventure Training," a variety of first-year courses, like weapons and marksmanship, mountaineering, rappelling, and orienteering, which many students find stimulating and can now use as a substitute for the traditionally required physical activity courses in their degree programs. Because of the attractiveness of ROTC on campus and Major Sauve's recruitment efforts, there were twelve juniors interested in some form of the military as a career, and thirty-seven other students enrolled in the basic courses in the fall of 1978. Since one of his female cadets decided- to marry and not remain in the program, Major Sauve had only eleven juniors during the spring semester, but ninety-seven underclassmen. The 108 students far surpassed the Major's goal of thirty-five students for the 1978-1979 academic year. It was obvious, too, that the Major needed more instructional help. In late February, Sergeant Howard Taylor arrived, and in July Captain John Wells, Captain John Fry, and Sergeant Regino Pizarro were added, bringing Sauve's instructional staff to five members. Each month the men of the local chapter of Blue Key National Honorary Fraternity traditionally recognize at a dinner a student, instructor, or administrator for making valid contributions to Northwest. Major Sauve received that honor in April 1979 for his successful implementation of ROTC on campus and for his indefatigable recruitment efforts. The program continued to grow. In the fall of 1979, ROTC had 141 students, including nine seniors, six juniors, and 126 undergraduates, and the following spring saw 236 students in the program, again with nine seniors and six juniors, but with 221 underclassmen, making it one of the fastest growing military science programs in the country. The substitution of first-year ROTC courses for physical activity courses, which became effective during the 1979 fall semester, is a major factor in the program's tremendous growth. Attractive trips for the group are an added lure, evoking the students' interest. One of their journeys, during the 1979 spring break, was a trip to Fort Carson, Colorado, where the students visited the military base and the Air Force Academy, trained with a mechanized infantry unit, and spent their leisure time skiing the slopes of the Colorado Rockies. Making the program more inviting for some students is the $100-a-month stipend that third and fourth-year cadets receive. Captain Wells, as enrollment officer, also plays an integral part in the growth. Northwest's cadets obviously are well-trained, talented, and diligent, for many of them, like cadets Dwight Durfey, Charles Bithos, Mike Lassiter, James MacNeil, Brady Snyder, Leslie Kirkland, George Knisley, Rebecca Shaver, Mark Worley, Patrick

Pijanowski, Judy Moning, Richard Loney, and Richard New, received their share of local and national honors in 1979 and 1980. On the morning of Saturday, May 10, 1980, Charles Bithos and Leslie Kirkland made history for themselves, their ROTC Unit, and their University when they became the first two officers commissioned into the United States Army from Northwest's two-year-old ROTC unit. Only hours before they were to receive their Bachelor of Science degrees at the University's Seventy-Fifth Anniversary Commencement, Bithos and Kirkland were commissioned Second Lieutenants in ceremonies conducted by Lt. Colonel Coombs, Major Sauve, and Captain Wells. Cadet Brady Snyder will receive his commission in August, and cadets Richard New, Dwight Durfey, Richard Loney, and James MacNeil expect theirs in the fall. On July 1, 1980, Major Sauve left his duties as Northwest's ROTC executive officer to enter the United States Army Command and General Staff College, the Army's prestigious career development school at Fort Leavenworth, Kansas, bringing honor to himself, Northwest, and the Army. Major Sauve will be remembered at Northwest for launching and implementing the highly successful ROTC program. His successor is Major Terry Fiest, a recent graduate of the Army Command and Staff College.

The Intensive English Language program, known as English as a Second Language (ESL), began on campus during the summer months of 1978. Since Northwest was experiencing 'an influx of foreign students, the program, coordinated by Dr. Rose Ann Wallace, assistant professor of English, was obviously needed to prepare foreign students for their American studies in higher education. Early in September, however, the program was reaching out to Maryville's St. Francis Hospital where eight Filipino women were nurses. Experiencing some problems with the English language, the eight nurses daily studied conversational skills and listening comprehension in English at the University for a ten-week period under the tutelage of Mr. Channing Horner and Mr. John Dougherty from the department of foreign languages.

Because of its willingness to help foreign students, as evidenced by the ESL program, Northwest became the willing recipient of a valuable collection of Chinese art representing more than 3,000 years of Chinese culture. The gift was presented by Consul General Robert C. J. Shih from the Republic of China in special September 27 ceremonies at the Gallery of the Olive DeLuce Fine Arts Building. The collection was given as a gesture of friendship from the Republic of China's Ministry of Education in recognition of the educational services that Northwest provides students from the Republic.

On Saturday, September 23, over 1,800 parents, brothers, sisters, and some grandparents and cousins of Northwest students spent the day on campus, helping to reintroduce the annual Parents' Day, a tradition that was absent at Northwest for many years. Coordinated by Dr. Phil Hayes, dean of students, the Day gave the relatives of the students an opportunity to become better acquainted with the faculty, staff, and students of Northwest. They were also able, in an efficiently planned series of activities, to visit classroom settings, participate in group activities, attend departmental open houses, see their loved ones' living arrangements, and view a variety of demonstrations and exhibits. The students' relatives also enjoyed the refuge of the newly decorated areas of the J. W. Jones Union. The East Den boasted a new Spanish motif, and its counterpart, the West Den, sported an American West design. The elegance of the third floor's Student Lounge and Ballroom was impressive to its beholders. Mr. Steve Easton, director of technical services, drew the mechanical plans for the rooms, while Interior Decorator Charlotte Pratt from Tampa, Florida, who also effectively had decorated the President's Home and the President's Office, was responsible for the decorating. The University's construction crew, headed by Mr. George Kiser, accomplished the work.

Students returning early for fall classes were avid spectators of something unusual hovering around the Administration Building. Five tons of an air-conditioning condenser were being hoisted by a huge crane onto the highest portion of the roof of the towered structure. Part of the Phase III renovation project of the lady's domain involving interior refurbishing of her first two floors, the air-conditioning unit replaced dozens of inefficient window units and kept her inhabitants comfortable. Many of those same student spectators quickly shook themselves from their summer lethargy and prepared themselves for classes and the big fall event—Homecoming. For Vincent Vaccaro, the 1978 Homecoming marked his first as executive director of alumni relations and he was ready. The newly chartered Bearcat Chapter of the Alumni Association composed of Northwest Missouri and Southwest Iowa alumni initiated the Homecoming events with a breakfast. Another new event was the post-game M Club reception, replacing the organization's traditional breakfast, and those same M Club members, along with other alumni and students, could dance that night in a popular Maryville "night spot" until midnight. Returning alumni saw something different at the football game, too. Bobby Bearcat, played so exuberantly and enthusiastically the past two seasons by the retired Steve Scroggins, was still present, but now it had a mate—Roberta Bearkitten. Linda Hernandez and Deb Irak donned their costumes, and, like Scroggins, were adept at involving the fans in the game's action. Hernandez, an accomplished dancer, and Irak added a new dimension to the mascots' roles with their dancing and gymnastics. The 1978 members of Blue Key also decided to do something different for Homecoming. Instead of the organization's usual coffee hour after the morning parade, this group initiated the annual homecoming post-game dinner in honor of its alumni. The event was held where the group traditionally meets for its monthly dinner meetings during the school year—the Cardinal Inn. Blue Key's alumni members were especially happy to "come home again" to the delectable home-cooked meal and the special attention provided by the restaurant's owner, Mrs. Mary Newton. Members of their families, too, were happy to be included in the nostalgic and delightful atmosphere where their husbands and sons spent so many happy moments during their undergraduate years. The alumni who attended the traditional Alumni Luncheon in the Ballroom of the J. W. Jones Union Building witnessed a special ceremony honoring a man who was president of Northwest when many of them were students. Dr. Robert P. Foster was presented the University's Distinguished Service Award by President B. D. Owens. Foster's Distinguished Service Award was the fifteenth given by the University in 1978, and it originally was to have been presented, along with eleven other Distinguished Service Awards, during inaugural ceremonies for President Owens the previous year, but President Emeritus Foster was traveling in Africa on American Legion business for the Freedom Foundation of South Africa. Many innovations were added to the 1978 Homecoming, but the traditional remained, too. Sponsored by Delta Chi fraternity, Diann Piper, a student from King City, Missouri, and a member of Alpha Sigma Alpha sorority, was crowned Homecoming Queen, thus making King City residents and members of the two organizations quite happy.

In late August, an editorial in Missouri Western's student newspaper, the *Griffon News,* called upon Northwest to compete with Missouri Western in sports, thus calling attention again to the absence of a friendly rivalry. Obviously upset with Northwest, the editorialist referred to Northwest as "that big dying University to the north." What the editorialist could not forecast, of course, was that a non-sports related rivalry would exist between the two schools in the fall and would culminate at a neutral site in December. The object of contention, at least for Missouri Western, was the first draft of Master Plan III, the Coordinating Board for Higher Education's document outlining goals and missions of state institutions of higher learning. Dr. Bruce Robertson, author of the draft and at the time the state commissioner of higher education, called for a December 5 public meeting at the Minnie Cline Elementary School in Savannah, Missouri, to hear the Coordinating Board's proposals concerning Northwest and Missouri Western. Of course, Master Plan III was already public knowledge in November, and Robertson explained that the purpose of the meeting was for people to tell him and the Coordinating Board whether they agreed or disagreed with it. The Savannah meeting would lead to the second draft of the plan and then finally the final draft. What the first draft of Master Plan III stressed was cooperation between Northwest and Missouri Western, and it very simply stated that Northwest was to continue to serve as a residential university offering its traditional baccalaureate and graduate degrees and phasing out existing two-year programs. Missouri Western was being asked to remain a commuter campus offering four-year degree programs and, in addition, to concentrate on developing a broad selection of two-year programs. This state master plan became an issue with Missouri Western followers because many of them believed it was designed to help Northwest at Missouri Western's expense. For Missouri Western President Marvin Looney, who was predicting an enrollment of 5,000 students in five years, it seemed an anathema on his school and the educational death of its baccalaureate program: obviously misreading the intent of the master plan, because it said nothing about Missouri Western dropping its four-year degree programs, Looney was frightened that his College, if the plan materialized, would revert to a junior college from which it evolved; whether he believed it or not is not the issue, but that at least is what he publicly stated. Robertson and Coordinating Board members must have grown weary of attempting to dispel Looney's so-called mistaken notion. Feeling that the plan was too restrictive for Missouri Western, President Looney also had fears that it implied a change in mission contrary to that indicated when Missouri Western became a four-year institution in 1969. Where Missouri Western officials' sounds of displeasure were quite audible, Northwest was relatively quiescent. President Owens did release portions of remarks he would deliver at the Savannah meeting. He stated that people at Northwest agreed that the plan's guidelines were logical and farsighted.

Attendance at the public meeting was well over 400, and it was a partisan Missouri Western crowd as the College's officials had actively solicited participation from their students, staff, and community citizens. A special December 1, 1978, edition of the *Griffon News* stated that the school's future was at stake and strongly urged people to attend. It was quite a show! President Looney set the tone by calling for "institutional autonomy," and Looney seemed to revel in his words and in his subsequent introductions and the utterances of the eleven other partisans, including the Mayor, members of the Board of Regents, prominent St. Joseph citizens, a professor of political science, and two students. For two hours the audience listened to the dozen reiterate, in their allotted ten-minute discussions, the same theme: remove the restrictions placed upon the College in the plan and "let the students vote with their tuition checks." Ten of the speakers walked quietly and quickly to the stage to join Looney when they were called to speak, but St. Joseph Mayor Gordon J. Wiser, attempting to be athletic, tough, urbane, and outspoken, apparently mistook the stage for a high jump pit. He theatrically vaulted onto the stage and immediately chided the members of the Missouri Coordinating Board for Higher Education. He referred to the commissioner of higher education in Missouri as "whatever your name is." Seemingly trapped in his own fatuities, the Mayor unsuccessfully attempted to intimidate the chairman of the coordinating board and moderator of the hearing, Robert Duesenberg, and belligerently asked why St. Joseph did not have a representative on the Coordinating Board. Duesenberg coolly met the charge by simply stating that the Governor makes those appointments. Undaunted, the Mayor proceeded to read his prepared, intemperate comments supporting Missouri Western and then jumped from the stage: Wiser seemed to represent the spoor of a system gone mad. He, incidentally, began his little scene of tacky ubiquity by stating, "I don't appreciate being here tonight." Obviously, a great number of St. Joseph citizens did not appreciate his presence, for they later apologized to Dr. Robertson and members of the Coordinating Board, especially Mr. Duesenberg. Although not lacking support from his school, President Owens was the lone official representative who spoke for Northwest Missouri State University, and he apparently was the only one the University needed. Stating that Northwest was committed to following the philosophies and goals outlined in the draft of the master plan, Owens clearly articulated that the University would continue as it had for seventy-three years to adhere to the charge by the state of Missouri "to provide the highest quality educational opportunities at the lowest possible cost consistent with sound educational policies and fiscal realities." Citing the existing cooperative graduate and ROTC programs being carried out by the two institutions, Owens called for full cooperation between the two schools and the avoidance and elimination of costly unnecessary duplication of state educational services in light of declining enrollment and tight fiscal policies. A part-time student from Northwest, claiming to represent no one, praised the plan for being removed from politics. He, however, awkwardly rambled, and his emotions obviously obfuscated his judgment. It was now Dr. Robertson's turn, and for several minutes he beautifully summarized the draft of Master Plan III and answered Missouri Western's objections. The pessimistic note, voiced by Missouri Western supporters, disturbed him. He attacked the College's argument for autonomy by saying that "unfettered, unlicensed autonomy" would be deleterious for Missouri colleges. Feeling that the dispute "could have been handled at a much lower key," Robertson then attempted to assure the audience that Missouri Western was not threatened by the plan but that it suggested a balanced approach to education, which meant compromise and cooperation among the various institutions of higher learning in the state. The capstone of Robertson's talk was his admonitory words, "You [Northwest and Missouri Western] need to work together more than most in order to solve a common problem."

On December 11, six days after the controversial meeting at Savannah, Missouri Western advocates appeared mollified when Dr. Robertson agreed to some changes in the Master Plan for Higher Education, but Robertson also explained that the alterations would be more in style than in content. In March, after the final version of Master Plan III was completed, both institutions seemed satisfied with the final results. President Looney was pleased that the plan included an individual mission statement for his school, defining it as a baccalaureate degree granting institution. The final version obviated a passage restricting dormitory expansion for Missouri Western, but the school, along with Missouri Southern at Joplin, was not to anticipate the development of extensive residential facilities. A large single section, so large that no one could possibly miss it, on institutional cooperation was also added. Dr. Robertson again reiterated that there were not any extensive changes in the plan, and President Owens felt that the overall substance of Master Plan III was basically the same as the first draft. The plan also promotes athletic competition between the two schools. In the summer of 1980, Northwest, meeting the spirit of Master Plan III, responded by offering Missouri Western a concrete proposal for the two institutions to compete in all sports. Hopefully, talk about playing each other will end, and Northwest and Missouri Western will encounter each other on the football field by the fall of 1981 and on the basketball court by 1982. In late July of 1980, Northwest was still awaiting its neighboring school's decision.

Today, Northwest functions in its traditional manner as the region's undergraduate and graduate level institution, and Missouri Western serves as a four-year liberal arts college with emphasis on two-year technical associate degrees for commuters. Ultimately, the solution to the problem is cooperation and caring—caring not about the enrollment figures, but about young people, caring about their being educated, and caring about the contributions they will be able to make to society.

One of Mayor Wiser's fears was allayed in the spring when Governor Joseph Teasdale appointed St. Joseph's Gerald Sprong to the Missouri Coordinating Board for Higher Education. Sprong, a graduate of Northwest and a 1977 recipient of its Distinguished Alumni Award, thought of himself as one person who was acceptable for all the colleges in the area and did not consider his appointment a compromise between Maryville and St. Joseph. He correctly saw his position, as any member of the Coordinating Board should, as representing the entire state with an emphasis, of course, on the northwest and the northeast sectors.

Northwest students, like any students, fretted about their finals during the middle of December, but they found something else more disruptive in their lives than finals. A wave of bomb threats was making it difficult for them to concentrate. As of December 14, twelve such phone threats occurred in four university buildings over a five-week period. False alarms or not, the buildings had to be evacuated while University Security and the Maryville Public Safety Department searched for explosives. The threats began again in the spring but stopped when the spring semester ended. The gagster was either finished with his fun or was one of those whose academic flaws finally caught up with him.

A pall was thrown over New Year's Day, January 1, 1979, by the death of eighty-five-year-old President Emeritus J. W. Jones. He was devoted to his school and in retirement continued to pay particular interest to it. He never forgot his dictum: "Once a Bearcat, always a Bearcat." Dr. Jones had been especially gratified that President Owens, the 1958-1959 student body president when Jones was head of Northwest, was now leading the University. Mrs. Jones echoes those same sentiments.

Faculty and administrative task forces, appointed by the President, were addressing themselves to the recruitment of quality undergraduate and graduate students, the retention of students, and the University's seventy-fifth anniversary in 1980. Before retention became such a concern with colleges and universities, Registrar Martha Cooper was concerned about freshmen dropouts. She was always uneasy when freshmen left school, for she felt if they could survive their first year most of them would remain until they received their degrees. Mrs. Cooper seemed to be a natural as the retention specialist on campus.

When she asked to be assigned duties concerning the retention of students, President Owens gladly accepted her offer. Mrs. Cooper, who now has the title of coordinator of special programs and services, assisted the retention committee with its efforts and continues to work with the retention problem as well as with teacher certification. She, in addition, advises students who are undecided about their courses of study.

Semester-opening faculty meetings usually offer no major surprises, but Dr. John Harr, head of the division of history and humanities, was probably more astonished than anyone else in the audience when President Owens announced that Harr was the recipient of Northwest's first Distinguished University Professor Honor, a new rank created by the Board of Regents to recognize long and distinguished service to the University. It seemed to be Dr. Harr's semester. In March, he was again singled out for distinction when a symposium, sponsored by his division, was held in his honor. Called "History át the Heart of It All," the symposium focused attention on some of the world's issues and featured Dr. John Taylor, professor of history, Ferris State College, Big Rapids, Michigan; Dr. J. Kelley Sowards, professor of humanities at Wichita State University; Dr. Richard Fulton, associate professor of political science at Northwest; and Dr. Byron Augustin, associate professor of geography at Southwest Texas State University. Taylor, Sowards, and Augustin, fine scholars and friends of Harr, formerly taught at Northwest. Due to Taylor's illness, his lecture was presented by video tape.

Twenty-nine law enforcement officers in the five-county Northwest Missouri area were on campus early in January of 1979. They were here, not to quell any disturbances or to find the one phoning in bomb threats, but to take a police training course in order to comply with a law passed by the Missouri General Assembly in 1978. Because of the law, officers across the state need a minimum of 120 hours of basic police training. The training was part of Northwest's continuing education program and was coordinated by Earl Brailey, who was then the University's security director. Dr. Pat McLaughlin from the school of business administration, Mr. David Coss from the department of English, Dr. David Smith, head of the division of sciences, and Brailey, along with several police officers and a prosecuting attorney, taught the courses.

On January 16, 1979, the Shah of Iran, Mohammed Riza Pahlevi, after thirty-seven years of ruling Iran, was driven from his country by a popular upheaval. On January 30, the United States ordered the evacuation of all dependents and nonessential American officials in Iran and urged others to leave. Early in 1979, the frenzied turmoil continued to exist, as it does in 1980, and twenty Iranian students attending the special intensive English program at Northwest were worried about more troublesome strictures than their capacity to handle the English language. The existing conflict in Iran involved their families and friends, and the students faced the possibility of bad news from their homes everyday. They also worried about being called home before their studies were completed or being unable to return home at all. Their strain would be even more considerable during the fall semester because of the American hostages seized by Iranian militant students at the American Embassy in Iran on November 4.

Late January and early February saw a mixture of something old and something new on campus. The seventh annual Bohlken Award Film Festival added a new twist to its award night by combining disco, films, and olio acts. Because Dr. Bob Bohlken introduced cinematography courses at Northwest, film instructor Rob Craig named the Festival for him in 1973. Craig, coordinator of the event, also had Bohlken open the 1979 ceremony with his rendition of John Travolta disco dancing to music from the movie *Saturday Night Fever*. Almost lost in the shuffle was the original intent of the program—honoring the most outstanding film in Craig's cinematography class. Bev Faust was the winner for her film creation, "I Was a Daytime Vampire." Five nights after the Festival, Northwest jazz fans heard nationally known woodwind performer Roger Pemberton in concert with Northwest's Jazz Band. The concert followed the first annual "Northwest Jazzfest," offering competition among fifteen high school bands from Missouri, Iowa, and Nebraska. The overall high school winner, Valley High School of West Des Moines, also played in concert with the above two. The Jazzfest, introduced and directed by Mr. William O'Hara, director of the NWMSU Jazz Band, is now an annual event.

Two members of Northwest's staff, Dr. Bob Bohlken, head of the communications division, and Mr. Jim Wyant, director of financial aids since 1978, developed, as members of the Maryville Optimist Club, an idea for fatherless boys eight to nine years of age. Because of the two men's efforts, eighteen Eugene Field Elementary School boys claimed "Big Buddies." Wyant, the Alpha Kappa Lambda fraternity sponsor, queried his members and received an enthusiastic response. Sixteen of the men volunteered to work with a "little buddy" from the elementary school, and the Optimist Club set up general guidelines for the "Big Buddies" to follow in the organized program. The men saw their little friends twice a week and were responsible for organizing weekly activities for them. It seemed to be a mutual admiration society.

The AKL men liked their participation in the "Big Buddies" program, and they also liked something else they had accomplished in recent months. Doing odd jobs and involving themselves in a variety of work projects, the men, after leasing their house on Walnut Street for the past fifteen years, bought a large house on West Sixteenth Street. They and their sponsor Jim Wyant were happy, and university officials voiced satisfaction over the move. Some of their neighbors vented displeasure at having forty-two extra inhabitants in such proximity, and they worried over the extra traffic and the possible late night parties. Other neighbors, however, did not seem to mind at all.

On March 28, 1979, a nuclear power plant accident at Three Mile Island near Harrisburg, Pennsylvania, released radioactivity causing the greatest amount of radioactive contamination of the atmosphere to that date from a commercial reactor breakdown. T-shirts with various types of inscriptions ranging from the inane to the esoteric were in vogue, and occasionally one could glimpse, in the spring of 1979, a wearer with the words, "I Survived Three Mile Island."

In May, a gasoline crisis in California caused long lines, incidents of violence, and the closing of filling stations in America's first fuel crisis since 1974. Northwest officials were not worried about energy accidents and, although they were apprehensive of a future shortage of energy, they were very concerned over the high costs of heating and cooling the campus buildings in 1979. Since the University spent almost a half million dollars on energy in the 1977-1978 school year and would spend considerably more in 1978 and 1979, Dr. Bob Bush, soon to be appointed to the University's newly created post of vice president for environmental development in August, was looking for a means to lessen the problem. Purchasing Agent Dwight Branson had an idea called the waste to energy plan, a system in use for decades in Europe. Solid waste, according to the plan, was to be collected and burned in an enclosed area, and the heat would supplement the current boiler system and provide the campus with hot water. It was, to be sure, not the total answer since the system would supply only approximately thirty percent of Northwest's heating requirements, but it could save the University $100,000 annually. It was a plan worth considering, but such a major move would take months of intensive study. In the meantime nine residence halls at Northwest consumed thirty-eight percent less electricity in February of 1979 than the previous February. The 2,000 residents of the halls, extremely aware of conservation, were involved in a three-month Inter-Residence Hall Council-sponsored energy saving program.

Clusters of high school students descended upon campus in the spring. More than 700 from Missouri, Kansas, Nebraska, and Iowa came to compete for scholarships in the eighth annual Mathematics Olympiad. And they were here for the seventh annual Journalism Day to listen to four Pulitzer prize winning journalists. At the end of March, the campus was inundated for two days with over 3,000 high school music students here for the annual Northwest Missouri District Evaluation Music Festival. The department of English tried something different in April—the Midlands Poetry Workshop. Directed by Mr. Craig Goad and Dr. Bill Trowbridge, two practicing poets and members of the department, the two-day workshop attracted high school creative writers and featured several poets, most notably Nebraska's William Kloefkorn, who read selections from their works and conducted special sessions where they could give critical commentary of the students' poems. Since the workshop was resoundingly successful, it has become an annual spring event. In June, Northwest swarmed with 400 high school cheerleaders from the four-state region who were participating in the nineteenth annual cheerleading clinic at Northwest under the direction of Mrs. Irma Merrick of the women's physical education department. The campus resounded with the young people's cheers, and their gyrations arrayed the landscape.

In 1977, it was an all-female contingent who retired from Northwest, and in the spring of 1979 the focus was a quartet of male retirees: Dr. John Harr, professor of history and the head of the division of history and humanities, a veteran with thirty-five years of service to Northwest; Mr. James Johnson, director of the library science program and former director of Wells Library, another veteran with thirty-one years; Dr. Howard George, associate professor of psychology, with twenty-two years; and Dr. James Lowe, professor and chairman of sociology for twenty years. (Mr. John Dougherty, associate professor of foreign languages for fourteen years, announced his early retirement during the summer and, therefore, missed the annual spring fete for the retirees.) Harr, George, Lowe, and Johnson were honored at the annual retirement dinner on March 30, where the University's Social Committee, headed by Miss Kathryn McKee for the past three years, saw to it that the evening was a gala one. Over a year later, Harr jogs, fishes, studies his Civil War history, and serves as general chairman of the University's 1980 Homecoming, a special event that highlights Northwest's diamond jubilee; George golfs, drinks coffee daily with his former colleagues, and enjoys whiling away the days at his home in Maryville; Lowe fishes and treks through the hilly country of Arkansas with his four-wheel Scout. The three are the quintessential contented men. Johnson shared that quintessence for a brief time as he, in his

Virginia home, followed his loves of reading, gardening, gourmet cooking, and sharing the good life with his wife, children, and grand-children. Unfortunately, that was all taken from him when he suffered a massive heart seizure and died on May 15, 1980.

Many activities dotted the March calendar, and many of them involved the science area. Dr. David Cargo, professor of earth science, wanted interested students to receive a very close view of a total eclipse of the sun. Cargo enlisted Dr. Bob Bush to pilot him and four of his students to a point sixty miles north of Winnipeg, Canada. The spot was chosen for its accessibility by air and for its forecasted ideal weather conditions. Cargo's science compatriots, Drs. Jim Smeltzer and Bob Mallory, were at the Jet Propulsion Laboratory in Pasadena to view Voyager I and its close encounter with Jupiter and its moons. Because of their increased involvement with NASA programs, Smeltzer and Mallory are now principal investigators for NASA, and in March they were extremely pleased with the news concerning one of their students. Joyce Murphy, a senior geology major from Kansas City, was selected by NASA to receive a summer internship at the United States Geological Survey's Center for Planetary Studies at the University of Northern Arizona. Only thirteen internships were given.

The airplane that took Cargo and the four students to Canada belongs to Northwest. Purchased for $87,500 in March 1978, the six-passenger Piper Aztec is not an extravagant frill, as some skeptics originally felt, but is saving the University transportation money. Because of the numerous trips President Owens and his top aides take to Jefferson City, airplane travel is proving more economical than driving an automobile to the state capital. It saves precious time, and an added advantage for Northwest is that both Owens and Bush are accomplished pilots. The Piper Aztec is used not only for official business trips to meet with the Missouri Legislature, but also academic departments are encouraged to use the plane.

Three different boards, two presidents, and a commissioner appeared on campus the morning of Friday, April 27. Northwest's and Missouri Western's Boards of Regents, the Coordinating Board for Higher Education, Presidents Owens and Looney, and Missouri Commissioner of Higher Education Bruce Robertson convened to tour the campus and discuss institutional cooperation and enrollment trends for the two schools. Robertson urged the two institutions to utilize resources to their maximum degree and to decrease costs without sacrificing quality education. The morning pattern was repeated at Missouri Western in the afternoon.

Northwest was again blessed with a productive cultural year. The venerable *Arsenic and Old Lace* as directed by Dr. Charles Schultz, and *A Flea in Her Ear,* a French farce directed by newcomer Mr. Theophil Ross, were the fall productions by the theater department. But the "show stopper" was the spring production of *Damn Yankees,* directed by Schultz. The first musical seen on campus in four years, the production combined the talents of three academic areas: theater, music, and dance.

The Bearcat basketball team pleased its home fans by winning all of its home games, and the team appeased its opponents' fans by losing all of its games away from home. The team had its first winning season in eight years as Coach Holley's men finished with 15 wins and 11 losses. Holley surprised Northwest by resigning in June to accept the head coaching position at William Jewell College, his alma mater. In July, Dr. Lionel Sinn, head coach and athletic director at Tennessee's Bethel College, was selected from a field of thirty applicants as the sixteenth coach in the Bearcats' sixty-four-year basketball history. Coach Jim Wasem's baseball men again won the MIAA Northern Division title with an 11-1 mark, lost the conference play-offs to South-west Missouri State University, but finished fourth in the NCAA Division II Regional Tournament, and capped the season with a 26-12 overall record. Vernon Darling, already an All-American cross-country runner, earned All-American honors again by running second in the 3,000 meter steeplechase at the NCAA Division II meet. His achievement was the highest national mark by a Northwest track performer since the late Herschel Neil, Northwest's track legend, won the NCAA triple jump title in 1936.

For the first time in the forty-year history of debate on campus, Northwest had a team qualify for the National Debate Tournament at the University of Kentucky in Lexington. Varsity debaters Ken Himes and Ward Smith, both coached by Dr. Jim Leu, were the only ones qualifying from Missouri, and they represented Northwest well as they finished twentieth.

Many of Northwest's students belong to the local chapters of national honorary fraternities, and agriculture was once again welcomed to the honorary roll call in the spring when nineteen of its members were initiated into the charter group of Alpha Tau Alpha, national professional honorary education fraternity.

In 1979, Northwest's 130 broadcasting majors studied under three full-time and several part-time instructors, and many of those students filled key roles at 100,000 watt KXCV-FM, a National Public Radio affiliate. KDLX continued as a campus station sending programs to the residence halls and the J. W. Jones Union Building. KXCV-FM through the years had won many first-place state awards for its "Alive and Living" daytime show, but, in May 1979, it claimed the coveted Corporation for Public Broadcasting first-place award for the magazine program, "Alive and Living . . . Evening Edition," co-produced by Program Coordinator Sharon Shipley and Operations Manager Perry Echelberger. The award was presented to both Shipley and Echelberger at CPB's annual conference in Washington, D.C. Sharing the two's joy at the national conference were Director of Broadcasting Rollie Stadlman and Chief Engineer Warren Stucki. National awards were not new to KXCV-FM. In 1975, the station was given an honorable mention in the Major Armstrong competition for its series on flamenco music.

Shipley and Echelberger, adept at coordinating and hosting programs, produced the seventh annual KXCV-FM Brain Bowl as Maryville High School captured first place, winning scholarships totaling $1,500. Dr. George Gayler still proficiently served as the quizmaster, and his colleague Dr. Harmon Mothershead was the judge.

Another national award winner that same spring was Northwest's *Tower* yearbook. Competing with four-year institutions with enrollments between 2,500 and 5,000 students, the *Tower,* edited by Salisbury, Missouri's Laura Widmer, received an All-American rating from the National Scholastic Press Association. Miss Renee Tackett was the faculty adviser.

The April 28, 1979, spring Commencement, one of the earliest in Northwest's history, was a memorable one, for the University paid homage to one of its most revered ladies. Miss Mattie Dykes, whose accomplishments are innumerable, was honored with the presentation of Northwest's Distinguished Alumni Award and the Distinguished Service Award. Professor Emeritus Dykes, founder of the local campus chapter of Sigma Tau Delta, national creative writing fraternity, in 1930, and well-known for her history of Northwest's first fifty years, *Behind the Birches,* responded to her honors and the audience's continued applause by telling the graduates how to solve many problems, "If you look at a thing long enough, you can find some way to get hold of it."

A renovation, the naming of two existing structures, and the naming of the streets through the university campus highlighted the month of June on campus. The final portion of Phase III, the renovation of the Administration Building Auditorium, was in its early stages and would be completed in November. Overseeing the major project, involving Northwest's own construction crews, were Mr. Steve Easton, director of technical services, and Mr. George Kiser, construction foreman. Two past presidents of the University were honored by naming campus structures for them. In November, upon completing the refurbishing of the Administration Building Auditorium, Northwest's theater would be called the Frank Deerwester Theatre for the first president of the University. And, in addition, the high-rise cafeteria building was named the Henry Kirby Taylor Commons after Northwest's third president. The ideas and the names for the two structures came from the University's Seventy-Fifth Anniversary Committee, and the Committee conceived yet another idea and more names for the streets on the campus proper. Some of the names were derived from the various titles of the University, including the periods when it was a Normal School and a College. They were familiar ones like University Drive, Normal Drive, College Park Drive, Northwest Drive, Memorial Drive, Farm Drive, Service Drive, and Bearcat Drive. Extremely useful for campus visitors were the new street signs and directional signs indicating campus buildings, as well as identifying markers at each building, other conceptions of the Anniversary Committee.

University people, happy with the theater renovation and the new names on campus, were extremely disappointed late in June when Governor Joseph Teasdale cut Northwest's budget to $9,272,000 from the $9,467,000 recommended by the Missouri General Assembly. Early July, however, brought the emotional barometer back to happiness again when Governor Teasdale signed the capital improvements portion of the budget containing $1,420,000 for the construction of a new swimming pool and the renovation of Lamkin Gymnasium. Northwest, after fifteen years of waiting, would finally have its new aquatic center. The edifice, to be built in the area north of Lamkin and Martindale Gymnasiums, would surely rescue Northwest's intercollegiate swimming program. Future runners would not have to brave the rigors of the basement running track in Lamkin, for part of the renovation project included the installation of a Tartan running surface around the Lamkin basketball court. Basketball, volleyball, and wrestling participants and their fans would find Lamkin more enticing, too, since its lighting, sound, and heating systems were to undergo extensive changes.

Prior to the spring of 1979, Northwest held graduate courses at St. Joseph's Lafayette High School; the Northwest Missouri State University Graduate Center was then established on the campus of Missouri Western State College. In the fall of 1978, Northwest, appreciative of being able to use Lafayette High School as a graduate center in past years, thanked the St. Joseph Public School District by offering five graduate scholarships to outstanding teachers in the St. Joseph Public Schools. An eight-member committee, comprised of public school teachers in St. Joseph, screened the applicants and was ready in April with its selections. The five outstanding teacher honorees were Margaret Artherton, Janet Bradshaw, Mary Ann Sadler, Ronald Starks, and Stanley Weston. It was a concrete gesture of appreciation by the University for the District's cooperation.

Since August of 1978, the technological life of the students, faculty, and staff was made more palatable with the installment of the new word processing software package, which was linked to the University's PDP 11-70 computer. The new system replaced the slow, antiquated method of rented automatic typewriters which utilized magnetic card devices. Planned by Mrs. Mary Jane Sunkel, chairman of office administration, and Dr. Jon Rickman, director of the computer and data processing center, the new computer word processing system is extremely effective, quick, and cost efficient. In June, the University was honored for its efforts in effectively implementing and using the word processing with a Cost Reduction Incentive Award by the National Association of College and University Business Officers at the group's national convention in Atlanta, Georgia. Since the inception of the new word processing system in 1978, Mrs. Sunkel has willingly taught word processing to numerous classes, seminars, special interest groups, and individuals. She has given talks and demonstrations in other states on the advantages of word processing and its effectiveness at Northwest. She is generous with her time.

In 1977, Mr. Tom Carneal, associate professor of history, conducted a comprehensive historic survey of historical buildings, sites, and objects in Nodaway County, believed to be the first such survey in Missouri and one of the first in the country. That survey and its proposal are considered model ones throughout Missouri by the Department of Natural Resources' Office of Historic Preservation. For his year's efforts, Carneal received a $3,200 grant for the project. In 1978, Carneal, branching out, embarked upon a comprehensive survey in an eight-county area of Northwest Missouri, including the counties of Buchanan, Andrew, Daviess, Holt, Atchison, Gentry, Worth, and a follow-up survey of Nodaway County. Because of his interest and historic specialty, Carneal and the University were the recipients of a $38,600 grant from the National Park Service of the United States Department of the Interior. The figure seemed magnanimous, but it was stretched to support the field research, for the photography and documentation, for obtaining the services of other specialists, for clerical help, and for a portion of Carneal's salary. Carneal, given some release time by Northwest to conduct the survey, spent the year identifying and marking the historic buildings, structures, sites, and objects in order to preserve history for the present and future generations. In July of 1979, Carneal was again the recipient of a grant. This one, totaling $16,840, was awarded jointly by the National Park Service and the Missouri Office of Historic Preservation for the Department of Natural Resources. This grant was awarded to help Carneal complete his historical survey of the eight-county area. Carneal, underplaying his importance to the historical inventories, felt that Northwest Missouri State University was selected for the three grants because of its available facilities for photography, maps, and resource personnel such as Social Historian John Harr and Architectural Historian Bob Sunkel. In June of 1980, Carneal did it again! This time he and the University received yet another grant from the same federal and state agencies. This grant, totaling approximately $44,000, is to be used by Carneal to conduct a historical survey of the counties of Clinton, Mercer, Livingston, DeKalb, and Harrison and also for him to finish the last of three counties in his original survey. Carneal's task, although it is one he cherishes, seems omnipresent.

In late June, the nation's independent truckers caused a work stoppage for a week by seeking a higher priority in their fuel allocations and a ten percent surcharge to meet high fuel prices. Northwest met the challenge of fuel allocations and high energy costs, however, by following its own plan to conserve. Its officials outlined recommendations to cut university vehicle use by at least ten percent, and two of the most significant recommendations, it seemed, were for personnel to walk the short distances on campus and to eliminate the really unnecessary trips to town and other locales. Of course, this was the year that President Carter issued the federal mandate that all thermostats in public buildings were to be adjusted to eighty degrees in the summer and sixty-five degrees in the winter. Colden Hall inhabitants certainly had no worries concerning the regulation of thermostats, for the building's cooling system worked irregularly in 1978, followed the same pattern in 1979, and initiated the 1980 summer session by malfunctioning.

Student laborers, both male and female, were swinging sledge hammers and using pneumatic drills to repair and construct campus streets and parking lots during the early summer months, and, because of their efforts, the campus had a new entrance through College Park Drive from College Avenue, thus eliminating the previously hazardous intersection there. For almost a year, no vehicle traversed in front of the Administration Building. That drive was closed, covered with dirt, and now in the summer of 1979 was planted with sod, so people could appreciate the environs in the foreground of the Administration Building for their aesthetic value.

The month of July in 1979 will not be remembered as the best of times in Northwest Missouri State University history. A harbinger for the month was death—the death of four stately birches on University Drive that were planted soon after Northwest was founded in 1905. New birch plantings, which would eventually replace the old trees, felled by age, dotted the campus. Three natural disasters that mankind dreads because of their destructive capabilities are extreme winds, damaging rains, and devastating fires. Northwest was the victim of all three in July, all within an eight-day period. Early in the morning on the sixteenth, high winds and rain attacked the Olive DeLuce Fine Arts Building, stripping nearly 1,200 square feet of its roofing. Because of the huge gap left by the absent roof, water poured onto the stage of the Charles Johnson Theater, leaving it engulfed with water. The stage was damaged and the curtains soiled, but quick action by Max Harris, director of maintenance services, and Steve Easton, director of technical services, and their workers kept the damages relatively low. However, 100 prints from the Percival DeLuce Memorial Collection received water damage. Wells Library was not immune to the elements' onslaught. The winds severed two ventilator covers from their anchors on the Library's roof, and unwanted water intruded in yet another of Northwest's buildings. Approximately 120 books received severe water damage, and a like number were marked with water and dirt. Many automobiles, owned by summer school students and parked near the high-rise residence halls, were damaged by the fury of the winds.

But the worst was yet to come! Northwest was quickly recovering from the force of nature's bombardments when it was hit by yet a greater tribulation. For several hours on July 24, an electrical malfunction above the fourth floor offices of the Speech and Hearing Clinic in the Administration Building was silently working up to a conflagration which would surpass any previous campus disaster. Her ailment was not detected until it was most obvious that something was dreadfully wrong with the favorite lady among the campus buildings.

At 8:14 p.m., smoke was discerned, and the Maryville Public Safety Department was notified by Campus Security. When the firemen arrived only minutes later, heavy smoke already prevailed throughout much of the building, serving as an ominous portent for what was to occur the next several hours and even days. University staff and faculty, townspeople, and area citizens immediately descended to the

Bill Bateman

Administration Building Fire, July 24, 1979

A shudder in the loins engenders
    there
The broken wall, the burning roof and
    tower . . .

— *William Butler Yeats*

Aftermath of Administration Building Fire

Brick by Brick, the Towers Stood.

—*V. Albertini*

calamitous scene to remove the valuable computer tapes of university records, Board of Regents' records, and student records. While these intrepid people were quickly removing contents from the sixty-nine-year-old edifice, hundreds were lined on the campus grounds watching the dancing flames along the ridge line of the building's west wing. It was not long before the participants became spectators because Maryville Public Safety Director Roger Stricker feared for their lives and ordered the building evacuated. The Maryville fire fighters, now aided by units from Conception Junction, Parnell, Burlington Junction, Polk Township, and the Riegel Textile Corporation's Maryville plant, were battling the flames both from the interior and the exterior. The firemen, too, obeyed Stricker's order, and on the outside it was heartbreaking for the battlers and the watchers. The flames were running amuck. They spread across the west roof area and into the north wing housing the 1,000-seat Frank Deerwester Theatre (seventy percent complete in the Phase III Administration Building renovation project). Feverishly attempting to thwart the onrush of destruction, the firemen were frustrated by clogged hydrants, low water pressure, and the lack of necessary equipment to reach the upper part of the structure. Flames continued to spread to the west and struck the attic area above KXCV-FM and KDLX before dropping into the two stations' studios and offices and destroying them. No one gave the grand matriarch, who once had survived the blows from a tornado and several major surgeries, much of a chance. When the roof of the Frank Deerwester Theatre collapsed, ascending a fantastic cloud of fire and sparks into the sky, everyone thought that this stately structure, that meant so much to so many people, was dead. The fire hungrily moved east through the upper parts of the towered middle portion of the building, and it looked as if it were ready to wreak more havoc in its ruinous path. The building was being broken apart, and the scene was enough to break a person in two. Adults were visibly weeping. But now there was an answer to this fury unleashed upon the revered building. An aerial truck, equipped with a 100-foot aerial ladder, arrived from the St. Joseph Fire Department. Director Stricker assigned the firemen from St. Joseph to the east end of the Administration Building. For hours the aerial truck played a stream of water on the roof of the east wing, and, finally, that section was rescued from imminent destruction. Later, President Owens would refer to the rescue as a splendid performance that prevented the fire from emerging into the east wing. Two weeks after the disaster, Maryville voters overwhelmingly approved a city sales tax which will eventually enable the Maryville Public Safety Department to have its own aerial truck to help fight fires involving tall buildings. Many people did not leave the scene until they were certain that the grand structure's four towers were not damaged by the excessive heat. Those towers seemed to symbolize pillars of strength, and a great majority of the viewers felt that if the towers were not damaged then somehow the lady could rise again. By two a.m., their hopes were realized. The towers were safe, but, as Walter Lord said of the *Titanic* disaster, "It was a night to remember."

The night, however, was far from over for Northwest's leading administrators. President Owens, Vice Presidents English, Mees, Bush, Graduate Dean Miller, Public Relations Officer Henry, and Maintenance Director Harris, exhausted and weary, proved their mettle that night and the days immediately following the fire, along with innumerable unsung heroes (including the firemen) who helped move items from the burning and burned-out building and the many who had to relocate their classrooms and offices. Northwest's leaders not only toiled, but they were responsible for keeping Northwest running as smoothly as possible, for summer school had to continue and the fall semester, looming like a giant shadow, was only a month away. But there is something in good men that enables them to perform well under duress. It was their finest hour. They worked their hearts out in an extremely debilitating situation. Plans were made at a staff meeting around the dining room table in President Owens' home to relocate classes and offices from the damaged building to other campus facilities. At 8 a.m., July 25, approximately twelve hours after the fire was reported, Owens called a faculty and staff meeting informing those in attendance that the east wing, despite damage, had been saved, that the first and second floors of the west wing were intact, and that the entire third and fourth floors of the west wing were unsalvageable. The final result was that the fire destroyed sixty percent of Northwest's oldest and proudest building. President Owens began the meeting with words that for several weeks became a rallying point for the University, "As of 8:00 this morning, it's business as usual." They were words of certitude.

For Rollie Stadlman, director of broadcasting, it certainly was "business as usual." When he and his staff realized that their radio and television studios were going to be lost, they, along with student broadcasting majors, resolved to be back on the air the next morning. Using equipment borrowed from radio stations KKJO and KFEQ in St. Joseph and a trailer from Maryville's O'Riley Construction Company, they did have KXCV-FM back on the air at 6:30 a.m., July 25. And on July 25, at 2 p.m., Director Stricker allowed people into the building to begin its evacuation. For forty-eight hours, students, townspeople, alumni, faculty, and staff splashed through water, breathed toxic fumes, and battled muggy humidity until they emptied the building of its salvageable contents. Thirty-eight hours after the fire was discovered, Governor Joseph Teasdale arrived to view the destruction, and he returned twelve days later to deliver a $20,000 check from the state's Emergency Appropriations Fund to help in the plans for the replacement of destroyed facilities. State legislators came in subsequent days to view the devastation, and they all shook their heads in disbelief. Yes, it was business as usual. No classes were missed, and administrative offices, student services, admissions, financial aids, news and information, the registrar, the mail room, data processing, the business office, speech, theater, broadcasting, home economics, and agriculture were quickly relocated. Immediate planning was obvious, but not immediately evident was that Northwest's administrators, led by President Owens, were doing some long-range planning, triggered by the disaster. Stadlman again rallied his forces and moved the studios from the trailer to Wilson Hall adjacent to Colbert and ironically only several yards from KDLX's 1960 birthplace—the "broom closet."

Personal losses, especially to members of speech pathology and theater, were plentiful, but fortunately there were no disabling injuries or fatalities. Bob Wiederholt, a member of the Maryville Public Safety Department, suffered a fractured ankle, and Graduate Dean Leon Miller broke a finger. Even the grand statue of Abraham Lincoln, which for years dignified the entrance to the Frank Deerwester Theatre, was unscathed. Firemen who fought the flames and battled the smoke until ordered out of the building rallied around the venerable replica of Lincoln. He seemed to offer a bond of strength—if he were all right, the firemen would be all right.

The removal of the rubble began in late August, and for days fall returnees could see truckloads of the debris being removed from the building and its perimeter. A temporary roof was installed over the building's exposed portions to protect it against the collection of water in cracks and winter freezing, which would cause additional heavy damage. Located north of the Thompson-Ringold Industrial Arts Building, a temporary metal building was completed in late fall to house the radio and television stations and the Speech and Hearing Clinic, which moved into the structure in January. Meanwhile, Homer Williams, the university architect, declared that it would cost approximately $15,000,000 to restore the Administration Building to its original condition. And all this time many thoughts about the restoration and the cost were being bandied in President Owens' mind. One prevalent thought emerged—examine alternatives for the replacement of the lost space. What seemed plausible to him was that the Administration Building could be reconstructed without a theater and yet be restored to retain its historic lines. What also seemed logical was that Northwest could add a badly needed new library, a new theater, and refurbish Wells Library for academic space lost in the Administration Building for less than the $15,000,000 necessary to restore the damaged structure and thus help solve Northwest's building problems. Owens, his high level administrators, and Mr. Williams, with his fellow architects, proceeded to design plans for the replacement of the lost facilities. Bob Henry helped by designing an emergency expenses and recovery options summary sheet, now jestingly called "The Henry Centerfold," that greatly aided Owens in his many visits with various members of the state legislature. They figured the cost for reconstruction and renovation of the first three floors of the Administration Building's east wing and the first two floors of the west wing, plus the reconstruction of the west wing roof line to its original appearance, would be $1,579,400; the construction of a new library building to cost $7,400,000; and remodeling of Wells Library for classrooms $477,000. In place of spending some $5,000,000 to reconstruct the theater to its original condition, a new modern design, free-standing auditorium could be constructed for $2,971,000. Of course, Northwest officials were concerned with non-structure losses and estimated a $1,180,281 replacement cost for such items as equipment, personal losses, demolition costs, technical fees, and the construction of a temporary storage facility. The steam tunnel needed repairs costing $200,000. Although many options were considered, this plan was a feasible one and was presented to Governor Teasdale before December 1, in order for him to include it in his January emergency appropriations request to the Missouri General Assembly. Northwest was asking $13,800,000 emergency funds to rescue itself from that devastating night of July 24, and Governor Teasdale, during his two visits to view the damage and to deliver the $20,000 check, pledged his support. Legislators, including Mr. Kenneth Rothman, speaker of the Missouri House of Representatives, did the same. Although extremely saddened by the disaster to the tradition-rich edifice, Northwest personnel were optimistic. Demonstrating excellence and rising to the occasion, President Owens, besides looking after the immediate needs of his University, made innumerable trips to Jefferson City to keep Northwest's necessities always present in the Governor's and the legislators' minds. And it was the swiftness of the university airplane, once denigrated by some as an unnecessary expense, that saved valuable time for him and Northwest and made those trips practicable.

State dignitaries did not stop coming to campus. On January 3, 1980, Mr. Rothman came and declared that he would not "walk away from this kind of tradition and heritage." One day after Rothman's visit, Governor Teasdale was at Northwest with the information that he was recommending that Northwest receive $13,800,000 in emergency funds to replace the space lost in the fire that destroyed over half of the Administration Building. By asking the Missouri General Assembly for emergency funds, Teasdale could make the money available immediately after he signed the bill into law. After receiving approval from both the Missouri Senate and the House of Representatives in March, Teasdale signed the emergency appropriations bill for the University at 3 p.m. on March 24, 1980. Cheers of joy resounded on campus with the good news. President Owens' plans, conceived shortly after the fire, were now tangible. Although new building committees were already working in anticipation that the state would approve the lower cost alternative that would best serve Northwest in the future, tentative plans could now become final ones for a new auditorium west of Rickenbrode Stadium and a new library between the Garrett-Strong Science Building and Cooper Hall. To be sure, the Administration Building would be partially restored, and Wells Library, containing approximately the same footage as the academic space lost in the Administration Building, was to be converted to academic classrooms. Other costs accrued by the July 24 devastation would also be covered by the emergency appropriations.

Several people whose offices were in the Administration Building suffered great personal losses the night of the fire, but for Mr. Theophil Ross, assistant professor of theater, the night was excruciatingly painful. Everything in his office was destroyed including rare books, works of art, and six years of research for his doctoral dissertation. Ross, however, proving the old adage that the show must go on, marshaled his student forces and presented on August 7 and 8, two weeks after the flaming debacle, the two dramas: *The Bald Soprano* and *The Lesson.*

As the summer session rapidly neared its end and summer commencement approached, it did appear to be "business as usual" on campus. The August 10 Commencement featured two outstanding alumni: Miss Mary McNeal and Dr. Fred Davis, recipients of the Distinguished Alumni Awards. Miss McNeal, who retired from a thirty-six-year teaching career in the spring, has shown her generosity toward her alma mater through the years by bestowing upon it a collection of

200 dolls from around the world, a scientifically classified insect collection, and a rock collection. Dr. Davis, the first and only president of State Fair Community College at Sedalia, Missouri, delivered the commencement address. Representatives from the St. Joseph, Maryville, Parnell, Conception Junction, Burlington Junction, Polk Township, and Riegel Textile Corporation fire departments were singled out for praise and given awards for their departments' splendid work the night of July 24 by Owens. This Commencement also marked the last one for Mr. E. D. Geyer, a member of the Board of Regents since 1975 and president of the group for two years. Although his term as a Regent had expired, Mr. Geyer was elected the first chairman of the Board of Fellows, newly established by Northwest's Board of Regents and recommended by President Owens. Comprised of former Regents, the Board of Fellows participates in fund raising and works with Missouri legislators and are, in Owens' words, "good-will ambassadors with the public."

Although some of Northwest's emeritus faculty move to retirement homes, many remain in Maryville and stay vitally interested in the University. Some, like Mr. Floyd Houghton, occasionally teach a course or are active on university committees. Retirees, like Mr. Herbert Dieterich, Mr. Ryland Milner, Dr. Irene Mueller, and Miss Ruth Miller, are sought by their former colleagues for advice concerning educational matters in their respective disciplines. Mrs. Opal Eckert is active as a free-lance writer and is known for her features in Maryville's *Daily Forum*. A recipient of many awards during her fifty-two-year teaching career, Mrs. Eckert received yet another one on August 13. The state of Missouri recognized her in Jefferson City as a Missouri Pioneer in Education. She received one of seven such awards in the state of Missouri.

President B. D. Owens was not the only leader in his family. Mrs. Sue Owens, Northwest's first lady, had ideas, too. Soon fall classes would be starting, and the home economics department needed help. Mrs. Owens formed a group of women, composed of townspeople and wives of faculty and staff members, to help clean up the damage caused by the July 24 fire. Armed with buckets, brooms, sponges, vacuum cleaners, soap, and disinfectant, they cleaned the home economics laboratory area and did not stop until it was ready for fall classes the following week. When Mrs. Owens thought of the idea, she simultaneously thought of a name for the women that would be appropriate for Northwest's forthcoming seventy-fifth anniversary—Diamond Damsels. After completing the first task, the Damsels moved on to sort and clean bricks that were felled by the fire and also scrubbed the floors and walls of the lower floors' east wing. Although the group was originally organized to help clean the Administration Building after the fire, it now considers itself as a source of service whenever help is needed at Northwest. Another group of Northwest's women, the Faculty Dames, a much older organization than the Diamond Damsels, was also active. The Dames were constructing, under the leadership of Mrs. Bonnie Carlile and Mrs. Virginia Dyche, two different sizes of commemorative plaques, resting on wooden easels, from the Administration Building's slate roofing debris. Profits from the sales of these items were to assist in the reconstruction of the Administration Building. Mrs. Carlile designed a drawing of a towered portion of the Administration Building and a compass for the face of the plaque. The back of the plaque listed a brief history of the Administration Building with a story of the Phoenix, the mythical Egyptian bird, and how it rose from its ashes with renewed life. The copy for this was written by Dr. Karen Fulton, and the message derived from the Phoenix's rebirth was that Northwest would rise again from its disaster, hopefully with new structures like a library and an auditorium. On November 1, 1979, the Dames really dazzled when members sponsored a Community Fair and Auction. Approximately 2,000 people spent the evening in the J. W. Jones Union Ballroom viewing the various exhibits and buying the homemade food, fresh country cream, honey, candles, stained glass, poetry, and books. The crowning success occurred later in the evening when local auctioneers offered their time and auctioned many donated items like hand-painted French plates, an English wool hooked rug, and a variety of afghans. On December 3, President Owens welcomed Mrs. Patty Schultz, Bill Barton, and Cindy Baessler, respective presidents of the Faculty Dames, Sigma Tau Gamma fraternity, and the Inter-Residence Hall Council, into his office. They came bearing a gift from their organizations to assist the University in the restoration of its fire-damaged building. No, it was not frankincense, gold, and myrrh, but a check totaling $8,279.79. The Faculty Dames raised $7,700 from their efforts at the November 1 Community Fair and Auction; Sigma Tau Gamma contributed $319.79 from money that was raised when members of the fraternity participated in a marathon run to Rolla, Missouri; and the Inter-Residence Hall Council gave $260.00 to the total with funds earned when its members hosted a chili supper the night of the Faculty Dames' Community Fair and Auction.

Even though buildings like Colden Hall were more crowded than usual because of the inconvenience caused by the July fire, more students seemed to be in evidence when the 1979 fall semester classes began on August 27. And they were here! Enrollment increased to 4,401 students, a nearly five percent growth over the 4,207 student number for the 1978 fall semester. The freshman class seemed to arrive in droves. The freshman enrollment showed an increase of 14.5 percent over its immediate predecessors and represented the largest class growth at Northwest in seven years. The large influx of freshmen seemed to be an unusual one among universities and colleges because of declining population, and if there is a declining population a shrinking enrollment can be expected. Some people at Northwest, however, refused to be daunted by population trends and concentrated on attracting quality students to a residential campus where they could live and learn. President Owens asked that student recruitment be made a top priority at Northwest. He, to be sure, was not talking about "hucksterism" employed by some institutions or the fairly widespread tendency by some schools to admit students who are not qualified. Director of Admissions Charles Veatch and his staff responded admirably to Owens' charge and fought the enrollment crunch that other schools were experiencing. His major weapons were accomplished staff recruiters, a communications center that became the center of student recruitment, an admissions office that remained open an extra twenty-five hours a week, a constant contact with the students interested in Northwest, and a total university effort with more faculty and students contributing to the recruitment program. The Undergraduate Recruiting Task Force, formed the previous fall and headed by Dr. Gene Stout, associate professor of business, was extremely helpful, for it drafted effective recommendations for an increase in the recruitment effort. Recruitment at Northwest early in 1979 was anything but passive, but the University did not try to be all things to all people or attempt to obtain students at all costs. A quality and traditional institution, like Northwest, does not soften admission requirements, or tacitly promise good grades, or give easy tests permitting students to leapfrog over undergraduate requirements so they can become instant sophomores. With the scramble for students, many colleges and universities are sorely tempted to lower their standards and seduce themselves into tailoring course offerings. But Northwest believes that the classic liberal arts courses still form the core of the curricula, and other courses do not stray from their traditional academic bases. Veatch, his staff, university personnel, and students worked assiduously, not only in the Northwest area but in Kansas City, St. Louis, Chicago, and other cities and states as well. Having a solid and quality school, however, certainly enhanced their efforts. In the fall of 1979, President Owens found his recruitment charge for an increase of qualified students, not merely numbers, resoundingly answered in the affirmative.

Concerning Northwest, President Owens had other thoughts besides recruitment, the aftereffects of the Administration Building fire, and what lay ahead for the 1979-1980 academic year. It was time, he felt, to begin a new tradition on campus by giving the Master Achievement Citation for Excellence (MACE), a name derived from the University's ceremonial mace, to Northwest faculty and staff for outstanding contributions in the areas of teaching, service, research, and student recruitment. Each honoree would receive a $1,000 check in recognition. Toward the end of the General Faculty and Staff Meeting on August 23, 1979, Owens surprised everyone in the packed Charles Johnson Theater by announcing the inception of the MACE Award, and when he finished six people from the faculty and staff were each on the stage receiving a handshake, a plaque, and a check from Owens and applause from their peers. Honored for excellence in teaching were Dr. Arthur Simonson, associate professor of mathematical sciences; Mrs. JoAnn Stamm Marion, assistant professor of elementary and special education; and Mr. Robert Findley, assistant professor of business. Mr. Richard New, associate professor of elementary and special education, received the MACE Award for excellence in student recruitment; Mr. Tom Carneal, associate professor of history was honored for research excellence; and Mr. Dwight Branson, director of purchasing, was the recipient for excellence in university service. The above were recognized for their valid service to Northwest during the 1978-1979 academic year.

Many faculty and staff members, students, and townspeople became avid spectators as they watched contractors removing the rubble left by the July 24 fire, and many of them were also watching something resembling the space age being installed in a grove of trees west of the University Greenhouse. What they saw was a satellite terminal—a parabolic disc aimed at a point in the sky—to allow KXCV-FM to receive information from National Public Radio via satellite. Funded by a $42,476 grant from the Corporation for Public Broadcasting, the new system was expected to improve the station's reception by 300 percent. Chief Engineer Warren Stucki helped with the installation of the parabolic disc, fifteen feet in diameter, that rests atop a twenty-foot steel tripod. Although the station's newest acquisition would not begin receiving signals from the Westar I satellite 23,000 miles above the equator until the first of December, Rollie Stadlman, director of broadcasting, was, nevertheless, reveling in excited anticipation because KXCV-FM, a National Public Radio station, was about to become a member of the world's first stereo network. Stadlman was also anticipating the move to the metal storage shed under construction, the station's third temporary home since the July fire.

Newness seemed to abound for Northwest in September. Mr. James Cremer, who served five years as the University of Tampa's security director, succeeded Mr. Earl Brailey as Northwest's security director. Dr. Guy D'Aurelio, in his first year as Northwest's director of bands, was showcasing his Marching Bearcats at pre-game ceremonies and at half times of the Bearcats' home football games; in addition, D'Aurelio was preparing his group for its first NWMSU Bearcat Marching Band Concert in November. Sigma Phi Epsilon, the nation's second largest fraternity, was attempting to add to Northwest's twelve Greek organizations—six fraternities and six sororities—by establishing a chapter on campus. It, however, was having trouble receiving recognition from the Inter-Fraternity Council and the Student Senate, but the group, with a good nucleus of men and a fine sponsor in Mr. Paul Read of the men's physical education department, was functioning as a colony while it was waiting to gain acceptance on campus. Seventeen graduate students, called tutorial assistants, became part of a program Northwest started in September as they helped some undergraduate students develop proper study habits and taught them basic knowledge in various disciplines such as English, mathematics, biology, history, chemistry, and geography. Since Northwest was unable to receive the space it had requested for a daytime graduate office on the Missouri Western State College campus where the cooperative graduate programs are held, the University opened a full-time office in downtown St. Joseph for the graduate program. Staffed by Colonel Frank Flesher, assistant to the vice president for academic affairs, the office handles requests and assists persons interested in taking graduate classes. President and Mrs. Owens were delighted to have Dr. Hsu Chia-yu, associate professor of medicine at Shanghai in the People's Republic of China, as their campus guest. Dr. Hsu, serving as the first Edgar Snow Professor of Medicine at the University of Missouri-Kansas City, was the first Chinese physician to visit the United States as an individual and not as part of a delegation. He visited with students and described his country's medical care to audiences at Northwest and was a special guest at a reception held in his honor at the Thomas W. Gaunt House, hosted by the Owens.

Northwest's recovery from its July calamity was commendable. There were crowded conditions but students, faculty, and staff seemed to be adjusting to their circumstances and pulling together toward their common goals. The total effort represented a magnetic chain of humanity. The aftereffects of the disaster, however, did take their toll in some quarters and weakened the chain somewhat. Chief Accountant Rod Hennegan and Comptroller John Drummond, both citing the fire as a definite setback to the business office, resigned from their positions in September because they felt that their work had become debilitating and onerous. Almost in conjunction with the two men's resignations was President Owens' request that Treasurer Don Henry, the head of the business office, take a six-month administrative leave of absence with full pay. Obviously, Henry had become a persona non grata in the administration's eyes for the enforced leave was in reality a release. When his six-month departure from his university duties was over, Henry asked that his leave be extended until the end of July, so he could accumulate ten years service at the University. His request was approved, and he remained on Northwest's payroll until July 31, 1980. Dr. John Paul Mees, vice president for student development, assumed top administrative leadership of the business office, while Mr. Jim Wyant, director of financial aids, was named acting comptroller, and Mrs. Jeanette Solheim, a member of the business office staff, assumed the role of acting treasurer. Meanwhile, Mrs. Ellen Mothershead, assistant director of financial aids, absorbed some of Wyant's duties until Mr. Ray Courter, internal auditor, was appointed comptroller, allowing Wyant to return to his full-time directorship.

President Owens discussed with his Board of Regents at their monthly meeting in September his plans to reorganize the business and financial operations of the University. The members approved his request for a vice president for financial affairs, thus creating a new administrative office for the University. The new vice president would oversee the treasurer's position with emphasis placed rather strongly on administration, forecasting, planning, budgeting, and general management of fiscal affairs and business operations. The key task for the new person would be forecasting the financial situation of Northwest not for a few months or a year in advance but for several years into the future. A search for the correct person to fill the position was launched in October, and, after several stops and starts, Northwest found a vice president for financial affairs seven months after the search began. Mr. Warren L. Gose, the audit manager in the Missouri state auditor's office, was appointed Northwest's newest vice president in May.

Over 350,000 people descended upon Des Moines, Iowa, on October 4. They were there to see Pope John Paul II. Very seldom does one have the opportunity to view a Pope from outside the confines of the Vatican, but this Pope, with his magnetic appeal, was different for he visited other countries. Twenty-one Catholic students from Northwest, not willing to pass up the experience of seeing an actual Pope, traveled, along with Father Chuck Jones, by the Bearcat bus to Des Moines to hopefully glimpse the head of the Roman Catholic Church. The students were lucky. Some of them came within three feet of one of history's most popular popes.

Homecoming 1979 was one that will be savored perhaps indefinitely by many. It was one that rang with anticipation for days preceding the event, for that October 20 day was once again marked with tradition but also laced with added attractions. Preceding the 9:30 a.m. parade, eight people, after listening to Father Chuck Jones, the director of the Newman Center, offer the prayer, approached the land immediately north of Martindale Gymnasium with shovels and participated in ground breaking ceremonies for the new aquatic center. Using those shovels and seemingly enjoying their task were State Senator Truman Wilson, Regents Dr. Harold Poynter and Mr. Al McKemy, University Architect Homer Williams, Professor Emeritus Bonnie Magill, Athletic Director Richard Flanagan, Professor Emeritus Ryland Milner, and President B. D. Owens. The hour-long parade was very possibly, according to veteran parade watchers, the best in the University's history. The noon Alumni Luncheon saw Dr. Jack Kinder elected as president of the Alumni Association, but there were two other people recognized at the Luncheon for what they meant to Northwest. Mr. Fred Parcher, a 1914 alumnus and grandson of the late Captain Lyman Parcher, who as a state senator introduced a bill in 1887 for a State Normal School in Maryville, was recognized as the earliest graduate in attendance and the one who traveled the longest distance—from Seattle, Washington. St. Joseph's Mr. Raymond Kinder, a 1941 alumnus, received an award that was unveiled for the first time. It was the University's Turret Award, recognizing "uncommon contributions" from an alumnus to Northwest. It was a fitting gesture, for Mr. Kinder worked so long and diligently in helping evacuate the Administration Building after the fire. The 1979 Alumni Luncheon also featured something that will probably never be erased from most of the participants' memories. They witnessed eight minutes of a touching slide presentation of the Administration Building fire and its aftermath, discreetly and adroitly prepared by Rollie Stadlman, director of broadcasting, with the help of Vincent Vaccaro, executive secretary of alumni relations. For Mr. John Green, a retired guidance counselor from California, who played on the 1938-1939 Bearcat football teams, the 1979 Homecoming was a time for him and his former teammates and coach to have a reunion. He organized reunion plans and was gratified to see thirty-one of those players from those two years arrive for the Friday night reunion dinner. Spectators were thrilled when the men, along with their venerable coach, Ryland Milner, ran onto the field as they were introduced during half time at the Homecoming game. Homecoming Queen Alice Barbee, a senior communication disorders major from St. Joseph, enjoyed their presence. The 1938 team posted a 9-0 record, and the 1939 squad duplicated it with another perfect season. Some of those former players, probably more familiar to area fans because they stayed close to the scene of their previous exploits, were Bob Gregory, Ivan Schottel, Quentin Goslee, Frank Baker, Gene Hiatt, Ralph Kurtright, Jack Padilla, Glenn Breckenridge, Andy Zembles, Dean Walker, Norman Preston, Ralph Strange, and Tony Rizzo. Vic Farrell from San Luis Obispo, California, who was one of the originators of the Ryland Milner Scholarship, and North Carolina's Marion Rogers and California's Bill Bernau, who were Little All-Americans, were also among their former teammates on the field at half time. Mr. Milner today cites Rogers as the best football player who ever performed for the Bearcats and claims that both Rogers and Bernau could have been "any kind of All-Americans they wanted to be." After the game between Northwest and Northeast, the men sat for several minutes in Rickenbrode Stadium and celebrated the young Bearcats' victory. They also knew that the win pushed Northwest's MIAA record to 3-0, the first time a Bearcat team had done that well in conference play since the 1939 team accomplished it. And, yes, the hallowed Hickory Stick was again in Northwest's possession, after a five-year absence, and Quarterback Mark Smith, the player who played so valiantly to push Northwest into the MIAA conference lead, was voted the Don Black Memorial Trophy winner. The men also learned of another honor. The assistant coach of those 1938-1939 teams, Wilbur "Sparky" Stalcup, was to be posthumously inducted into the Missouri Sports Hall of Fame the following month.

A cloud of sadness, however, struck university personnel and students on Homecoming Day, for they learned that Dr. William Fleming, the popular and fine professor of American history, had died suddenly at his home early that morning. It was known, too, that Fleming's colleague and good friend, Dr. Robert Killingsworth, also a professor of history, was ill and would undergo major surgery the following Monday. Dr. Killingsworth, respected and deeply appreciated by his colleagues and students for his academic abilities and for his likable gruffness, died on November 15.

In 1972, the men of the seventh floor in Phillips Hall were struck with the Halloween spirit and marshaled their energies by sponsoring a haunted house. They were so successful that it became an annual event. In 1979, over 1,000 toured the haunted house in the basement of Phillips Hall. The men were actually providing a service not only to the campus but to the community as many children delighted in the "chamber of horrors." In addition, the guests' contributions helped the seventh floor residents fund their future activities.

Football at Northwest in 1979 looked like more of the same as the Bearcats began the season with three losses, thereby extending its losing streak to fifteen consecutive games. The third loss by a lopsided score to powerful University of Nebraska at Omaha did nothing to whet the Bearcat supporters' appetites for winning, but Coach Jim Redd insisted that the game was a turning point and would guide his team into the head winds of winning. Of course, there were scoffers, but Redd and his staff also knew that their young players were maturing. The following week they traveled to Kansas and ended their losing ways by defeating the Fort Hays State Tigers. Once the young players felt the thrills that come with victory and the veterans remembered what winning was like, they were insuperable. They did not stop until they won the MIAA title, the first football crown at Northwest since 1974 and the eleventh in Northwest's history. Conference opponents reacted with alacrity because this was the same group that was picked to finish last in the MIAA. Southwest Missouri State was stupefied when the Bearcats accomplished a feat none of its predecessors could do in twenty years—win at Springfield! What Redd and his men did in the football season of 1979 ranks as one of the greatest athletic feats in Northwest Missouri State University history. The team did not emerge from the dark shadows of oblivion and into the bright sunshine of recognition by using magic wands. A larger and expanded recruiting staff—Redd and Defensive Coordinator Paul Read traveled to Florida and brought home twelve recruits—refinement and simplification of strategies, hard work, strong administrative backing and fan support, and a positive winning attitude were the principal factors contributing to the victorious season. The lack of debilitating injuries continuing throughout the season also helped the team's fortunes, and Athletic Trainer Sandy Miller, the highly professional and quiet man who sits unobtrusively on the sidelines, was the prime reason for keeping the athletes relatively free from incapacitating ailments. Togetherness seemed to be one of the important keys, too. The Pittsburgh Pirates, the 1979 World Series' winners, constantly pushed the words "family and togetherness." As mundane as it may sound, togetherness was evident to whoever watched this team play. Since recruiting players, whether it involves a Notre Dame, an Alabama, or Northwest Missouri State, is a football fact of life in contemporary times, Coach Redd and his top assistants, Paul Read and Dave Evans, immediately after the season ended, began looking for future Bearcats who would fill the positions left vacant by graduation.

Probably as active as Redd, Reed, and Evans but not as visible to the public were four other members of Northwest's staff—Jim Wyant, Don Carlile, Charles Veatch, and Martha Cooper. Wyant, as director of financial aids, was providing information, advisement, and help to students in need of some form of financial aid, and he, along with his assistant Mrs. Ellen Mothershead, was assisting eighty percent of Northwest's students with financial help through scholarships, loans, grants, and private programs amounting to $2,800,000. Carlile, director of the career/placement service, is the one to whom graduating seniors and alumni turn when they are seeking employment. In the fall of 1979, Carlile had found positions for all but ten of the year's graduating seniors, and those ten, for various reasons, were limited to finding employment in their chosen professions to a given geographical area. Director of Admissions Veatch, who had become somewhat of a legend on campus for the work he and his staff accomplished in helping Northwest experience the largest percentage increase in enrollment of any four-year state-supported university or college in Missouri for the 1979 fall semester, was launching a new recruitment campaign for new students with the theme "College Never Looked Better." In the spring of 1980, Veatch was appointed assistant to the president, a position Dr. Bob Bush held until he became the University's vice president for environmental development. Mr. Jim Goff, the assistant director of admissions, became Veatch's successor. Recruiting students in contemporary times is a necessity but retaining them is important, too. Largely because of the efforts of Martha Cooper, coordinator of special programs and services, and with the help of the special retention task force, three percent more freshmen were returning to complete their second semester work in the spring of 1980 than the previous spring. Cooper, of course, knew that to have every freshman return for spring semester studies was an impossibility. Twenty percent will never stay as Greg Hatten, a senior business major from St. Joseph, so clearly pointed out in his extensive research survey on freshmen, prepared for President Owens. Hatten's survey showed that, for the most part, those twenty percent were not enrolled at Northwest to complete a four-year program.

The decade of the seventies was rapidly drawing to a close, and it represented many things to many people. Inflation in 1979 was the biggest headache for most Americans. It rose to 13.3 percent, the worst annual increase in thirty-three years. What cost consumers $1.00 in 1967 cost them nearly $2.30 as 1979 ended. Much of the decade, to be sure, was marked by various forms of activities like streaking, jogging, tennis, disco, or waiting in gas lines. Northwest was deeply embedded with its own activities involving both the mind and the body at the end of 1979 and the beginning of 1980. Students were preparing for finals, plans for the emergency appropriations after the July 24 devastation to the Administration Building were being finalized, and the University was pursuing methods of financing its proposed waste to energy plant. It also bought, partly because of the July fire, $80,000,000 in insurance to cover all campus buildings. Northwest's thirty-nine Iranian students were concerned because of the ubiquitous political upheaval in their country. Iranian militant students still held the Americans as hostages in Iran, and the Iranian students on campus, like their fellow Iranian students at other American universities and colleges, feared some form of reprisal by the Americans. Although no major problems existed between the American and Iranian students at Northwest, the Iranian students—especially the vocal minority who claimed that the action by the militant students was justified—faced some annoyances such as graffiti on walls, signs and messages on their dormitory doors, and firecrackers exploding under their doors—all acts venting hostile feelings because of the American hostages' plight. The majority of Northwest's students, however, displayed sympathy for most of the thirty-nine students who worried about all the uncertainty and turmoil existing in their homeland.

The Bearkitten volleyball team, coached by Pam Stanek, was gaining respectability as it garnered a 28-26-3 record and capped its season with an invitation to participate in the AIAW Region 6 Division II Tournament where the Bearkittens managed a win against the eventual regional champion, the University of Minnesota at Duluth. The basketball Bearkittens, under their new coach Wayne Winstead, continued to make a shambles of the women's division of the Ryland Milner Tournament by winning the title for the third consecutive time and finishing the season with nineteen wins and eight losses. The Bearcat basketball team broke its jinx by finally winning a game away from home and pleasantly surprised its followers by not finishing, as it had for four years, in last place at the Christmas holidays MIAA Tournament in Springfield, Missouri. Finishing second, the team, under new mentor, Dr. Lionel Sinn, went on to record a 16-11 season, the team's best record in ten years.

Northwest's own faculty and staff members broke a record in December, and they were not competing for any laurel wreaths. What they did, however, gave them a warm feeling of victory because they contributed $2,700 to the University's Educational Foundation in the annual Holiday Greetings Campaign. It was not a total team effort, but the 104 who contributed toppled the 1978 record by $160.00.

Roberta Hall, Northwest's oldest residence hall and the domicile for the University's sororities, swirled with controversy early in 1980. Its female residents vociferously complained to the press about their abode's deteriorating condition. University officials knew for some time that Roberta Hall had become inefficient. The plumbing was bad, the wiring needed to be replaced, and the building was in a state of disrepair. It offered, to be sure, adverse living conditions. Since dormitories are supposedly self-supporting, the state of Missouri does not appropriate money for repairs for such structures. When Northwest appealed to the Department of Housing and Urban Development (HUD) for a loan to repair the dormitory, it was denied. Northwest could not afford to strain its budget further by underwriting the cost of extensive repairs. When the women residents were told, after they complained, that the University's only choice was to close Roberta Hall in February, the decision was met with a crescendo of protests. Some of the most demure of the coeds became very vocal in defense of their home, and several discussion meetings were held with approximately 100 of the young ladies who protested the closing and President Owens, Vice Presidents Mees and Bush, Director of Housing Bruce Wake, and Security Director James Cremer. The women simply did not want to leave the place that seemed to offer such warmth and closeness for each of them. The administrative officials, because of the women's sincerity, listened to their appeals and reversed the decision to close Roberta Hall. It would be kept open, they decided, until the end of the spring semester, but the young women were expected to follow stringent regulations such as smoking only in designated areas, using no appliances in their rooms, and keeping electrical circuit use to a minimum. They, in addition, had to maintain a volunteer fire patrol to check for safety transgressions. The women students accepted the administrative dicta, and relative harmony was restored. The women seemed appeased, for their togetherness would be maintained for three more months, and they did nothing to jeopardize their remaining days in Roberta Hall. When the women left their rooms in May, they knew they would not return to Roberta Hall in the fall but would relocate in Wilson, Richardson, and Colbert Halls, adjacent structures that would keep the sororities relatively close to each other. And what was to be the fate of Roberta Hall? A group of consulting engineers, after extensive study of the structure in the late summer or early fall of

1980, would inform Northwest of the financial feasibility of renovating Roberta. If their nod were negative, the oldest residence hall on campus might become history. If it were affirmative, she again would live to host effervescent female students. Remembering their happy times when living in the building once known as Residence Hall, many grandmothers and mothers hoped that their granddaughters and daughters would have the chance to live there. Northwest also hoped for their chance. Considering the administration's feeling for tradition, Roberta hall will probably remain as the University's second oldest structure.

For several months the Seventy-Fifth Anniversary Task Force, under the overall leadership of Mr. Bob Sunkel, head of the division of fine arts, was planning, with its various committees, for 1980 when Northwest would be celebrating its diamond jubilee. Centered around the theme "Our Tradition: The Environment for Student Excellence," the year would be marked by various activities highlighting Northwest's seventy-five-year history and tradition. The Faculty Dames staged its version of the University's history early in March with skits that depicted various epochs in the life of Northwest. The event that officially initiated the seven months of activities in observance of Northwest's jubilee, however, was the March 25 all-school Convocation, chaired by the department of music's Mrs. Mary Jane Sandford, chairman of the Anniversary Observances Committee. That day was significant, for on March .25, 1905, the bill authorizing the Normal School to the Northwest District was signed by Governor Joseph W. Folk. It had been some time since the University held a Convocation, and students, faculty and staff members, and townspeople overflowed the Charles Johnson Theater. Many media representatives were also present, including those from St. Joseph's television station, KQTV. The stage abounded with people, many who gave short speeches. It was a dignified yet entertaining affair. After Miss Peggy Bush from the department of music performed a prelude of organ music, Campus Minister David Bennett offered an opening prayer, and President Owens opened the Convocation with remarks. He then introduced Governor Joseph Teasdale who spoke of crises and made the crowd's pulses vibrate quickly when he said Northwest deserved the requested $13,800,000 in emergency appropriations. Professor Emeritus Mattie Dykes scintillated the assemblage with her story of why Maryville residents worked so arduously to secure a normal school in Maryville. She frankly stated that the town had the most to offer and evoked laughter with her remark that "Them that has gits." Miss Dykes, whom most everyone in the audience knew as the author of *Behind the*

Birches, the history of Northwest's first fifty years, finished her discussion by saying "But time's up—I must get Behind the Birches." Her end words were like a trigger, for everyone in the room responded to her and her remarks with a prolonged standing ovation. The following people then offered comments concerning Northwest and higher education: Dr. Robert Foster, president emeritus of Northwest; Mr. Robert Duesenberg, chairman of the Missouri Coordinating Board for Higher Education; Mr. Alfred McKemy, president of the Board of Regents; Dr. Jack Kinder, executive secretary of the Missouri State Teachers Association and president of the Northwest Alumni Association; and Mr. Steve Holle, a Northwest senior and president of Blue Key Honorary Fraternity. Additional remarks were made by President Owens, the University Chorale, under Byron Mitchell's direction, offered a closing song, and then Northwest's first observance of its diamond jubilee was over. Three ladies sat together during this March 25, 1980, Convocation. Two of those were former first ladies of Northwest Missouri State—Mrs. J. W. Jones and Mrs. Robert P. Foster. The third, of course, was the present first lady—Mrs. B. D. Owens.

That same night, the Charles Johnson Theater was again the setting for an overflowing crowd. Offering a contrast to the formal morning Convocation was Mark Russell, the nation's foremost political satirist. For two hours Russell, sponsored by the University's Performing Arts and Lecture Series, dazzled his audience with humorous comments and barbs.

The usual spring visits by area high school students were in evidence. Some were here for the annual events like Foreign Language Day, Journalism Day, and the Mathematics Olympiad, which was enlarged in 1980 from a one-day format to a two-day program that included computer science. A young event, however, was beginning to make its imprint. The second annual Science Fair, headed by Dr. David Smith, head of the division of sciences, attracted high school participants from Nebraska, Iowa, Kansas, and Missouri on March 22. Dr. Harmon Mothershead, head of the division of history and humanities, was gearing his colleagues for Missouri History Day, a state contest that included students in grades seven through twelve from fifteen counties.

The end of March offered a whirl of accomplishments for Northwest. Governor Teasdale, of course, signed the $13,800,000 emergency appropriations bill for Northwest. Northwest would, as originally promised by the General Assembly and the Governor, have its new structures—the library and the auditorium—plus the renovation of Wells Library and the restoration of the Administration Building. The

The Thomas W. Gaunt House
Home of Northwest Missouri State University Presidents

new buildings' committees were meeting weekly since January and would continue to meet until the structures were part of the family of campus buildings. The aquatic center, alas, should not be forgotten in this new building coterie. People did wonder during the winter months why there was no construction activity since ground for the center was broken on Homecoming morning. Bids were the problem. Those submitted by various contractors were higher than anticipated, but on March 27 the Board of Regents finally accepted a bid from O'Riley Brothers Construction of Maryville, and construction began in June for the 120x88 foot pre-cast concrete, brick veneer, free-standing building, that is scheduled for completion in the spring of 1981. Although the proposed aquatic center was welcomed wholeheartedly, its impending construction was causing negative ripples among the tennis set. Students, faculty, staff, and townspeople who regularly used the tennis courts east of the future aquatic center feared the loss of their beloved courts. What they finally discovered was that the facilities would quite likely become a casualty because the contractors needed the space for trucks to deliver construction materials. Their heavy apparatus assuredly would cause extensive damage to the courts, already badly in need of repair. President Owens felt that it would be less expensive to build new tennis courts than to attempt to repair heavily damaged ones. He, to be sure, liked the idea of removing the courts, for he found them less than aesthetically pleasing. A grass-covered mall, in their place, he thought, would add beauty to the campus grounds. But he did not plan to deny the tennis crowd. New lighted courts, he said, would be built near the aquatic center and the gymnasiums. In the meantime, two new indoor courts are to be ready in the fall of 1980 as part of the Lamkin Gymnasium renovation.

For some time university personnel and area residents knew that the President's Home, now officially called the Thomas W. Gaunt House, after the original owner and builder, was to be included in the National Register of Historic Places. As part of the University's seventy-fifth anniversary celebration, formal recognition for this honor was observed on April 2, 1980, in the Charles Johnson Theater with remarks by President Owens and a historical explanation of the significance of the naming by Mr. Tom Carneal, associate professor of history, the one who prepared the nomination for the House to be included in the National Register. Mr. Gilbert Whitney of the music department adeptly led the singing of the National Anthem, and several appropriate musical selections were provided by the University's Symphonic Band, directed by Dr. Guy D'Aurelio. The Reverends Robert Allen and Robert Ceperley, local ministers, presented the invocation and the benediction. President Owens, in his remarks, stressed the tradition of the Thomas Gaunt House and referred to the structure, since it has been the home for all eight of Northwest's presidents, as a vital link to the past. He mentioned, too, that thousands of people visit it each year. More numbers were certainly added on this day. After Mrs. Robert Foster, wife of President Owens' predecessor, and Mrs. Owens performed the ribbon-cutting ceremonies, hundreds trouped through the Thomas Gaunt House to view its interior.

Another event scheduled to coincide with the diamond jubilee celebration was the April 6 grand opening of a six-week exhibit of hand-crafted musical instruments from the Renwick Gallery of the Smithsonian Institute in the Gallery of the Olive DeLuce Fine Arts Building. Entitled "The Harmonious Craft: American Musical Instruments," the exhibit, with the appropriate number of seventy-five instruments, had not been seen outside the Smithsonian Institute until 1980.

KXCV-FM certainly proved its resiliency and its ability to thrive in adversity. Operating with minimal equipment and housed in three temporary homes since the Administration Building fire, the station's standard of excellence, however, was maintained. Two student reporters, Tim Hartnett and Laurie Peterson, won the Sigma Delta Chi honorary journalism fraternity's student broadcasting first place awards for Region VII, and Tim Parks, their fellow broadcaster, claimed a second. Region VII includes Missouri, Iowa, Nebraska, Kansas, and a part of Illinois. Within the state, the Missouri Radio and Television News Association awarded Suzie Zillner, Brad Pace, Kevin Bocqui, and Bob Hammond its number one trophy. The Missouri Broadcasters Association liked the work of Mike McLaughlin and John Coffey, and the two, not to be outdone by their peers, also won a first place rating. Operations Manager Perry Echelberger, a member of the staff, showed that he practiced what he taught as the Missouri Broadcasters Association also rated his work first. Jeff McCall, the station's news director, was displaying a smile of satisfaction for the work of his broadcasting crew. He was happy, too, for his protégée Kathy Brown was selected by *Newsweek* for a ten-week internship in New York City. In 1979, Miss Brown traveled to Las Vegas, Nevada, to receive the $1,000 Radio and TV News Directors Fund Scholarship. It was a good spring for McCall. He happily watched his wife, Cathy, walk across the stage at the Honors Assembly as she received the Kappa Omicron Phi Award, presented to a senior member of the organization for having made outstanding contributions to the club and for possessing an outstanding grade point average. Earlier McCall himself made the national news by picking the final rankings of the nation's top collegiate football teams. In so doing, he outpicked some of the country's top football prognosticators. Later in the spring, McCall received word that the Missouri Associated Press Broadcasters Association awarded him and his student news staff first place for their spot news coverage of the Administration Building fire.

A protest that received more media coverage than it probably deserved occurred on Thursday, April 24. A ragtag group calling itself "Students Are People Too" and numbering approximately forty students, organized and led by Jeff Sachs, was rallying against what Sachs called college student discrimination in Maryville. He said they were protesting against merchants who would not take checks from students, the conditions of some apartments, and the general attitude the town has toward students. Although the rally was discouraged by various campus organizations and was not sanctioned by the Student Senate, the group met at the Memorial Bell Tower and marched downtown to the Nodaway County Courthouse. Carrying signs, the group was orderly, for Sachs had warned them to follow three rules: no obscenity, no drugs, and no alcohol. One of the signs carried by a student, however, did elicit some comment by both students and townspeople. The sign and the student who carried it were lambasted in an editorial in the *Daily Forum* and in a letter to its editor. The placard that read "I'd Rather Live in Iran" was obviously tasteless and shameless, considering that the Americans taken as hostages in Iran on November 4 were still captives on April 24, 1980, the day of the protest march. When the event was over, Sachs met with approximately fifteen of his marchers and discussed methods to improve living conditions. These remnants of the march decided to publish a list of what they considered good housing and omit the names of those whom they felt were "bad" landlords.

Northwest's theatergoers saw such productions produced by the department of theater as *The Rivals, Cat on a Hot Tin Roof,* and *Antigone* during the 1979-1980 academic year. Although somewhat modified to meet twentieth-century tastes, *Antigone,* directed by Mr. Theophil Ross, was the first Greek tragedy seen for some time on campus. Incidentally, this tragedy, performed in the Charles Johnson Theater, was to have been the department of theater's first production in the Administration Building's newly renovated Frank Deerwester Theatre, which was seventy percent completed when it was destroyed in the July 24 fire. Usually the only reward theater people receive for their work is applause from the audience, and scene designers hardly ever obtain recognition except appreciation from the director and the performers. Mr. Ken Brown, however, garnered a Special Award for Excellence in Lighting Design, based on his lighting artistry for *Cat on a Hot Tin Roof,* from the American College of Theater Festival. Brown's award was the only one offered by the Festival in lighting design from forty-three entries in Kansas, Nebraska, Iowa, and Missouri. A bit of the broadway stage came to Northwest in April as Veteran Rita Gardner played the lead role in the theater department's production of *The Prime of Miss Jean Brodie,* directed by Dr. Charles Schultz. Gardner, sponsored by the University's Performing Arts and Lecture Series, was the imported star, but performances from students like Dussie Mackey were superb. This production completed a fine year for the theater group.

In the spring of 1979, only eighteen percent of Northwest's students voted in the Student Senate election. Although the students were called apathetic in some quarters, many could not trouble themselves to vote for anyone who was running unopposed for the presidency of the student body. The spring of 1980 was different. In an election that had a thirty-two percent voter turnout, Rhodes, Iowa's Joe Pickard won a resounding victory over his opponent. Pickard, it seemed to the voters, was the correct choice as he displayed a genuine concern for his peers and for campus issues. Maryville merchants found Pickard's platform pleasing, too. He promised better cooperation and interaction between the businessmen and the students, and he planned, along with his vice president, Dave Hart, to attend the Chamber of Commerce and the Maryville Citizens for Community Action meetings. Pickard, to be sure, promised to be a very visible and active president.

A long-standing tradition on campus is the University's recognition of its students for their scholastic achievements, leadership abilities, outstanding contributions, and their potential to the future. On Monday, April 28, Northwest for the thirty-first consecutive time, paid homage to those deserving students at the Honors Assembly. President Owens told the ninety-six honorees that twenty-one years earlier he, like them, was sitting and waiting in anticipation. Owens, as a student, received the Wall Street Journal Award, and he further remarked that the foundations of his education which were recognized with that award were serving him well in his post as the eighth president of Northwest Missouri State University.

Many of the students selected for the University's various honors were thrilled and visibly moved by their awards, and for Maryville's Cathy Miller it was a thrilling, enduring, and enchanting week. For the second year, she was cited at the Honors Assembly for winning the

Saville Scholarship. As a Saville Scholar, Miss Miller worked in Wells Library with Mr. Tom Carneal, associate professor of history, interpreting and preparing historical exhibits from the archives of the Missouriana Room Collection. The morning after the Honors Assembly, Miller received word of her appointment as a summer intern with the Missouri Department of Natural Resources' Division of Parks and Historic Preservation at the Watkins Mill State Historic Site at Lawson, Missouri. Of course, Carneal and his history colleagues at Northwest were exuberant, for Miss Miller was Northwest's first history intern. As a senior majoring in history and library science, in addition to her work with Carneal, Miller seemed ideal for the internship. Carneal felt that it would offer her sufficient experience to work effectively in the future at any historic site, and Miller's assignment undoubtedly would help break a new path for future Northwest history majors interested in historic preservation.

While the University was honoring its students in the spring, an honor bestowed upon a faculty member did not go unnoticed. Dr. Charles Kovich, assistant professor of English and director of freshman composition, was selected to Phi Beta Kappa, one of academe's highest honors.

Although Northwest's track and field team had brilliant individual performers, for seven consecutive years it could finish no better than sixth place in the MIAA outdoor championship meet. Coach Richard Flanagan's and Assistant Coach Richard Alsup's charges, however, accomplished something in the spring of 1980 that no Bearcat thinclad team had been able to do for twenty-five years—finish third in the conference. Coach Jim Wasem's baseball Bearcats ended its season in May when it lost in the finals of the NCAA Division II Midwest Regional Tournament to Minnesota's Mankato State. Coach Wasem and his men could take comfort, however, from the fact that the team finished with a 34-12 mark, the best in the University's history. Incidentally, the 1979-1980 Bearcat teams won the unofficial all-sports competition in the MIAA, a feat never before accomplished in the annals of Northwest.

Two faculty members who came to Northwest in the early fifties and one who joined them in the mid sixties retired during this seventy-fifth anniversary year. The three, Miss Dorothy Weigand, assistant professor of English; Mrs. Ruth Killingsworth, assistant professor of library science; and Mr. Gilbert Whitney, assistant professor of music; were honored by their peers and families at the University's Retirement Banquet on May 7 in the J. W. Jones Union Ballroom. Over 300 people shared the evening with the honorees, and, as a special treat, Mr. and

Mrs. Ken Bittiker, former students of Mr. Whitney's, sang and played old favorites. This extra touch was conceived by Mrs. Zelma Akes of the elementary education department, who headed the University Social Committee in charge of the Banquet. Miss Weigand, affectionately known as "Miss Dorothy" by her English colleagues and senior English majors, left as her legacy to Northwest thirty years of fine and dedicated teaching. On her last day of teaching, one of her classes offered her a standing ovation, a special and unusual accolade that a teacher anywhere rarely receives. If a trophy were given for the most reliable member of her department, Miss Weigand would have thirty of the mementos on her mantelpiece. Mrs. Killingsworth, a mainstay of the department of library science for fourteen years, effectively taught most of the courses the department offered, and in her last year not only taught library science courses, but headed the department and supervised the Horace Mann Learning Center Library. Mr. Whitney, during his twenty-nine-year tenure, directed the Tower Choir, College Chorus, University Singers, the University Swing Choir, and the Madraliers. By taking these groups at various times on singing tours to the region's high schools, Whitney helped serve as Northwest's "built-in" recruiter. Whitney, the founder and director of the traditional and happy Madrigal Feaste held each Christmas season, would be gone from the University but his footprint would be heavy.

Some of the people sharing the evening with Miss Weigand, Mrs. Killingsworth, and Mr. Whitney were also part of another recognition dinner the following month. On June 14, former students and colleagues gathered in the Ballroom to honor Professor Emeritus J. Gordon Strong, who retired in 1964 as chairman of the division of science and mathematics. Planned and coordinated by two of Dr. Strong's former students, Dr. Harlan Higginbotham, chairman of the department of chemistry and physics, and Mr. Robert James, a Cook Paint executive, the evening was one of tribute for Dr. Strong. Besides Higginbotham, Drs. Ed Farquhar and Ted Weichinger, two members of the chemistry and physics staff and former students of Dr. Strong's, were there, and the keynote speaker was yet another former student, Dr. Richard Leet, president of Standard Oil's Amoco Chemicals Corporation. Dr. Strong was happy, not so much for the recognition, but for the esteem in which his former students and colleagues regarded him. Mrs. Strong and their son, Melville, were happy for him, too, and the whole family reveled when Higginbotham announced the establishment of the J. Gordon Strong Scholarship in chemistry.

Late spring saw two other valuable members of the staff retire. The affable Mr. Earl Shannon, who served as custodian in the men's residence halls for fifteen continuous years, would be missed by the students. Mr. Richard Beason's absence would be noticed, too, for he steadily served the University in many different capacities for nineteen years.

Commencement ceremonies throughout Northwest's history had been held on various days of the week, but hardly anyone remembered graduation on a Saturday afternoon. The 1980 spring graduates, however, would remember this one for the Seventy-Fifth Anniversary Commencement was observed at 2 p.m. on Saturday, May 10. They also would not forget the heat and humidity of Lamkin Gymnasium on that day. Mr. E. D. Geyer, whom commencement watchers saw on the stage at the last spring commencement as the retiring president of the Board of Regents, returned as a recipient of the University's Distinguished Service Award. Two other Northwest graduates, Dr. Buford W. Garner and Dr. George R. Green, also returned to their alma mater to receive the Distinguished Alumni Awards and to deliver commencement remarks. Garner, administrator of area education No. 16 in Iowa, was honored for his contributions in the field of education. Green, a former Huebner Foundation Scholar and presently chief of the federal government's Business Outlook Division, received his award for contributions in the area of economics. His address was not the sometimes common glad tidings to the graduates, but he pessimistically forecasted a gloomy economic picture in America's future.

Northwest officials in the spring, after considering solid waste as a source of energy for more than a year, decided instead to burn wood waste products that would create steam to heat and cool the campus buildings. Wood appeared to be more attractive and cheaper as an energy source, and Dr. Robert Bush, vice president for environmental development, was cognizant of a source of wood wastes close to Maryville that would provide Northwest with the average forty tons of wood materials it would need daily. This source would be enough to supply the University's needs for five years, but other suppliers seemed to be in abundance. The proposed wood-burning plant, to be built at the site of the present offices of the physical plant, needed to be financed, and that in early summer was the only drawback. Northwest was considering various alternatives to finance the new energy plant and by waiting hoped to achieve considerable savings in interest rates. Financing, however, in the early summer of 1980, was being negotiated. But Northwest, disdaining to use again expensive natural gas and oil, would have its more efficient and less expensive energy alternative. The plant, when built, would pay for itself in seven years, and its equipment would possibly be durable enough to last a half century.

Northwest, because of the Administration Building fire, had found itself in a bit of a financial bind during the 1979-1980 academic year and adjusted to the strain accordingly. Usually individual departments were allowed to save for a special piece of equipment or project if the total amount of their budgeted money was not used during a given year. In 1979-1980, however, that money from the departments was used to help defray the expense of moving departments, to replace equipment lost due to the fire, and to prepare the Administration Building for the harshness of the winter months. The departmental financial paucity ended when the emergency appropriations were approved for the University. Northwest received $24,427,522 in appropriations from the eightieth Missouri General Assembly. Although its 1980-1981 operating budget of $9,866,371 is smaller than requested and represents an increase of approximately five percent over the 1979-1980 budget, Northwest filled its top priority with the $13,807,681 in emergency funds, to be used, of course, for the construction of the new library and the new auditorium and for the refurbishing of the Administration Building and the renovation of Wells Library for classrooms. Included in the General Assembly's package for Northwest is $333,500 for capital improvements for repairs; $235,000 to renovate and replace the utility distribution system to the Administration Building; and $185,000 to make modifications for the handicapped. The $24,427,522 total appropriations are the largest in Northwest Missouri State University's seventy-five-year history.

It is a truism that many instructors like their work so well that they would "do it for nothing if they could afford it." Although many of the professionals on Northwest's staff have this attitude, they care about the necessities of life, worry about the cost of living and inflation, and want to be paid well for what they do. Because Northwest's faculty salaries were the lowest among its sister institutions in the state for years, Northwest's present administration has repeatedly stated in the last three years that it is working to make salaries at Northwest the highest among its sister institutions in Missouri. Since Northwest's operating budget for the 1980-1981 academic year did not raise dramatically over the previous year, it looked as if faculty salary increases would be small. In August of 1979, however, the Board of Regents decreed, after listening to Owens' and English's recommendations, that Northwest's faculty would receive an eleven percent increase in 1980. Early in May, members of the University's instructional staff received their contracts, and what was reflected there was the school's highest percentage raise in history—11.2 percent. (In 1978 the increase averaged ten percent and in 1979, because of President Carter's salary lid, seven percent.) Although people—and teachers are no exception—never seem appeased with their salary levels, the increase was deemed by most as reasonably acceptable. It seems, however, that faculty members can at least believe what they are hearing from their administrative leaders because some fine gains in faculty salaries are being made. Many, too, according to the results of a questionnaire submitted by the University's Faculty Welfare Committee, were happy to see that their increases were not governed only by merit as they had been since 1978. Every faculty member received a 5.2 percent cost of living increase in 1980, and the remainder of the increase was based on merit. The present administration is a strong advocate of merit, for both Owens and English feel that their staff should be rewarded for effective teaching, worthwhile scholarship, and other valid contributions to the University. Heavily considered in the merit raises are student evaluations, division head and chairman recommendations, and the missive an instructor labors over annually—the annual report. The merit scale ranges from one to five. The fives are few and a happy group; the fours are not exactly sour; unless one is extremely complacent and likes to be average, no one revels in the three category; the twos are uncommon; and the ones would probably be better suited elsewhere. In 1978, Northwest's faculty salaries ranked thirty-sixth in a field of forty-nine higher education institutions in a nine-state area of the Midwest, and in 1979 the University moved to the twenty-eighth slot. With the 11.2 percent increase offered to the faculty in 1980, Northwest's faculty salaries, undoubtedly, will rank much higher on the rungs of the survey ladder.

The most important characteristic of any institution of learning is, of course, the teaching of men and women, young and old. One facet in the educational process, the news and information department, however, never seems to receive adequate recognition, nor does it appear to care to be recognized since its principal job is to inform the public of what is happening at the University. President Owens, recognizing the importance of media coverage, appointed Mr. Bob Henry in 1977 to the new position of public relations officer and gave him the additional supervisory responsibilities over the directors of alumni relations and radio and television broadcasting. Henry for three years carried the titles of public relations officer and director of news and information, but in June Mr. Tom Myers, the very capable media specialist in the office of news and information, was appointed to the directorship of that office. Miss Jane Kemp continues to serve as Northwest's first publications coordinator, a much-needed post that was created in 1978. Kemp efficiently fills the previous void with verve and vitality, and she has given Northwest a series of composite publications that reflect the image of Northwest Missouri State University. Mr. Larry Cain is Mr. Mike Kiser's successor as sports information director. Kiser, who won many national awards for his descriptive and informative Bearcat and Bearkitten brochures, resigned in May. The office, too, is fortunate to have the effectiveness of Executive Secretary Teresa Carter, who once received the Northwest presidential award as Secretary of the Month.

Observances of the University's diamond jubilee continue, and such activities will continue until the end of October. The Greater Maryville Association—the retail division of the Maryville Chamber of Commerce—and the Maryville community have been preparing for some time for a special observance of the University's seventy-fifth anniversary. On August 4, 1980, Maryville will commemorate the anniversary of the day Governor Folk notified the city that it had been selected as the site for the Northwest Missouri Normal School by recreating the celebration which took place in Maryville on August 4, 1905. The celebration, called University Day, will be no small affair. Unique features of University Day will include a special stamp cancellation, depicting an Administration Building tower, and a special commemorative envelope—both to be available on August 4. A special thirty-cent green stamp featuring a schoolhouse will be placed on each envelope. Other mementos to help highlight University Day are Anniversary buttons and reprinted copies of the August 10, 1905, issue of the *Nodaway Forum*. The Maryville community was ecstatic in 1905 when it received word that a normal school would be located in Maryville, and the community is no less happy that Northwest Missouri State University is here and thriving in 1980, seventy-five years later.

Summer Commencement will focus on Northwest's anniversary, and on September 12, 1980, the Board of Regents will hold a commemorative meeting and reenact the first meeting by the Board on September 12, 1905. On October 11, homecoming participants will see the day focusing on the anniversary theme, and individual departments throughout September and October will have special speakers and projects centering on Northwest's seventy-fifth anniversary.

6

Surmises

Strong as a tower in hope, I cry amen.

—Shakespeare

Since the University's legislative and gubernatorial creation in 1905, Northwest, at the end of the 1980 summer session, will have produced approximately 22,500 baccalaureate and master's degree graduates. At the end of the 1979-1980 academic year, the University possessed an instructional staff of 243 members. Of that number fifty-four were ranked full professors; sixty-one, associate professors; eighty-five, assistant professors; thirty-five, instructors; and eight were teaching assistants. Including two who retired in 1980, seventeen of Northwest's 1979-1980 faculty members answered roll call when *Towers in the Northwest* began in January of 1956. Since they were here throughout this twenty-five-year history, the following deserve mention: Mr. David Crozier, Miss Kathryn McKee, Dr. George Gayler, Miss Dorothy Weigand, Dr. Elwyn DeVore, Dr. Donald Sandford, Mrs. Mary Jane Sandford, Mr. Gilbert Whitney, Dr. Burton Richey, Dr. Ted Weichinger, Mr. Earle Moss, Mr. Robert Gregory, Mr. Myles Grabau, Dr. Wanda Walker, Mr. Calvin Widger, Mrs. Zelma Akes, and Dr. Berndt Angman. Dr. George Hinshaw can be listed as the tardy member since he joined the group in the fall of 1956. The hardy veterans of this club are the 1940's members. Mr. Crozier came in 1940 and ranks number one on Northwest's seniority list; number two is Miss McKee, who joined the faculty in 1946; and rounding out the forties is Dr. Gayler, who discovered Northwest in 1949. Northwest's students in 1980 claim more than thirty states and a like number of foreign countries as home, and the educational backgrounds of Northwest's faculty members represent more than 100 colleges and universities. Many of their degrees are from prestigious institutions.

Like any college or university in the country, Northwest has its share of students, who for various individual reasons, pack and head home for the weekends. There always seems to be, however, a plethora of activities on campus. The University's Performing Arts and Lecture Series supplies the culture; the Union Board brings in the concerts

271

and other especial student interests; the Inter-Residence Hall Council has helped in recent years with a myriad of activities. Academic departments use their allotted assembly budgets to host outstanding speakers and projects. The individual dormitories are strong in sponsoring their own brands of entertainment. Although the fraternities seem to overdo the party bit, they, the sororities, and the independents seem to have their share of fun, and there is always some intercollegiate contest involving either the Bearcats or the Bearkittens that students can attend. Intramural games are prevalent, too. The music and theater departments supply much entertainment throughout the school year, and theater always seems to help fill the summer void. The student who complains that "there is nothing to do" is probably not observant or is a rather obtuse individual and would probably make that comment wherever he is. Northwest's students also seem to have the capacity to entertain themselves as witnessed by the extensive number of joggers, tennis and racquetball players, and participants in pick-up basketball games at either Lamkin or Martindale Gymnasium. No, the social life and the cultural life at the University do not seem to interfere with its academic life although some members of the faculty probably think differently. Despite the distractions, time has been found for study. In addition to their regular classwork, some students even take advantage of the various departments' independent study programs. Northwest Missouri State University's graduates, as evidenced by the division of sciences' record, do well in graduate studies and lead satisfying and successful lives. Those, too, who have attained success have generally been the men and women who in their student days, while enjoying many of the activities, gave the highest priority to academic interests. The stronger accent at Northwest, to be sure, is on the academic.

Summer school enrollment in 1980 has increased twelve percent over 1979. In June, student applications for the fall were twenty percent ahead of what they were in 1979, and summer pre-registration for fall freshmen is running approximately eleven percent ahead of 1979 when Northwest's freshman class increased 14.5 percent. Administrators here are predicting a seven percent enrollment increase in the fall, and they are probably right. Although enrollment projections indicate there will be twelve percent fewer high school graduates in the state of Missouri by 1983, these same administrators see 5,000 students at Northwest in 1983 because they will want to enroll here for the school's quality programs. The 1980s, however, will pose a challenge for higher education. Given the demographic fact of a decreasing population of traditional college-age people, expected to continue for the next fifteen years, some colleges and universities will battle not for excellence but for bodies to fill their buildings. Northwest is not, to be sure, expected to be one of them. In studying the demography of the next decades, the Carnegie Council on Policy Studies in Higher Education envisions the 1980s as the "Golden Age" for students. The Council's report forecasts that students—because there will be fewer of them—will be sought more attentively, admitted more readily, counseled and taught more conscientiously, and will receive better help in obtaining jobs after graduation. One might worry about such optimistic assumptions, but the Council in making those predictions could have been using Northwest Missouri State University as its model. Of course, Northwest is not interested in accepting just anyone (as witnessed by the 400 students not welcomed back in 1978). But great attention is paid to quality recruits, and students are advised and taught rather conscientiously by most of the faculty members. As figures in the career/placement office show, graduates seldom want for positions.

The University is and will continue to serve as the cultural and academic center of the region. Northwest offers a traditional quality education, but it is not reticent to add new offerings or enrich existing programs so that its objective can be fulfilled to an even greater degree. The institution's latest academic development began in June of 1980 when it offered a unique graduate degree program, the Master of Science in School Computer Studies. Attracting approximately thirty full-time students this first summer, the program, coordinated by Dr. Merry McDonald, associate professor of mathematical sciences, is designed for students who want to teach computer science in secondary schools or junior colleges. Another graduate program, already approved by the Missouri Coordinating Board for Higher Education and awaiting the blessing of the North Central Association, when the group gathers on campus in the fall, is Northwest's own Specialist in Education degree. This additional year of study beyond the master's would, of course, be the University's highest degree. Because of what Northwest's ROTC program has accomplished in growth, leadership, enrichment, and strength during its two-year stay on campus, it is very likely that the local group, which began as a cross-enrollment agreement and then an extension of Missouri Western's ROTC program, will become a host unit in the near future. It is obvious, too, that people here will continue to receive an international flavor. Northwest's latest student trip took place in June when Dr. Luis Macias, associate professor of Spanish, led seventeen students, including fifteen Spanish majors and minors, on a fifteen-day study trip to Spain where they could absorb the Spanish culture and also receive three hours of academic credit. For seventeen days in July, President and Mrs. Owens were absorbing life in another country. The two, selected to be part of a twenty-five person scientific, cultural, and educational delegation from America, visited the People's Republic of China. The delegation was sponsored by the Edgar Snow Foundation at the University of Missouri at Kansas City. Owens was the only university president chosen and was there principally to discuss that country's educational policies with its dignitaries.

It is an exciting and stimulating period in the life of the University, and all the tangible elements beginning to materialize in the summer of 1980 are titillating reminders of Northwest's seventy-fifth birthday. By the summer of 1983, students (barring unforeseen calamities like construction strikes and extreme weather moods) will have full use of a highly technological yet traditional new library, a performing arts center (auditorium) that will offer many new cultural vistas, an aquatic center where people can swim in uncrowded conditions, a renovated Administration Building, a wood waste to energy plant, and a separate but permanent home for the speech department, the Speech and Hearing Clinic, and the broadcasting and television studios in the refurbished Wells Library. From his new communications' home, Rollie Stadlman, director of broadcasting, will be able to plan all kinds of ingenious devices for campus radio and television. KXCV-FM, of course, already receives National Public Radio by satellite, but by the middle of the eighties, with NASA as a resource, Stadlman and Chief Engineer Warren Stucki and Production Technician Larry Lewellen will very probably have developed a second parabolic disc (this one, however, for television) that will allow students to observe not one or two satellites, like Westar I or Comsat, but many. As a result of transmissions from the various satellites, Northwest's broadcasting students could have 110 different channels at their disposal. Since the people here are very capable in developing new technological areas and NASA is willing to help, the advancement in communications is economically feasible.

Although Northwest's alumni and friends have not been in the habit of making significant financial contributions to the University, another unfolding development is beginning to rise high in the future of Northwest. This development is not a structure made of bricks, pre-cast concrete, or limestone, but, nevertheless, it promises to have a solid foundation. In 1980, the University is launching a new organization, comprised of alumni and friends, called the Northwest Missouri State University Tower Society, a group dedicated to helping North-

west continue its "Margin for Excellence" by hopefully contributing
enough money to raise $2,200,000 in a five-year period. The Tower
Society would like to grow suddenly tall and then tower as a pinnacle
in the University's future. Appropriately named, the Tower Society
has as its symbol the Northwest tower of the Administration Building,
one of the four towers that proved its strength and durability by
staunchly withstanding the massive onslaught of the catastrophic July
24, 1979, fire. Even though the University is a state institution, private
financial sources in these economically harsh times are becoming
increasingly more important to institutions of higher education. Hoping
to help fill in the academic areas that student fees and state appropriations do not cover, the group certainly has towering and admirable
ideals. It plans to establish distinguished professorships, visiting
professorships, and faculty chairs; to build library resources; to
establish added scholarships, grants in aid, fellowships, and assistantships; to cultivate research enrichment; to institute more cultural
programs; to buy specialized equipment; and to supply money to
initiate new programs. The Northwest Missouri Alumni Association is
hopeful, too, that enough alumni and friends will pledge the necessary
money to enable the University to have an alumni center. In late July,
the Association was conducting a fund-raising drive to purchase the
Townsend House, located at 640 College Avenue—across the street
from the Thomas W. Gaunt House.

What Northwest Missouri State University has been and what it
will continue to be have been discussed—or, at least, strongly implied—
throughout the pages of this history. In an institution of higher learning, like this University, there is too much, in too great a depth, for
any one mind to fully comprehend. Men and women who have been
affiliated with Northwest as students, instructors, staff members,
or administrators must determine how the University affects its meaning in their own minds and define how the institution affects their lives.
If this University has not or does not bring important changes for
them, then the participants should examine both themselves and
Northwest.

Northwest's administrators, faculty, and staff view the future
with optimism. They are not as pessimistic as many people involved
with higher education because there is a feeling here that there is a
great deal more to commend higher education than merely numbers.
The pervading thought on campus is that if the quality is maintained
the students will be here. Northwest has a heritage of quality, and it
has no intention of slipping now. Even though many people are pessimistic about this decade, it will be one of opportunities for the Uni-

versity, opportunities to demonstrate what Northwest is about and what it has to offer. Northwest's entry into the 1980s may very well be the institution's most outstanding period. The fact that the Missouri General Assembly and the Governor have been strongly supportive suggests that Northwest Missouri State University is in good health and is doing a good job.

Many familiar strands run through this school's seventy-five-year history. Each generation of students, however, delineates its own disposition within the climate of its times. The hazing of freshmen and the wearing of beanies are probably gone forever but something similar may reoccur. There is no guarantee that a corresponding pattern will not happen again. Future dwindling enrollments may very possibly encourage a dangerous and self-damaging trend at some colleges and universities. Administrators and instructors could become so concerned with pleasing students that they fail in adequately provoking thought and maintaining high academic standards. There is little danger that these academic trespasses will ever be found or permitted at this University. There is something else here that many other campuses lack—the indomitable spirit of friendliness. As Northwest developed and matured and grew in complexity as a university, it did not lose the cozy atmosphere of a residential campus.

Historians tend not to forecast or predict, but national trends in higher education are quite well known. Higher education, to be sure, is in a state of flux. Our future will, for the next writer of Northwest's history, be past history, and it will be evaluated within the contexts of the trends now present. Population, energy, and ecology are some issues facing men and women in 1980. For years, college and university presidents tended to be affable and gregarious people in search of students, and they closely controlled their schools. Crises presidents then seemed to prevail, and those were replaced by managers in accountability. But there are those presidents, of course, who do not follow the trends. President B. D. Owens does not seem to be the average leader. He does not fit the stereotypes of the old-school college presidents, the crises presidents, nor the coolly aloof managerial types. He is blessed with managerial skills, as evidenced by his Ph.D. in applied economics, but he is also thoroughly academic. A special university, like this one, requires a special kind of leader. Although President Owens has already left a giant mark and helped propel this institution into the eighties with a gigantic thrust, history will pass judgment and determine if these observations in the summer of 1980 were totally correct.

One thing is certain. Northwest Missouri State University is well on its way to a viable future. Although it will expand its services regionally, nationally, and even internationally, this University will be strengthened and preserved as a living and learning residential institution of higher education.

APPENDIX

CONTENTS

APPENDIX 1
Members of the Board of Regents

1955-1957

M. E. Ford, Maryville, President
Harold M. Hull, Maryville, Vice President
Arlis B. Vogt, Stanberry
H. F. Simrall, Liberty
W. M. C. Dawson, Grant City
R. L. Douglas, St. Joseph
W. A. Rickenbrode, Maryville, Secretary
   (Deceased November, 1956)
J. W. Jones, Maryville, Acting Secretary
Luther G. Belcher, Maryville, Treasurer
Hubert Wheeler, Jefferson City,
   Ex Officio

1957-1959

M. E. Ford, President
Harold M. Hull, Vice President
Arlis B. Vogt
H. F. Simrall
W. M. C. Dawson
H. N. Stevenson, St. Joseph
J. W. Jones, Secretary
Luther G. Belcher, Treasurer
Hubert Wheeler, Ex Officio

1959-1961

W. M. C. Dawson, President
Harold M. Hull, Vice President
Arlis B. Vogt
H. F. Simrall
Garvin Williams, Maryville
H. N. Stevenson
Luther G. Belcher, Secretary-Treasurer
Hubert Wheeler, Ex Officio

1961-1963

W. M. C. Dawson, President
Harold M. Hull, Vice President
H. N. Stevenson
Garvin Williams
J. P. Morgan, Chillicothe

C. F. Russell, Trenton
Luther G. Belcher, Secretary-Treasurer
Hubert Wheeler, Ex Officio

1963-1965

Harold M. Hull, President
Garvin Williams, Vice President
W. M. C. Dawson
H. N. Stevenson
J. P. Morgan
C. F. Russell
Luther G. Belcher, Secretary-Treasurer
Hubert Wheeler, Ex Officio

1965-1967

Garvin Williams, President
C. F. Russell, Vice President
W. M. C. Dawson
J. P. Morgan
David W. Hopkins, St. Joseph
William F. Phares, Jr., Maryville
Luther G. Belcher, Secretary-Treasurer
Hubert Wheeler, Ex Officio

1967-1969

Garvin Williams, President
C. F. Russell, Vice President
W. M. C. Dawson
J. P. Morgan
David W. Hopkins
William F. Phares, Jr.
Luther G. Belcher, Secretary-Treasurer
Hubert Wheeler, Ex Officio

1969-1971

Garvin Williams, President
C. F. Russell, Vice President
W. M. C. Dawson
William F. Phares, Jr.
Arlis B. Vogt
Edgerton Welch, Chillicothe
Luther G. Belcher, Secretary-Treasurer
Hubert Wheeler, Ex Officio

1971-1973

C. F. Russell, President
W. M. C. Dawson, Vice President

William F. Phares, Jr.
Arlis B. Vogt
John M. Yeaman, Weston
James Stubbs, Chillicothe
Monica G. Zirfas, Maryville, Secretary
  (Appt. September, 1970)
Don L. Henry, Maryville, Treasurer
Arthur Mallory, Jefferson City,
  Ex Officio

1973-1975

W. M. C. Dawson, President
John M. Yeaman, Vice President
William F. Phares, Jr.
Arlis B. Vogt
James Stubbs
C. F. Russell
Monica G. Zirfas, Secretary
Don L. Henry, Treasurer
Arthur Mallory, Ex Officio

1975-1977

William F. Phares, Jr., President
E. D. Geyer, Trenton, Vice President
Mary Linn, Princeton
G. Raymond Speckman, Plattsburg
James Stubbs

John M. Yeaman
Monica G. Zirfas, Secretary
Don L. Henry, Treasurer
Arthur Mallory, Ex Officio

1977-1979

E. D. Geyer, President
Alfred McKemy, Hardin, Vice President
Mary Linn
Harold L. Poynter, Maryville
Welton Ideker, Mound City
John A. Dunlap, Stewartsville
Monica G. Zirfas, Secretary
Don L. Henry, Treasurer
Arthur Mallory, Ex Officio

1979-1981

Alfred McKemy, President
Mary Linn, Vice President
Welton Ideker
Harold L. Poynter
John A. Dunlap
J. Norvel Sayler, Maryville
Monica G. Zirfas, Secretary
Don L. Henry, Treasurer
Jeanette A. Solheim, Maryville,
  Acting Treasurer
Arthur Mallory, Ex Officio

APPENDIX 2

Administrative personnel, 1956-1980

NWMSU catalogs were the principal sources of information.

1955-1956
President
  J. W. Jones
Secretary to the President
  Mabel C. Winburn
Dean of Faculty
  W. A. Brandenburg
Director, Field Services
  Everett W. Brown
Registrar
  Robert P. Foster
Librarian
  James Johnson
Director, Instructional Materials Bureau
  Charles E. Campbell
Dietitian
  Ruth E. Burke

Horace Mann Nurse
  Pearl K. Dawson
Director, Guidance and Counseling
  Charles E. Koerble
Counselor, Residence Hall
  Elizabeth J. Luer
Director, Student Activities
  Lois A. Simons
College Nurse
  Thelma M. Smith
Dean of Men
  Lon Wilson

1956-1957
President
  J. W. Jones

Secretary to the President
Mabel C. Winburn
Dean of Faculty
Charles E. Koerble
Director, Field Services
Everett W. Brown
Registrar
Robert P. Foster
Treasurer
Luther G. Belcher
Librarian
James Johnson
Director, Instructional Materials Bureau
Charles E. Campbell
Dietitian
Ruth E. Burke
Horace Mann Nurse
Pearl K. Dawson
Director, Women's Housing
Elizabeth J. Luer
Director, Student Activities
Lois A. Simons
College Nurse
Thelma M. Smith
Dean of Men
Lon Wilson

1957-1958
President
J. W. Jones
Secretary to the President
Mabel C. Winburn
Dean of Faculty
Charles E. Koerble
Director, Field Services
Everett W. Brown
Registrar
Robert P. Foster
Treasurer
Luther G. Belcher
Librarian
James Johnson
Director, Instructional Materials Bureau
James Johnson
Director, Athletics
Ryland H. Milner
Dean of Women
Martha E. Bladt
Dean of Men
Lon Wilson
Director, Women's Housing
Elizabeth J. Luer
Dietitian
Annalu L. Sheldon
College Nurse
Thelma M. Smith

Horace Mann Nurse
Pearl K. Dawson

1958-1959
President
J. W. Jones
Secretary to the President
Mabel C. Winburn
Dean of Faculty
Charles E. Koerble
Director, Alumni, Correspondence,
Extension, and Placement
Everett W. Brown
Registrar
Robert P. Foster
Treasurer
Luther G. Belcher
Librarian
James Johnson
Director, Instructional Materials Bureau
Luke L. Boone
Director, Athletics
Ryland H. Milner
Dean of Women
Martha E. Bladt
Dean of Men
Lon Wilson
Director, Women's Housing
Elizabeth J. Luer
Dietitian
Annalu L. Sheldon
College Nurse
Thelma M. Smith
Horace Mann Nurse
Pearl K. Dawson
Residence Hall Nurse
Helen O'Connor

1959-1960
President
J. W. Jones
Secretary to the President
Emma R. Harris
Business Manager
Luther G. Belcher
Director, Placement and Alumni
Everett W. Brown
Dean of Administration
Robert P. Foster
Dean of Students
Charles E. Koerble
Director, Residence Facilities for Men,
Dean of Men
Lon Wilson
Dean of Women
Martha E. Bladt

Director, Residence Facilities for Women
  Elizabeth J. Luer
Assistant Registrar
  Ruth Nystrom
Assistant Director, Placement
  Esther Sellers
Librarian
  James Johnson
Director, Instructional Materials Bureau
  Luke L. Boone
Director, Athletics
  Ryland H. Milner
College Nurse
  Thelma M. Smith
Horace Mann Nurse
  Pearl K. Dawson
Residence Hall Nurse
  Helen O'Connor
Dietitian
  Annalu L. Sheldon

1960-1961
President
  J. W. Jones
Secretary to the President
  Emma R. Harris
Business Manager
  Luther G. Belcher
Director, Placement and Alumni
  Everett W. Brown
Dean of Administration
  Robert P. Foster
Dean of Instruction
  Leon F. Miller
Dean of Students
  Charles E. Koerble
Director, Residence Facilities for Men,
    Dean of Men
  Lon Wilson
Dean of Women
  Martha E. Bladt
Director, Residence Facilities for Women
  Elizabeth J. Luer
Registrar
  Ruth Nystrom
Assistant Director, Placement
  Esther Sellers
Librarian
  James Johnson
Director, Instructional Materials Bureau
  Luke L. Boone
Director, Athletics
  Ryland H. Milner
College Nurse
  Thelma M. Smith

Horace Mann Nurse
  Pearl K. Dawson
Residence Hall Nurse
  Helen O'Connor
Dietitian
  Annalu L. Sheldon

1961-1962
President
  J. W. Jones
Secretary to the President
  Emma R. Harris
Business Manager
  Luther G. Belcher
Dean of Administration
  Robert P. Foster
Registrar
  Ruth Nystrom
Assistant Registrar
  Monica G. Zirfas
Dean of Instruction
  Leon F. Miller
Dean of Students
  Charles E. Koerble
Dean of Men
  Jack L. Lasley
Dean of Women
  Martha E. Bladt
Director, Placement and Alumni
  Everett W. Brown
Assistant Director, Placement
  Esther Sellers
Librarian
  James Johnson
Director, Instructional Materials Bureau
  Luke L. Boone
Director, Athletics
  Ryland H. Milner
College Nurse
  Thelma M. Smith
Horace Mann Nurse
  Pearl K. Dawson
Women's Dormitory Nurse
  Helen O'Connor
Dietitian
  Annalu L. Sheldon

1962-1963
President
  J. W. Jones
Secretary to the President
  Emma R. Harris
Business Manager
  Luther G. Belcher
Dean of Administration
  Robert P. Foster

Registrar
  Ruth Nystrom
Assistant Registrar
  Monica G. Zirfas
Dean of Instruction
  Leon F. Miller
Dean of Students
  Charles E. Koerble
Dean of Men
  Jack L. Lasley
Dean of Women
  Martha E. Bladt
Director, Alumni, Correspondence,
    Extension, and Placement
  Everett W. Brown
Assistant Director, Placement
  Esther Sellers
Assistant Director, Correspondence
    and Extension
  M. T. Sheldon
Librarian
  James Johnson
Director, Instructional Materials Bureau
  Luke L. Boone
Director, Athletics
  Ryland H. Milner
College Nurse
  Thelma M. Smith
Horace Mann Nurse
  Pearl K. Dawson
Women's Dormitory Nurse
  Helen O'Connor
Men's Dormitory Nurse
  Patricia Kilpatrick
Dietitian
  Annalu L. Sheldon

1963-1964
President
  J. W. Jones
Secretary to the President
  Emma R. Harris
Business Manager
  Luther G. Belcher
Dean of Administration
  Robert P. Foster
Registrar
  Ruth Nystrom
Assistant Registrar
  Monica G. Zirfas
Dean of Instruction
  Leon F. Miller
Dean of Students
  Charles E. Koerble
Dean of Men
  Jack L. Lasley

Dean of Women
  Gimmie L. Atchley
Director, Alumni, Correspondence,
    Extension, and Placement
  Everett W. Brown
Assistant Director, Placement
  Esther Sellers
Assistant Director, Correspondence
    and Extension
  M. T. Sheldon
Librarian
  James Johnson
Director, Instructional Materials Bureau
  Luke L. Boone
Director, Athletics
  Ryland H. Milner
College Nurse
  Thelma M. Smith
Horace Mann Nurse
  Pearl K. Dawson
Women's Dormitory Nurse
  Helen O'Connor
Dietitian
  Annalu L. Sheldon
Director, Union Building
  William H. Needels

1964-1965
President
  Robert P. Foster
Secretary to the President
  Monica G. Zirfas
Business Manager
  Luther G. Belcher
Dean of Administration
  Charles H. Thate
Registrar
  Ruth Nystrom
Dean of Instruction
  Leon F. Miller
Dean of Students
  Charles E. Koerble
Dean of Men
  Jack L. Lasley
Dean of Women
  Karen L. Licklider
Director, Alumni, Correspondence,
    Extension, and Placement
  Everett W. Brown
Assistant Director, Placement
  Esther Sellers
Assistant Director, Field Services
  John E. Fuhrman
Librarian
  James Johnson

Director, Instructional Materials Bureau
 Luke L. Boone
Director, Athletics
 Ryland H. Milner
College Nurse
 Helen O'Connor
Horace Mann/College Nurse
 Pearl K. Dawson
Women's Dormitory/College Nurse
 C. Frances Steel
Director, Men's Residence Halls
 Bruce R. Wake
Director, Food Services
 Glen F. Vogt
Director, Union Building
 William H. Needels

1965-1966
President
 Robert P. Foster
Secretary to the President
 Monica G. Zirfas
Business Manager
 Luther G. Belcher
Dean of Administration
 Charles H. Thate
Assistant to Dean of Administration
 Oscar H. Kirschner
Registrar
 Ruth Nystrom
Dean of Instruction
 Leon F. Miller
Dean of Students
 Charles E. Koerble
Dean of Men
 Jack L. Lasley
Dean of Women
 Karen L. Licklider
Director, Alumni, Correspondence,
  Extension, and Placement
 Everett W. Brown
Assistant Director, Placement
 Esther Sellers
Assistant Director, Field Services
 John E. Fuhrman
Assistant Director, Alumni
 Jack B. Gray, Jr.
Librarian
 James Johnson
Director, Instructional Materials Bureau
 Luke L. Boone
Director, Athletics
 Ryland H. Milner
College Nurse
 Helen O'Connor

Horace Mann/College Nurse
 Pearl K. Dawson
Women's Dormitory/College Nurse
 C. Frances Steel
Men's Dormitory/College Nurse
 Patsy Johnson
Director, Men's Residence Halls
 Bruce R. Wake
Director, Food Services
 Glen F. Vogt
Director, Union Building
 William H. Needels

1966-1967
President
 Robert P. Foster
Secretary to the President
 Monica G. Zirfas
Business Manager
 Luther G. Belcher
Dean of Administration
 Charles H. Thate
Assistant to Dean of Administration
 Terry L. Myers
Registrar
 Ruth Nystrom
Dean of Instruction
 Leon F. Miller
Dean of Students
 Charles E. Koerble
Dean of Women
 Karen L. Licklider
Director, Alumni, Correspondence,
  Extension, and Placement
 Everett W. Brown
Assistant Director, Placement
 Esther Sellers
Assistant Director, Field Services
 John E. Fuhrman
Assistant Director, Alumni
 Jack B. Gray, Jr.
Librarian
 James Johnson
Director, Instructional Materials Bureau
 Luke L. Boone
Director, Athletics
 Ryland H. Milner
College Nurse
 Helen O'Connor
Horace Mann/College Nurse
 Pearl K. Dawson
Women's Residence Halls/College Nurse
 C. Frances Steel
Director, Men's Residence Halls
 Bruce R. Wake

Director, Food Services
    Glen F. Vogt
Director, Union Building
    Dan L. Greer

1968-1970
President
    Robert P. Foster
Secretary to the President
    Monica G. Zirfas
Business Manager
    Luther G. Belcher
Dean of Administration
    Charles H. Thate
Assistant to Dean of Administration
    Terry L. Myers
Registrar
    Ruth Nystrom
Director, Data Processing
    Myrl D. Cobb
Dean of Instruction
    Leon F. Miller
Dean of Students
    Charles E. Koerble
Dean of Men
    Bruce R. Wake
Dean of Women
    Karen L. Licklider
Director, Financial Aids
    Max R. Fuller
Director, Field Services, Extension,
    and Correspondence
    Everett W. Brown
Assistant Director, Field Services
    John E. Fuhrman
Assistant Director, Alumni
    Robert H. Cotter
Assistant Director, Placement
    Esther Sellers
Assistant Director, Publicity
    Jack B. Gray, Jr.
Librarian
    James Johnson
Director, Instructional Materials Bureau
    Luke L. Boone
Director, Athletics
    Ryland H. Milner
College Nurse
    Helen O'Connor
Horace Mann Nurse
    Pearl K. Dawson
Women's Residence Halls/College Nurse
    C. Frances Steel
Director, Food Services
    Glen F. Vogt

Director, Union Building
    Robert E. Dickey

1970-1972
President
    Robert P. Foster
Secretary to the President
    Monica G. Zirfas
Assistant to the President
    Everett W. Brown
Business Manager
    Luther G. Belcher
Dean of Administration
    Charles H. Thate
Associate Dean of Administration
    Donald D. Petry
Registrar
    Ruth Nystrom
Director, Data Processing
    Myrl D. Cobb
Director, Academic Advisement
    John K. Mobley
Director, Admissions
    Robert E. Bush
Director, Financial Aids
    Max R. Fuller
Dean of Men
    Bruce R. Wake
Dean of Women
    Louann B. Lewright
Director, Counseling Center
    Lawrence E. Zillner
Dean of Faculties
    Dwain E. Small
Dean of Graduate Studies
    Leon F. Miller
Director, Extension and Correspondence
    Everett W. Brown
Assistant Director, Field Services
    John E. Fuhrman
Assistant Director, Alumni
    Robert H. Cotter
Assistant Director, Placement
    Esther Sellers
Assistant Director, Publicity
    Robert M. Henry
Librarian
    James Johnson
Director, Instructional Materials Bureau
    Luke L. Boone
Director, Athletics
    Ryland H. Milner
College Nurse
    Helen O'Connor
Horace Mann Nurse
    Pearl K. Dawson

Women's Residence Halls/College Nurse
  Joyce Wilkerson
Director, Food Services
  Glen F. Vogt
Director, Union Building
  Marvin B. Silliman

1972-1974
President
  Robert P. Foster
Administrative Assistant
  Monica G. Zirfas
Assistant to the President
  Everett W. Brown
Director, Alumni
  Robert H. Cotter
Director, Field Services
  John E. Fuhrman
Director, News and Information
  Robert M. Henry
Director, Financial Aids
  Mark M. Maddox
Director, Placement
  Donald K. Carlile
Vice President for Business Affairs
  Donald D. Petry
Director, Security
  James Miller
Director, Data Processing
  William I. Churchill
Director, Physical Plant
  Robert Seipel
Director, Food Services
  Glen F. Vogt
Business Manager
  Don L. Henry
Vice President for Student Affairs
  Charles H. Thate
Director, Admissions
  Richard D. Buckridge
Director, Athletics
  Ryland H. Milner
Registrar
  Ruth Nystrom
Director, Academic Advisement
  Alan L. Peterson
Dean of Students
  Phillip H. Hayes
Director, Student Counseling Center
  Louann B. Lewright
Director, Student Union
  Marvin B. Silliman
Director, Housing and Student
    Administrative Affairs
  Bruce R. Wake

Director, Student Activities
  Camille F. Walton
Director, Health Services
  Ruth Zink
Vice President for Academic Affairs
  Dwain E. Small
Assistant to Vice President for
    Academic Affairs
  John P. Mees
Director, Institutional Research
  Robert L. Ontjes
Director, Library
  Charles W. Koch
Director, Instructional Materials Bureau
  Luke L. Boone
Dean of Graduate Studies
  Leon F. Miller

1974-1976
President
  Robert P. Foster
Administrative Assistant
  Monica G. Zirfas
Assistant to the President
  Everett W. Brown
Director, Financial Aids
  Doyle A. VanDyne
Director, Placement
  Donald K. Carlile
Director, Alumni Relations
  Robert H. Cotter
Director, News and Information Bureau
  Robert M. Henry
Director, Radio Broadcasting
  Rollie Stadlman
Vice President for Administration
  Donald D. Petry
Assistant to Vice President for
    Administration
  William I. Churchill
Director, Physical Plant
  Robert W. Brought
Director, Food Services
  Del E. Simmons
Director, Farm
  John C. Beeks
Business Manager
  Don L. Henry
Provost
  Charles H. Thate
Assistant Provost
  John P. Mees
Director, Learning Resources
  Charles W. Koch
Director, Instructional Television
  Carroll E. Fogal

Director, Instructional Material Services
  Luke L. Boone
Dean of Graduate Studies
  Leon F. Miller
Director, Athletics
  Ryland H. Milner
Director, Student Teaching
  Frank D. Grispino
Dean of Admissions and Records
  Robert E. Bush
Registrar
  Martha Cooper
Director, Admissions
  Richard D. Buckridge
Director, Industry Services Program
  Robert E. Bush
Coordinator of Veteran Affairs
  William C. Dizney
Dean of Students
  Phillip H. Hayes
Director, Housing
  Bruce R. Wake
Director, Counseling
  David C. Sundberg
Director, Student Activities
  Karen Hall
Director, Student Union
  Marvin B. Silliman
Director, Health Services
  Desmion M. Dizney
Director, Security
  James Miller

1976-1977
President
  Robert P. Foster
Administrative Assistant
  Monica G. Zirfas
Assistant to the President
  Richard D. Buckridge
Executive Vice President
  Donald D. Petry
Vice President for Academic Affairs
  John P. Mees
Business Manager
  Don L. Henry
Director, News and Information
  Robert M. Henry
Director, Admissions
  Charles W. Veatch
Director, Alumni Relations
  Robert H. Cotter
Associate Dean of Faculties
  Margaret A. Briggs
Director, Athletics
  Michael N. Hunter

Director, Broadcasting
  Rollie Stadlman
Director, Counseling
  David C. Sundberg
Director, Data Processing
  William I. Churchill
Dean of Admissions and Records
  Robert E. Bush
Dean of Students
  Phillip H. Hayes
Director, Financial Aids
  Doyle A. VanDyne
Director, Food Services
  Del E. Simmons
Dean of Graduate Studies
  Leon F. Miller
Director, Health Center
  Desmion M. Dizney
Director, Housing
  Bruce R. Wake
Director, Learning Resources Center
  Charles W. Koch
Director, Maintenance Services
  Robert W. Brought
Director, Personnel Services
  Sandra Cox
Director, Placement Services
  Donald K. Carlile
Registrar
  Martha Cooper
Director, Student Activities
  Irene P. Huk
Director, Student Union
  Marvin B. Silliman

1977-1978
President
  B. D. Owens
Administrative Assistant
  Monica G. Zirfas
Assistant to the President
  Robert E. Bush
Executive Vice President
  Donald D. Petry
Vice President for Student Development
  John P. Mees
Vice President for Academic Affairs
  George W. English
Business Manager
  Don L. Henry
Public Relations Officer
  Robert M. Henry
Director, Administrative Services
  Tom T. Catlett
Director, Admissions
  Charles W. Veatch

Director, Alumni Relations
  Robert H. Cotter
Associate Dean of Faculties
  Margaret A. Briggs
Director, Athletics
  Michael N. Hunter
Director, Broadcasting
  Rollie Stadlman
Director, Counseling
  David C. Sundberg
Director, Data Processing
  Jon T. Rickman
Dean of Students
  Phillip H. Hayes
Director, Financial Aids
  Doyle A. VanDyne
Dean of Graduate Studies
  Leon F. Miller
Director, Health Center
  Desmion M. Dizney
Director, Housing
  Bruce R. Wake
Director, Learning Resources Center
  Charles W. Koch
Director, Maintenance Services
  Robert W. Brought
Director, Personnel Services
  Sandra Cox
Director, Placement Services
  Donald K. Carlile
Registrar
  Martha Cooper
Director, Security
  Earl F. Brailey
Director, Student Activities
  Irene P. Huk
Director, Student Union
  Marvin B. Silliman

1978-1979
President
  B. D. Owens
Administrative Assistant
  Monica G. Zirfas
Assistant to the President
  Robert E. Bush
Vice President for Student Development
  John P. Mees
Vice President for Academic Affairs
  George W. English
Treasurer
  Don L. Henry
Public Relations Officer
  Robert M. Henry
Director, Admissions
  Charles W. Veatch

Director, Alumni Relations
  Vincent A. Vaccaro
Associate Dean of Faculties
  Peter A. Jackson
Director, Athletics
  Richard R. Flanagan
Director, Broadcasting
  Rollie Stadlman
Director, Custodial Services
  Edgar Friend
Director, Counseling
  David C. Sundberg
Director, Data Processing
  Jon T. Rickman
Dean of Students
  Phillip H. Hayes
Director, Financial Aids
  Doyle A. VanDyne
Dean of Graduate Studies
  Leon F. Miller
Director, Health Center
  Desmion M. Dizney
Director, Housing
  Bruce R. Wake
Director, Learning Resources Center
  Charles W. Koch
Director, Maintenance Services
  R. Max Harris
Director, Personnel Services
  Sandra Cox
Director, Placement Services
  Donald K. Carlile
Registrar (Acting)
  Phillip H. Hayes
Director, Security
  Earl F. Brailey
Director, Special Programs
  Martha Cooper
Director, Student Activities
  Irene P. Huk
Director, Student Union
  Marvin B. Silliman
Director, Technical Services
  Stephen B. Easton

1979-1980
President
  B. D. Owens
Administrative Assistant
  Monica G. Zirfas
Assistant to the President
  Robert E. Bush
Vice President for Student Development
  John P. Mees
Vice President for Academic Affairs
  George W. English

Treasurer
    Don L. Henry
Public Relations Officer
    Robert M. Henry
Director, Admissions
    Charles W. Veatch
Director, Alumni Relations
    Vincent A. Vaccaro
Associate Dean of Faculties
    Peter A. Jackson
Director, Athletics
    Richard R. Flanagan
Director, Broadcast Services
    Rollie Stadlman
Director, Custodial Services
    Edgar Friend
Director, Counseling Center
    David C. Sundberg
Director, Data Processing
    Jon T. Rickman
Dean of Students
    Phillip H. Hayes
Director, Financial Aids
    James R. Wyant
Dean of Graduate Studies
    Leon F. Miller
Director, Grounds Maintenance
    Wilbur Adams
Director, Health Center
    Desmion M. Dizney
Director, Housing Office
    Bruce R. Wake
Director, Learning Resources Center
    Charles W. Koch
Director, Maintenance Services
    R. Max Harris
Director, Personnel Office
    Sandra Cox
Director, Placement and Career Planning
    Donald K. Carlile
Registrar (Acting)
    Phillip H. Hayes
Director, Security
    Earl F. Brailey
Director, Special Programs
    Martha Cooper
Director, Student Activities
    Irene P. Huk
Director, Student Union and Intramurals
    Marvin B. Silliman
Director, Technical Services
    Stephen B. Easton

1980-1981

President
    B. D. Owens

Administrative Assistant
    Monica G. Zirfas
Assistant to the President
    Charles W. Veatch
Vice President for Student Development
    John P. Mees
Vice President for Academic Affairs
    George W. English
Vice President for Environmental
    Development
    Robert E. Bush
Vice President for Financial Affairs
    Warren L. Gose
Public Relations Officer
    Robert M. Henry
Director, Admissions
    James C. Goff
Director, Alumni Relations
    Vincent A. Vaccaro
Assistant to V. P. for Academic Affairs
    Franklin A. Flesher
Associate Dean of Faculties
    Peter A. Jackson
Director, Athletics
    Richard R. Flanagan
Director, Broadcast Services
    Rollie Stadlman
Business Manager
    Jeanette A. Solheim
Director, Counseling Center
    David C. Sundberg
Director, Data Processing
    Jon T. Rickman
Dean of Students
    Phillip H. Hayes
Director, Financial Aids
    James R. Wyant
Coordinator, Foreign Student Affairs
    William C. Dizney
Dean of Graduate Studies
    Leon F. Miller
Director, Grounds Maintenance
    Wilbur Adams
Director, Health Center
    Desmion M. Dizney
Director, Housing Office
    Bruce R. Wake
Director, Learning Resources Center
    Charles W. Koch
Director, Maintenance Services
    R. Max Harris
Director, News and Information
    Thomas M. Myers
Personnel and Payroll Officer
    Sandra Cox

Director, Physical Plant Personnel
   Training
   Edgar Friend

Director, Placement and Career Planning
   Donald K. Carlile

Registrar (Acting)
   Phillip H. Hayes

Director, Safety Office
   James A. Cremer

Director, Special Programs
   Martha Cooper

Director, Student Activities
   Irene P. Huk

Director, Student Union and Intramurals
   Marvin B. Silliman

Director, Technical Services
   Stephen B. Easton

Treasurer (Acting)
   Jeanette A. Solheim

APPENDIX 3

Faculty, 1956-1980

The following list includes names of persons who served at least one year as full-time faculty members at Northwest during the 1956-1980 time period. Date following each name indicates the beginning of service at this institution. Asterisks are used to denote people who once served or are currently serving as department chairmen or division heads.

Abrams, Ronald E., 1974
Achuthan, M. Radh, 1964
Adair, Charles D., 1969
Akes, Zelma O., 1955
Albertini, Dolores A., 1965
Albertini, Virgil R., 1965
Alcott, Muriel M., 1969
Allen, Ann M. *see* Brekke, Ann M.
Alsup, Richard R., 1977
Amsbury, Wayne P., 1972
Andersen, Paul R., 1971
Anderson, Mark J., 1972
Anderson, Marlys J., 1968
Angman, Berndt G., 1955
*Armstrong, Donald J., 1965
Arthur, Pauline R., 1947
Aufderheide, Lawrence, 1976
Augustin, Byron D., 1969
Aycock, Charles, 1969

Bahnemann, David W., 1968
Bailey, Nancy, 1976
Baisya, Hira L., 1963
Baker, Earl H., 1960
Baker, John W., Jr., 1977
Bales, Eugene F., 1979
Barker, Thomas M., 1956
Barnes, John W., 1969
Barratt, George W., 1962
Barrows, Floyd D., 1960
Basket, Georgia I., 1978
Bates, Oren L., 1968
Bauhs, Thomas H., 1972
Bauman, David L., 1971
Baumbach, Frances E., 1975

Bayha, Richard A., 1971
Beatty, Martha A. *see* Moss, Martha A.
Beebe, Dianna J., 1975
*Beeks, John C., 1958
Beeson, Richard O., 1966
Beeson, Valerie A., 1967
Behnke, Ralph R., 1972
Behnke, Susan B., 1972
Bejcek, Betty E., 1965
Belcher, Kathryn L., 1966
Bell, David M., 1966
Bell, Donald A., 1962
Bell, Linda J., 1969
Bell, Prudence, 1970
Bell, Rebecca, 1964
Bellamy, Robert V., Jr., 1979
Benner, Jean K. *see* Hurst, Jean K.
Bennett, Kathryn M., 1970
Bennett, William H., 1970
Bensusan, H. Guy, 1959
Benz, George A., 1956
Bereskin, C. Gregory, 1974
*Bernard, Barbara R., 1966
Bettis, Mervin D., 1977
Beuerman, Donald R., 1964
Birdsell, James F., 1967
Birru, Debela, 1979
Bitcon, Lawrence E., 1965
Blackman, Robert L., 1965
Blackwell, Dale J., 1948
Blades, Melvin L., 1968
Bladt, Luther G., 1957
Blankenship, Bill H., 1962
Bliss, Russell L., 1973
Blostein, Harold L., 1964

Griffith, John R., Jr., 1963
Grispino, Frank D., 1965
*Grube, Frank W., 1947
Gryder, Robert, 1955
Guilliams, Glenda R., 1976
*Gutzmer, Marvin D., 1962

Hackett, Maurice R., 1978
Hagan, Donald, 1965
*Hageman, Lee, 1967
Hagen, Kenneth M., 1969
Hale, Robert E., 1968
Hale, William C., 1979
Hall, Robert T., Jr., 1979
Hambrecht, Joanna R., 1975
Hamilton, Harold C., 1979
Handke, A. Frederic, 1962
Handke, Lillian W., 1966
Hansen, Jerry D., 1973
Harover, Phyllis, 1972
*Harr, John L., 1944
Harris, Jerry A., 1966
Harrison, Alton, Jr., 1965
Harristhal, Joann W., 1953
Hart, JoAnn, 1979
Hart, Richard A., 1962
Hartley, Susan S., 1977
Hassenplug, H. Fred, 1962
Hassenplug, Louise R., 1963
Hawkins, Charles E., 1975
Hayes, Hoyt K., 1975
Hefner, Donald R., 1965
Hemenway, Henry G., 1968
Henderson, Clarence M., 1965
Henlein, Paul C., 1965
Henney, Robert C., 1962
Herauf, James A., 1976
Herzig, John R., 1962
Hesler, Richard A., 1959
Hickman, Gerald W., 1969
Hicks, Diane K., 1974
*Higginbotham, Harlan K., 1964
Hilgenberg, Deborah D., 1971
Hillix, Virginia R., 1964
Hinckley, William L., 1968
Hinkhouse, James E., 1964
Hinshaw, George A., 1956
Hoadley, Carole B., 1968
Hoffman, Glenn J., 1953
Holley, Larry R., 1975
Holman, Richard W., 1965
Hooker, Lillian K., 1974
Hoover, Lester L., 1955
Hopper, John E., 1969
Horner, Channing J., 1967
Horner, Louise B., 1967

Hoskey, Marvin R., 1978
Hospodarsky, Theresa L., 1975
*Houghton, Floyd B., 1946
Houston, Richard D., 1966
Howey, Henry E., 1970
Hughes, Benjamin C., 1980
Hughes, Bettie B., 1965
Huk, Adrian I., 1975
Huneke, Leonard A., 1974
Hunter, Michael N., 1975
Hunter, Robert T., 1962
Hunter, Violette, 1946
Hurst, James A., 1962
Hurst, Jean K., 1962
Hutchinson, Robert, 1966
Hybels, Saundra K., 1965
Hyde, Charles L., 1957
Hysler, M. Doris, 1950

Iglehart, Robert W., 1965
*Imes, Johnie M., 1970
Ing, Dean C., 1974
Ingle, Dona A., 1969
Ingle, Josephine A., 1972
Irvin, Katherine, 1955
Isaac, Janice K., 1969

Jackson, Annette J., 1962
*Jackson, Harold, 1976
Jackson, Laura F., 1957
*Jackson, Mary H., 1962
*Jackson, Peter A., 1959
Janky, Donna L., 1969
Jenkins, Harold L., 1976
Jensen, Diane R., 1970
Jensen, Larry D., 1969
Jessen, William T., 1973
Jewett, Mike, 1969
*Johnson, Charles L., 1953
*Johnson, James, 1948
Jones, Carolea, 1971
Jones, Deborah J., 1974
Jones, Hershel L., 1969
Jones, Paul D., 1966
Jones, Walter T., Jr., 1973
Justice, John K., 1976

Kahng, Michael S. M., 1961
Kalisch, Philip A., 1964
Kannenburg, Barnabas E., 1972
Kauffman, Alice A., 1963
Keith, Mary E., 1924
Keller, Robert E., 1958
*Kelly, Alfred B., 1975
Kemp, Christopher, 1969
Kennedy, Russell R., 1961

Merkel, Edward T., 1974
Merrick, Irma M., 1969
Meyer, Paul F., 1973
Meyer, Richard E., 1969
Meyers, Laurie A. *see* Potter, Laurie A.
Middleton, James G., 1962
Midland, Dale L., 1961
Mier, Mary Jo, 1971
Millar, Robert S., Jr., 1966
Miller, Arnold R., 1972
Miller, Eleanor R., 1965
Miller, Gordon W., 1974
Miller, Larry E., 1969
*Miller, Leon F., 1950
Miller, Peggy S., 1969
Miller, Richard L., 1960
Miller, Roger A., 1963
Miller, Ruth M., 1948
Miller, Sanford E., 1975
Milligan, Terry G., 1978
Millikan, Chloe E., 1928
Mills, Lois P., 1974
Milner, Ryland H., 1937
*Minter, Kenneth W., 1963
Minyard, Donald H., 1979
Mitch, Patricia E., 1966
Mitchell, Byron F., 1964
Mitchell, Corinne, 1970
Mitchell, Frances F., 1964
Mobley, John K., 1966
Mocciola, Michael R., 1979
Monk, Richard C., 1979
Moor, E. Dean, 1958
Moore, Catherine O., 1968
Moore, Clarence C., 1967
Moore, Dorothy T., 1976
Morey, Russell W., 1966
Morgan, Jane E., 1968
Morley, Gordon E., 1962
Morris, David C., 1975
Morris, Gay L., 1968
Morris, Homer H., 1963
Morris, Larry D., 1976
Morris, Mike, 1972
Morse, Lincoln B., 1970
Moss, Earle I., 1954
Moss, Janet L., 1966
Moss, Marion L., 1958
Moss, Martha A., 1958
Moss, Robert J., 1964
*Moss, Ron L., 1966
Moss, Shela D., 1958
*Mothershead, Harmon R., 1965
Mueller, Irene M., 1943
Mulford, Harold A., Jr., 1950
Mull, Sandra S., 1969

Murphy, Kathryn L., 1964

Nagle, Jean S., 1965
Nagle, Robert D., 1965
Nair, Lola, 1976
Neatherlin, James W., 1965
Nelsen, Kenneth M., 1975
Nelson, Harold, 1964
Nelson, Paula D., 1965
Neustadt, Helen A., 1967
New, Richard M., 1967
Newcomer, Patricia R., 1972
Nichols, Michael G., 1969
Nincehelser, Floyd I., 1968
Nixon, Harold W., 1971
Noah, Ronald D., 1966
Nolte, Carol J., 1978
Nothstine, Donald E., 1970
Nothstine, Sue A., 1970
Novak, Michael, 1977
Nowak, Rita, 1960
Null, Linda M., 1979

Oblinger, Carl D., 1972
O'Dell, Charles A., 1968
O'Grady, Edna, 1945
O'Hara, William J., 1977
Oomens, Fred W., 1970
Orr, Leonard R., 1978
Oschwald, Karamaneh I., 1957
Oschwald, Richard A., 1956

Padelford, Walton M., 1975
Padgitt, Dennis D., 1967
Padgitt, Janice, 1978
Pagel, Evelyn A., 1964
Palling, Barbara R., 1955
Palmer, Neil H., 1958
Papathanasis, Anastasios, 1979
Parete, Jesse D., 1978
Parker, David E., 1961
Parks, Paula S., 1961
Parmelee, Bruce D., 1969
Patterson, Mary J., 1963
Patterson, Paul W., 1971
Pederson, Glen A., 1970
Peel, Donald F., 1957
Pendleton, William R., Jr., 1964
Pener, Michael A., 1970
Perez, Samuel A., 1979
Perkins, John E., 1955
Perkins, Laurence J., 1958
Perrett, James W., 1963
Person, Marjorie P., 1954
Petersen, Charles G., 1972
Peterson, Carolyn S., 1962

Stadlman, Rollie, 1970
Stamm, JoAnn *see* Marion, JoAnn
Stanek, Pamela J., 1977
Stanton, Leola R., 1972
Stein, Jared M., 1969
Stephens, Larry N., 1969
Stewart, Glen C., 1958
Stout, R. Gene, 1974
*Strong, J. Gordon, 1943
Stuart, James W., 1969
Sullivan, Ann M., 1956
Sunderman, Mark A., 1977
*Sunkel, Mary J., 1961
*Sunkel, Robert C., 1960
Surphlis, Ross C. C., 1963
*Surrey, Sterling, 1936
Syed, Bashir A., 1962
Szawara, Mary J., 1975

Tackett, Natalie J., 1970
Tackett, Renee R., 1978
Tackett, W. Marshall, 1964
Taft, Thomas B., 1968
Taylor, Bettie, 1971
Taylor, John S., 1946
Taylor, Myron L., 1966
Temple, Mary M., 1966
Temple, Paul A., 1965
Terrell, Rebecca L., 1965
*Thate, Charles H., 1960
Thomason, Terry L., 1978
Thomasson, Ellen H., 1966
Thompson, Herbert M., Jr., 1964
Thompson, JoLynne, 1979
Thompson, Kenneth T., 1942
Thummel, Carol J., 1968
Tice, Willard C., 1970
Timmons, Clara E., 1962
Timmons, Timothy M., 1975
Tollman, Thomas A., 1974
Treese, William D., 1964
Tremble, Neal C., 1956
Trowbridge, William L., 1971
Troxell, Jerry J., 1966
Trubey, Donald W., 1964
Tucker, Douglas R., 1972
Turner, J. Paul, 1958
Turney, Jerry L., 1977

Underwood, Robert A., 1975

*Valk, Donald N., 1932
Van-Dieren, Kenn W., 1979
VanDyke, Patricia A., 1969
Vanice, Bettie *see* Taylor, Bettie
VanVoorst, Phillip J., 1969

VanZomeren, Wayne C., 1966
Vassian, Edwin G., 1960
Viele, Daniel F., 1979
Vint, Virginia H., 1966
Vitaska, Charles R., 1965

Wacker, John G., 1974
Wade, Stanley L., 1967
Wahrer, John W., 1965
Waldron, Joyce J., 1966
Walker, Dorothy J., 1958
Walker, John H., 1965
Walker, Roy L., 1966
Walker, Wanda C., 1955
Wallace, Rose A., 1971
Wallace, Wayne A., 1963
Walrafen, Phyllis J., 1960
Walston, Sydney C., 1967
Walter, James E., 1971
Walters, Stephen P., 1976
Walton, Cecil E., 1960
Wang, Guang-Nay, 1978
Wantz, Richard A., 1976
Wasem, James L., 1972
Weaver, Arden W., 1972
Weaver, Richard A., 1967
*Webster, Kathie A., 1976
Wegner, Gary G., 1977
Wegner, Jane R., 1977
*Weichinger, Theodore, Jr., 1954
Weigand, Dorothy L., 1950
Weil, Norman E., 1971
Weir, E. Lee, 1964
Welding, John C., 1977
Wells, John L., 1979
West, Robert W., 1967
Wetzel, Joseph F., 1966
White, Joyce M., 1966
Whitmore, E. L., 1970
Whitney, Gilbert A., 1951
Wickman, John E., 1962
*Widger, Calvin R., 1955
Williams, Emelda L., 1969
Williams, Harriett T., 1948
Williams, Jeanne P., 1979
Williams, John R., 1970
Williams, Ray N., 1967
Williams, William M., 1969
Williford, Sherry A., 1971
Wilson, Alice G., 1957
Wilson, Barbara, 1954
Wilson, L. Neville, 1978
Wilson, Lynn M., 1974
Wilson, Rodney M., 1966
Winsor, Jerry L., 1964
Winstead, Wayne, 1979

Winzenread, Marvin R., 1964
Wirth, Marion G., 1969
Wirth, Sandra L., 1975
Wispe, Ruby V., 1954
Wolfe, Michael J., 1975
Wood, Betty J., 1968
Woodruff, Ernest R., 1976
Worley, George W., 1969
Wrather, Charles B., 1973
Wright, Gerald D., 1969
*Wright, Richard T., 1935
Wujek, Joseph B., Jr., 1979
Wyant, James R., 1975
Wynne, Johanne W., 1977

Wynne, Patrick F., 1972

Yates, William O., 1959
Youland, Jane L., 1970
Young, Philip W., 1970

Zabel, Jacquelyn, 1970
Zach, David K., 1979
Zahnd, Carole E., 1961
Zeglin, Suzanne C., 1970
*Zillner, Lawrence E., 1965
Zimmerman, Muriel E., 1978
Zindel, David L., 1976

APPENDIX 4

Emeritus Faculty

But I have promises to keep, . . .
—Robert Frost

The first date following each name indicates the beginning of service at this institution and the second date the year of retirement.

Arthur, Pauline R., 1947-1974
Brown, Leta, 1964-1977
Cook, Mabel G., 1947-1971
Cushman, Cathran E., 1967-1975
Dieterich, H. R., 1928-1969
Dougherty, John M., 1965-1979
Dunbar, Vida E., 1950-1975
Dykes, Mattie M., 1922-1957
Eckert, Opal E., 1965-1974
Fulsom, Ralph E., 1951-1976
Geiger, Vance E., 1969-1974
George, Howard A., 1957-1979
Gorsuch, Anna J., 1945-1975
Graham, Avis L., 1945-1975
Grube, Frank W., 1947-1973
Handke, A. Frederic, 1962-1976
Harr, John L., 1944-1979
Houghton, Floyd B., 1946-1974
Hunter, Violette, 1946-1975
Jackson, Mary H., 1962-1977

Keith, Mary E., 1924-1960
Kensinger, Clifford A., 1946-1967
Killingsworth, A. Ruth, 1966-1980
Knittl, Esther N., 1939-1977
Long, Myrl D., 1948-1975
Lowe, James L., 1959-1979
Magill, Bonnie, 1943-1976
Mauzey, Elaine, 1945-1976
Miller, Ruth M., 1948-1977
Milner, Ryland H., 1937-1975
Mueller, Irene M., 1943-1975
Riddle, Kathryn S., 1956-1975
Ringold, Howard W., 1945-1975
Rivers, Charles L., 1956-1975
Ross, Neva M., 1942-1971
Smay, John L., 1947-1975
Strong, J. Gordon, 1943-1964
Thompson, Kenneth T., 1942-1975
Weigand, Dorothy L., 1950-1980
Whitney, Gilbert A., 1951-1980

APPENDIX 5

Necrology

O may I join the choir invisible
Of those immortal dead who live again
In minds made better by their presence.
—George Eliot

The following list includes the names and dates of death of members of Northwest's faculty and administration who died during the 1956-1980 time period. Extensive searches were made to locate necrology information only on persons known to be deceased.

Hettie M. Anthony, March 29, 1960
Edith A. Barnard, February 11, 1962
Kenneth E. Bird, April 8, 1976
Luther G. Bladt, September 18, 1966
Harry W. Bomar, August 3, 1969
Estella Bowman, January 19, 1968
William A. Brandenburg, January 19, 1975
Hazel E. Carter, November 1, 1968
Arthur J. Cauffield, April 29, 1962
W. Wallace Cook, June 8, 1968
Albert H. "Bert" Cooper,
    October 26, 1956
E. A. "Lefty" Davis, February 13, 1965
Reven S. DeJarnette, unknown
Olive S. DeLuce, February 22, 1970
Harry G. Dildine, July 7, 1968
Virginia Dorman, September 6, 1979
Blanche H. Dow, May 24, 1973
Joseph A. Dreps, April 11, 1980
Helen Dvorak (Talley), April 20, 1977
Dorothy L. Dyke, January 17, 1979
Durward H. Dyke, January 9, 1970
Lauris M. Eek, February 22, 1963
Mary M. Fisher, unknown
William F. Fleming, October 19, 1979
Katherine A. Franken, November 22, 1960
M. Margaret Franken, July 23, 1980
William T. Garrett, December 20, 1979
William C. George, July 25, 1970
Clarence M. Henderson, April 15, 1975
Carrie E. Hopkins, February 5, 1956
Nell Hudson, July 10, 1964
Robert Hutchinson, January 24, 1975
Laura F. Jackson, November 12, 1972
Minnie B. James (Cryder), March 8, 1980
Charles L. Johnson, August 28, 1963
James Johnson, May 15, 1980
J. W. Jones, January 1, 1979
Alice A. Kauffman, November 7, 1971
Joseph P. Kelly, September 6, 1969
Robert B. Killingsworth,
    November 15, 1979
Charles E. Koerble, September 18, 1975
William A. Lafferty, October 9, 1966

R. Lucile L'air (McKinney), July 31, 1977
Uel W. Lamkin, September 16, 1956
Ruth O. Lane, February 17, 1973
H. F. "Shorty" Lawrence, August 8, 1970
Leonard Levy, July 10, 1958
Thelma F. Long, September 18, 1963
Elizabeth J. Luer, April 14, 1967
Joseph C. MacCoy, February 5, 1969
Nell Martindale (Kuchs), July 25, 1976
Carol Y. Mason, November 26, 1956
Cyrus M. McDonald, Jr.,
    September 11, 1971
Arthur J. McGehee, November 12, 1974
J. C. Miller, November 15, 1956
Chloe E. Millikan, November 24, 1969
Gordon E. Morley, June 5, 1964
Helen O'Connor, January 10, 1979
Edna O'Grady, May 14, 1979
Richard A. Oschwald, April 3, 1979
Anna M. Painter, June 7, 1962
Neil H. Palmer, February 7, 1960
Homer T. Phillips, December 18, 1961
Theodore C. "Tad" Reid, May 16, 1971
Anita M. Rice (Javier), April 16, 1978
William A. Rickenbrode,
    November 29, 1956
Lula M. Sheetz, February 24, 1966
M. T. Sheldon, August 13, 1966
Dora B. Smith, August 31, 1977
Wilbur "Sparky" Stalcup,
    April 21, 1972
Sterling Surrey, August 15, 1962
W. Marshall Tackett, July 20, 1975
Donald N. Valk, September 22, 1976
E. L. Whitmore, May 13, 1978
Harriett Williams, May 15, 1978
Lon E. Wilson, June 9, 1961
Mabel C. Winburn, May 20, 1973
Beatrix Winn (Ford), December 6, 1975
Marion G. Wirth, December 25, 1976
Sandra L. Wirth, December 25, 1976
Randall L. Wolcott, February 28, 1979
Richard T. Wright, December 4, 1973

APPENDIX 6

Chairmen of the Faculty Senate (instituted 1974)

1974-1975
Robert C. Sunkel
1975-1976
Merry G. McDonald
1976-1977
Roger W. Corley

1977-1978
Dale W. Rosenburg
1978-1979
Robert H. Findley

1979-1980
James A. Herauf
1980-1981
Ronald J. Ferris

APPENDIX 7

Presidents of the Student Senate

1955-1956
Kenneth Moore, Macksburg, Iowa
1956-1957
Arthur Buckingham, St. Joseph,
Missouri
1957-1958
Jerry Overton, Atchison, Kansas
1958-1959
B. D. Owens, Grant City, Missouri
1959-1960
Donald Kixmiller, Carson, Iowa
1960-1961
Robert Dale Cramer, Chillicothe,
Missouri
1961-1962
Joe Merrigan, Stanberry, Missouri
1962-1963
Ivan Lyddon, Stuart, Iowa
1963-1964
Jim Sanders, Maryville, Missouri
1964-1965
Glenn Acksel, St. Louis, Missouri
1965-1966
Jerry Taylor, Indianola, Iowa
1966-1967
Nick Erganian, St. Joseph, Missouri
1967-1968
Tom Frank, Union Star, Missouri

1968-1969
Mike Wilson, Chillicothe, Missouri
1969-1970
Steve Schottel, Maryville, Missouri
1970-1971
Jim Oliver, Guilford, Missouri
1971-1972
Stan Barton, Independence, Missouri
1972-1973
Jim Spurlock, Indianola, Iowa
1973-1974
Ed Douglas, St. Joseph, Missouri
1974-1975
Mike Snodgrass, Chariton, Iowa
1975-1976
Dwight Tompkins, Bolckow, Missouri
1976-1977
Leo Brooker, Jefferson, Iowa
1977-1978
Rex Gwinn, Des Moines, Iowa
John Moore, Kansas City, Missouri
1978-1979
Darrell Zellers, Kansas City, Missouri
1979-1980
Roger Scarbrough, Shenandoah, Iowa
1980-1981
Joe Pickard, Rhodes, Iowa

APPENDIX 8
Homecoming Queens

1956
Velma Swartz, Graham, Missouri
1957
Donna Sue Jones, St. Joseph, Missouri
1958
Joan Hall, Watson, Missouri
1959
Gay Laughery, Bayard, Iowa
1960
Barbara Loyd, Kansas City, Missouri
1961
Anne Chick, Shenandoah, Iowa
1962
Lana Green, Prescott, Iowa
1963
Sandra Kelly, Kansas City, Missouri
1964
Barbara Knox, Casey, Iowa
1965
Dorothy Hardyman, Storm Lake, Iowa
Marlene Kelly, Excelsior Springs, Missouri
1966
Elaine Sherman, Maryville, Missouri
1967
Donna Merritt, Rosendale, Missouri

1968
Betsy Thompson, Cainsville, Missouri
1969
Cheryl Jackson, Weldon, Iowa
1970
Paula Moyer, Maryville, Missouri
1971
Christine Clark, Booneville, Iowa
1972
Margaret Rooney, Cameron, Missouri
1973
Melody Ann Gabel, Chillicothe, Missouri
1974
Sally Grace, Albany, Missouri
1975
Melissa Jane Koepnick, Fenton, Missouri
1976
Catherine Locke, Kansas City, Missouri
1977
Nancy Cole, Cameron, Missouri
1978
Diann Piper, King City, Missouri
1979
Alice Barbee, St. Joseph, Missouri

APPENDIX 9
Spirits of Christmas

These senior coeds were selected by their peers to reign over the traditional annual "Hanging of the Greens" Christmas festivities in Residence Hall, later called Roberta Hall.

1956
Sue Wright, Graham, Missouri
1957
Beverly Murphy, St. Joseph, Missouri
1958
Delivee Cramer, Chillicothe, Missouri
1959
Margaret Boyd, Shenandoah, Iowa
1960
Betty McCaig, New Hampton, Missouri
1961
Sue Crone, Winston, Missouri
1962
Carolyn Holst, Avoca, Iowa
1963
Jerilyn Irvin, Westboro, Missouri

1964
Sandra Herzog, Kent, Iowa
1965
Judy Salfrank, Shenandoah, Iowa
1966
Gano Whetstone, Casey, Iowa
1967
Martha Geyer, Wamego, Kansas
1968
Betty VerSteeg, Orange City, Iowa
1969
Wanda Weldon, Graham, Missouri
1970
Susan Johnson, Lewis, Iowa

Discontinued in 1971.

APPENDIX 10
Tower Queens

1956
Shirley Motsinger, Grant City, Missouri
1957
Carolyn Ogden, Maryville, Missouri
1958
Eva Lee Hess, Skidmore, Missouri
1959
Barbara Burgess, Smithville, Missouri
1960
Peggy Humphreys, Manilla, Iowa
1961
Merle Imamoto, Lahaina, Maui,
    Hawaii
1962
Sue Crone, Winston, Missouri
1963
Carolyn Holst, Avoca, Iowa
1964
Nancy Timberlake, Bedford, Iowa

1965
Susan McConkey, Barnard, Missouri
1966
Dianna Brown, Hamburg, Iowa
1967
Carolyn Kading, Des Moines, Iowa
1968
Anne Morgan, Elliott, Iowa
1969
Janet Wilson, Lathrop, Missouri
1970
Deborah Lambright, Bolckow, Missouri
1971
None
1972
Sue Kroeger, Lake View, Iowa
1973
Brenda DeWeerdt, Lathrop, Missouri
Discontinued in 1974.

APPENDIX 11
Student Organizations Currently on Campus

DEPARTMENTAL:

Accounting Society
Agriculture Club
American Society for Personnel
    Administration
Art Club
Collegiate FFA
Geology-Geography Club
Horticulture Club
Industrial Arts Club (including The Bear-
    cat High Performance Team)
Kids—Elementary Education
Music Educators National Conference
National Student Speech and Hearing
    Association
People Related to Nursing
Pi Beta Alpha—Business
Pro PR—Public Relations
Psychology/Sociology Club
Student Affiliates of the American
    Chemical Society
Student Chapter of the Soil Conservation
    Society of America
Student/Faculty Interface—Home
    Economics
Student Home Economics Association
Student MSTA—Education
Student Practical Nurses Association

Theta Mu Gamma Math Club
University Players

LEADERSHIP HONORARY:

Blue Key—National Men's Honorary
    Fraternity
Cardinal Key—Senior Honor Society

MUSICAL:

Brass Ensemble
Concert Band
Madraliers
Marching Band
Opera Workshop Ensemble
Phi Mu Alpha Sinfonia
Piano Repertoire
Progressive Jazz Ensemble
Sigma Alpha Iota
Tower Choir
University Chorus
Woodwind Ensemble

RELIGIOUS:

Baptist Student Union
Campus Bible Fellowship
Chi Alpha

Fellowship of Christian Athletes
Latter-Day Saint Student Association
Liahona Student Fellowship
Messengers
The Navigator Chapter of NWMSU
New Covenant Campus Fellowship
Newman House
Religious Life Council
Sunday Night Supper Club
Wesley Foundation of Maryville, Inc.

SCHOLASTIC HONOR:

Alpha Beta Alpha—Library Science
Alpha Mu Gamma—Foreign Language
Alpha Psi Omega—Drama
Alpha Tau Alpha—Agriculture
Beta Beta Beta—Biology
Delta Psi Kappa—Physical Education
Delta Tau Alpha—Agriculture
English Honor Society
Gamma Theta Upsilon—Geography
Kappa Delta Pi—Education
Kappa Omicron Phi—Home Economics
Pi Gamma Mu—Social Science
Pi Kappa Delta—Debate
Pi Mu Epsilon—Mathematics
Pi Omega Pi—Business Education
Sigma Tau Delta—English (Writing)
Society for Collegiate Journalists
Student Chapter of the Association for
    Computing Machinery

SERVICE:

Alpha Phi Omega
Circle K
Sigma Society
Youth Association for Retarded Citizens

SOCIAL:

Alpha Kappa Lambda Fraternity
Alpha Omicron Pi Sorority
Alpha Sigma Alpha Sorority
Delta Chi Fraternity
Delta Sigma Phi Fraternity
Delta Zeta Sorority

Omega Psi Phi Colony
Phi Mu Fraternity
Phi Sigma Epsilon Fraternity
Sigma Gamma Rho Sorority
Sigma Phi Epsilon Fraternity
Sigma Sigma Sigma Sorority
Sigma Tau Gamma Fraternity
Tau Kappa Epsilon Fraternity

SPECIAL INTEREST:

Afrikan Kultural Enlightenment and
    Tourism
Bearcat Steppers
The Chinese Student Club
Fencing Club
The Flying Bearcats
Golf Club
Gymnastic Club
Harambee House
Jogging Club
M Club
Nigerian Students Union
Orchesis Club
Pre-Law Club
Pre-Medical Professions Club
Sigma Phi Dolphin Swim Club
Soccer Club
Student International Meditation Society
Student Union Board
Swim Club
Third Foundation Science-Fiction Club
Tower 4-H
Varsity Cheerleaders
Veterans' Club
Volleyball Club
Weightlifting Club
Wrestling Grappelettes
Youth For Political Action

STUDENT GOVERNING:

Inter-Fraternity Council
Inter-Residence Hall Council
Panhellenic Council
Residence Hall Councils
Student Senate

APPENDIX 12

Directors of the Northwest Missouri State University Educational Foundation, Inc.

Date following each name and address indicates beginning of service as a director.

The Northwest Missouri State Educational Foundation, Inc. was incorporated April 21, 1971, as a non-profit organization to promote the welfare, goals, and programs of the University.

Leigh Wilson, Maryville, 1971 (President)
Larry A. Jones, St. Joseph, 1972 (Vice President)
Harold W. Voggesser, Maryville, 1973 (Treasurer)
Donald K. Carlile, Maryville, 1971 (Secretary)
Anita Aldrich, Bloomington, Indiana, 1976
Frank E. Babb, Chicago, 1974
Charles R. Bell, Maryville, 1972
James Cline, Maryville, 1971
Robert H. Cotter, St. Joseph, 1979
Victor M. Farrell, San Luis Obispo, California, 1972
Maxine McDermott Hill, Kansas City, Missouri, 1977
C. E. Kavanaugh, Kansas City, Missouri, 1973
Kenneth Lepley, Des Moines, 1972
Edward P. Morgan, Washington, D.C., 1978
Austin Mutz, Maryville, 1975

J. J. O'Connor, Atlantic, Iowa, 1972
Stanley K. Ogden, San Francisco, 1973
Wilbur L. Pollard, Kansas City, Missouri, 1972
Margaret Porter Polsky, Santa Barbara, California, 1972
Gerald R. Sprong, St. Joseph, 1974
Merrill Ostrus Staton, Morristown, New Jersey, 1972
Frank H. Strong, Maryville, 1976
Frances Stuart, Chesterfield, Missouri, 1972

FORMER DIRECTORS:

B. J. Alcott, Maryville, 1971-1975
J. Norvel Sayler, Maryville, 1971-1979
Everett W. Brown, Maryville, 1971-1976
Paul Fields, Maryville, 1971-1973
Elbert Barrett, Sun City, Arizona, 1972-1977
Max Kinney, Omaha, 1976-1978

APPENDIX 13

Presidents of the Alumni Association

1960
  Earl Bridgewater (1959)
1961
  Ed Hiner (1939)
1962
  Mabel Clair Winburn (1929)
1963
  Florence (Abarr) Lawhead (1942)
1964
  Don Johnson (1941)
1965
  Noma (Robison) Sawyers (1952)
1966
  John Russell (1950)
1967
  Max Buckner (1962)

1968
  Irene (Neal) Groom (1952)
1969
  Russ Noblet (1933)
1970
  Bob Gill (1949)
1971
  Betty (Drennan) Jackson (1943)
1972
  Morris Walton (1950)
1973
  Ron O'Dell (1957)
1974
  Frances Stuart (1937)
1975
  Wilbur Pollard (1951)

1976
   Lana Babcock (1965)
1977
   Barbara (Nixon) Sprong (1956)
1978
   Bob Severson (1959)

1979
   Byron "Bud" Baker (1949)
1980
   Jack A. Kinder (1955)

APPENDIX 14

Distinguished Alumni Award Recipients

1970
   George H. Adams (1931)
1970
   Mildred (Sandison) Fenner Reid (1931)
1971
   Elbert Barrett (1936)
1971
   Richard E. Miller (1941)
1971
   Frances R. Stuart (1937)
1972
   B. D. Owens (1959)
1972
   Merrill Ostrus Staton (1940)
1973
   Jack A. Kinder (1955)
1973
   J. P. Morgan (1940)
1974
   Vane B. Lucas (1961)
1974
   C. F. Russell (1931)
1975
   Kenneth Lepley (1947)
1975
   Lucile Lindberg (1936)

1976
   J. D. Hammond (1955)
1976
   Wilbur L. Pollard (1951)
1976
   J. Norvel Sayler (1932)
1977
   Larry A. Jones (1957)
1977
   Gerald R. Sprong (1956)
1977
   Eileen (Elliott) Vivers (1937)
1978
   Henry Iba (1928)
1978
   Truman E. Wilson (1950)
1979
   Fred E. Davis (1949)
1979
   Mattie M. Dykes (1919)
1979
   Mary McNeal (1943)
1980
   Buford W. Garner (1939)
1980
   George R. Green (1958)

APPENDIX 15
Distinguished Service Award Recipients

1977
  Everett W. Brown
1977
  E. Thomas Coleman
1977
  Hardin Cox
1977
  W. M. C. Dawson
1977
  J. W. Jones
1977
  James C. Kirkpatrick
1977
  J. P. Morgan
1977
  William F. Phares, Jr.
1977
  C. F. Russell
1977
  James Russell

1977
  Garvin Williams
1978
  Lela Bell
1978
  Robert P. Foster
1978
  Harold M. Hull
1978
  Henry Iba
1978
  M. E. Morris
1978
  Joe M. Roberts
1978
  Jack Stapleton
1978
  H. N. Stevenson

1978
  James Stubbs
1978
  Arlis B. Vogt
1978
  Edgerton Welch
1978
  Alan F. Wherritt
1978
  Harry Wiggins
1978
  Truman E. Wilson
1978
  John M. Yeaman
1979
  Mattie M. Dykes
1980
  E. D. Geyer

APPENDIX 16
Fall Semester Enrollments, 1956-1979

1956	1561	1968	4842
1957	1592	1969	5136
1958	1820	1970	5530
1959	1952	1971	5632
1960	1848	1972	5341
1961	2247	1973	4696
1962	2503	1974	4592
1963	2841	1975	4505
1964	3341	1976	4682
1965	3809	1977	4360
1966	3897	1978	4207
1967	4194	1979	4401

APPENDIX 17

University Oath

We will never bring disgrace to this, our University, by any act of cowardice or dishonesty. We will fight for the ideals and sacred things of the University. We will transmit this University to those who come after us, greater, better, and more beautiful than it was transmitted to us.

Alma Mater

Let your voices loudly ringing, echo far and near,
Songs of praise thy children singing to thy mem'ry dear.

Alma Mater! Alma Mater! tender, fair and true;
Grateful ones with love unfailing all their vows renew.

Years may dim our recollections, Time its change may bring,
Still thy name in fond affection, evermore we sing.

Alma Mater! Alma Mater! tender, fair and true;
Grateful ones with love unfailing all their vows renew.

INDEX